The Collected Courses of the Academy of European Law
Series Editors: Professor Philip Alston, *New York University School of Law*; Professor Gráinne de Búrca, *European University Institute, Florence*; and Professor Bruno de Witte, *European University Institute, Florence*

VOLUME XII/4

Executive Power of the European Union

The Collected Courses of the Academy of European Law
Edited by Professor Philip Alston, Professor Gráinne de Búrca, and Professor Bruno de Witte

This series brings together the Collected Courses of the Academy of European Law in Florence. The Academy's mission is to produce scholarly analyses which are at the cutting edge of the two fields in which it works: European Union law and human rights law. A 'general course' is given each year in each field, by a distinguished scholar and/or practitioner, who either examines the field as a whole through a particular thematic, conceptual or philosophical lens, or who looks at a particular theme in the context of the overall body of law in the field. The Academy also publishes each year a volume of collected essays with a specific theme in each of the two fields.

Executive Power of the European Union

Law, Practices, and the Living Constitution

DEIRDRE CURTIN

OXFORD
UNIVERSITY PRESS

This book has been printed digitally and produced in a standard specification in order to ensure its continuing availability

OXFORD
UNIVERSITY PRESS

Great Clarendon Street, Oxford OX2 6DP

Oxford University Press is a department of the University of Oxford. It furthers the University's objective of excellence in research, scholarship, and education by publishing worldwide in

Oxford New York

Auckland Cape Town Dar es Salaam Hong Kong Karachi Kuala Lumpur Madrid Melbourne Mexico City Nairobi New Delhi Shanghai Taipei Toronto

With offices in

Argentina Austria Brazil Chile Czech Republic France Greece Guatemala Hungary Italy Japan South Korea Poland Portugal Singapore Switzerland Thailand Turkey Ukraine Vietnam

Oxford is a registered trade mark of Oxford University Press in the UK and in certain other countries

Published in the United States by Oxford University Press Inc., New York

Reprinted 2010

ISBN 978-0-19-926408-7

Cover illustration: René Magritte, *La clef des champs*, 1936. Museo Thyssen-Bornemisza, Madrid. © by SIAE 2009.

Do m'athair agus mo mháthair

To Onno, Aisling, Analivia, Owen, and Jeremy

Preface

This book has had a lengthy gestation period by any standards. The idea for this book started life initially as a publication commitment following upon the general course on European Law I gave at the Academy of European Law in Florence in 2001. This course focused on how our understanding of emerging constitutionalism and the EU had to factor in the legal and institutional practices emerging below the level of treaty level reform. This was an approach to understanding the European Union and its evolution in practice that was developed during my time as Professor of International Organisations at the Law Faculty of the University of Utrecht (1992–2002). In collaboration with colleagues such as Ige Dekker and the doctoral and subsequent work of Ramses Wessel this rather institutional approach was given flesh and substance and applied, in particular, in the context of the emerging 'new' and often only formally 'intergovernmental pillars' of the EU: justice and home affairs as it was generically known and foreign and defence policy.

My focus in particular on the executive power of the EU was in retrospect inspired by the secrecy and the lack of real accountability forums of any kind at any level surrounding much of the initial implementation of the Treaty of Maastricht. My sense that this was normatively problematic was fed by, at times, close collaboration with civil society organizations trying, in the general public interest, to perform a fire-alarm role, both vis-à-vis national and European parliaments and more generally in the (barely nascent) public sphere. In this context I would like to pay tribute in particular to the seminal and important work performed—for two decades now—by the Dutch Standing Committee of Experts on International Immigration, Refugee and Criminal Law and its initiator, the late Professor Herman Meijers, a relentless and inspiring siren, of an expert kind. In addition Statewatch, the UK-based civil liberties organization, has persistently and systematically over two decades, brought to public attention (through its exemplary web site and through expert opinions, evidence and otherwise) the hidden or barely visible activities of EU executive power in its various components and manifestations. Often working behind the scenes, quietly, with little to no public funding, from the basis of an organization with a charitable status, individuals, such as Tony Bunyan, Professor Steve Peers and Dr Ben Hayes, and others, have tirelessly worked to bring information and facts into the public domain.

This book would not have moved beyond a rather legal and formal approach to understanding the manner in which the EU has evolved, in particular its executive power, but for two complementary further, multi-disciplinary, inputs. First, in 2002 I moved to take up the new chair of European and International

Governance in the recently established and largely nationally focused, Utrecht School of Governance. This forced me to leave the cosy haven of legalistic analysis and to explain, justify, and discuss my research in much broader thematic terms—at times it felt under constant methodological assault. Eventually this experience (battleground it sometimes felt like) left me able to engage in a hopefully constructive and genuinely bilateral dialogue with political scientists that has born some fruit. Collaboration with scholars such as Mark Bovens, Paul 't Hart, Albert Meijers and Sebastiaan Princen in particular has led to a series of scholarly publications and books (in the offing). Moreover it has been incredibly beneficial, as a lawyer, to be exposed to their much more sustained interest in and exploration of the empirical facts, without at the same time losing sight of the bigger picture and possible normative implications. At the same time my involvement with Connex, the EU-funded Network of Excellence expertly led by Beata Kohler Koch, facilitated in very practical ways the collaboration with leading EU focused political scientists and lawyers resulting in a series of workshops, thematic conferences, joint publications and guest edited special issues of legal and political science journals. In this context I would like to pay particular tribute to colleagues such as Morten Egeberg, Renaud Dehousse, Carol Harlow, Ioannis Papadopoulos, Peter Mair, Andre Nollkaemper, Antje Wiener, and Anchrit Wille, for stimulating cross-disciplinary discussions, debate and output.

Bringing these three strands together and the book not only acquired a mission but also in some sense a method. First a word on the mission, then on the method. The mission of the book was to focus explicitly and in a manner not done hitherto on broad-brush executive power of the European Union as such and in a sense by so doing let the sunshine in on the nature and reach of this power as a whole, the 'ugly sister' in conceptual terms at least in terms of the specific EU political system and the two other powers (legislative and judicial). At the same time this must have appeared to many an impossibly ambitious task in terms of its sheer reach: the full spectrum of executive actors, both political and bureaucratic/administrative, juxtaposed against one another and not just explored side by side in distinct, discrete studies. Yet even though certainly ambitious in terms of its reach, my task was greatly facilitated by various discrete studies on specific actors that separately add greatly to the state of the art knowledge on EU executive actors. Books such as those by Brandsma (2010, forthcoming), Busuioc (2010, forthcoming), Egeberg (2006), Hayes-Renshaw and Wallace (1997), Naurin and Wallace (2008), and Wille (2010, forthcoming) have all shed untold light on (often) previously dark institutions/actors. The finalization of this book was also facilitated by interviews carried out with various members of staff of both of the Commission and the Council. I would thank in particular Catherine Day, Paolo Ponzano, Bernardus Smulders, Hilary Majewska, and Michael Duoro who were especially helpful, also in enabling me to complete some of the tables included throughout the book.

It was however, alas and alack, not only the reach of the book that was ambitious—it was also the timing. The subject proved over the course of almost a decade to be one in constant movement and subject to interstitial change. Not only the series of treaty reforms but also the 'misses' (the Constitutional Treaty defeated by two separate referenda in France and in the Netherlands) and the near miss (the first Irish defeat of the Lisbon Treaty in June 2008, while I was on the last lap towards completion of the final manuscript). What to do? To wait for Godot or to push on even further? Quite a dilemma! I chose the latter, not only in the belief that the second Irish referendum to be held on 2 October 2009 would be positive but also that in any event the broader narrative of the book remains virtually the same irrespective of the final entry into force or otherwise of the Treaty of Lisbon. If ever it did not enter into force as planned then the future would be even further underground and darker, making the story of the book, incomplete though it may well be, even more relevant. The fate of this book is almost quintessentially and by definition to be incomplete and patchy. A broad-brush narrative can never at the same time be systematically in-depth and complete.

The mission has however been not only to map the broad reach of executive power of the EU but also to frame it within an understanding of checks and balances, of an organically growing 'living constitution'. The method of both the map and the frame has however unquestionably been eclectic. The approach is essentially legal but digging deeper into the institutional and legal undergrowth than many European lawyers tend to do: it includes analysis and relevance of case law but its essential thrust is one of institutional evolution and mutation. It is not in any sense a political science book (it could not be since I am no political scientist) but its essential message and thrust has been enriched and enlightened by the methodologically sound empirical analyses carried out by many political scientists. I hope I have done them justice. The law is as stated on 1 May 2009.

It remains for me to thank the many and varied people who have read and commented on various bits of the book at various times. Four people deserve special thanks for having read and commented on considerable portions of the book as a whole. First thanks to the anonymous reviewer for OUP for having read the manuscript more or less as a whole and for making really helpful suggestions and comments. Second to Paul Craig of the University of Oxford who diligently and altruistically ploughed through most of the book manuscript and commented in detail on many aspects. I am very grateful to him for taking time out from his own very busy schedule of commitments for doing this and his comments were greatly to my profit. Third, Steve Peers of the University of Essex has systematically been very helpful in providing me with information and commenting on the details of many chapters over the course of the years. Finally Ronald van Ooik of the University of Amsterdam has done Trojan work in correcting some specific errors or inaccuracies that remained and being overall very helpful.

To those who have at various stages commented on discrete parts of the book I am equally grateful and in their debt. The usual disclaimer applies, any errors are truly mine. I wish to thank in particular Mark Bovens, Gijs Jan Brandsma, Tony Bunyan, Madalina Busiouc, Christina Eckes, Ige Dekker, Paul 't Hart, Ben Hayes, Herwig Hofmann, Christian Joerges, Madeleine de Leeuw, Albert Meijer, Sebastian Princen, Ramses Wessels, Bruno de Witte, and Anchrit Wille. I also wish to thank my three student assistants who were so helpful especially in the final stages: Franz Ebert, Liesa Veldman, and Zsofia Zsorias. I could not have done it without them. My management assistant, Angela Moisl is a gem and I thank her in particular for all her help—and patience—with the bibliography and with the tables and the figures.

Warmest thanks go to the Director and staff of NIAS (the Netherlands Institute for Advanced Study), where I spent my sabbatical year 2007–8 as a fellow. This 'paradise' in the sand dunes in Wassenaar provided a safe haven to write, reflect, and finalize what otherwise I fear would have been a never-ending project.

The (various) Directors of the Academy of European Law have maintained faith that a book would finally emerge from the chrysalis woven over quite some years but especially over the last two years. And I thank too all at OUP for their patience and help: John Louth, Chris Champion and Bethan Cousins. Jeremy Langworthy who copy-edited the book did a splendid job and managed to keep me on the straight and narrow and (more or less) to the deadlines!

Finally I dedicate this book to my Irish roots and my Dutch branches: to my parents for always stimulating an interest in education, language and intellectual endeavour and facilitating those early crucial years—I am delighted that they witness the completion of this project; and to my family in the Netherlands, my partner Onno Brouwer and our children, Aisling, Analivia, Owen, and Jeremy for living, enduring, coping, and emerging at the other side! To our future together—minus the obsessive quest this particular book involved!

Haarlem, The Netherlands

9 May 2009

Contents

List of Tables and Figures

Abbreviations

ACER	Agency for the Cooperation of Energy Regulators
BEREC	Body of European Regulators for Electronic Communications
CAP	Common Agricultural Policy
CdT	Translation Centre for Bodies of the European Union
CEDEFOB	European Centre for Development of Vocational Training
CEPOL	European Police College
CESR	Committee of European Securities Regulators
CFCA	Community Fisheries Control Agency
CFI	Court of First Instance
CFSP	Common Foreign and Security Policy
CIE	Committee of Independent Experts
CJHA	Cooperation in Justice and Home Affairs
COMCEN	Communication Centre of the EU
COREPER	Committee of Permanent Representatives
COSAC	Conference of Community and European Affairs Committees of Parliaments of the European Union
COSI	Standing Committee on Operational Cooperation on Internal Security
CPVO	Community Plant Variety Office
CT	Treaty establishing a Constitution for the European Union
DG	Directorate General
EAR	European Agency for Reconstruction
EASA	European Aviation Safety Agency
EC	European Community
ECA	European Chemicals Agency
ECB	European Central Bank
ECDC	European Centre for Disease Prevention and Control
ECHO	European Community Humanitarian Assistance Office
ECJ	European Court of Justice
ECN	European Competition Network
ECOWAS	Economic Community of West African States
ECSB	European System of Central Banks
ECSC	European Coal and Steel Community
EDA	European Defence Agency
EEA	European Environment Agency
EEC	European Economic Community
EFA	European Fund Ad ministration
EFSA	European Food and Safety Authority

EMCDDA	European Monitoring Centre for Drugs and Drug Addiction
EMEA	European Agency for the Evaluation of Medicinal Products
EMSA	European Maritime Safety Agency
EMU	Economic and Monetary Union
ENISA	European Network and Information Security Agency
EP	European Parliament
EPC	European Political Cooperation
ERA	European Railway Agency
ESCB	European System of Central Banks
ESDP	European Security and Defence Policy
ETF	European Training Foundation
ETI	European Transparency Initiative
EU	European Union
EUMC	European Monitoring Centre on Racism and Xenophobia
EUMS	European Union Military Staff
EU-OSHA	European Agency for Safety and Health at Work
EURATOM	European Atomic Energy Community
EUROJUST	The European Union's Judicial Cooperation Unit
EUROFOUND	European Foundation for the Improvement of Living and Working Conditions
EUROPOL	European Police Office
EUSC	European Union Satellite Centre
FRA	European Union Agency for Fundamental Rights
FRONTEX	European Agency for the Management of Operational Cooperation at the External Borders
GAC	General Affairs Council
GERT	Group of European Regulators in Telecoms
GNSS	Global Navigation Satellite System
GSA	European GNSS Supervisory Authority
IGC	Intergovernmental Conference
IGO	Intergovernmental organization
IIA	Integrated Impact Assessment
ISS	Institute for Security Studies
LGAC	Legislative General Affairs Council
NAFTA	North American Free Trade Agreement
NATO	North Atlantic Treaty Organisation
OHIM	Office for Harmonization in the Internal Market
OLAF	European Anti-fraud Office
OMC	Open method of coordination
PJCC	Police and judicial cooperation in criminal matters
PRAC	Regulatory procedure with scrutiny
PSC	Political and Security Committee
QMV	Qualified majority voting

SCIFA	Strategic Committee on Immigration, Frontiers and Asylum
SG	Secretariat General
SG/HR	Secretary General/High Representative
SIS	Schengen Information System
SITCEN	Joint Situation Centre of the EU
SNE	Seconded National Experts
SPP	Strategic Planning and Programming
TAO	Technical Assistance Office
TEC	Consolidated Version of the Treaty establishing the European Community (Nice Treaty)
TEU	Consolidated Version of the Treaty on European Union (Nice Treaty)
TEU, Lisbon	Treaty on the European Union (Lisbon Treaty)
TFEU	Treaty on the Functioning of the European Union (Lisbon Treaty)
UN	United Nations
UNESCO	United Nations Educational Scientific and Cultural Organization
WCO	World Customs Organization

Table of Cases

Court of First Instance

European Court of Justice

European Court of Human Rights

United Kingdom

Table of Legislation

DECISIONS (CHRONOLOGICAL ORDER)

REGULATIONS (CHRONOLOGICAL ORDER)

COMMON POSITIONS

JOINT ACTIONS

Table of Treaties and Conventions

PART I

TOPOGRAPHY AND LAYERED SEDIMENTS

1

Geology of the European Union

1.1 The Unseen and Many Layers

The scope of the power that is exercised by actors and institutions under the auspices of the European Union (EU) may be fuzzy for many citizens, consumers, and third states. Decisions are taken in the EU by a wide variety of actors in a wide variety of forums and institutions. Much of the reform debate in recent years in the context of EU decision-making has been on the *legislative* process: who adopts what, when, and according to what procedure? The focus in terms of reform tended to be rather mono-institutional and to involve giving the European Parliament more of a role in a wide spectrum of European legislative processes. What has remained much more invisible in structural terms and also in terms of public perception and public understanding is the fact that *non-legislation* has moved much more to the centre stage in terms of the actual overall output of the EU. Non-legislation basically refers to executive action in one form or another from implementation and standard setting to operational decisions by both majoritarian and non-majoritarian actors.

In the EU there are core—political and administrative—EU institutions with far-reaching non-legislative powers. The European Commission (the Commission) can for example impose fines of in excess of $900 million on Microsoft, the US based multinational, on top of the original fine of $500 million.[1] Compared to other international organizations the EU is unusually effective both in its ability to adopt rules and in its ability to ensure that its Member States *comply* with those rules—and even to ensure that a multinational as powerful as Microsoft not only pays astronomical fines but actually changes its anti-competitive behaviour.

The Commission will be empowered—after entry into force of the Lisbon Treaty—to adopt so-called 'delegated legislation' across the full spectrum of EU policy areas, without having to employ the current system of committees of national civil servants (the so-called 'comitology' system, its very name suggesting hidden corridors of power) in order to fill in the details of legislation. In

[1] See further European Commission, Microsoft case: <http://ec.europa.eu/competition/antitrust/cases/microsoft/index.html>.

this context too the mushrooming of EU-level agencies (often linked to networks of national agencies) and the consolidation and reinforcement of their powers of decision taking are noteworthy. Like some of the existing agencies, the new EU Agency for Cooperation of Energy Regulators (ACER)—it has been agreed—will be able to adopt individual decisions and will have an important regulatory role to play, as will the European Commission.[2] Such agencies are populated by EU-level as well as national-level civil servants but may enjoy executive and regulatory power at the EU level. Another example of mushrooming power is the proposal to empower the existing Committee of European Securities Regulators (CESR) with the task of licensing Credit Rating Agencies in the EU and monitoring their performance.[3]

Some actors are thus both European and national. They consist both of politicians and of bureaucrats. Some may be wearing two hats, others not. A good example is the Council of Ministers itself (often known simply as 'the Council') composed of national ministers as well as a shadow bureaucracy with both Eurocrats and national civil servants (also known as 'new Eurocrats'). The Council has sometimes surprisingly specific and even operational type powers. It can for example compile EU-level lists of suspected terrorists whose assets are then frozen by national authorities as a direct consequence of EU-level lists. The European Council, which prior to the entry into force of the Lisbon Treaty is not even a formal institution of the EU as such, sometimes gives rather specific instructions to both the Commission and the Council as to (legislative) agenda-setting.[4] The European Council sets the agenda in a very streamlined and structural fashion as well for whole policy areas and also for the inter-linkages between broad policy areas (for example the Tampere programme 1999–2004, in the field of justice and home affairs and also with regard to climate change via thematic 'strategies'[5]).

Secretive and 'hidden' (comitology) committees can agree rules on the use of body scanners,[6] for example, as well as on what travellers may and may not take on board aircraft in the interests of security; technical requirements may subsequently not be published so citizens are unaware of the rules

[2] See further the proposed Agency for the Cooperation of Energy Regulators, Proposal for a Regulation of the European Parliament and of the Council establishing an Agency for the Cooperation of Energy Regulators (SEC (2007) 1179) (SEC (2007) 1180), COM/2007/0530 final—COD 2007/197. See too the new EU telecoms agency, BEREC (Body of European Regulators for Electronic Communications), <http://euobserver.com/9/27887>.

[3] See J de Larosière et al, *The High-Level Group on Financial Supervision in the EU—Report*, Brussels, 25 February 2009, para 67, <http://ec.europa.eu/commission_barroso/president/pdf/statement_20090225_en.pdf>. See further, European Commission (2009a), Communication, European Financial Supervision, COM/2009/252 final, 27 May 2009.

[4] See for example the far-reaching European Council conclusions, 10–12 December 2008.

[5] See further, I von Homeyer (2009), 'The Evolution of EU Environmental Governance' in J Scott (ed), *Environmental Protection: European law and governance*, Oxford: Oxford University Press, pp 1–26, at p 26.

[6] See, however, the resolution adopted by the European Parliament on 23 October 2008 that led to the withdrawal by the Commission of the draft implementing measures on this issue.

on aviation safety that may apply to them when they board aircraft.[7] EU-level border guards cooperate with Member State border guards under the auspices of an EU-level agency, Frontex, and carry out a rapidly increasing number of joint operational activities. In the year 2007 for example the EU borders agency initiated itself 21 joint operations (compared to only 7 in the year 2006).[8]

National actors step outside their national political systems when they participate in joint decision-making at the European level to varying degrees. That may mean more political decision-making by national prime ministers in the context of the European Council, national ministers in the Council of Ministers, national civil servants in the 'comitology' committees that implement the details of legislation, and national agencies or others networking with their infra-national counterparts. In this sense they jump the fence of national electoral politics. They were not elected to take these decisions; they have no mandate from the citizens and no overt and visible political program in this regard.

At the same time, decisions are also taken by European-level actors. These European actors may be to some extent politicized but in a context where political contestation and debate are missing. There is no overt link with the national level of politics; they have not jumped the national fence but have been constructed and put in place in order to function in what appears to be a relatively autonomous fashion at the specifically European level of governance. Formal institutions may take flesh and shape in ways that are not originally envisaged in the formal legal rules. They may spawn new actors who, through various informal processes and legal and institutional practices, acquire and exercise tasks. Institutions become 'living' and acquire a life of their own by virtue of their *empirical practices.* At the same time, part of the 'living' context is also the concrete manner that the various actors interact across the different governance levels.

1.2 The Evolving EU

As an object of research it is certainly true to say that the EU is *unidentified* and *travels at great speed.* The EU is largely *unidentified* in that it escapes the conventional labels such as nation, state, empire, region, federation. Yet it possesses elements of several of these categorizations (international organizations, state, political system etc). The *speed* of institutional change is undeniable; from a weak advisory parliamentary assembly to a more powerful European Parliament with co-legislative rights; from a weak court to a strong court, a court that can, for example, rule on issues that would appear purely national. The EU has moved

[7] See the facts underlying case C-345/06, *Gottfried Heinrich*, judgment of 10 March 2009, nyr.
[8] J Pollak and Slominski, P (2009) 'Experimentalist but not accountable governance? The role of Frontex in managing the EU's external borders' *West European Politics*, 32/5, pp 904–24.

in less than 50 years from being a trade regime with a common market to a political union by now covering, in varying degrees, the length and breadth of state policies.[9]

The contemporary EU is a *political union* that is constantly and incrementally evolving. In a political union there is almost no area of national policymaking that is not related in some fashion with policymaking at the European level. The EU polity has expanded almost to the point that there is virtually no area of political or social life that is *potentially* not within its remit. This includes matters from the purely regulatory to the redistributive and almost everything in between. The EU has built up a considerable body of independent policy and regulation in fields like environmental protection, consumer protection, occupational health, and safety. In addition, the EU has branched out to include issues such as immigration policies, justice and home affairs, and a common foreign and defence policy. In terms of output the EU issues the equivalent of national legislation as well as measures that can be considered to be more of a secondary or tertiary nature (via implementation and comitology for example). In terms of representing this visually the following table (Table 1.1, 'legislative' output of the EU) may help in the realization that the formal more 'legislative' type measures (by the Council alone, including measures of justice and home affairs or the Council and European Parliament under the joint legislative procedure) is far inferior to the output of the Commission acting alone and in a more executive capacity. It emerges from this table for example that whereas the Council (with or without the European Parliament) adopted some 363 legal instruments in 2007 and 525 in 2008, the Commission adopted respectively 1,329 and 1,203 instruments, as published in the Official Journal.[10]

The EU may be considered in terms of its nature as a peculiar hybrid: in some aspects it still, even today, resembles the rather classical intergovernmentalism of other international organizations;[11] in other respects it displays features of a polity or 'would be' (federal) state more comparable in essence to what happens in national political systems.[12] This can be translated as a conflict or struggle between a more 'diplomatic' understanding of the EU and a more 'democratic' one. The EU has, moreover, evolved as a system in its own right and, by virtue of autonomous institutions, into what has been termed an autonomous and new

[9] L Hooghe and G Marks (2008), 'European Union?', *West European Politics* 31/1–2, pp 108–29, at p 108.

[10] Despite the best assistance of the services of the Commission in compiling these tables it must be noted that it is very difficult on the basis of the information available to be more precise than this.

[11] See further P Magnette (2005), *What is the European Union? Nature and prospects* (London: Palgrave Macmillan).

[12] See, for example, T Koopmans (2008), 'Confederalisme: Van de "Articles of Confederation" naar het Verdrag van Maastricht' in F Judo and G Geudens, *Confederalisme?* (Gent: Larcier), pp 1–18.

Table 1.1 Legislative acts adopted 2005–8

	2005	2006	2007	2008
EP + Council Regulations	19	44	21	48
EP + Council Directives	26	39	18	53
EP + Council Decisions	14	19	18	30
Council Regulations	118	164	129	137
Council Directives	10	26	5	14
Council Decisions	252	245	272	244
Commission Regulations	675	610	628	574
Commission Directives	54	75	53	53
Commission Decisions	645	698	644	609
Total	1813	1920	1788	1762

Source: EUR-LEX, the inter-institutional computerized documentation system on Community law, excluding acts not published in the Official Journal and acts published in light type (routine management acts valid for a limited period).

This table is based on the official figures provided by Eurolex and given by the Commission services. But if a calculation is done including all acts that Eur-Lex seems not to display anymore (for whatever reason), but which were still adopted, a considerably higher number of regulations is shown to have been adopted by the Commission (between 1400 and 2000 over the past few years instead of 600 plus). This discrepancy may be explained by the fact that temporary measures etc not published in the Official Journal are not included in the official figures. Data compiled from EUR-LEX by Dimiter Toshkov, Leiden University. See further, GJ Brandsma (2010).

'executive order'.[13] As the realization grew, in the decades after the Maastricht Treaty, that the remit of the EU had been expanded beyond economic issues to core issues of national polities, to issues of both external and internal security, anxiety grew among populations in different Member States as to how such decision-taking processes were being legitimated and within what context.

It is generally assumed that on the map of international organizations the EU still today occupies a distinctive position due, in particular, to what has been termed its supranational normative order and specific—and far-reaching—judicial power. One of the defining features of the EU is precisely the manner in which the Court of Justice crafted the bald legal provisions laid down in the original treaties into a new—and 'constitutional'—legal system, the legal system of the European Communities. This can be considered an example of a process of judicial construction of *an institutional normative order*—but then, at the supranational level, the EU indeed represents the most advanced example of 'institutionalized normative order' beyond bounded territories (states).[14]

[13] See further on the use of this term, D Curtin and M Egeberg (2008), 'Tradition and innovation: Europe's accumulated executive order' in D Curtin and M Egeberg (eds), 'Towards a new executive order in Europe?', *West European Politics*, 31/4, pp 639–61.

[14] See further on this term 'institutional normative order', N MacCormick (2007), *Institutions of Law: An essay in legal theory* (Oxford: Oxford University Press), pp 59–60.

This book focuses on the shadowy side of EU decision-making—the part that is not so visible even in the unwritten constitution, and the role multiple actors play at different levels and wearing different hats. Who are they, what are they doing, and how can one even begin to structure a debate on their democratic and political embedding within a political system, at which governance level or at multiple governance levels? What is the EU precisely; how can we understand it in holistic terms; and what are these actors, European and national, doing in this context? How can we frame it so as to relate it to the institutional normative order?

The subject of EU executive power is currently unmapped in two senses: first it is topographically undefined in all its plurality and fragmentation. Secondly, the extent to which there exists a visible—and at the same time invisible—small 'c' constitution that frames some checks and balances is also not mapped or understood in the light of incremental (legal and institutional) practices evolving over time. This is what this book attempts to do with regard to a previously unmapped subject, the executive power of the EU: to reveal the piecemeal nature of the growth of a certain type of power, also at times in unexpected places, as well as its broader constitutional framing and evolving checks and balances at various levels.

1.3 The Metaphor of 'Sedimentation'

A metaphor implies the use of language that directly compares seemingly unrelated subjects. They are usually understood as figures of speech that present one thing as another thing and may be used either at the abstract, conceptual level or as a highly specific expression of a phenomenon.[15] Many metaphors have been used in the context of the EU in the highly abstract conceptual sense. Thus representations (often by national politicians) of the EU as motion or constant forward movement is made concrete in the metaphor of a bicycle or a ship. One very early metaphor involved the use of tidal ecosystems to suggest the intensity of the relationship between national and Community (at that time) legal systems as well as its irreversibility. Lord Denning referred to the EU as long ago as 1974, as 'an incoming tide. It flows into the estuaries and up the rivers. It cannot be held back.'[16] More recently the metaphor of ecology has been (re)used to suggest

[15] See, for a detailed study, P Drulák (2004), 'Metaphors Europe lives by: Language and institutional change of the European Union', available at <http://www.arena.uio.no/events/documents/Paper_001.pdf>.

[16] *Bulmer v Bollinger* [1974] 2 WLR 202.

a broadly fluid and penetrating effect of EU rule-making ('governance').[17] Other metaphors are more static and solid, implying brick-by-brick construction. They traditionally present the EU in the architectural—and seemingly unmoving—terms of a Greek temple or a Gothic cathedral suggesting complexity yet unity.[18]

A geological metaphor is not unrelated to a biological or ecological one and suggests movement and evolution as well as layers of meaning and practice. Darwin's *On the Origin of Species* and his theories of evolution were very much influenced by his experience as a field geologist. Geology provided the vast time frame needed for natural selection to produce the biodiversity we see today. Geology also provided evidence that the planet's topography is not best understood by virtue of the 'big bangs' of history and catastrophic events but rather in a more organic way as being the result of the daily operation of wind, rain, erosion, and sedimentation, as well as the usually imperceptible movement of land masses over millions of years.[19] The metaphor of 'sedimentation' refers to the geological process of an accumulation of layers of 'deposits' being piled upon one another and involving the settling of solid particles from fluids. In applying the notion of 'sedimentation' in the context of the evolving legal and political systems of the EU, I have been inspired by a not dissimilar debate in the US context where more than a decade ago two legal writers used the term 'The Sedimentary Constitution' for the US Constitution.[20]

The geological metaphor raises the question of the overall processes of transformation of political order in Europe and the emergent topography of the EU as it evolves over time. The time perspective of geological movements is of course sobering and incomparable with the—minute—time frame involved in the process of constitutionalization in the EU to date. The issue of time is clearly crucial.[21] The time scale is hugely different, particularly in the case of the EU—a very new and in many ways unprecedented type of political experiment. That said, some analogy is in my view possible, tracing the evolution of the past and the present, not only in its wrenching transformative events but also in the slow and organic process of gradual and incremental change. The metaphor of the sedimentary 'living' constitution conjures up the image of organic and incremental

[17] A Sbragia (2008), 'Distributed governance: The changing ecology of the European Union' in B Kohler-Koch and F Larat (eds), *Efficient and Democratic Governance in the European Union*, Connex Report Series No 09 (Mannheim: Connex Report Series), pp 339–55.

[18] See, for example, B de Witte (1998), 'The pillar structure and the nature of the European Union: Greek temple or French gothic cathedral?' in T Heukels, N Blokker, and M Brus (eds), *The European Union after Amsterdam: A legal analysis* (The Hague: Kluwer Law International), pp 51–68.

[19] C Lyell (1990), *Principles of Geology* (Chicago: University of Chicago) (originally published 1830–3).

[20] B Friedman and S Smith (1998), 'The sedimentary constitution', University of Pennsylvania L Rev, 147/1, pp 1–90.

[21] WT Eijsbouts (1996), 'Constitutional sedimentation', Legal Issues of European Integration, 23/1, pp 51–60.

growth: gradual rather than sudden (although there may well be distinct and specific impulses, also treaty-based), piecemeal rather than a 'big bang'.

1.4 The Living Constitution

Legal and structural change is important but so too are the arrangements and procedures of what can be termed the 'living constitution' (or of a 'living tree') as opposed to the written and formal constitution. The 'living Constitution' is an extremely commonplace metaphor in the US context: as Chief Justice William Rehnquist of the US Supreme Court remarked: 'the phrase "living Constitution" has about it a teasing imprecision that makes it a coat of many colours'.[22] The metaphor of the 'living tree' does not necessarily imply that everything in constitutional law is constantly open to change; rather, 'the very possibility of growth depends on the trunk and roots remaining firmly in place'.[23] The use of the organic growth implied in the use of the term a 'living constitution' is inevitably different in the context of the EU as opposed to its use in the context of, for example, the United States.

In the US there is a written, formal, and political Constitution, adopted democratically. But there is also an unwritten constitution that ensures that the written Constitution is not frozen in its contents but evolves over time to meet social, political, and historical realities unimagined by the framers.[24] In the EU context the roots and trunk are more difficult to locate and were not framed—originally at any rate—in constitutional terms. In Europe there is not (nor is there likely to be in the foreseeable future) a written, formal, political constitution—we have by now a series of treaties that have been de facto supplemented by judicial interpretation in line not necessarily with the original intentions of the framers, but also with evolving understandings by the judges in particular. Already *twenty* years ago the late Judge Federico Mancini eloquently described his view of the making of a constitution for Europe—by the judges in Luxembourg.[25] But this is a largely judge-made, lower 'c' constitution that may at times, particularly in recent years, take some surprising turns indicating a different status of European integration as opposed to the norms of public international law in general—again in the minds and deeds of the judiciary.

[22] W Rehnquist (1976), 'The notion of a living Constitution', Texas L Rev, 54, p 693.

[23] J Goldsworthy (1997), 'Originalism in constitutional interpretation', Federal L Rev, 25/1, p 29.

[24] See, for example, TC Grey (1974–1975), 'Do we have an unwritten constitution?' Stanford L Rev, 27, pp 703–18.

[25] GF Mancini (1989), 'The making of a constitution for Europe', Common Market L Rev, 26, pp 596–614. See more generally GF Mancini (2000), *Democracy and Constitutionalism in the European Union* (Oxford: Hart Publishers). See too JHH Weiler (1999), *The Constitution for Europe* (Cambridge: Cambridge University Press).

The metaphor of a living entity is however used in this book not only to refer to the manner in which judges may interpret—and develop—the provisions of a constitution (or treaty) over time[26]—but also, more generally, to refer to various incremental 'practices' of institutions that indicate an evolving understanding of the nature of the polity.[27] These lower-level, and at times hidden, practices may too contribute to the organic growth of the EU and its smooth functioning. Or they may not and may indeed reflect more a Darwinian evolution that is random, undirected, non-progressive and indifferent.[28]

The metaphor of sedimentation suggests that layered under the superficial outer crust of core understandings (treaty texts as revised over the years) we may find more complex sediments of 'living' institutions and empirical practices. Examples include the manner in which, for example, non-formal instruments such as inter-institutional agreements are used by the core institutions in a structurally invisible fashion in order to agree salient institutional matters among themselves and to apply them in practice, long before the formal political and legal system catches up (if at all). This living political (and non-political) matrix is an essential part of understanding what the EU is becoming and the nature and scope of the changes that it has effected on the national systems as a result.

1.5 Dark Matter

Treaty amendments can provide for a framework for institutional change and development but it takes tradition, conventions, and implementing law to provide the glue to hold it together in overall constitutional terms. Inter-institutional conventions or agreements have been referred to as the 'cartilage enabling the legal bones to move. Without it a certain constitutional arthritis is bound to occur.'[29] The instrument of 'inter-institutional agreements' has been much used as a relatively informal instrument to oil and even change the interrelationships among the institutions and introduce more checks and balances into the political system as a whole.[30]

In recent years inter-institutional dialogue and in particular the instrument of inter-institutional agreements has gained considerably in importance in the EU's

[26] See further on this use of the metaphor of the 'living constitution', A Kavenagh (2003), 'The idea of a living constitution', Canadian J of L and Juris, 16/1, pp 55–89.

[27] For a different more general—political—use of the term 'living constitution' in the context of the EU, see S Gustavsson (2008), 'The living constitution of the EU' in B Kohler-Koch and F Larat (eds), *Efficient and Democratic Governance in the European Union*, Connex Report Series No 09, (Mannheim: Connex Report Series), pp 325–38.

[28] For a nuanced view of the relationship between a Darwinian view of evolution and the metaphor of a living Constitution see, S Dodson, (2008) 'A Darwinist View of the Living Constitution', Vanderbilt Law Review, 61/5, pp 1319–47.

[29] B Driessen (2007), *Inter-Institutional Conventions in EU Law* (London: Cameron May).

[30] Ibid, p 266.

legal and political system. One role that such agreements may fulfill in the EU's institutional architecture is that of 'engineering' a particular result or practice that is agreed and carried out at what has been termed the 'sub-constitutional level'.[31] At the same time, endogenous institutional change involving informal and interstitial dynamics can in certain circumstances feed back into subsequent (treaty level) institutional change as the detailed work of political scientists Farrell and Héritier has shown us.[32] The argument has been made that the European Parliament in particular has 'used' the instrument of inter-institutional agreements in order to precook, in a sense, the content in certain respects of intergovernmental (treaty reform) conferences.[33] A similar phenomenon can be discerned with the Commission in the driving seat, attempting to put and keep on the agenda the issue of the so-called 'operational framework' of regulatory agencies, first via a draft inter-institutional agreement and, when the Council objected that there was no legal basis for the rather far-reaching measures proposed, an inter-institutional 'declaration' (see Chapter 6 below for details).

The question may be put: is the very invisibility and shadowy nature of this 'dark' process not problematic? The Court of Justice, after all, is itself a non-majoritarian institution that constitutes the 'oracle' of EU law in a manner that has no link with democratic process. At the same time, it might be argued the ongoing and evolving practices of 'living' institutions in the interstices of formal rules may also be problematic for its very invisibility and perhaps unpredictability. With regard to rule-making, in particular via the method of inter-institutional agreements, it is sometimes argued that these are concocted and applied with a non-democratic 'cocoon of power'.[34] The very fact that institutions meet largely behind closed doors to agree and apply rules with uncertain binding legal effect is regarded by some scholars as problematic from a democratic point of view.[35] In the words of one scholar:

> The findings about these 'sub-constitutional' changes as part of a self-referential interinstitutional game do not endorse the democratic quality of the EU *per se*. They rather seem to enhance integration by stealth, or to put it differently, while the cocoon of power is ever growing through the formalisation of informal practices by creating legal instruments as

[31] I Eiselt and P Slominski (2006), 'Sub-constitutional engineering: Negotiation, content and legal value of interinstitutional agreements in the EU' European LJ, 12/2, pp 209–25. See too, W Hummer, (2007), 'From "Interinstitutional Agreements" to "Interinstitutional Agencies/Offices"'? European LJ 13/1, pp 47–74.

[32] H Farrell and A Héritier (2003), 'Formal and informal institutions under co-decision: Continuous constitution-building in Europe', *Governance: An international journal of policy, administration and institutions*, 16/4, pp 577–600; H Farrell and A Héritier (2007), 'Co-decision and institutional change', *West European Politics*, 30/2, pp 285–300.

[33] See further D Kietz and A Maurer (2007), 'The European Parliament in treaty reform: Predefining IGC's through interinstitutional agreements', European LJ, 13/1, pp 20–46.

[34] See, in particular, S Puntscher Riekmann (2007), 'The cocoon of power: Democratic implications of interinstitutional agreements', European LJ, 13/1, pp 4–19.

[35] See further I Eiselt and P Slominski (2006).

sources of legitimacy, it does not resolve the problem of responsiveness and accountability *vis-à-vis* European citizens.[36]

Other efforts were however made in parallel to these ongoing processes to bring the entire process more out in the open, as to the evolving nature of the EU as a polity, and to give it an overt 'constitutional' framing in one way or another, including the adoption of a 'big bang' European constitution.

1.6 A 'Big Bang' Constitution?

The material constitution of the EU in a juridical or functional sense refers to the idea that the existing treaties form a constitution for the institutional structure of Council, European Parliament, Commission, and Court. The role of the Court in this regard has traditionally been viewed as truly revolutionary, already 'declaring' and interpreting years ago the constitutional effects of these treaties, as a 'Constitutional Charter' in one of its more famed pronouncements.[37] In particular the famous *van Gend en Loos* and *Costa* judgments affirmed Community law as an autonomous legal order, implying that the Community legal order had a material constitution of its own. When the Court in its path-breaking decisions took EC law to be an autonomous legal order, it did so on the basis of a presumed direct relation with the peoples of Europe. It was this premise that accorded an independent normative authority to the EU and its legal order. The assumption of independent normative authority has required the adoption of constitutional doctrines to constrain and legitimate that authority—it was thus a constitutionalism instrumental to and limited by the claim of normative authority.[38]

Part of the constitutional fabric that has been knitted together over the years by the Court has related however not only to the legal order but also to the more political order. The Court has discovered and applied a fundamental ordering principle with political implications, namely the *principle of institutional balance*. It has used that principle to mark out, in a rather preliminary and basic fashion, a certain balance in the powers of political institutions, rationalized particularly in terms of the interests or constituencies represented.

In conclusion, the material constitution of the EU, as shaped by the Court in particular, was there in outline form before the turn of the century. The problem however with this approach to constitution-making is twofold. First, it represents a rather haphazard and ad hoc approach to constitution-making. The strong

[36] S Puntscher Riekmann (2007), p 19.

[37] See further D Curtin (2006b), 'Making a political constitution for the European Union', European J of L Ref, 8/1, pp 65–76.

[38] See further N Walker (2006), 'EU constitutionalism in the state constitutional tradition', Current Legal Problems, 59, pp 51–60.

aspect has been the conceptualization and implementation of an autonomous legal order. The weak point has been the conceptualization and implementation of a balanced and accountable political system. The latter can also be considered a step too far—simply too much to expect of judges as the oracle of the law in a context where the political authority has been left at the level of the national political systems. At the same time, that reality was being outmatched by an evolving empirical reality of increasingly centralized sources of executive and regulatory power at the EU level itself.

The second problem with the largely judicial approach to constitution-making is the elitist and closed process itself. In other words, this legal habit of viewing the treaties as a juridical or functional constitution never received the kind of popular endorsement that would have legitimized it as a political constitution. According to this view, constitutionalized Europe to the extent that it exists, exists as an affront to democracy rather than as a product of it.[39] It is, indeed, rather difficult to determine what are the norms which citizens could see themselves as the authors of in the absence of a formal constitution. Moreover it is hard to argue that European citizens have endorsed the material constitution of the Union in any meaningful sense. European citizens do not see themselves as authors of the existing material constitution of the EU. The type of constitutionalism involved was low-intensity rather defensive, in the words of one author.[40] The constitutional concepts did not affect the way in which the political process operated—the domain of politics was dominated by their intergovernmental nature and constitutionalism, as a form of deliberation, was left to the domain of national political communities.

What the EU does not have, therefore, is a formal documentary constitution and one, moreover, the product of a subjective act of approval by the people or their representatives. This idea of a (big 'C') Constitution can be referred to as a democratic or normative or political constitution and the EU does not have a normative constitution in this democratic sense. Almost a decade ago, the German Foreign Minister Joschka Fischer delivered a speech in which he interpreted the underlying social discontent with the EU as an unarticulated will to enact a constitution for the EU. It was necessary, according to Joschka Fischer, to engage in a thorough discussion of the future of the EU, in which the *finalité*, or purpose, of Europe could be discussed and decided upon. The crowning outcome of such a process would be the drafting of a constitution for the Union 'which will deserve its name': in other words it would not be unlike national constitutions. The idea was that the constitution would be a final political form

[39] N MacCormick (2004–2005), 'The health of nations and the health of Europe', The Cambridge Yearbook of European Law Studies 7, pp 1–16.

[40] MP Maduro (2004), 'How constitutional can the European Union be? The tension between intergovernmentalism and constitutionalism in the European Union' in J Weiler and C Eisgruber (eds), *Altneuland: The EU Constitution in a contextual perspective*, Jean Monnet Working Paper 5/04, <http://www.jeanmonnetprogram.org/papers/04/040501-18.html>.

appropriate to its maturity—a sort of coming of age of the EU. The latter is often referred to as a *political* or democratic 'Constitution', a 'big C' Constitution and is very contested—and contestable.[41]

In the political system of the Union, the powers of the core institutions are amended in intergovernmental conferences agreeing changes to the existing treaties. Intergovernmental conferences are, as the name already suggests, diplomatic arenas with conclusions being reached on the basis of diplomatic inter-state bargaining processes. Exceptionally in terms of treaty revision processes, the precursor of the Lisbon Treaty, the treaty establishing a Constitution for Europe, was prepared by a 'Convention' composed of members of national parliaments as well as members of Union institutions and 'representatives' of the Member States.[42] The Treaty establishing a Constitution for Europe was adopted largely after a much more open and deliberative process than the normal treaty-amendment process. In substantive terms it attempted in Part 1 to lay down in relatively understandable terms the basic elements of its political and institutional system in a manner that, at least potentially, was accessible to the non-specialist.

The point is however that even the 'Treaty establishing a Constitution for Europe' was not a big 'C' Constitution that could be compared to the deep structures of national 'Constitutions'. It included language and a few distinct provisions that were state-like in their symbolism.[43] Especially in Part 1 it structured and ordered the basic principles of 'government' in a visible and largely accessible fashion. But for the rest it consisted in the main of institutional and substantive provisions that could have been adopted by the normal treaty-amendment process (both Parts 1 and 3).

As is well known—with two negative referendum results in France and the Netherlands—the EU did not get its big 'C' formal political Constitution but instead with the adoption of the replacement 'Basic Treaty' got another amending treaty, the Treaty of Lisbon, with many of the same substantive provisions. The latter clearly does not aim to be a political or democratic constitution in the sense of some of the provisions and rhetoric surrounding the failed Constitution for the EU. Much of the focus since the Lisbon Treaty has been adopted (and signed) has been on whether it is not the Constitution for the EU in disguise. In my view this is the wrong question and departure point, despite the fact that it can—initially—seem a big issue especially in those countries where it has to

[41] See, in general, A Wiener (2007), 'Contested meaning of norms: A research framework', *Comparative European Politics*, 5/1, pp 1–17.

[42] The precedent for this convention method was the Convention that deliberated on the content of the EU Charter of Fundamental Rights concluded in December 2000. See further: <http://www.europarl.europa.eu/charter/default_en.htm>.

[43] T Christiansen (2005), 'Towards statehood? The EU's move towards constitutionalisation and territorialisation', *ARENA Working Paper, No 21*, available at <http://www.arena.uio.no/publications/working-papers2005/papers/05_21.xml>.

be decided whether or not to hold a referendum another time round.[44] But it is regarded as following the same trajectory as the previously existing one: that of a material, juridical (small 'c') constitution—EU constitutionalism without a Constitutional Treaty.[45]

1.7 The Phoenix Arises

At the time this book went to press the Treaty of Lisbon had not entered into force. Yet quite irrespective of this fact its provisions cannot be ignored in a book on executive power of the EU. The Treaty of Lisbon is but the latest layer potentially to be added to the most visible part of the EU constitution. It is an overlay that will strengthen, consolidate, and rationalize the existing political system in particular to varying degrees. If it never happens then it can simply be excised and the underlying narrative both of visible and invisible constitution making as well as the incremental growth of executive power in the EU political system as such remains equally valid and indeed equally strong. In other words the underlying narrative of this book is not dependent on the Treaty of Lisbon entering into force; yet, given the fact that it most probably will enter into force in one form or another,[46] it is imperative, given the scope and subject matter of this book, that it be considered in an upstream fashion and in some of its detail.

The details of the Treaty of Lisbon were hammered out in diplomatic negotiations behind closed doors, with little possibility for input by national parliaments or civil society at that point. In procedural terms it constitutes a legally convoluted amendment to the two (pre-)existing treaties but substantively it took over at least 90 per cent of the Treaty for a Constitution for Europe that had been rejected in two referendum processes (in France and in the Netherlands), albeit ordered in a less coherent and transparent fashion in structural terms in the case of the Lisbon Treaty, as well as a number of extra (rather discrete) provisions.

This means that even for the specialist it is a considerable challenge to piece the various changes together as well as their relationship with the previously existing institutional and constitutional order. On top of that is the fact that the new institutional set-up under the Treaty of Lisbon has raised a whole series of implementation questions about support structures and others that will require to be

[44] See, for example, the opinion of the Dutch Council of State on this question, answering it, conveniently for the Dutch government, in the negative: Advisory Opinion of 15 February 2008 (W01.08.0004/I/K), available at <http://www.raadvanstate.nl>.

[45] See too S Griller and J Ziller (eds) (2008), *The Lisbon Treaty: EU constitutionalism without a constitutional treaty?* (Vienna: Springer).

[46] See in the same sense, A Dashwood (2009), 'What can be salvaged if the Treaty of Lisbon is lost?' in MK Bulterman et al (eds), *Views of European Law from the Mountain* (The Hague: Kluwer), pp 335–44.

worked out—behind the scenes—in principle in advance of the treaty actually entering into force.

It is beyond the scope of this book to analyse these provisions in any detail with the exception of those relating to executive power.[47] The approach that has been taken is to describe in any event the status quo, the situation after the Treaty of Nice. In addition, the substantive discussion of the manner in which an evolution was conceived to take place, more in the nature and numbers of formal political actors, their roles, and tasks, both in the run-up to the Treaty of Lisbon and in the actual provisions of the Treaty of Lisbon itself, are incorporated into the substantive and thematic discussion throughout the book.[48] The reality however at the time this book went to press was that it was not known conclusively whether indeed the Treaty of Lisbon will enter as such into force, although the indicators are auspicious.[49] The outcome of the Brussels Summit in December 2008—in particular the Irish 'decision' contained in the European Council conclusions and the special protocol(s) planned to be included in a future accession treaty with Croatia—have increased the likelihood that when the Irish vote in a second referendum in Autumn 2009 the outcome will be positive.[50]

In the event however that Ireland does not ratify, the expectation is that the substance of what was agreed in the Lisbon Treaty will enter into force in some manner—possibly without the participation of Ireland (or in a lesser institutional context, for example in the outer chamber of the European Economic Area). Moreover the specific provisions of the Lisbon Treaty, certainly with regard to executive power, form part of a wider and deeper narrative that is ongoing and will continue quite irrespective of the formal entry into force of the formal provisions of the treaty as such. Very often such formal treaties represent an opportunity for 'catch-up' in formal treaty provisions for what has to a large extent being going on in practice anyway. The story is, of course, ongoing and to be continued. The fact that this is so in my view removes none of the salience of an underlying examination of the nature and scope of executive power in the EU and the manner of its evolution both in primary law (treaty-level amendment)

[47] See, for chapter and verse, R Barents (2008), *Het Verdrag van Lissabon: Achtergronden en Commentaar* (Deventer: Kluwer); KH Fischer (2008), *Der Vertrag von Lissabon: Text und Kommentar zum Europäischen Reformvertrag* (Baden-Baden: Nomos). See too S Griller and J Ziller (eds), *The Lisbon Treaty: EU Constitutionalism without a Constitutional Treaty?* (Vienna: Springer).

[48] This book refers to the new numbering of the (consolidated) Treaty of European Union as TEU, Lisbon and the Treaty on the Functioning of the European Union as (TFEU). The Nice Treaty is referred to simply as TEU and TEC.

[49] See further Presidency Conclusions, Brussels European Council 11 and 12 December 2008, available at <http://www.consilium.europa.eu/ueDocs/cms_Data/docs/pressData/en/ec/104692.pdf>. See too, J Crosbie (2009), 'Support for Lisbon rises in Ireland', EuropeanVoice.com (1 June 2009) showing that 54% of Irish voters) are now in favour of the Lisbon Treaty.

[50] See for a more detailed analysis, D Curtin (2009), 'The Irish "no" to the Lisbon Treaty: Ireland's voice and Europe's exit', *Zeitschrift für Staats- und Europawissenschaften/Journal for Comparative Government and European Policy*, pp 31–50.

and in (legal and institutional) secondary 'practices'. The underlying narrative in the various and multiple tides of treaty and other reforms is quite simply that of the expansive nature of executive power, moving in and out of the shadow, and encased in various layers and sediments.

Moreover, there is nothing specific to the EU about this situation. One of the overall trends of our times is the expansiveness of executive power, at the national level, at the European level, and even at the international level. The Treaty of Lisbon makes this element of executive power more visible but it does not create it; failure to ratify it will also not eliminate it. On the contrary, failure to ratify may well aggravate it and force it more underground and less subject to checks and balances in a constitutional sense. Taken as a whole, the Lisbon Treaty does not aggravate the democratic deficit but improves it in a few distinct ways without by any means eliminating it. The rule of law is strengthened as a result of the more streamlined role given to the courts in Luxembourg in partnership with national courts. It makes more visible than was previously the case what the political system of the EU is, who the actors are, what their powers are, and the nature of their decisions in language that can be compared to what happens in national political and constitutional systems. This does not mean that a super-state is being created, rather that we find at the European level the same phenomena that we find at the national level—and indeed increasingly at the international level too.

The difference with the EU level of governance as opposed to either the formal or the informal international levels of governance is that in the former we have a political, constitutional, and legal system at that level of governance capable of providing countervailing power to the 'impetuous vortex' at times of expanding executive power. Only in the European system can, as a result of sustained case law by the European Courts, the Council be forced as an ultimate sanction to 'remove' a suspected terrorist organization from the European 'black list'.[51] In the United Nations system a similar remedy is not available to individuals (and groups of individuals) who feel that their human rights and rights of criminal procedure have been hollowed out from above.

1.8 Mapping the Existing Literature

In the existing literature on the EU, the contours and map of EU executive power in both its political and administrative components is a surprisingly under-researched subject.[52] The formal structure and contours of the executive,

[51] This was as a result of the OMPI line of case law. See Cases T-228/02 *Organisation des Modjahedines du peuple d'Iran v Council and UK* [2006] ECR II-4665 and T-256/07 *People's Mojahedin Organization of Iran v Council*, judgment of 23 October 2008, not yet reported. See too T-284/08 *People's Mojahedin Organization of Iran v Council*, judgment of 4 December 2008, nyr.

[52] Executive bodies' policy formulation and implementation activities are thought to be at least partly accounted for by considering the way that they are organized and staffed, and by viewing

understood as embracing both the political and administrative levels, are rarely the subject of explicit focus in legal or constitutional law textbooks—this has perhaps to do with the fact that constitutional law in particular tends to focus often on certain core constitutional doctrines (such as that of ministerial responsibility to Parliament) or to look at (aspects of) executive behaviour through the prism of judicial review. Lawyers tend to focus, when using the term 'executive', on the core political level as opposed to the underlying bureaucracy. For example, Craig and Tomkins in their edited volume on *The Executive and Public Law*[53] focus above all on the power and accountability of the political level of the executive. There are many legal textbooks, however, that look only at the 'administration' in terms of administrative law proper[54] rather than, more broadly, law and administration in a general constitutional perspective.[55] To my knowledge, *The Executive in the Constitution* is one of the few (legal) books to take a holistic approach to both political and administrative levels and the interconnections between both in the specific (unwritten) constitutional context of the United Kingdom.[56] The work of political scientist Egeberg is however exemplary of a more holistic approach in the EU context.[57]

There is no existing book that focuses in a broad-brush manner on the executive power at the exclusively EU level of governance and across its entire spectrum, although this may well be changing.[58] There is a certain tendency among political scientists when describing aspects of the political system of the EU to focus on one or more aspects of what can be described as executive power of the EU and to map it empirically in a detailed fashion, using either (or both in some cases) quantitative research methods (surveys, etc) or qualitative methods (interviews, etc). This has been done, for example, with regard to (aspects of) the Commission, comitology committees, agencies, networks, etc. In addition, political scientists will tend to focus on 'power' and 'behaviour'

their relationship with other institutions of government (for example parliament or the courts). Understanding how executive institutions and their inter-institutional arrangements themselves change constitutes a rather common focus point for subgroups within political science and public administration. See, for example, M Egeberg (ed) (2007), *Institutional Dynamics and the Transformation of Executive Politics in Europe* (Mannheim: Connex Report Series, 3).

[53] P Craig and A Tomkins (2006), *The Executive and Public Law: Power and accountability in comparative perspective* (Oxford: Oxford University Press).

[54] See, for example, P Craig (2006), *EU Administrative Law* (Oxford: Oxford University Press).

[55] See, for example, P Craig and R Rawlings (2003), *Law and Administration in Europe: Essays in honour of Carol Harlow* (Oxford: Oxford University Press); H Hofmann and A Türk (2006), *EU Administrative Governance* (Cheltenham: Edgar Elgar).

[56] T Daintith and A Page (1999), *The Executive in the Constitution: Structure, autonomy and internal control* (Oxford: Oxford University Press).

[57] M Egeberg (ed) (2006c), *Multilevel Union Administration: The transformation of executive politics in Europe* (Basingstoke: Palgrave Macmillan).

[58] See, for example, the edited monograph by M Egeberg (ed) (2006c) and the special issue of *West European Politics* (2008) edited by D Curtin and M Egeberg (2008), both of which largely focus on the EU institutional level of executive activity.

and often on measuring or understanding the 'real world' map of how power is exercised in practice or to locate aspects of that phenomenon in a 'grand theory' of European integration (of which there are by now many competing forms).[59] But there is no existing work that attempts to view the admittedly fragmentary executive power of the EU (and its component Member States) in a holistic fashion from a constitutional perspective. Nor is there an existing book that looks for EU executive power in unexpected places. Rather than assuming that executive power rests exclusively with the Commission for example, this book will reveal the fact that EU executive power has, in fact and as a matter of practice, developed in different institutions to form a veritable 'patchwork' of EU executive power.

The delimitation of executive power as it has evolved over time involves discussion of a possible politics–administration dichotomy that may not be very visible at the formal treaty level. The executive is generally considered to comprise the individuals—mostly ministers and the civil servants—who actually control, from day to day, the state's instruments of coercion, wealth, and information.[60] The term governance can be used to describe the phenomenon of 'administration unbounded'—in other words, the practice of actors other than the administration as such (government) being included in a process of reaching decisions.[61] This obviously covers a wide range of phenomenon and does not just refer to what is termed within the specific context of the EU, the OMC (the open method of coordination), but covers also, for example, aspects of economic governance and other hard-core policy areas.[62]

1.9 Out of the Shadow

The perspective adopted in this book is that, at this stage in its evolution, the EU is best analysed as an evolving political system in its own right, as something that can be compared to (aspects of) national political systems and not merely as an order external to the national domestic order. Rather it can be compared in certain respects to aspects of the national internal order—without making the argument that it is 'replacing' it. It is neither new nor radical to study the EU and its predecessors from the perspective of comparative politics

[59] See further, for an overview, M Jachtenfuchs (2007), 'The European Union as a Polity (II)' in KE Jørgensen, MA Pollack, and B Rosamund (eds), *Handbook of European Union Politics* (London: Sage Publications), pp 159–73.

[60] T Daintith (1997), 'Regulation' in R Buxbaum and F Mádl (eds), *International Encyclopaedia of Comparative Law*, vol xvii: *State and Economy* (Tübingen: Mohr Siebeck), Ch 10, quoted in T Daintith and A Page (1999), p 2.

[61] This definition was given by M Shapiro (2001), 'Administrative law unbounded: Reflections on government and governance,' *Indiana Journal of Global Legal Studies*, 8, pp 369–77.

[62] On economic governance within the EU see further, I Maher (2007), 'Economic governance: Hybridity, accountability and control', Columbia J of European L, 13/3, pp 679–703.

rather than that of international relations.[63] Even among (some) lawyers, this qualification is accepted nowadays as an accurate description of the nature of the evolving EU.[64]

It has been accepted from the relatively early days of the EU and its predecessors that it possesses 'legislative power' and also 'judicial power';[65] in my view the time has come to re-evaluate 'executive power' at the level of the EU itself. In terms of the EU political system, the emphasis is on the executive power in this book for two main reasons. First, as we have seen it is a surprisingly under-researched topic as a whole. There are many detailed studies in EU studies of specific institutions or actors, either empirical or more legal, but none that looks at the evolving executive power in a holistic fashion as a patchwork of legal provisions and institutional practices. In this sense it was time to redress the balance somewhat and draw attention to the executive power of the EU alongside the clearer and more sharply defined EU legislative power and EU judicial power. It is hoped that this book is a modest—and by no means comprehensive—first step in helping to consider an agenda for further research.

Secondly, as in other political systems across the world, we see that the locus of power is shifting from the legislative power to the often more in shadow executive power. This is true of some national systems but also of the international system of governance, both informal and formal (international organizations). Indeed with regard to the latter—international level—the vacuum in terms of countervailing powers seems greatest. In this sense too we can speak of a certain incremental 'hour of the executive', a phenomenon that this book draws attention to.

This book deliberately adopts a wide and dynamic view of the evolving EU political system and is not limited, as in much of the existing academic work, to the activities of a particular institution, policy sector, or a specific type of decision-making. Rather, the aim of this book—the first to attempt to delimit executive power at the EU level itself in a broad brush and inclusive fashion[66]—is

[63] See, for example, S Hix (1994), 'The study of the European Community: The challenge to comparative politics', *West European Politics*, 17/1, pp 1–30 and his subsequent monograph, S Hix (2005), *The Political System of the European Union*, 2nd edn, The European Union Series (Basingstoke: Palgrave Macmillan).

[64] See, for example, W van Gerven (2005), *The European Union: A polity of states and peoples* (Oxford: Hart Publishing).

[65] See, for example, P Pescatore and C Dwyer (1974), *The Law of Integration: Emergence of a new phenomenon in international relations, based on the experience of the European Communities* (Leiden: AW Sijthoff) who describe the emergence of a 'multinational *legislative power*' (author's emphasis) and a 'European *judicial power*' (author's emphasis).

[66] To my knowledge there is no full-length monograph on the subject either in law or political science other than the doctoral thesis defended some years ago in France: J Jorda (2001), *Le pouvoir exécutif de l'Union Européenne* (Aix-en-Provence: Presses Universitaires d'Aix Marseille). Although a valuable contribution this thesis focuses largely on what I would term the administrative executive and in particular comitology. Understanding how executive institutions (in particular the Commission) and their inter-institutional arrangements themselves change constitutes a rather common focus point for sub-groups within political science and public administration. See, for

to contribute to a process of bringing the EU Executive as inclusively understood out 'of the shadow' by mapping the form and evolution of various executive actors as well as analysing the manner in which this institutional and legal map fits within a constitutional perspective on the rule of law and accountability. At the same time this book does not have the ambition—or the illusion—to be fully comprehensive in undertaking this mapping exercise on a constantly moving—and often hidden—target.

Thirdly, this book is arguably unusual—certainly for a legal book—in the emphasis placed on subterranean legal and institutional practices that evolve incrementally. Attempting to document these legal practices is, however, no easy task for a lawyer more comfortable with the formal and hierarchically superior provisions. Like Sherlock Holmes, magnifying glass in hand, it has required looking behind the treaty provisions to the actual decisions adopted and behind that again to the looser 'practices' of the institutions themselves that make the legal structure operational. All of this detective work has been to facilitate the piecing together of small sediments in order to produce a clearer picture, a core understanding, of complex and often hidden interactions—in unexpected places more often than not. At the same time the type of largely legal and institutional mapping that has taken place is to be distinguished from the type of empirical study of informal practices and understandings that are often carried out by political scientists (via qualitative and quantitative methods of research). Where possible, where such work exists, it is referred to as providing further valuable insight into how often hidden interactions are to be understood or how 'living' institutions and actors actually evolve in empirical practice. At the same time, the more legal and institutional approach based largely on an analysis of published or available documents is supplemented by a series of qualitative interviews with key actors in Brussels (both at the Commission and the Council) in order to supplement the more document-based research and to cross-check both facts and understandings.

1.10 The Book's Mission

The mission of this book is a dual one. First of all, it sets out to reveal the different layers of sedimentation that exist in and around a broad understanding of the 'executive' power at the level of the EU political system both in its political and administrative (or bureaucratic) components (and ultimately including as well actors in the regulatory arena, what I term the 'satellite executive'). It attempts to draw together the 'bits and pieces' of executive power in the EU and in so doing it does not share the Commission's avowedly unitary view of executive power in the

example, the edited monograph by M Egeberg (ed) (2007), and the special issue of *West European Politics* edited by D Curtin and M Egeberg (2008).

EU (namely that *it* is the unique and sole possessor of executive power in the EU political system). Rather it looks in an open fashion at how various (executive) institutions and actors have evolved over time or were 'squatted' with a growing number of executive type powers and tasks. In so doing it hopes to complement our current understanding of the nature of the EU integration process in the highly salient area of executive power, both autonomous and stemming from the constituent Member States.

In focusing specifically on the changing contours of executive power *of* the EU, this book aims above all to make visible in a coherent and systematic fashion the fact that, anyway at this stage of institutionalization and practice of European integration, the nature and scope of executive power in the EU is substantial. It is often underplayed in the debate on treaty reform with much emphasis traditionally being placed on lawmaking and legislative processes and actors as well as the primordial nature of judicial power. But this book puts the spotlight on EU executive powers as such and its organic development, also in unexpected places, without attempting to develop or latch onto a 'grand theory' of European integration. Its approach is more deliberately bottom-up and explorative, even if the exercise is undertaken to all intents and purposes only at the level of the EU political system itself. At the same time it is robustly broad-brush, attempting to outline the bigger picture in terms that hopefully can be comprehensible to someone interested in evolving systems of law and politics at any governance level. It is neither purely legal in its analysis—and those looking for a very detailed account of the applicable legal provisions in all their sophisticated detail may be disappointed—nor purely grounded in a political-science approach.

As with all mapping exercises, the depth of the surface revealed may well be limited. This is almost inevitable in a study that attempts above all to put the subject in its wide spectrum on the map. It in no sense attempts to be exhaustive or even comprehensive. By its very nature although broad-brush, it is also selective and can be criticized for lack of depth within layers, corridors, and shafts. In so doing it reveals the urgent need for further, detailed, complementary empirical work within a variety of disciplines. A number of such empirical studies have already taken place and will be referred to where available; others are still being carried out and there is still enormous scope for new and complementary empirical research projects. At the same time an 'empirical turn' on its own is not necessarily going to increase our understanding of the overall topography. We need to be able to also understand and see the broad contours of the map in order to have a more profound and comparative understanding of the evolution of the EU as a matter of practice. This book is the beginning of a conversation, across certain adjacent disciplines—in particular law, political science and public administration—around the broad topic of executive power in the EU and the various constitutional implications, and is not in any sense an end point.

As a lawyer my methodologies are, almost by definition, limited and, despite having carried out a series of qualitative interviews with actors (mainly in 'Brussels') in order to enhance my understanding of specific features of the political system, my sources are primarily the legal and institutional texts and documents that I have been able to track down. In this regard it must be said that although not always easy or obvious, this task has been greatly facilitated in recent years by the increased accessibility of information (documents) available via the Internet and in particular the register of documents of the Council. I see these sources of 'evidence', the bits of the surface patchwork, as unveiling a layer often hidden but relatively close to the surface, adding an extra element to the—often more informal—empirical sources of political scientists and other disciplines. Informal governance is certainly central to a deeper understanding of how institutions and actors function in practice but so too are the lower-level 'practices' that may take paper form (and thus be accessible to the outsider). In the context of the EU political scientist, Adrienne Héretier has focused on what she terms 'the numerous inconspicuous changes of European institutional rules that are occurring on a daily basis between the large-scale treaty revisions. These small-scale changes may have consequences for the overall change of institutions, albeit not occurring in "a big bang" institutional change, but in small steps.'[67] In other words, such small-scale changes occur in the 'shadow' and are often only (much) later pieced together in a fashion that becomes (constitutionally) visible.

The second mission of this book is to place the layers and bits and pieces of executive power that have been excavated within the framing of a broadly 'constitutional' approach. The constitutional framework postulated in this book is a relatively low-key and small 'c' one. I borrow some of the core precepts of classic constitutionalism as it has evolved over the centuries (rule of law, checks and balances, etc) but my purpose is not to make a contribution to the (many) 'grand theories'—or otherwise—of EU constitutionalism.[68] Rather, at a more basic level, I wish to make visible what often remains invisible and fragmentary in terms of a number of different ways that countervailing power is introduced and fleshed out in the contemporary state of evolution of the EU political system. The extent to which a variety of actors provide a form of checks and balances or countervailing powers to incremental executive power being exercised in a scattered fashion at the level of the EU political system is also mapped, at least in outline form and with regard to a number of key constitutional limits on the exercise of power (rule of law, transparency, and accountability).

What is in fact the relationship of the EU plural executive power with the two other main branches of government, the legislative and the judicial, as a matter

[67] A Héritier (2007), *Explaining Institutional Change in Europe* (Oxford: Oxford University Press).

[68] See further, for example, N Walker (2006).

of living and evolving practice? This involves not only boundary issues and overlapping (or even shared) powers but also the crucial 'constitutional' issue of the extent to which executive power is balanced in a web of relationships and interactions by countervailing powers in the political and legal systems of the EU. Have organic and incremental practices developed over the years that lead to a more profound understanding of the manner in which EU executive power is subject to some countervailing power at the EU level?

1.11 Structure of this Book

The further structure of the book is as follows. Chapter 2 highlights the salience and centrality of contemporary executive power in the EU and aims to provide an overview of how executive power has jumped arenas over the course of time. This does not indicate a replacement of executive powers at other levels or in other arenas but rather an accumulation of executive power (or 'executive order'[69]). The picture is more one of overlapping orders and arenas and not neatly ordered substitution. Chapter 3 focuses on the internal ordering of executive power within the EU political system and discusses the manner in which executive power is balanced by the other 'countervailing' powers in the constitutional system of checks and balances. It focuses on the key 'executive' institutions in terms of their original conception and in terms of the interests they were representing, as well as the manner in which that has evolved to become what can be referred to as a composite executive order of sorts.

Chapters 4, 5, and 6 constitute the core of the institutional mapping that Part II of the book seeks to provide, revealing in the process the various layers and depth to the sedimentation that is already accrued. The emphasis in this part of the book is on the so-called 'tides of reform'[70]—both at treaty level and below, in secondary laws and in what is termed legal and institutional 'practices'. The ebb and flow of the tides, the pace and mix of reform strategies and practices, all in their own way throw up 'sediments' of executive tasks and actors that need to be mapped. Chapter 4 focuses on the political layer, the 'political executive', close to the top layer of the European Council, the Council of Ministers, and the Commission and associated actors (the High Representative of the Union for Foreign Affairs and Security Policy). It is here that the tides of treaty reform have been most prominent and visible and these are detailed if relevant. In addition an impression is given of evolving inter-institutional practices in the relationships

[69] For more specific use of this term, see further D Curtin and M Egeberg (2008).

[70] The use of this term is inspired by reading PC Light (1997), *The Tides of Reform: Making government work, 1945–1995* (New Haven, CT: Yale University). Thanks to Utrecht colleague Dr Kutsal Yesilkagit for drawing this book to my attention.

between different bodies—especially between the political institutions and the European Parliament.

Chapter 5 moves down a layer to the assumed hierarchically inferior 'administrative executive' in its various configurations that are sketched in impressionistic fashion. The administrative executive is composed of the civil servants that go to form the public administration and actually implement and execute public policy in practice. These civil servants are found both at the European level itself (mainly in the Commission but also increasingly in other EU institutions) as well as coming from the national level: the hordes of *national* civil servants and scientific and technical 'experts' that participate in one way or another in EU policymaking processes. Part of the administrative executive may form part of the so-called 'core executive' although clearly not all. Chapter 6 introduces a further layer in institution-building and maps those institutions and actors who, on the whole, have been delegated powers by the political actors, often with the explicit intention of placing their rule-making activities at one remove from political decision-making. Such non-majoritarian agencies, as they are often referred to, have become in recent years an important part of the overall political and legal systems of the EU, without however being reflected at the treaty level.

In continuing the metaphor of sedimentation, the subject of study, the EU Executive, is placed in Part III of the book within the broader framework of constitutionalism and the manner in which, bit by bit and by various 'practices' of different actors, fundamental tenets of executive power may be given shape and substance. The whole point in using the terminology of a visible and invisible constitution is to emphasize the fact that there is an ongoing constitutional narrative, quite irrespective of the adoption or otherwise of a formal democratic big 'C' EU Constitution. The lines of the visible and living constitution are also clear—and becoming clearer—in, for example, recent case law of the Court of Justice where it emphasizes the primordial position of the rule of law within the Union legal order, building on existing case law and interpretations of the underlying constitutional values of the EU system (see Chapter 7 below). The lines of the invisible constitution are understandably more opaque, and often hidden somewhat, so may require more active rooting-out and reconstruction. This can involve issues such as the evolving case law of the Court giving shape to a principle of legal unity across the various 'pillars' (leading to further 'depillarization' in practice, in a manner not easily visible to an outsider: see Chapter 7 below). At the same time, other (political) actors may be involved in this process too as the manner in which the tool of inter-institutional agreements are used illustrates.

Chapter 8 deals with the issue of 'transparency' and the manner in which this principle has evolved, both in law and in practice, to constitute a salient part of the evolving operating system of the EU. It provides clear examples of how the notion of openness or transparency is now, in the contemporary understanding of the EU as a political system, regarded as necessary to confer greater legitimacy on the institutions in the eyes of the citizens. Finally Chapter 9 highlights the manner of the evolution of certain practices of public 'accountability' in the context of a diffuse and fragmented understanding of EU executive power in the Union political system. The invisible constitution of the EU can also include relatively subterranean processes and practices by non-executive institutions, such as the European Parliament for example, that gradually and incrementally is becoming an accountability forum of some significance with regard to various EU satellite actors (in particular the agencies: see Chapter 9 below).

The concluding chapter, Chapter 10, looks to the overall ecology of EU executive power and its relationship with its surrounding environment. The perspective adopted is, in the final analysis, one of the compound or composite nature of this power, in the sense not only of a shared and plural executive at the EU level but also of very often the same actors performing different roles and tasks at different governance levels without this being very clearly visible or generally understood. This fact, or perspective, is then further considered in the light of a number of the so-called 'meta-principles' of the overall political order (such as the principles of legitimacy and of democracy) as well as the arguably lower-level 'organizing principle' (at least in procedural terms) of accountability as quite succinctly and precisely defined and applied. This chapter encapsulates the broader narrative of this book, that is to further contribute and analyse the process of making the invisible visible across the wide spectrum of executive power in the EU political system as a whole.

2

Externalizing National Executive Power

2.1 Locating Executive Power

Executive power in nation states was traditionally cleaved in two: *internal* executive power (national constitutional law) and *external* executive power (international law and international relations). In approximately the same time frame that the concept and practice of internal executive power was delimited more sharply and ultimately 'tamed' to some extent by constitutional principles such as the separation of powers, checks and balances, and the pre-eminence of the rule of law within territorial states, something else was happening in the arena of foreign policy or international relations. The executive power was not only beginning a process of externalization of its functions and tasks in the international arena in cooperation with the executive powers of other Member States; it was doing so in a manner that gradually became subject to certain rules and customs at the international arena, different from those that evolved over time in the internal national arena.

After the Peace of Westphalia in 1648, the intergovernmental order became increasingly sophisticated as regards its institutional characteristics. However, it was not until the advent of the EU and its predecessors that Europe's executive order started to transcend its basically intergovernmental pattern inherited from the past. The EU can be considered distinctive in the family of international organizations as having evolved as a system in its own right, and by virtue of autonomous institutions, into what has been termed an autonomous and new 'executive order'.[1] This can, in particular, be ascribed to the consolidation of the European Commission (the Commission) as a new and distinctive executive centre at the European level,[2] although there are certainly other organs being 'squatted' with executive functions. This phenomenon embraces both specifically European-level civil servants (Eurocrats) as well as national civil servants coming from national sectoral or functional ministries and agencies (the so-called

[1] See further on the use of this term, D Curtin and M Egeberg (2008), 'Tradition and innovation: Europe's accumulated executive order' in D Curtin and M Egeberg (eds), *Towards a New Executive Order in Europe?*, *West European Politics*, 31/4, pp 639–61.

[2] See further, M Egeberg (ed) (2006c), *Multilevel Union Administration: The transformation of executive politics in Europe* (Basingstoke: Palgrave Macmillan).

'new Eurocrats'[3]). The new executive order does not seem to replace former (diplomatic) orders; instead it tends to be layered around already existing—executive—orders so that the result is an increasingly compound and *accumulated* 'executive order' in Europe.[4]

2.2 Executive Power External to the State[5]

One of the defining powers of the executive in virtually all political systems is that relating to defence and security of the 'state' externally. Among early political scientists the word 'diplomacy' was used interchangeably with 'international relations'.[6] After the signing of the Peace of Westphalia, and the division of Europe into a system of territorial states, a system of bilateral diplomacy evolved. This classic model of diplomacy was of a distinct and unified national diplomatic service that 'represented' the state internationally and at the same time could be distinguished from the normal (internal) civil service dealing with governmental policy within the limits of the territorial state.[7]

At the Congress of Vienna in 1815 the diplomatic institution became more formalized; for example, the senior ambassador, ie the ambassador who had been longest at the post in a particular capital, became the *doyen* or dean of the diplomatic body, or corps, in that particular country.[8] The fact that this person represents the other ambassadors in any disputes affecting their corporate rights and interests reflects very well the existence of a community. 'Even as scientists, philatelists and other experts find, when they meet together, that the interests of their calling transcend all differences of nationality or language, so also do the diplomatic services of the several countries evolve a form of solidarity and establish certain tacit standards which they all respect.[9] In her study of key international congresses from 1648 onwards Cross found that diplomats tended to share opinions more often than their respective political masters.[10] The congress semi-institutionalized multilateral diplomacy in the form of conferences at the ministerial and ambassadorial level among Europe's great powers (the Concert of Europe).

3 See further, KP Geuijen et al (2008), *The New Eurocrats: National civil servants in EU policy-making* (Amsterdam: Amsterdam University Press).

4 See further D Curtin and M Egeberg (2008).

5 In these paragraphs I draw heavily from recent work co-authored with political scientist Morten Egeberg. See D Curtin and M Egeberg (2008) where we discuss in more detail the historical evolution of executive power in the international relations arena.

6 See further MKD Cross (2007), *The European Diplomatic Corps: Diplomats and international cooperation from Westphalia to Maastricht* (Basingstoke: Palgrave Macmillan), p 3.

7 See too K Geuijen, P Hart, S Princen and K Yesilkagit (2007).

8 H Nicolson (1969), *Diplomacy* (London: Oxford University Press).

9 H Nicolson (1969), p 40.

10 See further MKD Cross (2007).

National diplomats, coming from the ministries of foreign affairs, gradually became part of a diplomatic community beyond their respective territorial states.[11] Common norms and codes of conduct gradually developed so that diplomats came to perceive themselves as being grounded in two distinct worlds: their respective home state (and administration) on the one hand and the (trans-national) diplomatic community on the other.[12] This model of diplomacy took bilateral relations between states as its foundation. The diplomats operated nationally within the Department of Foreign Affairs and at the same time represented the (unitary) state in its external relations. This model draws a clear distinction between international representation and internal areas of government policy.

According to Claude, 'nothing essentially new has been added by the multilateralization and regularization of diplomacy until the secretariat is introduced; this is the innovation that transforms the series of conferences into *an organization*'.[13] The reason that international organizations are created in the first place is the result of the need felt by states to cooperate within an institutional framework. This need arises because states no longer consider themselves capable of performing a given task independently.[14] In contradistinction to the open-ended and general public tasks of states, international organizations are created to perform specific functional tasks.[15]

The term 'intergovernmental organization' (IGO) already indicates two aspects of international organizations: first, the joining together of the 'governmental' functions of (sovereign) states at the international level. In general, in Europe, the term 'governmental' in this context is used in a restrictive sense as only covering the executive branch of government. On this understanding intergovernmental organizations are concerned with cooperation between the executive branches of the governments of the Member States.[16] Although some may prefer to describe such organizations as merely 'arenas' for lawmaking action, they have also been described as 'for all practical purposes a new kind of lawmaking actor, to some degree autonomous from the states that establish them.[17]

[11] See further J Bátora (2005), 'Does the European Union transform the institution of diplomacy?', *Journal of European Public Policy*, 12/1, pp 44–6; C Jönsson and M Hall (2005), *Essence of Diplomacy* (Basingstoke: Palgrave Macmillan).

[12] See further J Bátora (2005); C Jönsson and M Hall (2005).

[13] IL Claude (1964), *Swords into Plowshares: The Problems and Progress of International Organisation* (New York: Random House), p 175. Author's emphasis.

[14] HG Schermers and NM Blokker (2003), *International Institutional Law: Unity Within Diversity*, 4th rev edn (Leiden: Martinus Nijhoff), p 11.

[15] See, in general, M Virally (1977), 'La notion de fonction dans la théorie de l'organisation internationale' in *Mélanges offerts a Charles Rousseau: La communauté internationale* (Paris: Pedone), pp 277–300.

[16] HG Schermers and NM Blokker (2003).

[17] See, for example, JE Alvarez (2006), 'International Organizations: Then and now', American Journal of International Law, 100/2, pp 324–47, p 333.

Secondly, the institutionalization implied by the term of an 'organization' implied a separate and new entity with legal personality. It was the specific functions to be carried out by the IGO in question that determined the optimal institutional structure of international organizations.[18] These organizations constitute legal orders in themselves which, in the words of Schermers and Blokker:

> are not similar to domestic legal orders, but are instead partial legal orders, concerning only the field of activity of the organization and only those states which choose to participate. The constitutions of these organizations lay down a number of substantive ground rules. Organs are created with their own powers. An institutional framework is established within which the member states can further the objectives of the organization, adapt its substantive rules to changing circumstances and supervise the implementation of obligations by the member states.[19]

There are, in effect, two models operating side by side in contemporary international relations. One model still assumes that states act as relatively unitary actors and may delegate powers to a limited number of international organizations that will then often be directly enforceable. This is in line with the general tendency in IGO's that the organ representing the separate governmental interests—a council of ministers in one form or the other—was the central decision-maker. Decision-making will traditionally take place pursuant to the unanimous consensus (or vote) by all the representatives of the constituent governments. Organs composed of persons independent of the Member States, committees of experts or parliamentary assemblies may play an advisory role, but they will generally not have the power to take final decisions.[20] It has, however, been documented that expert-based permanent secretariats contribute significantly to task-expansion at the international level and that they may also be able to forge transnational coalitions by linking previously disconnected actors.[21] Thus, although international organizations are created by states, once established, they do not necessarily operate as straightforward tools or agents of those states.

The second model of international relations may be termed the 'complex interdependence' model.[22] Slaughter's portrayal of a 'new world order', consisting of disaggregated states that interact in a compound manner within and alongside IGOs, builds heavily on the complex interdependence perspective.[23] It assumes largely disaggregated states in which national civil servants and experts 'interact intensively with one another and adopt codes of best practices and agree on

[18] HG Schermers and NM Blokker, p 8.

[19] Ibid, p 6.

[20] See further HG Schermers and NM Blokker (2003).

[21] RW Cox and HK Jacobson (eds) (1973), *The Anatomy of Influence: Decision making in international organization* (New Haven: Yale University Press); M Barnett and M Finnemore (2004), *Rules for the World: International organizations in global politics* (Ithaca and London: Cornell University Press); J Trondal, M Marcussen, and F Veggeland (2005), 'Re-discovering international executive institutions', *Comparative European Politics*, 3, pp 232–58.

[22] See, for example, RO Keohane and JS Nye (1977), *Power and Independence: World politics in transition* (Boston: Little, Brown and Company).

[23] A-M Slaughter (2004), *A New World Order* (Princeton: Princeton University Press).

coordinated solutions to common problems—agreements that have no legal force but that can be directly implemented by the officials who negotiated them'.[24] Such disaggregated actors include a huge number of non-diplomatic civil servants coming from sectoral or functional ministries, other state actors and agencies who network and collaborate with their own counterparts both transnationally and within IGO's, as well as vast numbers of national scientific experts. In this new model of international relations it is not possible to draw a clear line anymore between international representation of the state externally and the internal policies of the state as applied by government departments (and agencies) other than the department of foreign affairs.

This is the general picture of the kind of executive order that had evolved over the centuries to its current rather institutionalized form of (general) international organizations. It has been argued elsewhere[25] that with the EU and its predecessors Europe's executive order started to transcend its basically intergovernmental pattern inherited from the past. This transformation phenomenon is due, in particular, to the consolidation of the Commission as a new and distinctive executive centre at the European level, outside of the inter-governmental locus, the Council of Ministers (the Council). This raises the need to consider more generally the question as to the nature of the EU (and its predecessors) as such. Must we understand it as a sophisticated international organization and seek comfort in the further refinement of the notion of an international organization (for example a constitutional international organization with citizens and members)?[26] Or is it more accurate, in the current stage of development both of its own institutional system and powers as well as its impact on national political (and legal) systems, to analyse it more in comparative political terms as an evolving political system or (non-state) 'polity'?

2.3 The European Union as an International Organization

One recurring theme in the vast literature on the EU system is the apparent exceptionalism of what has actually developed in post-war Europe. Historians may deny this on the grounds that there are in any event parallels that can be made with ancient times and the rise of the Holy Roman Empire. This may be the first example of a polycentrical order with no fixed hierarchical relations.[27] Another parallel is with the rise of the Catholic Church from the eleventh to

[24] Ibid, p 263. [25] D Curtin and Morten Egeberg (2008).

[26] See, for example, J Hoeksma (2007) on the status of the EU as a constitutional international organization, *De Uitvinding van Europa: De Europese Unie als Nieuw Verschijnsel in het Volkenrecht* (Assen: Van Gorcum).

[27] See, for example, H Zahle (1995), 'The polycentricity of the law or the importance of legal pluralism for legal dogmatics' in H Petersen and H Zahle (eds), *Legal Polycentricity: Consequences of pluralism in law* (Dartmouth: Aldershot).

the fourteenth centuries in Europe and its state-like ambitions. At this time of 'fragmented authority' in Europe, power was shared across several (governance) levels with their own rule-making authority, at times overlapping and at times conflicting.[28]

It can be argued—and often is—that, even in terms of the comparison with other international organizations, the EU is *sui generis*. This label does not identify the distinctive features of the new phenomenon itself. Lawyers are particularly attached to the label of uniqueness. After all, it was the European Court of Justice that as long ago as 1962 ordained that the European Community constitutes 'a new legal order of international law for the benefit of which the states have limited their sovereign rights'.[29] That legal order, in its own words, has a 'special and original nature'. Political scientists phrase the issue a little differently. They commonly refer to the European Community, and its successor the EU, as being unique, representing an *n of 1*, arguably requiring a theory and framing all of its own.[30] This line of reasoning has recently been extended in terms of a constitutional 'core' that may derogate from the norms of general public international law by the Court of Justice in its judgment in the *Kadi* case (see Chapter 7 below).

It is, of course, possible to argue that the processes of integration in Europe are specialized and qualitatively different from processes elsewhere. To say that the EU is unique is simply shorthand for saying that we have not yet developed the categories abstract enough to see the EU as an instance of a more general class of phenomena.[31] It is not part of the national political systems in Europe nor does it (yet) constitute a distinct and fully fledged political unit in its own right. Above all it is seen to be exceptional in that it lacks a so-called '*demos*', a European people, and hence by definition, or so it is asserted, it is a system that *cannot* function democratically. This strange and ill-defined polity was moreover deliberately constructed in this way from the very beginning by national executive politicians.[32] Some authors go so far as to claim this is the national interest, its *raison d'Etat*.[33] This is the idea that national governments use international cooperation to gain influence in the domestic political arena and to overcome internal opposition to their preferred policies.

[28] I am grateful to Jan Luiten van Zanden, Professor in Economic History, University of Utrecht, for drawing this historical parallel to my attention.

[29] See C-26/62 *Van Gend en Loos v Nederlandse Administratie der Belastingen* [1963] ECR 1.

[30] See, for example, JA Caporaso (1997), 'Does the European Union represent an n of 1?', *ECSA Review*, X/3 (Fall 1997), pp 1–5, available at <http://aei.pitt.edu/s4/01/n1debate.htm>.

[31] Ibid.

[32] P Mair (2005), 'Popular democracy and the European Union polity', *Eurogov Working Papers*, No C-05-03, available at <http://www.connex-network.org/eurogov/>.

[33] See, for example, M Koenig-Archibugi (2004), 'International governance as new *raison d'etat?* The case of the EU common foreign and security policy', *European Journal of International Relations*, 10/2, pp 147–88.

But what is the case for the uniqueness of the contemporary EU? Different perspectives will in any event give radically different answers. An international-relations scholar will tend to view the EU as an *external order* that impacts on domestic policies and political institutions. This is the rather classical view that it is still today best analysed as an international organization no matter how sophisticated it has become in these terms.[34] Seeing the EU through the lens of an international organization (and thus as intrinsically something that can be compared to other international organizations) helps, in the words of Paul Magnette, to 'avoid optical illusion, highlight its originality and understand its proper value'.[35]

It does not take much effort to conceptualize the EU as an international organization and indeed, at the formal level, it simply is one in remarkably sophisticated form. If one wishes to be more specific then the EU can be described as an 'international integration-organization'.[36] This label is used for those international organizations that do not merely purport to establish cooperation between their member states but aim to go beyond this cooperation by establishing *integration* in one or more policy areas. The Oxford English Dictionary defines the verb 'to integrate' as the combining of parts into a whole. The element of completeness and unity ('whole') which integration includes does not negate, but rather implies, the possibility of compositeness (the various independent 'parts').[37] 'Integration' can thus range from mere cooperation to ultimately almost complete unification. Federalism has been construed as a particular way of bringing together previously separate, autonomous, or independent territorial units to constitute new forms of union based upon principles that, broadly speaking, can be summarized in the dictum 'unity in diversity'.[38] Both the process of integrating and the end results (the degree of integration achieved) can be considered essential to an analysis of integration. But that can take place in a wide variety of ways with the basic spectrum running from a confederation—a union of states, rather than a single state—to a federation.

An essential feature of so-called integration organizations is that competences are transferred from the member states to the organization or that new competences of the organization are created, for example to set rules to harmonize the

[34] See, for a recent example, W Werner and R Wessel (2005), *Internationaal en Europees Recht: Een verkenning van grondslagen en kenmerken* (Groningen: Europa Law Publishing). See too A Moravcsik (1993), 'Preferences and power in the European Community: A liberal intergovernmental approach', *Journal of Common Market Studies*, (31), p 473.

[35] P Magnette (2005), *What is the European Union? Nature and prospects* (Basingstoke: Palgrave Macmillan), p viii.

[36] The term is used by M Virally (1981), 'Definition and classification of international organisations: A legal approach' in G Abi-Saab (ed), *The Concept of International Organization* (Paris: UNESCO), pp 50–66.

[37] M Cappelletti, M Seccombe, and J Weiler (eds) (1986), *Integration Through Law: Europe and the American federal experience* (Berlin: Walter de Gruyter).

[38] See further M Burgess (2004), 'Federalism' in A Wiener and T Diez (eds), *European Integration Theory* (Oxford: Oxford University Press), pp 25–6.

legal systems of the member states in certain areas.[39] A number of international organizations have evolved into autonomous legal entities with competences to govern the behaviour of the member states. This may be not only at the level of the international legal order but also within the national legal orders of the member states.

The EU is in any event no longer the only (regional) international organization with such competences: NAFTA, Mercosur, and the WTO can all be placed along a continuum with the EU with regard to the level of integration aimed at, with the EU still in the vanguard. It is such integrator organizations in particular 'that are in need of a whole toolbox of governance instruments to steer, stimulate or enforce the cooperation between member states and to get a grip on the actions of their citizens... this means that a larger number of legal acts in a variety of shades conceivably form part of the legal system of international organizations... and thus of the national legal systems'.[40]

2.4 Vertical Delegation of Powers

The executive functions of national governments of policy initiation, policy decision, and policy implementation have to a considerable degree been removed from the domestic arenas and 'delegated' in one form or another to international (and European) arenas. That this has tended to be framed within the parameters of *delegation of powers* is perhaps not surprising as in its literal dictionary meaning executive power implies a power that is not autonomous but that is exercised *on behalf of* someone or something else—God or the people or the law.[41] An executive is he who 'carries out' the intention of others, often that of the law. It will be subordinate to the will of others—of the legislature—and ultimately the people. In other words the executive will formally be an *agent* and logically there must be a principal somewhere that has formally or informally delegated power to the executive agent (the people in a democratic political system).

Political scientists indeed commonly employ a 'principal–agent' analysis to frame delegation and accountability in political systems, both internal and external. Lawyers on the other hand tend to analyse the delegation of powers in terms of legal principles (and in particular the principle of institutional balance in the EU context). At its core in terms of policymaking and rule-making there is an ongoing struggle between notions of diplomatic negotiations among sovereign member states and a more 'democratic' vision of involvement by democratic

[39] I Dekker and R Wessel (2004), 'Governance by international organisations: Rethinking the normative force of international decisions' in I Dekker and W Werner (eds), *Governance and International Legal Theory* (Martinus Nijhoff), pp 215–36.

[40] Ibid, p 236.

[41] HC Mansfield (1989), *Taming the prince: The ambivalence of modern executive power* (The Free Press), p xxvii.

institutions at the level of the political system itself. This struggle between the locus of the 'political' (even if denatured compared to the national level) and the locus of the 'administrative' has been a persistent theme in understanding the ongoing processes of European integration and their qualification, especially in the qualification of the delegation of power that was said to have taken place both vertically (from the Member States) and horizontally (within the EU political system itself).

Delegation is often understood as involving an actor, called a *principal*, relying on another actor, called an *agent*, to act on the principal's behalf. From the early days of the European Community some political scientists defended a rather dominant theory of understanding the process of European integration as a series of (vertical) delegations of powers from the—political—Member States to (most specifically) the Commission as a supranational (administrative executive) actor.[42] On a principal–agent reading, a seemingly supranational actor such as the Commission is constructed as being in fact driven by the political will of the Member States in a dependent relationship. Scholars operating from neo-realist assumptions assert a relationship between the will of the Member States to achieve a common market and the process of European integration.[43] On this view, the mechanism driving forward integration of any kind, legal or political, is the national interests of the (dominant) Member States.[44]

From a (European) lawyer's perspective the political-science approach to a principal–agent framework of analysis may miss important nuances in how the role and tasks of the Commission and other actors, both political and legal, have evolved in the institutional system of the EU and of its interaction with the Member States.[45] Moreover it does not take account of a perspective drawn more from comparative politics rather than (realist) international relations, namely that delegation can be analysed at the level of the EU evolving political system itself (see further below). This would seem to be more in line with the approach taken as well by those political scientists who reject 'high-politics' theories of liberal intergovernmentalism in favour of more 'low-politics' and empirically grounded multilevel governance.[46]

Even lawyers may, however, take a different view. For example, an American legal scholar built on the putative separation of the political from the

[42] See further M Pollack (2003), *The Engines of European Integration: Delegation, agency and agenda-setting in the EU* (Oxford: Oxford University Press).

[43] A Moravcsik (1993), 'Preferences and power in the European Community: A liberal intergovernmental approach', *Journal of Common Market Studies*, 31/4, pp 473–524.

[44] A Moravcsik (2004), 'Is there a "democratic deficit" in world politics? A framework for analysis', *Government and Opposition*, 39/2, pp 336–63.

[45] D Halberstam (2004), 'The Bride of Messina or European democracy and the limits of liberal intergovernmentalism', *Jean Monnet Working Paper No 5/04* (New York: NYU School of Law), available at <http://www.jeanmonnetprogram.org/papers/04/040501.html>.

[46] See, for example, I Bache and M Flinders (eds) (2004), *Multi-Level Governance* (Oxford: Oxford University Press). See too L Hooghe and G Marks (2003), 'Unravelling the central state, but how? Types of multi-level governance', *American Science Review*, 97/2, pp 233–43.

administrative and the subordination of the latter to the former to argue that the powers that are exercised at the EU level are fundamentally considered as being quintessentially non-political (non-majoritarian) and thus of an *administrative* character. The political principals, the Member States, had in this view limited the normative autonomy of their 'agents', the institutions of the EC (EU) to the administrative level.[47] This view seems to represent a rather American approach to administration that traditionally views it as *an appendage* to the three distinct powers (executive, legislative and judicial).[48] It goes very far, arguing that 'the EC as a whole—including its purportedly political branches as well as its judiciary—should be understood as a supranational administrative agency of the Member States severally'.[49]

When applied to the EU and its predecessors this view denies that the EU is a fully fledged political venture and reveals a highly specific understanding of delegation and accountability chains pertaining to the EU, downplaying the possibility, or indeed the value, of parliamentary (majoritarian) forms of democracy at the EU level itself. This approach is in line with the reality that it was not possible to construct in the context of European integration a single chain of delegation and a chain of accountability (running in opposite directions), from the voters to the civil servants that ultimately implement public policy even with multiple links in the chains.[50] Even if we view the national legislature (connected to the voters) as delegating power upwards via the national governments to the EU supranational executive actors (in particular the Commission), it is difficult to link that same authorization by the national legislature with the output of the EU actors in any substantive fashion. It is thus, in any event, difficult to analyse directly elected legislatures as transferring policymaking authority to a non parliamentary (majoritarian) institution in the sense that it would happen in national political systems.

2.5 Complementarity of Politics and Administration

The argument that the EU and its predecessor's powers of policymaking and executive functions are exercised in a delegated relationship of agency for the politically legitimated Member States would seem to be premised on an assumption of 'separation' rather than complementarity of politics and

[47] PL Lindseth (1999), 'Democratic legitimacy and the administrative character of supranationalism: The example of the European Community', Columbia L Rev, 99/3, pp 628–739.

[48] M Rutgers (2000), 'Public administration and the separation of powers in a cross-atlantic perspective', *Administrative Theory and Praxis*, 22/2, pp 287–308, p 297.

[49] A Verhoeven (2002), *The European Union in Search of a Democratic and Constitutional Theory* (The Hague: Kluwer), pp 658–9.

[50] See, in general, K Strom (2000), 'Delegation and accountability in parliamentary democracies', *European Journal of Political Research*, 37/3, pp 261–89.

administration. The administrative power is separate from the executive power in the political sense and subordinate to it.[51] Europeans tend however to use *politics* and *administration* as an internal subdivision of the executive.[52] On the European view the executive is considered to have two types of power: *political*, the leadership of society through the proposal of policy and legislation (agenda-setting and initiative—and adoption—of measures); and *administrative*, the implementation of law, the distribution of public revenues, and the passing of secondary and tertiary rules and regulations.[53] The executive on this understanding comprises the individuals—mostly ministers and the civil servants—who actually control, from day to day, the state's instruments of coercion, wealth, and information.[54] In general terms, administration plays a significant role in West European political systems, as it is an elementary part in the functioning of modern governments. The administration is part of the system of government and administrators *complement* the political role of those who are either elected or appointed by those who are elected. Another way of describing the distinction politics–administration is politics and bureaucracy, which stresses the organizational–structural element as opposed to the substantive tasks.[55] Table 2.1 provides an overview of the politics–administration divide in the EU.

The relationship between politics (or the political executive) and administration is traditionally framed in terms of a clear *hierarchical* distinction between the sphere of politics and the—subordinate—sphere of administration.[56] In this framing the administration serves as a mere transmission belt for the normative judgments made by parliamentary legislation. This 'legitimating myth' has long been exposed and challenged with some scholars advocating an approach based rather on complementarity. Complementarity entails separate parts, but parts that come together in a mutually supportive way. One fills out the other to create the whole. The complementarity of politics and administration is based on the premise that elected executives and administrators join together in the common pursuit of sound governance.[57] This seems much more in line with contemporary realities than any notion of a strict 'separation' of powers.

Rather than distinguishing the 'political' and the 'administrative'/bureaucratic, they can be joined together. According to Joerges, the oxymoron

[51] PL Lindseth (1999). [52] See further, M Rutgers (2000).

[53] S Hix (2005).

[54] T Daintith (1997), 'Regulation' in R Buxbaum and F Mádl (eds), *International Encyclopaedia of Comparative Law*, vol xvii: *State and Economy* (Tübingen: Mohr Siebeck), Ch 10, quoted in T Daintith and A Page (1999), *The Executive in the Constitution: Structure, autonomy and internal control* (Oxford: Oxford University Press), p 2.

[55] This is the approach taken for example by A Wille (2010), *The Normalization of the European Commission: Politics and bureaucracy in an evolving executive* (forthcoming). See further on the term 'core executive', RAW Rhodes and P Dunleavy (1995), *Prime Minister, Cabinet and Core Executive* (Basingstoke: Palgrave Macmillan).

[56] W Wilson (1887), 'The study of Administration', *Political Science Quarterly*, 2/2, pp 197–222.

[57] See, in general, JH Svara (2001), 'The myth of the dichotomy: Complementarity of politics and administration in the past and future of public administration', *Public Administration Review*, 61/2, pp 176–83.

Table 2.1 Executive power in the EU

	Executive power	
	Political	Administrative
Tasks	Agenda-setting Policy initiative Policy decision External representation	Policy implementation Policy application Distribution of public funds Policy supervision

'political administration' refers to the tension between the adoption and implementation of the purely technical decisions based on expertise ('administration') and decisions involving the balancing of certain values ('politics'). The concept of 'political administration' originates from the German term *politische Verwaltung* which was developed by the legal theorist Rudolf Wiethölter.[58] This notion is, according to Joerges, rooted in the concept of 'administration' by Max Weber and the concepts of 'social state administration' and Wiethölter's notion of politics as 'good order' (*gute Ordnung*). This concept contrasts with the notion of a 'strong state' developed by the national-socialist theorist Carl Schmitt.[59] Joerges has used the composite concept of *political administration* in particular to characterize the comitology phenomenon (see Chapter 5 below) but arguably it is of wider application in the EU context. The adoption of seemingly technical regulation of certain (delegated) legislative measures frequently requires addressing issues that are politically sensitive. A second dimension of this concept concerns the implementation of these regulations, which often requires integrating expert knowledge and certain additional considerations in increasingly complex decisions. In Joerges' view, these elements and the tasks resulting thereof can be qualified as 'political' elements if one understands this term in the sense of an Aristotelian 'good practice'.[60]

[58] The original German term is *politische Verwaltung* and was developed by R Wiethölter (1972), 'Wirtschaftsrecht' in A Görlitz (ed), *Handlexikon zur Rechtswissenschaft* (München: Ehrenwirt), pp 531–9.

[59] C Joerges (2001), '"Economic order"—"technical realization"—"the hour of the executive": Some legal historical observations on the Commission White Paper on European Governance', *Jean Monnet Working Paper No 6/01*, available at <http://www.jeanmonnetprogram.org/papers/01/012201.rtf>, p 10 *et seq*. Joerges also points out that the concept of 'political administration' has to be read in the light of the work of Hans Peter Ipsen, the major authority on EU/EC law in Germany. Ipsen's reasoning on supremacy (*Durchgriffswirkung*) is said to have influenced the ECJ's doctrine of supremacy. In Joerges' opinion, Ipsen's reasoning is, however, rooted in the author's authoritarian thinking dating back to 1937 when this author published his habilitation 'Justice and Politics' (*Justiz und Politik: Das Problem der justizlosen Hoheitskakte* (Hamburg: Hanseatische Verlagsanstalt)).

[60] C Joerges (2000), 'Zusammenfassung und Perspektiven: Gutes Regieren im Binnenmarkt' in C Joerges and J Falke (eds), *Das Ausschusswesen der Europäischen Union: Praxis der Risikoregulierung im Binnenmarkt und ihre rechtliche Verfassung* (Baden-Baden: Nomos), pp 349–382, p 364.

Much of the detailed empirical work that has been undertaken by those political scientists (and others, some lawyers) that follow an approach more grounded in the realities of the interactions that actually take place across levels and by different types of actors (in networks or otherwise) of multilevel governance would support the more 'complementary' approach. A number of empirical studies have shown varying intermeshing of the two spheres of politics and administration suggesting that the interaction between the two 'levels' is more complex and differentiated.[61] For example, recent empirical work that has also been carried out in the context of the EU, in particular with regard to the European Commission, has inter alia shown a growing involvement of civil servants in what is traditionally described as 'political' roles.[62]

2.6 The EU as an Evolving 'Political System'

A relatively new perspective grounded in *comparative politics* analyses the evolving nature of the EU in a manner that does not compare it to either international organizations nor states and state formation.[63] This approach analyses the EU not as an external (international) order but as something comparable to *internal* (national) political orders. The purpose of using the term 'political system' is precisely, by using a more abstract category, to avoid the confines of other more precise categories and offices that might not seem to be overtly connected with the state.[64] By using the conceptual language of a 'political system' rather than that of a (federal) state to frame the component parts of the EU[65] it is possible to 'encompass pre-state/non-state societies, as well as roles and offices that might not seem to be overtly connected with the state'.[66]

In the EU context, the use of this classic language in political-science terms as well as its set terms of reference has the major advantage of allowing the EU to be treated as a political system and in this sense as something that is also comparable

[61] See, for example, JD Aberbach et al (1981), *Bureaucrats and Politicians in Western Democracies*, (Cambridge: Harvard University Press); PE Mouritzen and JH Svara (2002), *Leadership at the Apex*, (Pittsburgh: University of Pittsburgh Press).

[62] See further A Wille (2007a), 'Bridging the gap: Political and administrative leadership in a reinvented commission' in M Egeberg (ed), *Institutional Dynamics and the Transformation of Executive Politics in Europe* (Mannheim: Connex Report Series 3), pp 7–41.

[63] For an early example, see S Hix (1994), 'The study of the European Community: The challenge to comparative politics', *West European Politics*, 17/1, pp 1–30.

[64] Ibid.

[65] This term is accepted by both political scientists (S Hix (2005), *The Political System of the European Union*, 2nd edn, The European Union Series (Basingstoke: Palgrave Macmillan); P Mair (2005), 'Popular democracy and the European Union polity', *Eurogov Working Papers*, No C-05-03, available at <http://www.connex-network.org/eurogov/>) and lawyers (W van Gerven (2005), *The European Union: A polity of states and peoples* (Oxford: Hart Publishing), Ch 1).

[66] SE Finer (1970), 'Almond's concept of the political system', *Government and Opposition*, 5/1, p 5.

to *other* political systems. Given this helpful theoretical framework, enabling one to analyse the EU in substantive terms as a (would-be) political system, it is possible to address to the EU the questions that can be addressed to any political system. The attractiveness of understanding the EU as an evolving political system is that it may be divorced from specifically state-building exercises and be viewed at a different level of abstraction. At the same time as a self-standing political system we can address to the Union the questions that can be addressed to any political system. We can expect of the Union the standards of legitimacy and accountability that are expected of other political systems.[67]

A political system in the classic definition of political scientist David Easton has three components: (1) the political system allocates values (by means of policies); (2) its allocations are authoritative; and (3) its authoritative allocations are binding on the society as a whole.[68] When this definition is used then it is not problematic to conclude that the EU indeed constitutes a 'political system' in this sense: its policies are clearly both authoritative and binding.[69] This reasoning applies not only in the context of the traditional 'European Community' and the 'Community method' of decision-making but also to the newer policy areas formally institutionalized as part of the EU with the Treaty of Maastricht. With regard to the area generically known as 'justice and home affairs' it became obvious early on that this area—despite not being fully integrated into the 'Community method' could be considered as an integral part of the evolving EU political system as defined above by virtue of its 'values', its 'authoritative' allocations, and its binding nature on the Union as a whole.[70] Even with regard to the putatively more intergovernmental common foreign and security policy (CFSP) it was also argued, already a number of years ago, that it too makes authoritative allocations that are binding on all the EU Member States.[71] As Allen once put it, the EU 'is now trying to reproduce foreign policy governance without an actual government'.[72]

A political system defined in Easton's abstract general manner does not imply the creation of a state as such; indeed the purpose of this understanding of the nature of the EU is to avoid characterizing the EU as becoming a state as such, federal or otherwise, but to stick to the more neutral and abstract qualification

[67] See, in general, P Mair (2005).

[68] D Easton (1953), *The Political System: An inquiry into the state of political science* (New York: Alfred Knopf), p 130. See too P Mair (2005).

[69] See too, in this sense, A Follesdal and S Hix (2005), 'Why is there a democratic deficit in the EU: A response to Majone and Moravcsik', *CONNEX*, No C-05-02, available at <http://www.connex-network.org/eurogov/pdf/egp-connex-C-05-02.pdf>.

[70] See further, for details of the evolution of this policy area, S Peers (2006), *EU Justice and Home Affairs Law* (Oxford: Oxford University Press).

[71] See further ME Schmidt (2004), *Europe's Foreign and Security Policy: The institutionalization of cooperation* (Cambridge: Cambridge University Press), p 176 *et seq.*

[72] D Allen (1998), '"Who Speaks for Europe?" The search for an effective and coherent external policy' in J Peterson and H Sjursen (eds), *A Common Foreign Policy for Europe?* (London, New York: Routledge), pp 41–58, at p 48.

of a political system, which also applies to non-state systems. But the categorization of the EU as a political system in its own right does point to the fact that the dichotomy between (external) international relations and (internal) democratic politics is no longer apposite in all its simplicity to the Europeanization processes that take place in and around the EU. Nor does the use of the term 'political system' imply necessarily the search for the equivalent of an EU 'government' in any individual institution; rather a less institutional and more functional approach to executive power is preferred and considered more fitting to the specifics of the EU political system and the manner it has evolved—bit by bit—over time.

Hix gives one of the most elaborate accounts of the political system of the EU in his full length monograph on the subject. His elaboration (from 2005) of the basic interests, institutions and processes in the EU political system (the arrows indicate the directions of the connections: complete arrows indicate a strong/direct link, and non-continuous arrows indicate a weaker/non-direct connection) is reproduced in an adapted and modified version in Fig 2.1 below. In my view this illustrates well the plural nature of EU executive power as well as its inter-connections both at the national level and at the European level. Under 'government' I think the European Council needs to be factored in more prominently even before the Lisbon Treaty enters into force. In addition under 'policymaking' what I term the administrative and satellite executive could be included more explicitly, in particular the central role played by comitology committees as well as the increasingly powerful (at least in their ability to take binding decisions) EU level agencies.

When we look at the EU and compare it to other political systems in the post-industrial world the most striking point is its non-responsiveness in terms of elections, parties, and the conventional procedures of popular democracy. At the same time the Union is institutionally part of the national political systems of the Member States. At present we only find the conditions for electoral and party democracy at the national level and even these are weakening. Even at the national level where politics is located, the EU, in common with an increasing number of issue areas, is not in fact the subject of contestation in real elections by the national political parties. In neither national elections nor European elections are citizens given a decisive vote. This leads to what political scientist Peter Mair has termed the 'depoliticization of the Europeanization dimension in the national sphere'.[73] Depoliticization refers to 'the process of placing at one remove the political character of decision-making'.[74]

There is a whole strand of literature—particularly in political science—that seeks to show both how there are no real 'politics' in the sense of electoral and other contestation at the EU level and how this is the 'medicine' the EU needs

[73] P Mair (2004), 'The Europeanization dimension', *Journal of European Public Policy*, 11/2, pp 337–48, p 339.

[74] P Burnham (2001), 'New Labour and the politics of depoliticisation', *British Journal of Politics and International Relations*, 3/2, pp 127–49, p 128.

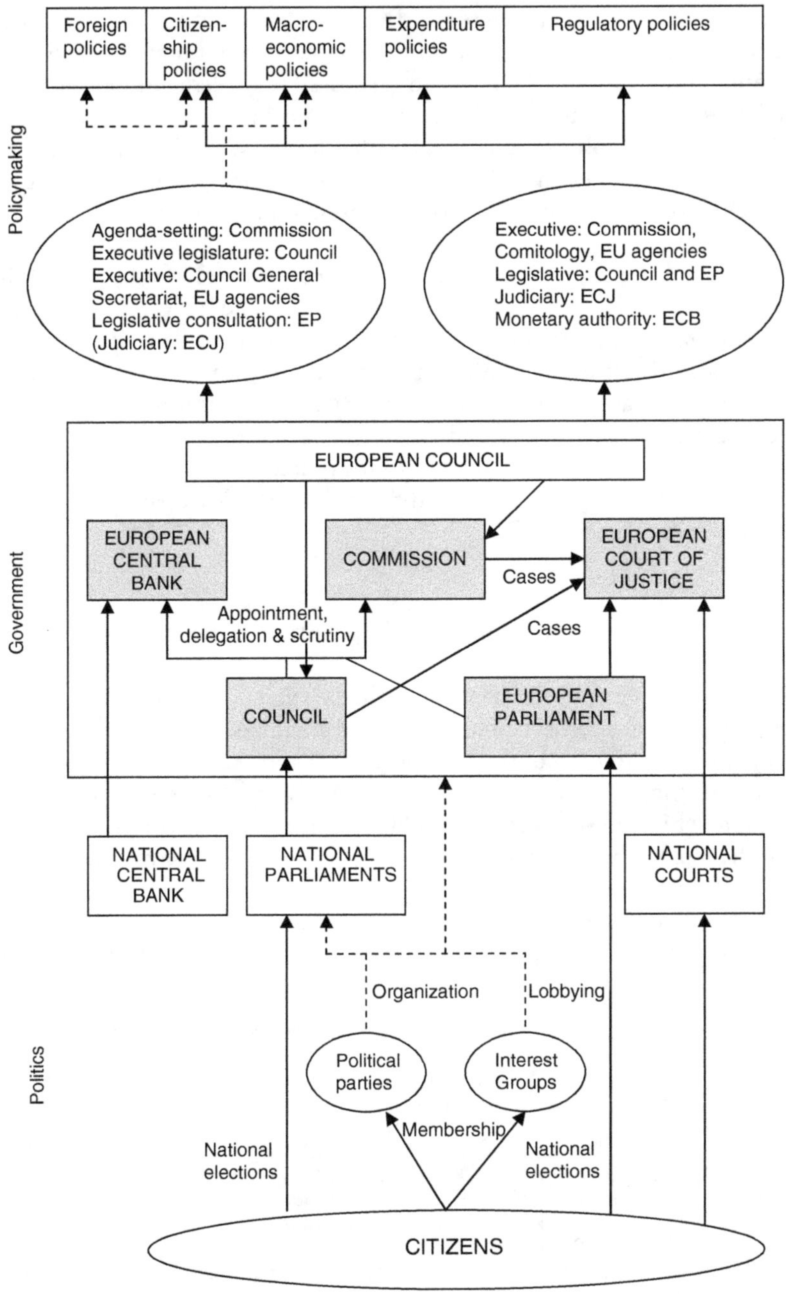

Fig 2.1 The EU political system

Source: A modified and amended version of S Hix (2005), *The Political System of the European Union* (Palgrave MacMillan), Fig 1.1, p 6.

and how that can be administered.[75] The political system of the EU contains elements of parliamentary democracies (that have been augmented in recent years, especially in recent treaty-reform exercises)[76] and elements of (semi-) presidential systems (that have likewise been increased in recent treaty-reform exercises in particular).[77] But it remains a peculiar hybrid with, at its very core, what has been termed a deficit in 'politics' in the sense that it is not in any meaningful sense premised on a system of electoral accountability, political contestation, or party politics.[78]

This aspect of its original design is however compensated for by the emphasis put on law and legal integration. The ultimate goal of the EU (previously the EC) may always have been political (ever-closer union among the peoples of Europe), its immediate objectives economic and social, but the means and techniques used to achieve them have traditionally been 'legal': the application and progressive development of common rules and enforcement procedures. Moreover, the law defines the framework within which political actors operate, 'controlling and limiting their actions and relations and determining, at least partially, the effects and effectiveness of their acts'.[79]

2.7 Horizontal Delegation of Powers

Lawyers tended in any event from the early days to take a different approach to the principal–agent approach of some political scientists. The classic legal analysis started with the founding of the European Coal and Steel Community (ECSC) in 1951 with the ECSC functioning as if it were a law (often called a *traite-loi*) pursuant to which powers were delegated to institutions that could only function within the scope of those powers and within the policy framework set out in the treaty itself. As Advocate-General Lagrange put it in those early days: 'The Treaty is based upon delegation, with the consent of the Member States, of *sovereignty* to supranational institutions for a strictly defined purpose.'[80] Lawyers tended to

[75] See, for example, S Hix (2007), *What is Wrong with the European Union and How to Fix It* (Cambridge: Polity Press).

[76] See, for example, B Crum and JE Fossum (2009), 'The multilevel parliamentary field: A framework for theorizing representative democracy in the EU', *European Political Science Review,* 1/2, pp 249–71.

[77] See, for example, WT Eijsbouts (2005), 'De Macht, de Mensen, het Model: Europa's Grondwet à l'Américaine', *Nederlandsch Juristenblad,* 80/20, pp 1024–34.

[78] P Mair and J Thomassen (2010), 'Electoral democracy and political representation in the European Union' in P Mair and J Thomassen (eds), *Representation and the European Union,* special issue of *Journal of European Public Policy* (forthcoming).

[79] M Cappelletti, M Seccombe, and J Weiler (eds) (1986), *Integration Through Law: Europe and the American federal experience* (Berlin: Walter de Gruyter).

[80] See Opinion of Mr Advocate General Lagrange delivered on 14 June 1957 in Joined Cases 7/56 and 3–7/57 *Dineke Algera et al v Common Assembly of the European Coal and Steel Community* [1957] ECR 39. Author's emphasis.

analyse the powers and tasks of the Commission above all as 'constituting the most original and most supranational institution', acting independently from the Member States with its main mission to protect and serve the *general interest* of the EU and its predecessors. At the same time they stress its eclectic nature in terms of the mixed bag of functions it has been conferred with by the original EC Treaty, as subsequently amended—legislative, executive, and (quasi-) judicial.[81] Legally speaking, powers had in fact been 'delegated' by the Member States to this autonomous actor subject to a number of legal and political constraints but the powers could not be reclaimed or repatriated by the Member States.[82]

The political system of the EU has in any event evolved quite substantially in practice in recent years to the point where the EU unquestionably possesses rather full-scale legislative power and increasingly expansive executive power. The distinctive feature of the horizontal EU political system as it has evolved is precisely the fact that it constitutes a political system without a single and clear political principal at that level (whether Member States/national parliaments, the Commission or the Council or—even—the European Council).[83] This absence of a single political principal within the EU institutional configuration is a corollary of the spirit that inspired European construction itself, namely balance and compromise. If anything, when it comes to the politics of delegation at the level of the horizontal EU political system, it is characterized by a multiplicity of—at times competing—principals.[84] These principals have delegated powers to various 'agents' within the EU political system itself and, in so doing, are bound by certain legal principles. Is there another way to give effect to democratic input by referring to a principle of balance between interests represented and between the institutions that represent those interests?

In the context of the EU political system there are two contexts in which a 'delegation of powers' can be said to take place at the horizontal level. First, the attempts made by the Commission (and the Council) in particular to delegate de facto some of its own administrative executive power to other actors (see Chapter 5 below). Over the course of at least the past decade it has been engaged in a process of trying to refocus its own work on what it considers to be its more 'political' tasks such as policy initiation, policymaking, etc and to delegate away its perceived non-political tasks of management and 'administration' to 'satellite' actors such as executive agencies. The institutional context of 'comitology'

[81] See for example, the descriptions of formal composition and powers or tasks in P Craig and G de Búrca (2003), *EU Law: Text, cases and materials*, 3rd edn (Oxford: Oxford University Press), pp 54–65 and the similar approach taken in D Chalmers et al (2006), *European Union Law: Text and material* (Cambridge: Cambridge University Press), pp 87–101.

[82] See, for example, J de Zwaan (2004), 'The role of the European Commission over the years: Changes and challenges' in J de Zwaan et al (eds), *The European Union: An ongoing process of integration* (TMC Asser Press), pp 53–69.

[83] See, in particular, R Dehousse (2008), 'Delegation of powers in the European Union: The need for a multi-principals model', *West European Politics*, 31/4, pp 789–805.

[84] Ibid.

committees may be relevant in this context too. Such 'practices' are hugely relevant to understanding the evolving nature of the Commission as an executive institution and the fragmentation of certain aspects of executive power within the Union institutional system as a whole.

The other salient context of 'delegation' is in relation to the array of 'agencies' created over the course of the past decades, some exercising tasks previously exercised by the Commission and other exercising 'new' tasks at the European level or tasks exercised previously by the Member States and their administration (see Chapter 6 below). Some delegation attempted to be 'internal' to the institution delegating (for example, delegation by the Commission to 'executive agencies' and to previously existing 'private' actors) while others are clearly external and involve the setting up of new institutions and actors that go on to acquire a life and practice of their own. A proliferation in the creation and tasking of actors carrying out rule-making and even legislative functions,[85] at the specifically European level of governance, has taken place. Such European-level administrative actors constitute 'depoliticized' decision-making arenas that are insulated to some degree from political decision-making.

2.8 Beyond the Visible

In the evolving political system of the EU, certain actors have always to some extent taken shape and substance *outside* the formal treaty provisions. This is the case of the European Council and of early variants of comitology committees in particular. In recent years, however, this phenomenon has accelerated and expanded. The manner in which powers and tasks are being delegated in addition to what I term 'satellite' committees, agencies, and networks established and active at the European level of governance, is a striking illustration of the development in practice of institutional structures in layers outside (on the whole) the formal treaty framework.[86] Actors such as comitology committees and agencies are not grounded in a legal basis in the Union treaties as such but in an array of formal and more informal secondary- and tertiary-level texts and rules. They are increasingly being given tasks that go beyond the purely informational to the regulatory (decision-making) and even operational.[87] If anything, this process is currently in acceleration, not the contrary—and quite irrespective of whether the

[85] R van Schendelen and R Scully (eds) (2003), *The Unseen Hand: Unelected EU legislators* (London: Frank Cass Publishers).

[86] See too G de Búrca (1999), 'The institutional development of the European Union: A constitutional analysis' in G de Búrca and P Craig (eds), *European Union Law: An evolutionary perspective* (Oxford: Oxford University Press), pp 55–82.

[87] See further D Curtin (2006a), 'Delegation to EU non-majoritarian agencies and emerging practices of public accountability' in D Geradin, R Munoz, and N Petit (eds), *Regulation Through Agencies: A new paradigm of European governance* (Cheltenham: Edgar Elgar), pp 88–119.

Treaty of Lisbon enters into force or not.[88] Even in the case of policies where the formal decision-making rules resemble the standard 'community method', it can be a struggle to keep the locus of decision-making within the formal rules of the political system. These 'satellites' are not at the heart of the 'community method' as such but in orbit around it, with differing ties back to the core political actors and the formal decision-making processes depending on the actor involved.

There is, of course, nothing specific or unique to the EU about non-majoritarian decision-making. It happens at the national level too and also at the level of (intergovernmental) international organizations. But national, technocratic bureaucracies are embedded in democratic states and, in some fashion, in national governments. At the levels of governance beyond the nation states there may be either no link or only a very weak link with electoral accountable government. They have, however, on the whole become more 'visible' in recent years thanks to extensive information made available on the Internet, both passively and actively.[89] They are part of the understanding of the expansive vortex of power in and around core executives and also at the level of the political system of the EU. Their accelerated growth and the absence of any overall institutional design structure is all part of the landscape of the 'hour of the executive'.

[88] See, for example, the scope of the (autonomous) rule-making powers that are being given to the new so-called Lamfalussy agencies currently under construction. See the proposed Agency for the Cooperation of Energy Regulators, Proposal for a Regulation of the European Parliament and of the Council establishing an Agency for the Cooperation of Energy Regulators (SEC(2007) 1179) (SEC(2007) 1180), COM/2007/0530 final—COD 2007/197, and the proposed Telecoms Agency, Common position adopted by the Council with a view to the adoption of a Regulation of the European Parliament and of the Council establishing the Group of European Regulators in Telecoms (GERT), 9 February 2009, 2007/0249 (COD).

[89] See further G de Búrca (1999); P Craig (2006), *EU Administrative Law* (Oxford: Oxford University Press).

3

Balancing Executive Power

3.1 The Impetuous 'Vortex' of Power

Niccolo Machiavelli (1469–1527) was the first writer on politics to use the word 'execute' frequently and thematically in its modern sense.[1] In his case, the use of the word 'execute' implied an outsized executive who, because the function of punishment must be understood politically, is not confined to carrying out the laws. Machiavelli's *Prince* governed by reminding his subjects that necessity is stronger than principle. Machiavelli's executive government is not ordinarily visible unlike, for example, the Aristotelian regime where the form of politics shows the character of politics and political appearance in general corresponds to political reality. Yet executive power is not entirely invisible either, revealing itself in a myriad of ways on important occasions. Nonetheless the scope and nature of executive power in a given political system is difficult to define in substantive terms and may be highly ambivalent.

The inadequacy of formal, constitutional definitions of executive power is a widely shared phenomenon, as study of various national systems from a comparative perspective has shown.[2] This may have something to do with the fact that the executive power is rarely fixed and determinate but evolves over time, shaped by social and political circumstances, legal and institutional practices, as well as the letter of a constitution. Even in national political and constitutional systems that have been designed to have one core executive organ (a president, a government, etc) it appears that the formal (constitutional) texts reveal little by way of detail in terms of definition.

Alexander Hamilton wrote that the judiciary was 'the least dangerous' branch of government.[3] James Madison was however in no doubt that it was the legislative branch that was 'the most dangerous'. 'The legislative department', he wrote, 'is everywhere extending the sphere of its activity and drawing all power into its

[1] See further HC Mansfield (1989), *Taming the Prince: The ambivalence of modern executive power* (New York: The Free Press), Ch 1.

[2] P Craig and A Tomkins (eds) (2006), *The Executive and Public Law: Power and accountability in comparative perspective* (Oxford: Oxford University Press), p 4

[3] A Hamilton, J Madison, and J Jay (1961), *The Federalist*, BF Wright (ed), Essay No 78 (Alexander Hamilton) (Cambridge, MA: The Belknap Press of Harvard University Press), p 490. See too <http://thomas.loc.gov/home/histdox/fedpapers.html>.

impetuous vortex.'[4] From a contemporary perspective the picture has changed rather dramatically. Never has the executive branch been more powerful nor more dominant over its two counterparts, not only in the United States but also worldwide. The executive branch of government arguably subsumes much of the contemporary tripartite structure of government, constituting 'the most dangerous branch'[5] compared to the legislative and judicial branches. The suggestion is that the long tentacles of executive power are both encroaching and tenacious and that the executive power is, in any event by early in the 21st century, the most powerful organ of nation states.[6]

This 'impetuous vortex' of executive power also exists at the international and European levels of governance. The result of the obedience claim of international law coupled with the conflation of government and State which international law posits results in 'a monstrous empowerment of the executive branch at the expense of other political estates.'[7] Part of the problem lies in the fact that the borderlines between the different levels of governance—international, European and national—are increasingly grey, uneven, and porous. Indeed it is often the same political actors that appear on the various political stages, even though they may play different roles in each. The connections between these levels are mainly made by members of the national executive power and not by relationships between the legislative bodies at the various governance levels.

3.2 The Separation of Powers

The classic formulation in modern times is that there are three distinct branches of 'government'—the legislative power, the executive power and the judicial power—which should be discharged by three separate agencies—the legislature, the executive and the judiciary—and that no individual should be a member of more than one of them. The separation of state powers has been a central concept

[4] These are the words originally used by James Madison to describe the 'legislative department'. See A Hamilton, J Madison, and J Jay (1961), *The Federalist*, BF Wright (ed), Essay No 48 (Alexander Hamilton) (Cambridge, MA: The Belknap Press of Harvard University Press), p 343. See too <http://thomas.loc.gov/home/histdox/fedpapers.html>.

[5] See, for example, MS Flaherty (1996), 'The most dangerous branch', Yale LJ, 105/7, pp 1725–839; and, more recently, J Coleman (2006), 'The most dangerous branch? Mayors, governors, presidents and the rule of law. A symposium on executive power: Introduction', Yale LJ, 115/9, pp 2215–16, at p 2215. Alexander Hamilton wrote in The Federalist Papers that the judiciary was 'the least dangerous' branch. See A Hamilton, J Madison, and J Jay (1961), *The Federalist*, BF Wright (ed), Essay No 78 (Alexander Hamilton) (Cambridge, MA: The Belknap Press of Harvard University Press), p 490. See too <http://thomas.loc.gov/home/histdox/fedpapers.html>.

[6] See too P Craig and A Tomkins (eds) (2006), p 1.

[7] JHH Weiler and J Motoc (2003), 'Taking democracy seriously: The normative challenges to the international legal system' in *International Economic Governance and Non-Economic Concerns: New challenges for the international legal order* (Vienna: Springer), pp 47–77, pp 47 and 67.

of modern constitutionalism ever since Montesquieu[8] and has been intricately tied up with attempts to delimit the scope of inter alia executive power. The separation of the executive from the legislature in particular was used as a means to avoid tyranny denying the executive the privilege of law making and ensuring that the legislative power serves the rule of law and not ambitious men. The primacy of human legislative power was devised in order to ensure the sovereignty of the rule of law.[9]

The separation of powers as it is classically understood includes the idea that one branch of government will be checked and balanced by the action of another.[10] The essential constitutional 'value' behind the principle is that it functions as a guarantee against tyranny—or put more positively—in order to ensure the protection of liberty.[11] As James Madison put it in *The Federalist Papers* 'if men were angels, no government would be necessary. If angels were to govern men, neither external nor internal controls on government would be necessary.'[12]

It should however be recalled that the principle of the separation of powers as originally conceived is, in any event, not often respected in practice or only weakly. As Vile put it in his classic work:

> The pure doctrine of the separation of powers implied, that the functions of government could be uniquely divided up between the branches of government in such a way that no branch need ever exercise the function of another. In practice such a division of functions has never been achieved, nor indeed is it desirable that it should be, for it would involve a disjuncture in the actions of government which would be intolerable.[13]

The numerous instances of fusion rather than separation of powers are well known and there are also many functional overlaps in different constitutions.[14] This is also the case in the political system of the EU where no rigid or formal

[8] See, for example, MJC Vile (1967), *Constitutionalism and the Separation of Powers* (Oxford: Clarendon Press); E Barendt (1995), 'Separation of powers and constitutional government', Public Law, 21, pp 599–619. A clear expression may be found in Art 16 of the French Declaration of the Rights of Man of 1789: 'Any society in which the safeguarding of rights is not assured, and the separation of powers is not observed, has no constitution.' The principle of the separation of powers was also discussed extensively in *The Federalist Papers* and is reflected in Articles I (legislative power), II (executive power) and III (judicial power) of the US Constitution. This organic understanding of the separation of powers is also found in various other constitutions around the world, both written and unwritten.

[9] See further HC Mansfield (1989).

[10] See G Marshall (1971), *Constitutional Theory* (Oxford: Clarendon Press).

[11] See further HC Mansfield (1989).

[12] A Hamilton, J Madison and J Jay (1961), *The Federalist*, BF Wright (ed), Essay No 51 (James Madison) (Cambridge, MA: The Belknap Press of Harvard University Press), p 356, <http://www.constitution.org/fed/federa51.htm>.

[13] See MJC Vile (1967), p 318.

[14] For examples drawn from the field of British constitutional law, see A Tomkins (2001), 'Separation of powers, ancient and modern', St Catherine's College, Oxford, available at <http://www.utexas.edu/law/conferences/oxford/>.

system of separation of powers exists,[15] at least not in the sense of an organic assessment of executive power.

One aspect as we have seen of the dominance of executive power is the intensity of the powers it acquires in certain exceptional conditions (eg the so-called 'war on terrorism'). Another is the fact that it has simply proliferated way beyond the original conception of the executive as something profoundly political to embrace the administrative (civil servants) and the technical (experts and science advisers). These categories were not originally included in the tripartite principle. Indeed the American approach has been to regard 'administration' (or bureaucracy) as an appendage to executive power and not as at its core.[16]

3.3 A Residual Approach to Executive Power

Over the years, various attempts have been made to brand the increased influence of such 'new' actors as requiring further categorizations in terms of 'new' branches of government. These include what has been variously called the 'fourth' branch of government (public administration and civil servants),[17] the 'fifth branch' of government (science advisers and experts as policymakers)[18] and even a further (sub) branch (autonomous 'unelected organs').[19] The latter can also include more (mixed) private bodies performing in some sense public functions as well as the more classic non-majoritarian (unelected) agencies.

Non-majoriarian agencies are the term political scientists use to refer to all those bodies and organs that are 'unelected' in the national political processes.[20] It denotes the set of institutions—commissions, agencies, boards, and

[15] See too K Lenaerts (1991), 'Some reflections on the separation of powers in the European Community', Common Market L Rev, 28/1, pp 11–35, p 13.

[16] M Rutgers (2000), 'Public administration and the separation of powers in a cross-Atlantic perspective', *Administrative Theory and Praxis*, 22/2, pp 287–308.

[17] What has been called the 'fourth branch' of government has been variously described: already in 1937 *The President's Committee on Administrative Management* referred to independent regulatory committees as a 'headless Fourth Branch of Government' and in the 1960s it was variously used to refer to the press and media on decision-making (see D Cater (1963), *The Fourth Branch of Government* (Boston: Houghton Mifflin)) and the (federal) civil service (see P Woll (1963), *American Bureaucracy* (New York: Norton). See too the work in Dutch by R Crince Le Roy (1969), *De Vierde Macht* (Den Haag: Vuga-Boekerij); R Crince Le Roy (1976), *De Vierde Macht: Een Hernieuwde Kennismaking* (Den Haag: Vuga-Boekerij); and M Bovens (13.08.2000), 'De Vierde Macht Revisited: Over Ambtelijke Macht en Publieke Verantwoording', *Inaugural Lecture, University of Utrecht.*

[18] S Jasanoff (1990), *The Fifth Branch: Science advisers as policymakers* (Cambridge, MA: Harvard University Press). The term 'fifth branch' is also used by some authors to refer to the phenomenon of interest groups as part of a broader governance process.

[19] F Vibert (2007), *The Rise of the Unelected: Democracy and the new separation of powers* (Cambridge: Cambridge University Press).

[20] Ibid.

tribunals—that perform regulatory and other functions.[21] The idea is often that the input of (unelected) independent expertise into decision-making will contribute to better risk assessment and risk management.[22] They may exist in layers in and around the formal political institutions—with differing degrees of autonomy de facto and *de jure*. A public non-majoritarian institution is a wide term for all those organizations that spend public money and fulfil a public function but exist with some degree of independence from elected politicians. The Commission can itself be considered as a non-majoritarian institution but there are also many others operational within the EU political system itself with looser affiliations with a 'political' core. In recent years the empirical range of such depoliticized or 'non-majoritarian' actors has increased considerably as has the type of task that is conferred or delegated by the EU institutions and by the EU Member States as the overview provided in Table 3.1 illustrates.

Table 3.1 Tasks of EU agencies

	European Union		
	EC	CFSP	PJCC
Information Providing/ Advisory	CEDEFOP, EEA, EU-OSHA, ECDC, EUROFOUND, FRA, EMCDDA, ENISA	EUSC, ISS	
Management	EAR, ETF, GSA, CdT		CEPOL
Operational/(Judicial) Cooperation	FRONTEX, CFCA, EMSA, EASA	EDA	EUROPOL, EUROJUST
Decision-making	CPVO, EASA, OHIM, EMEA, ECHA		
(Quasi-) Regulatory	EASA, EFSA, EMEA, EMSA, ERA		

What is noteworthy with regard to the so-called 'new' branches of government is that they can all in some sense be considered as types of 'satellite' actors around the executive power as such, rather than one of the other core branches, legislative or judicial (see Chapter 6 below). This may have something to do with

[21] G Majone (2002), 'The European Commission: The limits of centralization and the perils of parliamentarization', *Governance: An International Journal of Policy, Administration and Institutions*, 15/3, pp 375–92, p 385.

[22] F Wendler and E Vos (eds) (2006), *Food Safety Regulation in Europe* (Antwerpen: Intersentia).

the fact that it is much easier to define and delimit the 'judicial power' or tasks of a judicial nature, 'legislative power', and a legislative assembly than the executive power as such or the scope of governmental (and non-governmental) power. Both courts and legislatures can be defined and written about, extrapolated from particular constitutions—even if there are, of course, a number of institutional differences in different contexts. This is in real contrast with the executive: the diversity of executives between states and the variety of institutions within the executive makes an abstract approach outside the bounds of an actual constitution impossible.[23]

The 'residual' approach to executive power is, in my view, the approach that most aptly describes the manner in which the EU institutional systems have been conceived and applied in practice. The 'residual' approach sees executive power as the power that is not exercised by anyone else—what is 'left over'. Indeed the provisions of the Treaty establishing a Constitution for Europe (and subsequently those of the Lisbon Treaty) explicitly came up with a category of functions or powers that were what was left over after the legislative had been defined. These were defined in the negative as the 'non legislative'. Two specific instances were then given of such non-legislative powers—delegated legislation that could be conferred on the Commission and the existing comitology procedures. But in addition what were not mentioned explicitly in this part of the treaty were all the other powers or jurisdiction that are identified and attributed (but clearly not legislative or judicial powers). Some of these latter powers are in line with the fact that executives in modern political systems are given specific powers that are neither 'executive' in nature in this literal meaning nor subordinate or delegated. Thus executives may initiate legislation, they may in some circumstances veto legislation, and they have a monopoly on foreign policy.

This approach takes into account the reality that it is very difficult to delineate executive power with a comparable degree of precision to legislative power or judicial power. The topography of executive power is quite simply more messy and fragmented and consists of more 'bits and pieces' than any other branch of government. This is in line moreover with the reality of the expansive nature of executive power across governance levels and countries.[24]

My approach to the mapping of executive power does not involve the addition of new layers or branches of government nor indeed accept the need for a so-called 'new separation of powers' as argued by Vibert in particular. Rather, I accept that the executive power is more fragmented and more plural than either its legislative or judicial counterpart. This approach leaves at least the rhetoric and underlying thrust of separation of powers unchanged (the need for countervailing powers

[23] See too NW Barber (2001), 'Prelude to the separation of powers', Cambridge LJ, 60/1, pp 59–88, p 87.

[24] P Poguntke and P Webb (eds) (2005), *The Presidentialisation of Politics: A comparative study of modern democracies* (Oxford: Oxford University Press), pp 336–56.

and checks and balances, also in a constitutional sense) and avoids the need for a 'new' separation of powers.[25]

3.4 Checks and Balances

The most relevant aspect of the general principle of separation of powers, as it has evolved over time and abstracted from any one specific political system, is the idea that one branch of government will be checked and balanced by the action of another.[26] This point is of particular relevance in the context of the executive power: indeed it can be said that the notion of control ('taming') of the executive power is part of the way that executive power has come to be delimited over the years. 'Checks and balances' does not presuppose a radical division of government into three separate parts, with particular functions neatly parcelled out amongst them. Rather, 'the focus is on *relationships and interconnections*, on maintaining the conditions in which the intended struggle at the apex may continue'.[27] The relational and balancing aspect is of particular importance to the point where one may speak more of a *balancing* than of a separation of powers.

In normative terms a lot of emphasis has been traditionally put on an idea of democracy in the EC/EU context based upon what is referred to as a (constitutional) principle of 'institutional balance'.[28] Does this notion have substantive meaning in the context of the EU legal and political systems or is the reference to 'institutional balance' in this context 'simply a device which enables the Community to move forward in an incremental manner, without ever really resolving the issues of democracy and legitimacy which lie at the heart of the debate about its future'?[29] The normative vision of democracy that takes a principle of institutional balance seriously stems from republican thought and political theory. Republicanism is a political doctrine principally concerned with freedom and its realization through self-government.[30] It reflects an idea with a strong historical lineage both in the United States and in Europe and a rich history with the important substantive meaning of balanced government or

[25] See, however, contra F Vibert (2007), who advocates the need for a 'new separation of powers'.

[26] G Marshall (1971).

[27] P Strauss (1984), 'The place of agencies in government: Separation of powers and the fourth branch', Columbia L Rev, 84/3, pp 573–669, p 578. Author's emphasis.

[28] See, for the latter, G de Búrca (1996), 'The quest for legitimacy in the European Union', The Modern L Rev, 59/3, pp 349–76.

[29] P Craig (1997), 'Democracy and rulemaking within the EC: An empirical and normative assessment', Jean Monnet Working Papers No 2/97, available at <http://www.jeanmonnet program.org/papers/97/97-02-.html>. See further P Craig (1990), *Public Law and Democracy in the United Kingdom and the United States of America* (Oxford: Oxford University Press).

[30] ML Rogers (2008), 'Republicanism' in WA Darity (ed), *International Encyclopedia of the Social Sciences*, 2nd edn (Detroit: Macmillian Reference USA), pp 188–189, available at <http://www.melvinlrogers.com/files/PublishedRepublicanism.pdf>.

balanced constitutionalism.[31] It was traditionally one of the central elements in the republican conception of democratic ordering, another being the idea that democratic deliberation should be designed to achieve public interest rather than narrow sectional desires.[32]

In so far as the EU institutions are concerned, the key constitutional principle referred to by the Court is that of 'institutional balance'. This phrase does not appear in the treaties but it has become the accepted term for describing the complex allocation of power amongst the various institutions established within the Community (and later Union) context.[33] The emphasis traditionally put on what was termed the 'principle of institutional balance' in the evolving EU political system was the perceived necessity to create a stable form of political ordering for a system in which there are different interests or constituencies to be represented.[34] The principle of institutional balance was conceived and applied in order to establish a balance of sorts between the different (decision-making) institutions as well as a relationship with the powers and input of the Member States as such (big and small).

The nature of the legal principle of institutional balance is basically that of 'a constitutional principle which must be respected by the institutions and the Member States; infringements may be condemned and sanctioned by the Court of Justice'.[35] It is regarded as one manifestation of the rule that the institutions must act within the limits of their competences.[36] The role of the Court of Justice is both to ensure that the system of distribution of powers as laid down in the treaties is maintained and, rather proactively at times, to reinterpret that principle in the light of a changing balance among the institutions as reflected in institutional practice and further treaty amendments. Moreover, given the centrality of the legal-basis requirement, there is no such thing as a single institutional balance or fixed structure of institutional interaction. For each subject matter the legal basis (treaty provision) decides whether the Union can act, which institutions must be involved, and how.

It follows from the need to respect this principle of institutional balance that, for example, horizontal delegation of powers is not permitted within the EU political system—neither of the power to adopt secondary legislation nor the power to formulate rules for implementing legislation to independent agencies. Delegation

[31] For a discussion of republican thought see in general JGA Pocock (1975), *The Machiavellian Moment: Florentine political thought and the Atlantic Republican tradition* (Princeton, NJ: Princeton University Press).

[32] For a detailed treatment see P Craig (1990).

[33] See too G de Búrca (1999), 'the institutional development of the European Union: A constitutional analysis' in P Craig and G de Búrca (eds), *The Evolution of European Union Law: An evolutionary perspective* (Oxford: Oxford University Press), pp 55–82.

[34] See, in general terms, G Majone (2005), *Dilemmas of European Integration: The ambiguities and pitfalls of integration by stealth* (Oxford: Oxford University Press).

[35] See J-P Jacqué (2004), 'The principle of institutional balance', Common Market L Rev, 41/2, pp 383–91, p 383.

[36] See Art 13(2) TEU, Lisbon.

of powers in the EU political system has been legally constrained by the ECJ's ruling in *Meroni*[37] (delivered more than 50 years ago and still 'good law'). It is only permissible when it involves 'clearly defined executive powers the exercise of which can, therefore, be subject to strict review in the light of criteria determined by the delegating authority' whereas delegation of 'a discretionary power, implying a wide margin of discretion' is to be excluded in all cases. As a result, lawyers tend to analyse the creation of EU-level agencies in terms of a transfer of authority from the Commission, in particular, to the new agency and the need to ensure that the 'institutional balance' established by the treaties is not upset. It follows from the need to respect this principle of institutional balance that delegation is not permitted either of the power to adopt secondary legislation nor the power to formulate rules for implementing legislation to 'independent' agencies.

The underlying concern of *Meroni's* prohibition for the Commission to delegate more power than it has itself and of its distinction between 'clearly defined executive powers' and 'discretionary powers' seems to be the notion of democratic legitimacy. Law is made by politically elected or at least publicly accountable officials (both the Council and the Commission) and any delegation of rule-making power should be traceable, in the final analysis, to that superior source of legitimacy.[38]

It should be noted however that this principle of an institutional balance of powers has always been strongly criticized, especially in its legal formalistic anchoring in the notion of the exercise of treaty-enumerated competences and the weakening of its power as a normative principle of governmental organization within the EU.[39] This legal principle has however been of limited utility in defining very clearly and limiting the parameters of the evolving political system. Indeed it can be argued that the legal principle of institutional balance remains a rather elusive and contested principle, of uncertain scope.[40] The inherent instrumentalism weakens its powers as a normative principle of governmental organization within the EU. The risk is that with each successive treaty-revision process the changing institutional balance is a mere 'snapshot'

[37] Case 9/56 *Meroni & Co, Industrie Metallurgiche, SpA v High Authority of the ECSC* [1957–58] ECR 133 and Case 10/56 *Meroni & Co, Industrie Metallurgiche, SpA v High Authority of the ECSC* [1957–58] *ECR* 157.

[38] C Joerges, H Schepel, and E Vos (1998), 'The law's problems with the involvement of non-governmental actors in Europe's legislative processes: The case of standardization under the "new approach"', *Working paper EUI*, June, available at <http://cadmus.iue.it/dspace/handle/1814/154>.

[39] See further T Läufer (1990), *Die Organe der EG: Rechtsetzung und Haushaltverfahren zwischen Kooperation und Konflikt* (Bonn: éditions Europa-Union); G Majone, and M Everson (2001), 'Institutional reform: Independent agencies, oversight, coordination and procedural control' in O de Schutter, N Lebessis, and J Paterson (eds), *Governance in the European Union* (Luxembourg: Office for Official Publications of the European Union), pp 129–68.

[40] See too K Lenaerts and A Verhoeven (2002), 'Institutional balance as a guarantee for democracy in EU governance' in C Joerges and R Dehousse, *Good Governance in Europe's Integrated Market* (Oxford: Oxford University Press), pp 35–88, p 38.

of the most recent set of institutional arrangements as reflected in treaty provisions.[41]

A more dynamic interpretation than the traditional one reads the principle not merely as a negative obligation to limit the encroachment of state power into a civil sphere 'but more as a positive duty to ensure... the continuing credibility of the European integration project, as well as a core place within that project of the Member States'.[42] A more dynamic interpretation of the principle of institutional balance does seem to include the (positive) duty to read the provisions of the treaty in such a way as to preserve the integrity of the powers of each institution and the power balance between them and this notwithstanding that there may be contestation as to what the precise power balance may be. For example, in recent case law the Court has rather proactively policed, in the name of the principle of institutional balance, how certain institutions behave (viz the Council) in order to ensure that it does not seek to acquire extra (legislative) powers in addition to those laid down in the treaty.[43] The principle of institutional balance enables the Court to ensure that one institution does not undertake an act of institutional 'self-aggrandizement' so as to 'deprive the other institutions of a prerogative granted to them by the Treaties themselves'.[44]

As a political principle the scope and potential of institutional balance is however considerably broader than the traditional legal understanding. On one reading (by lawyers!) institutional balance requires the makers of the European Constitution 'to shape institutions and the interactions between them in such a manner that each interest and constituency present in the Union is duly represented and cooperates with others in the frame of an institutionalized debate geared towards the formulation of the common good'.[45] In other words, it requires a reflection on the particular role(s) the various institutions are called upon to play in the EU decision-making process and the manner in which the interests it represents are carried out in practice.

As a political principle, institutional balance can also be viewed more broadly as a means of describing the way the relationship between the institutions is organized.[46] If we now turn to each of the main 'political' institutions then the following 'balance' in terms of interests represented broadly emerges. In terms of 'representation of interests' it can be said that there is no one view of 'representation' in the EU political system but it includes a motley array of provisions and institutional 'balances' embracing electoral, territorial (constituent Member States and or parliament(s)), and functional representation (specific private interests or

[41] See, in this sense, G Majone and M Everson (2001), p 145.

[42] G Majone and M Everson (2001).

[43] See Case C-133/06 *European Parliament v Council of Ministers* [2008] ECR I-3189, paras 56–7.

[44] Case 149/85 *Wybot* [1986] ECR 2391, para 23.

[45] K Lenaerts and A Verhoeven (2002), p 47. Author's emphasis.

[46] JP Jacqué (2004), p 383.

public and more general purposes). It is hard to formulate an overall—or even remotely even—'balance' in the three traditional channels of representation found in the EU political system.[47]

3.5 The Balancing of Executive Power

3.5.1 The Council of Ministers and the European Council

The Council of Ministers was not conceived in particularly innovative terms institutionally; rather it was meant to do what councils of ministers traditionally did in intergovernmental organizations, namely to provide for the formal representation of Member States in the EU.[48] The Council of Ministers represented institutionalized intergovernmentalism by the Member States acting collectively[49] and was meant to counterbalance the much more innovative and 'supranational' Commission where the general 'Community' interest was to prevail. Its task was to ensure that the interests of the Member States remained predominant and that they could 'control' (by participating in decision-making and ultimately by exercising a veto) the output of the organization.

The Council of Ministers is not only to be understood as a profoundly political institution, with the Member States de facto in the steering seat but also as an EU executive institution which has gained (oversight over) not insignificant administrative and even operational-type powers particularly in the past decade or more.[50] In other words, a certain consolidation of the Council of Ministers as a new and distinctive executive centre is taking place at the European level, alongside that of the European Commission and alongside pre-existing (national and international) executive orders. The Council of Ministers can arguably also be analysed in terms of a politics–administration/bureaucracy dichotomy in the sense that the level of the ministers is the obvious political (and intergovernmental, albeit qualified with the advent of widespread qualified majority voting) level and the administration is the General Secretariat of the Council of Ministers that for a long time was considered merely a supporting secretariat along the model of many international organizations (see further Chapter 5 below).

[47] See further M Martensson (2007), 'Mixed representation and legitimacy in the European Union', *European Integration*, 29/3, pp 285–302.

[48] T Christiansen (2001a), 'The Council of Ministers: The politics of institutionalised intergovernmentalism' in J Richardson (ed), *European Union: Power and Policy-Making* (London: Routledge), pp 135–54, p 136.

[49] T Christiansen (2001a), p 136.

[50] See generally F Hayes-Renshaw and H Wallace (2006), *The Council of Ministers*, 2nd edn (Basingstoke.: Palgrave Macmillan). See too, for its evolutionary powers in the area of freedom, security, and justice, S Peers (2006), *EU Justice and Home Affairs Law* (Oxford: Oxford University Press).

Despite the fact that the Council of Ministers has also, from the very beginning, been the core of the legislative power of the EU and its predecessors, it has traditionally behaved—even when adopting legislation—as an executive organ of the traditional intergovernmental mode known also from other international organizations. Thus, a defining feature of the Council of Ministers is that, by a process of diplomatic negotiation, it distils the bottom line in terms of the collective of national interests. The Council of Ministers institutionalized a decision-making process whereby members of the national executive power adopted decisions, many of which gradually came to be regarded as being legislative in nature, by processes of diplomatic negotiations. In other words, given that there was never one single Member State point of view on any given policy initiative the Council was, *ipso facto*, the main forum for negotiation in the EU.

Considerable improvements have indeed have taken place in recent years as a result of a variety of 'transparency' provisions but, nonetheless, one often needs the mindset of a private investigator to unearth relevant information both about processes and about its various (sub-)actors. Even in 2009, it still remains 'shrouded' in secrecy in many salient respects (see Chapter 8 below). This observation pertains both to the legislative processes and also to the 'non-legislative' processes and output. Article 16(8) TEU, Lisbon provides that Council meetings where legislative acts are adopted must be held in public; this has pre-emptively entered into force prior to the entry into force of the Treaty of Lisbon itself, thus illustrating the fact that many of the latter's provisions can be introduced into the EU legal and political systems in a different—and easier—manner than a treaty-reform process.

With regard to the putative new status of the European Council as a fully fledged institution of the Union[51] it is specifically provided in the Treaty of Lisbon that 'it shall not exercise legislative functions'. In this case, and using a residual approach to executive power, 'not legislative' is to be equated with executive functions—in any event political and, possibly at times, more administrative in nature. It might be thought that the executive functions of the European Council would necessarily be 'political', given both its (high-level) political composition and the fact that it lacked any permanent administrative structure of its own, but in fact other institutions have complained in recent years that this is not necessarily the case. Thus, Javier Solana, the Council Secretary General and the High Representative, noted some years ago that the European Council was increasingly 'asked to spend time on laborious *low-level* drafting work which adversely affects normal Community procedures'.[52] In other words, there is a clear example here of the growing confusion in practice of the roles and responsibilities of the different institutions and associated bodies. Institutions

[51] Art 13 TEU, Lisbon.

[52] Report by J Solana (2002), *Preparing the Council for Enlargement,* Council of the European Union, General Secretariat, S0044/02, available at <http://ue.eu.int/ueDocs/cms_Data/docs/pressdata/EN/reports/69889.pdf>. Author's emphasis.

are after all not just passive environments for action but may develop a life of their own ('living' institutions) that may be extremely difficult for their architects to control.

The political nature of both the Council of Ministers and of the European Council comes from the fact that it is composed of members of the national executive power. But is its power 'politicized' in the sense we know from national political systems where elections take place on the basis of a system of political parties with left–right cleavages? And what do we mean by 'representation' in this context: are the (prime) ministers really 'representing' the citizens when they take decisions at the EU level? Throughout Europe representation is commonly understood to work via the 'responsible party government' model, in which the electorate selects from two or more parties based on their policy promises and performance.[53] This mechanism provides a link between the preferences of citizens and the actions of governments. Parties in power remain accountable on a day-to-day basis to parliaments and at regular intervals to the electorate, who retain ultimate control. This model is—as we have seen—highly problematic when applied in the context of the EU both in the indirect channel (national elections) and the direct one (direct elections to the European Parliament).[54]

At the ministerial level, the Council of Ministers is composed of 'representatives' of the constituent Member States who have (in general) been elected in the national political processes (or appointed by those elected). Those representatives are drawn from governments in office and the national civil servants taking part in working groups and committees are under a duty to pursue the policies of their current governments. In other words, there is no role for the political opposition at the level of the Council of Ministers. One might assume then that the government in office is elected also on the basis of its European policies and that it receives a mandate in that regard too from its political principals—the citizens—in the respective Member States. But this appears not to be the case in the real world patterns of contestation. Political scientist Peter Mair puts it like this: 'The choices . . . become increasingly irrelevant to the outputs of the system, and the behavior and preferences of citizens constitute virtually no formal constraint on or mandate for the relevant policy makers'.[55]

This leads to 'depoliticization' at the European level, in which there is no political debate or possibility of opposition being expressed in the context of decision-making by the Council of Ministers. The only political opposition that can come

[53] See further M March and P Norris (1997), 'Political representation in the European Parliament', *European Journal of Political Research*, 32/6, pp 153–64.

[54] See further, on the latter, ibid and, more recently and generally, C van Eijk and H Schmitt (eds) (2008), *The Multilevel Electoral System of the EU* (Mannheim: CONNEX Report Series No 4).

[55] P Mair (2007), 'Political opposition and the European Union', *Government and Opposition*, 42/1, pp 1–17, p 11.

is from the European Parliament and this too has a long way to go in terms of becoming politicized in the sense we know from national polities.[56] So we have two core institutions at the EU level, the European Council and the Council of Ministers that consist of members that have been elected in national elections or appointed by those elected but *not* on the issues that they decide on as the main decision maker at the EU level.

The Council has in fact two different types of bureaucratic support or input into its political decisions. First, like the Commission, it has a (much smaller) staff of European civil servants, responsible for 'public administration' largely in its General Secretariat. In recent years the role of the Secretariat has evolved to the point where it has assumed more significant tasks in policymaking and implementation that would traditionally have been carried out by the Commission as an executive actor in other (Community) policy fields.[57] Secondly, the system of working parties and committees that participate in formulating and sometimes finalizing the contents of its (political) decisions, are also 'administrative' in the sense of being populated by national civil servants. They are linked via the diplomatic COREPER to the more political Council. The Council of Ministers is indeed a more chameleon-like institution than the Commission since it also houses within it committees, working groups, etc that are populated by national civil servants ('new Eurocrats') acting, presumably, within the web of national politics (and not European politics).[58]

3.5.2 The Commission

The High Authority of the European Coal and Steel Community (ECSC) and its successors were conceived from the very beginning as original and distinctive institutions in the world of international organizations. When Robert Schumann presented the 'Schumann Plan' in 1950, its central element was a High Authority composed of independent experts and authorized by the governments of the prospective Member States to regulate the market for coal and steel by issuing decisions that would be binding for the Member States.[59] Jean Monnet was a champion of a technocratic approach to policymaking according to which government action follows the advice of experts and technocrats and his conception of the High Authority was 'of a permanent international *secretariat of*

[56] See further M Marsh and P Norris (1997).

[57] See further, for example, T Christiansen (2006), 'Out of the shadows: The General Secretariat of the Council of Ministers', Journal of Legislative Studies, 8/4, pp 80–97 and T Christiansen, and S Vanhoonacker (2008), 'At a critical juncture? Change and continuity in the institutional development of the Council Secretariat', *West European Politics*, 31/4, pp 751–70.

[58] See further H Wallace (2002), 'The Council: An institutional chameleon', *Governance: An International Journal of Policy, Administration and Institutions*, 15/3, pp 325–44.

[59] See, in general, B Rittberger (2001), 'Which institutions for post-war Europe? Explaining the institutional design of Europe's first community', *Journal of European Public Policy*, 8/5, pp 673–708.

experts working for the common good'.[60] He tended to downplay its managerial and administrative tasks and to stress the political leadership role that it would play by being the champion of the European cause and the beholder of the true European interest.[61] Monnet stressed time and again that the High Authority had to be independent from governments.[62] In that sense (national) 'politics' had been rather effectively 'organized out'.

It was the Belgian and Dutch delegations that insisted during the ECSC negotiations on superimposing an intergovernmental council of ministers representing the territorial and political interests of the respective Member States in the institutional design.[63] Be that as it may, it seemed that for the first time an 'executive body' with its *own* leadership had been established outside the national ministers' council.[64] In the words of Egeberg, the uniqueness of the European Commission and its predecessors lies in the fact that it is 'the only multipurpose executive body at the international level that is organizationally separated from councils of ministers. Given that this institution has the potential to act relatively independently as an executive, this means that the executive branch of the EU Member States has a new and higher layer of executive organization with which to relate.'[65]

Not only was the central role of the Commission conceived traditionally as a manner of ensuring that the general Community interest was taken into account (and thus of the many small Member States) and not only those of the (few) large Member States, but also the fact that the presidency of the Council of Ministers rotated among all the Member States equally every six months had the aim of serving as a counterweight to the power of the large states and ensuring political equality in this regard between the small and large Member States. This balance of power between small and large Member States enabled the EU to function effectively in practice, and was also built into the Community method from the very beginning in the manner that the system of 'qualified' majority voting was calculated (and explicitly not based only on size of population). In addition, the relatively central role of the Commission was from the very beginning considered crucial in ensuring balance between the large and small Member States in the exercise of the treaty-conferred competences.[66]

[60] K Featherstone (1994), 'Jean Monnet and the "democratic deficit" in the European Union', *Journal of Common Market Studies*, 32/2, pp 149–70, p 156. Author's emphasis.

[61] See too L de Hooghe (2001), *The European Commission and the Integration of Europe* (Cambridge: Cambridge University Press), pp 153–4.

[62] See, in general, B Rittberger (2007b), 'Original meanings: Ideas about representation in the making of Europe's first community', Paper presented at CONNEX Thematic Conference on Accountability, EUI, Florence, 29–30 June 2007.

[63] B Rittberger (2001).

[64] M Egeberg (2006b), 'Europe's executive branch of government in the melting pot: An overview' in M Egeberg (ed), *Multilevel Union Administration: The transformation of executive politics in Europe* (Basingstoke: Palgrave Macmillan), p 1.

[65] Ibid.

[66] See, in particular the old literature on this subject, W Hallstein (1965), 'The EEC Commission: A new factor in international life', Int'l and Comp LQ, 14/3, pp 727–41.

The Commission was designed as a technocratic body composed of independent experts to propose solutions to policy problems, to broker deals, to constitute the 'motor of integration', and to be the guardian of the common European interest. In the words of Anchrit Wille, the integration and mediating function of the Commission:

> was to be guided by the judgment of a technocratic elite rather then by political judgment since politicians are bound to be short-sighted and self-seeking, as they are subject to electoral mechanisms. It would make for better governance to take the impartial, the overall and long-term view of the 'technocrat' as a guardian of the European interest. The Commission's role would hence depend on its expertise and its credibility as an impartial mediator between political views, conflicting national interests and interest group pressures.[67]

According to Milward, 'Monnet's attachment to . . . a small and powerful committee able to take far-reaching decisions sprang from his lack of conviction that the politics of the nation-state were genuinely capable of evolving into those of supranationality except over too long a period of time to serve his purpose.'[68]

For a long time the European Commission was not analysed as constituting something in any way comparable to a 'government' or 'executive board' of the Union and its predecessors.[69] It was the public administration of the Union, its civil service with limited and defined powers, nothing more than an administrative executive. In other words, whereas it was recognized that the European Commission possessed powers that could only be described as executive in nature, it was the administrative component of executive power that was stressed, not the political component (except perhaps with regard to its exclusive power to initiate legislation in the legislative process). In addition, the European Commission possessed powers that were more of a judicial and supervisory nature, less common in a public administration at the national level. It has only in recent years been overtly recognized that the European Commission is a very important part of executive power in the EU institutional configuration.

In the words of a report by the European Parliament-appointed Committee of Independent Experts a decade ago: 'the Commission plays the part of the executive branch and holds sole power of legislative initiative. It thus bears especially well-developed duties of responsibility and accountability towards the other

[67] A Wille (2007a), 'Bridging the gap: Political and administrative leadership in a reinvented commission' in M Egeberg (ed), *Institutional Dynamics and the Transformation of Executive Politics in Europe* (Mannheim: CONNEX Report Series 3), pp 7–41.

[68] A Milward (2000), *The European Rescue of the Nation-State*, 2nd edn (London: Routledge), p 336.

[69] J de Zwaan (2004), 'The role of the European Commission over the years: Changes and challenges' in J de Zwaan et al (eds), *The European Union: An ongoing process of integration. Liber Amicorum Fred Kellermann* (Cambridge: Cambridge University Press), pp 53–69.

participants in the political structure: Parliament and Council, and, above all, the citizens of Europe.'[70]

The Commission it seems is best understood if compared with a national executive: 'The Commission consists of a series of executive politicians who are in charge of various administrative services. Similar to national executives the Commission is authorized to initiate and formulate policy proposals and to implement policies, or more commonly, to monitor their implementation.'[71] The Commission is considered to have reached the point in its evolution that it is considered a 'normalized' core executive.[72] A core executive in this sense has both political and purely administrative, even managerial, tasks with, at times, blurred political–administrative roles.[73] The Commission embodies many of the organizational and behavioural patterns that are highly typical of executives, as we know them from national settings.[74] Indeed, the bureaucratic divisions of the Commission are comparable to ministries in national administrations and the role of Commissioners to those of Ministers.

The nature of the Commission and its role within the EU has, in particular, often been the subject of contestation. The Commission is clearly not the EU's government in a singular organic sense, although there have been attempts to portray it in these terms from time to time.[75] It is difficult to regard the Commission as a kind of parliamentary 'government', even if there are clear signs that the College of Commissioners is gradually becoming more and more dependent on the European Parliament. This is especially the case with regard to new provisions providing for the election of the Commission president by the European Parliament.[76] These new provisions stem essentially from an effort to enhance the democratic legitimacy of the Commission in particular—the belief is that increasing the 'politicization' of the Commission in this manner will attenuate, in one respect at any rate, the 'democratic deficit' of the Union.

[70] Committee of Independent Experts (1999), *Second Report on the Reform of the Commission: Analysis of current practice and proposals for tackling mismanagement, irregularities and fraud*, vol II, available at <http://www.europarl.europa.eu/experts/default_en.htm>.

[71] M Egeberg (2002), 'The European Commission: The evolving EU executive', *ARENA Working Papers, WP 02/30*, available at: <http://www.arena.uio.no/publications/wp02_30.htm>.

[72] A Wille (2010), *The Normalization of the European Commission: Politics and bureaucracy in an evolving executive*, forthcoming. See too S Hix (2005), *The Political System of the European Union*, 2nd edn, The European Union Series (Basingstoke: Palgrave Macmillan), p 32.

[73] See further A Wille (2007a).

[74] M Egeberg (ed) (2006b) and S Suavierol (2007), *Beyond the Myth of Nationality: A study on the networks of European Commission officials* (Delft: Eburon), p 14.

[75] See, for example, KH Neunreither (1971), 'Transformation of a political role: Reconsidering the case of the Commission of the European Communities', *Journal of Common Market Studies*, 10/3, pp 233–48. See more recently, G Grevi (2003), 'Time for a government of the Union', *European Policy Center, Working Paper No 4*, 10 April 2003, available at <http://www.epc.eu>.

[76] Art 17(7) TEU, Lisbon.

In fact, there is no equivalent of a national government at the level of the EU political system; rather, executive power is fragmented and dispersed across an increasing number of institutions and actors. In the original conception, the Commission was designed to be a very central decision-making institution with a variety of tasks. Chief among these were 'its own power of decision' and its participation 'in the shaping of measures taken by the Council and the European Parliament in the manner provided for in this Treaty'. In addition it was to 'exercise the powers conferred on it by the Council for the implementation of the rules laid down by the latter'.[77] None of the subsequent treaties, including the Treaty of Lisbon, made any specific or significant alteration to this broad framework or the manner of their exercise as a collegial and independent body.

3.6 Composite Executive Power

The notion of composite orders, rather than a metaphor using architecture or the descriptive but hierarchical reality of 'levels', can bring a fresh look at things and broaden horizons in a cross-cutting fashion beyond that of an analysis grounded in separate, vertical 'levels'.[78] The idea of the composite or compound nature of the power raises the expectation of close interaction but also symbiosis to some extent between the European levels and the national levels. The metaphor of ecology ties together in a fluid, and not necessarily hierarchical, manner a whole motley array of connections between different layers and spaces, between law and practices—national, European, and even international in some instances.[79] This incorporates not only problem-solving networks of public and private actors and the so-called 'satellite' actors but is also underpinned in some fashion by a more old-style hierarchical form of public administration, national and European, linked and separate. We find both old-fashioned hierarchy (at times in the shade) intertwined with what is sometimes called new 'governance'. All are part of the compound ecological system we are dealing with.

Executive power at the EU level as well as its interaction with national executive power has, however, remained largely 'in shadow', when compared to its legislative and judicial counterparts. This is not only because of its scattered and fragmentary nature but also because there is no single instance of EU executive power that can (yet) be characterized as the EU 'government' in a way that can

77 These are the original wordings of Art 155 EEC. See now Art 17 TEU, Lisbon that provides, inter alia, that it 'shall exercise coordinating, executive and management functions, as laid down in the Treaties'.

78 It was developed by a Dutch colleague, L Besselink (2008), *A Composite European Constitution* (Groningen: Europa Law Publishers).

79 See too A Sbragia (2008), 'Distributed governance: The changing ecology of the European Union' in B Kohler-Koch and F Larat (eds), *Efficient and Democratic Governance in the European Union* (Mannheim, CONNEX Report Series No. 09), pp 339–55, p 348.

be compared in a sustained fashion to a 'government' (as such) in national political systems. Executive power in terms of the institutions and actors of the EU consists of various bits and pieces that have been cobbled together across a spectrum of institutions, sub-actors, and policy areas. No fewer than three institutions of the EU and its predecessors can claim to exercise executive (in both its political and administrative components) authority within the EU, albeit to varying degrees and with varying emphasis: the Commission, the Council, and the European Council. In addition there are a number of 'satellite' actors who have in a variety of ways had executive powers delegated to them but whose role is even more 'in shadow'.[80]

Attempts to describe single institutions (the European Council, the Commission) as constituting the EU government as such are, in my view, misguided.[81] This is not the same as saying that, overall and viewed in a holistic fashion, the political system of the EU does not reveal the existence of the three traditional branches of government—a legislative power, a judicial power, and an (increasingly visible, albeit fragmentary) executive power.

It is striking however that the EU political system has been deliberately crafted not with a single executive but with a plural executive. Moreover, it strikes a distinctive balance between electoral and territorial representation in the sense that territorial representation determines policy to a much greater extent than political competition within the electoral channel. This fact is often a key element in the democratic deficit criticism of the EU (see Chapter 10 below). It has emerged from studies in recent years that in fact both the Commission and the Council of Ministers can both be analysed in terms of a 'core executive'. Moving beyond the myth of separation of politics and administration, a modern view of constitutionalism will integrate the crucial dimensions of normative bureaucratic judgment and attempt to discipline it by a host of techniques ranging from public participation in decision-making to judicial review.[82] This involves acceptance of the fact that administrators/bureaucrats can be held responsible autonomously in a way that the classic Weberian dichotomy between politics and administration could never have envisaged.

[80] See further D Curtin (2007), 'Holding (quasi-)autonomous EU administrative actors to public account', European LJ, 13/4, pp 523–41.

[81] See, for example, S Hix, (2005), who categorizes in his monograph both the Commission and the Council as the 'government' of the EU. See too WT Eijsbouts (2005), 'De Macht, de Mensen, het Model: Europa's Grondwet à l'Américaine', *Nederlandsch Juristenblad*, 80/20, pp 1024–34, who treats the European Council and its evolving powers as the nascent 'government' of the EU in a presidential political system.

[82] See too B Ackerman (2000), 'The new separation of powers', Harvard L Rev, 113/3, pp 634–729, pp 696–7.

PART II

TIDES OF EU REFORM

4

Political Executive Power

4.1 The Political Top

Executive power as it was originally conceived is in fact 'the power of *governments*. It is the legal authority vested in, and exercised by, for example, prime ministers, presidents, cabinets and councils. It is the political power that all those who embark on a career in politics dream of wielding.'[1] This understanding of the *political executive* as fulfilling a separate and distinct government power (as opposed to legislative power and judicial power) is sometimes also referred to as the *core executive*.[2] This chapter limits its focus to this 'core' executive power and the manner in which this has been (further) institutionalized in the provisions of the Treaty of Nice and of the Treaty of Lisbon. The main focuses of the chapter are on the institutional 'actors', and the manner in which their executive powers have been consolidated in processes of further institutionalization at the 'top' political and legal level; the Nice Treaty, the formal status quo, and the Lisbon Treaty—if it enters into force. In order to from the very beginning make clear the main changes to the EU political executive both before and after the Treaty of Lisbon a detailed overview per institution is provided in Table 4.1.

This chapter begins by focusing on the manner in which processes of informal governance are salient in understanding further the manner in which the power of two key political executive institutions have developed in recent years—the European Council (and its agenda-setting function) and the Council of Ministers (and its legislative function, in conjunction with a directly elected parliament). After that, the role of the Commission as a 'normalized core executive' will be analysed. A key part of the 'institutional balance' of the EU system as a whole (as defended by the Court in *Meroni* and subsequent case law: see Chapter 3 above) is the balance between the Commission and the Council (with the European Parliament coming subsequently into the equation).

[1] P Craig and A Tomkins (eds) (2006), *The Executive and Public Law: Power and accountability in comparative perspective* (Oxford: Oxford University Press), p 1.

[2] L Helms (2005), *Presidents, Prime Ministers and Chancellors: Executive leadership in Western democracies* (Basingstoke: Palgrave Macmillan).

Table 4.1 EU political executive before and after the Treaty of Lisbon

	Nice Treaty	Lisbon Treaty
European Council	• Not formal institution • Rotating presidency 6 months • Limited EU role *de jure* • De facto steering role • Support Council General Secretariat • Commission president ex officio member • Ministers Foreign Affairs and member Commission participants (not members) • Political impetus and 'guidelines' • Consensus • Report to EP: after meeting and annually • At least 2 meetings each year	• Formal EU institution • President to be appointed for max 5 years • Expanded role *de jure* • De facto steering role • Expanded support Council General Secretariat • Commission president ex officio member • Ministers and member Commission participants (not members), if so requested • High Representative CFSP ex officio participant (not member) • Political impetus and guidelines; no 'legislative' functions • Consensus • Report by president to EP: after meeting • At least 4 meetings each year
Council of Ministers	• Co-legislator • Budgetary authority • Presidency troika • Incremental role General Secretariat • Executive tasks, CFSP and CJHA • COREPER and high level committees • Operational collaboration • Council Departments attached to High Representative/General Secretariat (EUMS, etc) • Simple majority • QMV: weighting of votes	• Co-legislator (expanded role EP) • Budgetary authority (expanded role EP) • Presidency troika, except for Foreign Affairs Council • Expanded role General Secretariat • Executive tasks EU wide (pillars removed) • COREPER and high level committees • Operational collaboration (COSI) • Council Departments attached to Secretariat General • QMV • QMV: 55% and 65%
European Commission	• Core executive • Supervision application EC law • Exclusive initiation legislative process • President nominated by QMV Council (in composition heads of state and government)	• Core executive (EU wide) • Supervision application EU law (except CFSP) • Exclusive initiation legislative process (somewhat expanded) • Account to be taken of results of EP elections in choice president designate • President nominated by QMV European Council

(contd.)

Table 4.1 (*Continued*)

	Nice Treaty	Lisbon Treaty
	• President appointed by QMV Council	• President elected by EP
	• Members appointed by QMV Council	• Members appointed by QMV European Council
	• College and president subject as body to vote of approval EP	• College and president subject as body to vote of approval EP
	• College works under political guidance of president	• College works under political guidance of president
	• Number of Commissioners to be less than number of MS	• Number of Commissioners to be same as number of MS (subject to Irish Protocol)
High Representative CFSP	• High Representative CFSP and Secretary General Council	• Separate 'double-hatted' office High representative CFSP
	• Agenda setter	• Agenda setter
		• President of Foreign Affairs Council
	• Executive decision-taker	• Executive decision-taker
	• Within Council General Secretariat	• Outside Council General Secretariat but External Action Service
	• Appointed QMV Council	• Appointed QMV European Council, with agreement of president of Commission

What this chapter shows is that this institutional balance, as originally conceived, has been quite consistently and incrementally undermined (although rarely openly acknowledged) as a result of the emergence and growth in power and stature of what still today—2009—is formally not an 'institution' of the EU as such: the European Council. This may consist in undermining the position of the Commission in terms of its powers of legislative initiative, but the position and role of the Council of Ministers may also be affected. It too is given tasks by the European Council in a sometimes surprisingly specific fashion. The European Council is in many ways the alpha and the omega of executive power in the EU political system. This is not how the institutional balance was originally conceived; rather, in very broad brush terms, it could be said that the Council possessed the core legislative power (other than the right of initiative) and the Commission the core 'executive' power of preparation and implementation. These originally relatively broad lines have become blurred and fuzzy. Though they may be foundational understandings, they have had, at times, a coach and horses driven through them.

4.2 The 'European Council': The 'Queen Bee' Directs and Controls

4.2.1 A hive of activity

The European Council is the most 'high-politics' actor there is, by virtue of its composition. It is composed of the prime ministers of all the national political systems, the French president and the president of the European Commission. All of these members are either elected directly in national elections or are appointed by national parliaments or, in the case of the president of the European Commission, by the European Council itself. Some years ago this is how the EU website described the European Council:

> only the European Council can give the EU a shot in the arm... It plays a vital role in all EU fields of activity whether it be by giving impetus to the Union, or defining general political guidelines, or by coordinating, arbitrating or disentangling difficult questions... It has acquired such importance and legitimacy today that it is difficult to imagine that there was a time when it did not exist.[3]

Moreover, each of these various tasks/roles has incrementally acquired more shape and substance, first as a matter of informal practice and latterly in tides of treaty reform.

Its key agenda-setting role is evident from Art 4 TEU:[4] it 'shall provide the Union with the necessary impetus for its development and define the general political guidelines thereof'. Agenda-setting is, of course, a crucial stage in the policy process for any political system.[5] But the European Council can also act as type of 'court of appeal' in certain specified—and limited—circumstances (for example, when a Member State has breached the core values of the EU[6] or when a Member State alleges specific national interests[7]). And it takes (or will take) absolutely key decisions concerning the EU and its Member States outside of the legislative procedure as such.[8] In addition, through the medium of the conclusions of its summits, it steers the other decision-making institutions and more or less tells them what to do and where the priorities lie.[9] At other times its role is

[3] Quoted by P de Schoutheete and H Wallace (2002), *The European Council* (Paris: Research and Policy Group—Notre Europe), available at <http://www.notre-europe.eu>. The current entry (31 January 2009) on the *Europa* website has changed and is more factual and sober in its presentation of the European Council.

[4] This would be renumbered as Art 15(1) TEU, Lisbon.

[5] See further B Guy Peters (1994), 'Agenda-setting in the European Community', *Journal of European Public Policy*, 1/1, pp 9–26.

[6] Art 7(2) TEU, Lisbon

[7] See, for example, Art 31(2) TEU, Lisbon and Arts 48 (social security systems), 82(3) (judicial cooperation in criminal matters), 83(2) (minimal rules for crimes), 86(1) (European public prosecutor's office), and 87(3) (police cooperation) of the TFEU.

[8] See, for example, Art 7 TEU, Lisbon.

[9] For a clear recent example see Presidency Conclusions, Brussels European Council Summit, 11 and 12 December 2008, available at <http://www.consilium.europa.eu/ueDocs/cms_Data/docs/pressData/en/ec/104692.pdf>. See further, J Werts (2008), *The European Council* (London: John Harper Publishing).

more invisible given that it cannot formally take decisions within the EC and as a result the Council will sometimes take decisions in the composition of heads of state and government (Art 121(3) TEU on the Euro and Art 214(2) TEU on the appointment of members of the Commission).

Ludlow describes already several years ago the European Council as 'the arbiter of systemic change, the principal agenda setter, the ultimate negotiating body and the core of the EU's executive'.[10] It can be said to have executive functions as regards its broad agenda-setting role and other non-legislative tasks yet it is not an executive in the sense that it usually works out concrete policy proposals or has the responsibility for implementing EU policies.[11] This does not mean that some of its 'conclusions' are not very detailed in substance[12] leaving little margin for discretion for the Union institutions required to implement them. In the view of some, this has shifted the original 'institutional balance' in the EU towards that of the Member States united in the European Council.[13]

The European Council was created—in the 1970's—as an intergovernmental initiative in response to what has been termed the failure of the Community method and the weakening of the Commission as a result of the Luxembourg accords.[14] It evolved during subsequent decades in largely informal fashion to become 'a locus of power second to none in the EU's institutional system today'.[15] It was for many years considered to operate outside the framework of the formal treaty provisions and to constitute an 'informal' organ with a highly political role. Gradually, though, the European Council was given specific powers and competences in various treaty amendments, a position which was consolidated and expanded in the provisions of the Lisbon Treaty with the European Council finally being formally categorized as a full 'institution' of the EU, of equal status to the Commission, Council, and European Parliament etc.[16]

The European Council came into existence precisely because the Commission could not set the broad political agenda ('high politics') of the Union on its own,

[10] See, in general, P Ludlow (2002), *The Laeken Council* (Brussels: European Council Commentary), p 5, and subsequent books on other European Council meetings. See, more recently, J Werts (2008), *The European Council* (London: John Harper Publishing).

[11] M Egeberg (ed) (2006c), *Multilevel Union Administration: The transformation of executive politics in Europe* (Basingstoke: Palgrave Macmillan), p 5.

[12] See too H Pahre (2008), *Das Recht des Europäischen Rates: Eine Untersuchung im Lichte aktueller Entwicklungen der Europäischen Union* (Frankfurt: Verlag Peter Lang).

[13] See, for example, J Werts (2008), pp 194–6.

[14] R Barents (2008), *Het Verdrag van Lissabon: Achtergronden en Commentaar* (Deventer: Kluwer), p 238 *et seq.*

[15] F Hayes-Renshaw and H Wallace (2006), *The Council of Ministers*, 2nd edn (Basingstoke: Palgrave Macmillan), p 165.

[16] Art 13(1) TEU, Lisbon.

lacking as it did clear democratic legitimacy,[17] and presumably because the Council did not have the status or means to do so either (with its changing formations and its rotating and very short-term presidencies). In the words of Dashwood, 'the democratically accountable leaders of the Member States, meeting with the Commission President, are the right agenda-setting body'.[18] This does not mean that the Council's agenda-setting role is in practice negligible—indeed this has become more streamlined since the European Council conclusions at the Seville summit in 2002 when the preparatory role of the new General Affairs and External Relations Council was consolidated.[19] The latter adopts an annual operating programme of Council activities since then, and the Commission an annual legislative programme. The adoption (since December 2003) of multi-annual strategic programmes by the European Council has meant that both the Council and the Commission are involved in the preparatory consultative process leading to the adoption of these multi-annual strategic programmes. At the same time, the adoption of such new working methods post-Seville has contributed to the phenomenon of an 'all powerful European Council'.[20] Nowadays the General Affairs Council, and in particular COREPER, finalize the draft conclusions in advance, except for some important remaining points.

What is not clear, as a matter of empirical practice, is the extent to which the Commission, for example, as formal agenda-setter under the treaties, actually has to change its draft legislative agenda in a given year as a result of the input by other institutions. Majone has, in any event, shown that the Commission is not very 'autonomous' in its exercise of its own agenda-setting function and that, in this sense, one can speak of a not insignificant 'dilution' in the Commission's original power of legislative monopoly as a key element in the Community method as originally conceived.[21]

The European Council has been referred to 'as the most visible face of the Council today'[22] and ensures coordination between the various (sub-)Councils and the many policy areas incrementally subject to European integration. From the very early days it seems that the Council General Secretariat was involved in helping to prepare a meeting of the European Council.[23] The support provided was primarily administrative and logistical, although depending on the size and experience of the Member State in office the support could also be more substantive.

[17] A Dashwood (2006), 'The EU Constitution: What will really change?', *Cambridge Yearbook of Legal Studies*, 7, pp 33–56, p 49.

[18] Ibid.

[19] See Presidency Conclusions, Seville European Council 21 and 22 June 2002, available at <http://ue.eu.int/ueDocs/cms_Data/docs/pressdata/en/ec/72638.pdf>.

[20] J Werts (2008), p 163.

[21] G Majone (2002), 'The European Commission: The limits of centralization and the perils of parliamentarization', *Governance: An International Journal of Policy, Administration and Institutions*, 15/3, pp 375–92.

[22] F Hayes-Renshaw and H Wallace (1997), *The Council of Ministers*, 1st edn (Basingstoke: Palgrave Macmillan), p 158.

[23] See further T Christiansen and S Vanhoonacker (2008), 'At a critical juncture? Change and continuity in the institutional development of the Council Secretariat', *West European Politics*, 31/4, pp 751–70.

Nowadays the European Council can be said to operate increasingly as the senior branch of the Council.[24] Indeed in many ways this was reflected in the provisions of the Lisbon Treaty which provided for a huge reinforcement of—and linking with the Council of Ministers—of the position of the European Council.

The incremental consolidation of the tasks of the European Council both as an agenda-setter and otherwise culminated in the provisions of the Treaty of Lisbon with a much more detailed description of its role than existed hitherto—at least in formal treaty provisions. Its primordial political role is explicated as defining 'the general political directions and priorities' of the Union.[25] The addition of the word 'priorities' is significant, although it can be argued it reflects current practice with the European Council exercising a leading agenda-setting power in the Union, despite the lack of formal provisions to date.[26] At the same time, the sentence that 'it shall not exercise legislative functions' explicitly indicates that it in any event exercises 'non-legislative' or executive functions.[27] Those executive functions may be both political and administrative. It includes decision-making at various levels and in various ways. Sometimes it adopts decisions on the basis of formally conferred powers, especially in the field of common foreign and security policy (CFSP). At other times it adopts positions that have no formal legal status but are treated as legally binding. A good example of the latter is constituted by the Copenhagen criteria setting conditions for enlargement to the Union. Dashwood does not mince his words in this regard: 'it is highly unsatisfactory that such decisions should be taken by a body lacking rules of procedure . . . which does not keep minutes, and from which national officials and all but a tiny number of Council officials are excluded.'[28]

The Treaty establishing a Constitution for Europe (and in a more opaque way the Lisbon Treaty too) attempted to inculcate a clearer and more visible distinction between in particular EU legislative power and what is in fact EU executive power. Legal acts adopted by the legislative procedure shall constitute legislative acts.[29] The executive power is defined more in terms of what it is not—ie, it is not the legislature and does not adopt legislative acts; it adopts non-legislative acts.[30] This definition is entirely formal[31] and does not mean that formally 'non-legislative' acts could not be considered as constituting 'legislation' if a substantive

[24] These are the words of leading commentators F Hayes-Renshaw and H Wallace (2006), *The Council of Ministers*, p 2.

[25] Art 15(1) TEU, Lisbon.

[26] See further, for the practice to date, P de Schoutheete and H Wallace (2002). See also A Dashwood (2006), p 49.

[27] Art 15(1) TEU, Lisbon.

[28] A Dashwood (2006), p 49. See further A Dashwood (2000), 'Decision-making at the summit', Cambridge Yearbook of European Legal Studies, 3, pp 79–106.

[29] This is taken over in the Treaty of Lisbon; see, Art 289(3) TFEU.

[30] Title V, Ch I, Art I-35 of the Treaty Establishing a Constitution for Europe. This is less explicitly phrased in the Treaty of Lisbon but as a matter of substance it is the same.

[31] See, contra, A van den Brink (2008), 'Van Rechtsinstrument naar Rechtshandelingen: "Lissabon" en de Introductie van een Europees Primaat van de Wetgever', *Sociaal-Economische Wetgeving*, 56/5, pp 166–70.

approach to the content of legislation is preferred. Legislation is after all normally constituted by norms of a general nature affecting a range of people and categories of acts for the future. In other words the dividing line is fuzzy and conceptually unsatisfactory. The Treaty of Lisbon provision that states that the European Council 'shall not adopt legislative measures'[32] may not correspond with reality in the sense that a close reading of the various amending provisions of the Treaty of Lisbon reveal that in fact the European Council does adopt decisions that come very close indeed to being of a general legislative nature—on a substantive understanding of what constitutes 'legislation'.[33] Indeed, specific provisions are clearly in substantive terms effectively legislative type decisions although this is hidden by using the opaque language of decisions (see, for example, Art 48(7) TEU, Lisbon that enables the European Council to decide whether the Council acts by unanimity or by qualified majority voting).[34]

One of the most important reasons to attempt to radically reorganize the European Council in the recent treaty reform processes was to institutionalize and constitutionalize it further in the EU system so that such overlapping of respective competences could be better avoided in the future. In one fell swoop the European Council, as a formal EU institution, would become subject, upon entry into force of the Treaty of Lisbon, to the provisions of Art 13(2) TEU, namely that 'each institution shall act within the limits of the powers conferred on it in the Treaties, and in conformity with the procedures, conditions and objectives set out in them. The institutions shall practice mutual sincere cooperation.' In this manner the European Council will become further embedded formally within the institutional structure of the EU and the legal guarantees offered by the EU legal system as well as the—rather open-ended—duty to act in good faith.

4.2.2 President of the European Council

One of the most important innovations in the Treaty of Lisbon as a whole has been the formal institution of a new actor in the executive order of the EU and

[32] Art 15(1) TEU, Lisbon.

[33] I am grateful to Paul Craig for this point. See too on the same phenomenon and the Constitutional Treaty, D Curtin (2005b), 'Mind the gap: The evolving EU Executive and the Constitution', Third Walter van Gerven Public Lecture, University of Leuven, available at <http://www.usg.uu.nl/download/Mind%20the%20Gap_The%20Evolving%20Executive%20and%20the%20Constitutional%20Treaty.pdf>. On the practice of the European Council in this regard, sees WT Eijsbouts (2000), 'De Raad van Opperhoofden: Over het Regeringsstelsel van de Unie' in AK Koekoek (ed), *Bijdragen aan een Europese Grondwet: Staatsrechtconferentie 2000* (Deventer: Tjeenk Willink), pp 59–87.

[34] See too, R Barents (2008), pp 458–9.

one that in many respects is to be considered at the very pinnacle of executive power in the EU: the president of the European Council as a distinct (semi-permanent) actor.[35] These provisions are the result of extensive discussions about the need for a visible 'president' for the Union as a whole.[36] Moreover it probably confirms the success of the French in pushing their own governmental model of a leading role for presidents and heads of state.[37] In the view of some commentators this success leads to the conclusion that the EU political system is clearly evolving towards a presidential model of government and not a parliamentary one.[38] They will moreover be the external spokesman on the international political scene on behalf of the Union as such.[39] This president will convey increased authority externally as a person personifying the whole EU and will project internationally an image of continuity and coherence that should address concerns about who 'speaks for Europe'.[40] They will be the person Henry Kissinger would hypothetically call.

The institution of this new actor can also be understood against the background of the ephemeral nature of the presidency of the Council, not a single post, but held by a Member State's government (see further below). In effect, this new actor 'won' from those who had argued that it was more logical in structural and constitutional terms that the powers of the Commission president be expanded to be able to fulfil this role. After all, the Commission president was the one connected both in formal and substantive terms with the core exercise of executive power in the Union. In the compromise that was finally reached there will be a 'king-pin' president of the European Council that is juxtaposed with the (weakened?) president of the Commission, and squeezed in between them will be a 'double-hatted' Janus-faced High Representative of the Union for Foreign Affairs and Security Policy (see further on both these other actors below).

The Treaty of Lisbon provides for a semi-permanent presidency of the European Council with its own bureaucratic support mechanism in the form of the General Secretariat of the Council of Ministers.[41] This key role of the Council Secretariat, which will function as interface and communication channel between the semi-permanent European Council presidency and the largely more transient six-month Council presidency, will increase the role and significance of this already increasingly powerful (but somewhat hidden) actor.[42] Almost inevitably

[35] See further S Blavoukos, D Bourantonis, and G Pagoulatos (2007), 'A president for the European Union: A new actor in town?', *Journal of Common Market Studies*, 45/2, pp 231–52.

[36] See further P Lequiller (2003), *Un Président pour l'Europe* (Paris: Fondation Robert Schuman); F Dehousse and W Coussens (2003), *Which Presidency for the European Union? The Convention's dilemmas* (Brussels: Studia Diplomatica), p 97.

[37] See too J Werts (2008), p 147.

[38] See, for example, WT Eijsbouts (2000), pp 59–87.

[39] Art 15(6)(d) TEU, Lisbon.

[40] S Blavoukos, D Bourantonis, and G Pagoulatos (2007), p 240.

[41] Art 235(4) TFEU.

[42] See too Joint Study EPC, EGMONT and CEPS (2007), *Treaty of Lisbon: Implementing the institutional innovations*, Brussels, November 2007, available at <http://www.irri-kiib.be/SD/Joint_Study_complet.pdf>, p 50.

it will play a key role in ensuring cooperation and coordination between the two sets of presidents, one more permanent in nature and the other rotating periodically. The expectation is that the relevant officials of the Council General Secretariat will have an important (but hidden) role to play in the preparation of European Council decisions and in their implementation (see further below on the evolving role in general of the Council General Secretariat). The 'follow-up' to its decisions will thus become much more institutionalized than is currently the case. At the same time, the expectation is that the European Council will have its own specific expenditure that will need to be separately itemized in the overall budget and that the president may well have their own 'cabinet'.[43]

It is not excluded moreover that at some point in the future the presidency may formally acquire its own autonomous secretariat, separate to that of the Council and even perhaps a kind of all-powerful 'bureau'.[44] In terms of institutional design the French (and Giscard d'Estaing as Convention president and indeed the large Member States) dream of an all-powerful EU executive with the Commission being controlled not only by the European Parliament but also by a further reinforced European Council—may come back to haunt it. The dream is effectively of the European Council as the 'government' of the EU.[45] The alternative was of a genuinely single executive—the creation of a single post combining the presidency of the European Council with that of the Commission—and was favoured by the smaller Member States. The choice between these two alternatives can be considered part of the future institutional design choices facing the Union and an integral part of the ongoing and deeper narrative and tension between different visions as to the construction of the EU political system.

Article 15(5) TEU, Lisbon (Treaty of Lisbon) stipulates that the European Council shall elect its president, by qualified majority, for two and a half years, renewable once. The president's tasks are, inter alia, to chair the European Council and 'drive forward its work' on the basis of 'the work of the General Affairs Council'. Leadership is understood as 'an asymmetrical relationship of influence in which one actor guides or directs the behaviour of others towards a certain goal over a certain period of time'.[46] Successful formal leadership does not follow a single pattern and is heavily context- and personality-dependent.[47] In terms of the possible European Council presidency functions it seems that these will, in any event, include an overarching administration and coordinating

[43] See European Parliament (2009), Committee on Constitutional Affairs, *Draft Report on the Impact of the Treaty of Lisbon on the Development of the Institutional Balance of the European Union*, 26 January 2009, PE405.890v02–00, para 20.

[44] See further, the various plans discussed and rejected for the moment at the European Convention, J Werts (2008), pp 151 *et seq*.

[45] Ibid, pp 190–1; WT Eijsbouts (2000), pp 76–7.

[46] A Underdal (1994), 'Leadership theory: Rediscovering the arts of management' in IW Zartman (ed), *International Multilateral Negotiation: Approaches to the management of complexity* (San Francisco: Jossey-Bass), pp 178–97.

[47] S Blavoukos, D Bourantonis, and G Pagoulatos (2007), p 234.

role ('shall ensure the preparation and continuity in the work of the European Council'[48]). One of the key unresolved issues is what precise consultation and coordination procedures will be put in place in legal and institutional 'practices' for all those involved in the presidency. One of the key issues in this context will be the need for regular meetings between in any event the permanent president of the European Council, representatives of the rotating presidency, the High Representative, the president of the Commission and the Secretary General of the Council. In addition, the European Parliament is particularly keen to improve the inter-institutional cooperation between the European Parliament and the European Council as a whole. It favours the adoption of an inter-institutional agreement on the relations between the two institutions and in particular that the president of the European Parliament be enabled to attend discussions in the European Council itself.[49]

Leaving aside the issue of foreign policy for the moment, it is clear that the president will prepare and control their own agenda. A crucial issue for the manner in which executive power will be led is the relationship between the president of the Commission and the president of the European Council and the nature of their respective powers. With regard to the Commission the position is continued that the Commission president is *ex officio* a member of the European Council. Further, there will be a special new relationship between the Commission and the European Council by virtue of the 'two hats' worn by the new High Representative of the Union for Foreign Affairs and Security Policy (see further below) but this is in a specific policy field. Much will depend on the manner in which this relationship is implemented in practice, for example in the new rules of procedure of the European Council and the revised ones of the Commission—to be adopted, presumably, once the Treaty of Lisbon has entered into force.

Similarly, the nature of the relationship between the president and the Council of Ministers and its administration is not yet precisely determined other than that it will be close. There is only limited personal overlap in the actual work of the Council of Ministers in the sense that no provision is made for joint membership of Council formations and the European Council, although the heads of states 'shall be assisted' by the ministers of foreign affairs (members of the Council).[50] The European Council has no power over the running of the Council as such but it does have a special relationship with the General Affairs Council.[51] The president of the European Council shall ensure the preparation

[48] Art 15(6)(b) TEU, Lisbon.

[49] See too European Parliament (2009), para 15.

[50] Art 4 TEU. In the Lisbon Treaty it is at the discretion of members of the European Council whether they want to be assisted by a minister: Art 15(3) TEU, Lisbon.

[51] The General Affairs Council composed of the ministers of foreign affairs has attempted to coordinate overall policy and priorities. In the Treaty establishing a Constitution for Europe it was proposed to establish a Legislative General Affairs Council (LGAC) that would have had a more visible role in terms of the adoption by the Council of legislative measures, as opposed to the prior

and continuity (follow-up) of the meetings of the European Council 'on the basis of the work of the General Affairs Council'.[52] This has to be read in conjunction with the provision that the General Affairs Council must prepare and ensure the follow-up to meetings of the European Council, in liaison with the Commission and the president of the European Council.[53] In the view of Craig, this creates (for the Constitutional Treaty precursor) 'a cognizable legal obligation on the [L]GAC, when it meets in its General Affairs function, to ensure that the conclusions reached by the European Council are followed up. It creates a more formal mechanism than hitherto for the European Council to influence the priorities of the EU. It may enable the European Council to influence the detail of executive matters.'[54] This would include pressing for legislation specific priorities of the European Council and its president despite the fact it has no formal powers to start the legislative process. As a matter of fact, this is the case already with the European Council clearly requesting that legislation be adopted in specific areas, as a study of European Council practice already shows.[55]

The overlapping of responsibilities and the fragmentation of executive power would seem to point towards the need to further develop the role of the president of the European Council as the *oppercommando* of the system[56] as it has been conceived and enshrined in the Treaty of Lisbon. Logically the president of the European Council will be the driving force of the various collegial presidencies and will act as its arbiter since 'he is ultimately accountable to the highest body'.[57] The European Council in its turn is the *Oberrat* that will in the final analysis take political decisions and lead them to the respective competent Council formations.[58]

Much will depend on the first incumbent and the manner in which the various possibilities will be operationalized in a concrete manner. On the one hand nothing in the Lisbon Treaty prevents the president from establishing the necessary structures in order to bring their position in line with the requirements of their task: to exercise leadership at the highest level.[59] At the same time nothing excludes the contrary evolution: a function more modestly modelled, for

and current practice of any configuration whatsoever of the Council adopting legislation irrespective of the policy area at issue.

[52] Art 15(6) TEU, Lisbon. [53] Art 16 (6) TEU, Lisbon.

[54] P Craig (2004b), 'The Constitutional Treaty: Legislative and executive power in the emerging constitutional order', EUI Working Paper, Law no 2004/7, available at <http://papers.ssrn.com/sol3/papers.cfm?abstract_id=635342>.

[55] P de Schoutheete and H Wallace (2002). See too G Majone (2002); J Werts (2008), pp 46–8.

[56] R Barents (2008), p 211, uses this term in relation to the European Council as a whole and not just its president. I take it one step further in terms of leadership potential.

[57] Joint Study EPC, EGMONT, and CEPS (2007), p 52.

[58] See, in this sense, A Maurer (2008), 'Vermittlung, Steuerung und demokratische Verantwortung: Die Sollbruchstellen des Reformvertages' in I Pernice (ed), *Der Vertrag von Lissabon: Reform der EU ohne Verfassung?* (Berlin: Nomos Verlag).

[59] J Werts (2008), p 175.

example, upon that of the Secretary General of NATO, lacking effective—and more autonomous—political power. Only time will tell what narrative emerges. Even without the Treaty of Lisbon, this narrative will continue given the very clear support by the larger Member States for this visualization and reinforcement of the role of the European Council in this manner.

4.3 The 'Council of Ministers': An Institutional 'Chameleon'

4.3.1 Institutional 'chameleon'[60]

Below the European Council in the national executive hierarchy of the EU is the Council of Ministers—the body conceived originally as the principal legislative body for European integration. The Council of Ministers was, as we saw in Chapter 3, from the very beginning, designed as the *political* decision-making centre among the institutions of the Union and its predecessors.[61] In the national political systems, government ministers (in some systems) and members of national parliaments will tend to be directly elected. At the level of the political system of the EU the situation is more varied: the 'politicians' are either the ministers participating in the Council of Ministers (or the prime-ministers/French president—and Commission president—in the European Council), all of whom will have been either directly elected in the national system or appointed by those who have been directly elected. The Council of Ministers continues to be perceived as mainly a political organ (consisting of national ministers, *ipso facto* executive politicians) with (both formal and substantive) legislative power (either autonomous or shared with the European Parliament depending on the policy area).

Lawyers have traditionally tended to analyse the Council of Ministers in rather formal terms, relying very much on the formal treaty rules where the rules as to composition, decision-making, and so on are defined.[62] In addition, what Héretier calls 'overt and formal modes of changing rules'[63] will tend to be taken into account. This will mainly include third-party adjudication by the European Court of Justice in particular but other formal and overt sources such as the

[60] The term is that of H Wallace (2002), 'The Council: An institutional chameleon', *Governance: An International Journal of Policy, Administration and Institutions*, 15/3, pp 325–44.

[61] W Wessels (1991), 'The EC Council: The community's decision-making centre' in RO Keohane and S Hoffmann (eds), *The New European Community: Decision-making and institutional change* (Boulder, CO: Westview), p 133. See, in general terms, F Hayes-Renshaw and H Wallace (2006).

[62] See, for example, K Lenaerts and P van Nuffel (2005), *The Constitutional Law of the European Union*, 2nd edn (London: Sweet and Maxwell), pp 409–27; P Craig and G de Búrca (2003), *EU Law: Text, cases and materials*, 3rd edn (Oxford: Oxford University Press), pp 65–75; D Chalmers et al (2006), *European Union Law* (Cambridge: Cambridge University Press), pp 101–7.

[63] A Héretier (2001), 'Overt and covert institutionalization in Europe' in A Stone-Sweet, W Sandholtz, and N Fligstein, *The Institutionalization of Europe* (Oxford: Oxford University Press), pp 56–70.

institution's rules of procedure or relevant inter-institutional agreements will also be referred to where relevant. Informal rules or what is termed 'soft institutions' will to some extent also be taken into account in analytical descriptions, such as for example the use of the Luxembourg compromise in practice and other more informal arrangements especially in the area of voting. Long-established 'institutions' such as COREPER, explicitly mentioned in the treaties, tend in the legal literature to be referred—and even analysed in great detail[64]—to the exclusion of newer and perhaps more fragmentary features of further institutionalization (eg various high-level committees, working parties, and the growing and changing role of the General Secretariat). That said lawyers are leading the way in terms of analysing the implications of new formal treaty provisions and new actors tied in closely with the evolution of the Council of Ministers in formal terms.[65]

Covert institutionalization in the sense of what happens behind closed doors and what is not easily accessible or understandable to outsiders is less explicitly put on the map in legal analyses of the various facets of the Council as an institution. In recent years it has been political scientists in particular who have dug deeper into emerging institutional practices and structures in an attempt to analyse more profoundly the manner in which the nature of the Council of Ministers as an institution and in practice has evolved over time.[66] My approach in this (and the next) chapter is not to attempt to give chapter and verse of the legal rules, both formal and informal, governing the composition and operation of the Council of Ministers and its core tasks.[67] Rather, I aim to give a sense, in a necessarily selective fashion, of the manner in which its nature has evolved as an executive institution over the course of the past decade, in particular in its practices, taking into account the new roles—and even (covert) structures—it acquired in the aftermath of the entry into force of the Treaty of Maastricht and indeed subsequent reform treaties.

The extent to which the Council of Ministers changes its colour may not only be dependent on changes in the surrounding environment but may occur also in response to changing physical and physiological conditions. The metaphor of a chameleon is apt because it suggests that it is possible to read the evolution that

[64] See, for example, the work by J de Zwaan (1995), *The Permanent Representatives Committee: Its role in European Union decision-making* (Amsterdam: Elsevier). See too D Bostock (2002), 'COREPER revisited', *Journal of Common Market Studies*, 40/2, pp 215–34.

[65] See, for example, R Lauwaars (2004), 'The President of the European Council: The beginning of a European government?' in J de Zwaan et al (eds), *The European Union: An ongoing process of integration. Liber Amicorum Fred Kellermann* (Cambridge: Cambridge University Press), pp 71–6; J Wouters (2004), 'The Union Minister for Foreign Affairs: Europe's single voice or Trojan horse?' in J de Zwaan et al (eds), *The European Union: An ongoing process of integration. Liber Amicorum Fred Kellermann* (Cambridge: Cambridge University Press), pp 77–86; see too various articles in European Constitutional L Rev (2005) 1/1.

[66] See, for example, D Naurin and H Wallace (eds) (2008), *Unveiling the Council of the European Union: Games governments play in Brussels* (Basingstoke: Palgrave Macmillan).

[67] There are excellent accounts of these to be found elsewhere: see references cited above plus the book by F Hayes-Renshaw and H Wallace (2006).

has taken place in the nature of the Council of Ministers as changes in colours in certain contexts or settings while recognizing that the original understanding (colour) may also be visible at times and that a certain mixing of colours may also take place.

4.3.2 The 'presidency': A composite carousel

The 'presidency of the Council' is not a single post, but is held by a Member State's *government*. Every six months the presidency rotates between the states, in an order predefined by the Council's members, allowing each state to preside over the body in turn. Article 16(9) TEU, Lisbon stipulates that the presidency of all council configurations, except foreign affairs, is to be held by Member State representatives on the basis of equal rotation.[68]

Due to this rotating system, national governments are given the opportunity to influence the political priorities and the visibility of the EU is increased due to the involvement of national politicians. The structural weaknesses inherent in the rotating presidency, linked to the shortness of the mandate and the resulting lack of continuity both in terms of representation and action, may have been improved somewhat by measures going in the direction of *team* presidencies. From 2007 groups of three Member States (the presidency *troika*) cooperate for a combined 18 months on a common agenda, although only one formally holds the presidency for the normal six-month period.

The main functions of the rotating Council presidency, as described systematically in the 1979 report by the Three Wise Men[69] are to:

- supervise the practical organization of the proceedings of the Council, the European Council and the Council's preparatory bodies
- represent the Council in dealings with the other institutions and with non-member countries
- play the part of an honest broker in negotiations
- set the Union's political agenda (within limits).

These functions have come to be exercised in a rapidly evolving institutional context and are of three different orders in terms of the type of role exercised—agenda-setter, organizer, and mediator. It has been pointed out that these tasks correspond very broadly to those of the new (semi-)permanent president of the European Council 'with however the very important addition of the organization of work in the medium and long-term, which is linked to the permanent nature

[68] The conditions for rotation are established in accordance with Art 236 TFEU. See also Declaration No 9 annexed to the Lisbon Treaty.

[69] B Biesheuvel, E Dell, and R Marjolin (1980), *Report on European Institutions: Presented by the Committee of Three to the European Council* (Luxembourg: Office for Official Publications of the European Communities), available at <http://www.ena.lu/conclusions_wise_men_committee_dublin_29_30_november_1979–020003121.html>.

of the function'.[70] The advent and practice of the European Council has obviously affected the ability of a Council presidency changing hands every six months to perform a concerted agenda-setting role that is long-term-oriented and aims to find solutions beyond the common denominator. The European Council has in effect provided such political leadership in recent years and not the Council presidency. On the other hand, useful management and organization tasks are efficiently performed by the rotating Council presidency. In addition the Council presidency must seek to find solutions aimed at the common denominator and facilitate wider group processes (including increasingly negotiating with the European Parliament in co-decision).[71] At the same time it has been shown that the Member State governments have developed the presidency office in order to address collective-action problems in European integration, generally at the expense of the Commission.[72]

The Council presidency is supported by the General Secretariat of the Council. All presidencies rely on the Council Secretariat to advise them on procedures, to draw up minutes and other reports of meetings and for functions such as arranging the production, translation and circulation of Council documents. The Council General Secretariat developed into the Council's institutional memory and also functions as a bridge between various chairs. Its officials do not only support the Council in all its formations but also its preparatory bodies such as the Committee of Permanent Representatives (COREPER) and the various working groups. As a result the Secretariat also becomes a source of coordination, coherence, and continuity in the Council's work.[73] In addition, the fact that from 1982 onwards the General Secretariat started to play a key role in the preparation of the draft presidency conclusions[74] meant that its role at a high political level grew in importance. This political status increased with the advent of CFSP and the fact that after the entry into force of the Treaty of Maastricht and subsequent treaties the European Council acquired an incrementally more important role in deciding on common strategies and taking decisions in that regard. Through long-term involvement in a dossier and informal communication with government representatives, the Secretariat gains an in-depth and horizontal picture of state preferences. 'At the same time, there may well be powerful self-referential

[70] Joint Study EPC, EGMONT and CEPS (2007), p 50.

[71] See further A Schout and L van Schaik (2008), 'Reforming the EU presidency?', *Journal of Comparative Government and European Policy*, 6/1, pp 35–56.

[72] See further, J Talberg (2004), 'the power of the chair: Formal leadership in international cooperation', Paper prepared for presentation at the Annual ISA Convention, Montreal, March 17–20 2004, on file with author.

[73] See too T Christiansen and S Vanhoonacker (2008), 'At a critical juncture? Change and continuity in the institutional development of the Council Secretariat', *West European Politics*, 31/4, pp 751–70.

[74] See further J Werts (1992), *The European Council* (Amsterdam: Elsevier); and M Mangenot (2002), 'L'affirmation du Secrétariat du Conseil de l'Union européenne: Les transformations du rôle d'une institution non codifiée', Paper presented at the 'VIIe congrès de l'Association française de science politique', Lille, 18–21 September 2002.

concepts at work—the idea that the Council General Secretariat considers its role as being one of an 'honest broker' may heavily influence how the actor and those working for it operate in practice.[75]

The rather ephemeral Council leadership will share centre stage and the spotlight with no less than two new executive actors brought to life in the Treaty of Lisbon, assuming it enters into force in one form or another. First, as we have seen above, the (semi-)permanent and non-rotating president of the European Council represents a quantum leap in terms of institutionalization and visibility. Nothing terribly explicit is said in the Treaty of Lisbon regarding the issue of relationship between the presidencies of the European Council and the Council of Ministers other than in the context of the tasking of the GAC when the European Council presidency would seem to have a leading role. Unlike some proposals made in the context of the European Convention, there is no overlap with the work of the Council itself—the only explicit interface is with the GAC and in one direction: it must prepare and implement European Council work. Given, however, the fact that one presidency will be more or less permanent (and be supported by the same Council Secretariat) and the other will change every six months (even if embedded in teams of three) it is relatively clear that the latter will de facto be in a subordinate position. This is also made apparent in a number of explicit provisions, such as that it is the European Council that adopts the decision establishing further formations in which the Council may meet.[76] Secondly, the rather Janus-faced figure of the new High Representative of the Union for Foreign Affairs and Security Policy (the High Representative, see further below) shall not only chair the Foreign Affairs Council but also at the same time be one of the vice presidents of the Commission. It may be doubted whether these various pieces (and hats) will be compatible and coherent in practice.

4.3.3 Legislative and executive tasks: Blurring boundaries

In the 'community method', the role of the Council of Ministers is largely as legislative decision-maker (incrementally in some aspects of policy fields in 'co-decision' with the European Parliament). In other putatively 'intergovernmental' policy areas, such as CFSP and justice and home affairs, it is the only 'decision-maker' (also of legislative decisions, as it emerged in practice). Evidence of the indivisibility of the Council as an institution is provided by certain cross-'pillar' practices that developed over the years.[77] Yet it is only with the entry into force of the Lisbon Treaty that the ordinary legislative procedure

[75] J Talberg (2006), 'The power of the chair: Formal leadership in international cooperation', Paper presented at the Third Pan-European Conference in EU Politics, Istanbul, p 45, quoted by T Christiansen and S Vanhoonacker (2008).

[76] Art 236 TFEU.

[77] See further for specific examples in CFSP and CJHA, D Curtin and IF Dekker (1999), 'The EU as a "layered" international organization: Institutional unity in disguise' in P Craig and G de Búrca (eds), *The Evolution of EU Law* (Oxford: Oxford University Press), pp 83–136.

will often apply in the policy area of freedom, security, and justice. In any event, the legislative role of the Council is not focused on one Council formation but is scattered across the respective Council formations in the specific policy fields. The fact that, as a matter of practice, specific pieces of legislation are actually often adopted by a Council formation other than the one dealing with the specific policy field does not increase the coherence or visibility of the Council's role in EU legislation.[78]

At the same time it has been gradually understood that the Council's role in non-legislative and even operational decisions has grown greatly since the entry into force of the Treaty of Maastricht and subsequent tides of treaty reform. Jacqué, the director of the Legal Service of the Council of the EU, acknowledges in his scholarly writings that the Council of the EU can be considered to also exercise executive power, alongside its law-making powers.[79] What had indeed begun to take shape—in the shadow of legal and institutional practices—over the years with regard to the executive functions of the Council was confirmed ultimately in the provisions of the Treaty of Lisbon.[80] The fact that new rules and practices are developing incrementally and almost continuously creates new opportunities as well as constraints for the actors involved.[81] In the words of Sjursen, 'the risk is that what we will observe in the future is a multi-level process of self-reinforcing executive dominance'.[82]

It is clear that the Council's executive powers do not only involve implementation of laws. Indeed, the recent practice of the Council has been to delegate such implementation tasks to the Commission, even with regard to the newer policy areas of justice and home affairs. In an increasing number of cases, the Council as an executive power has a function independent of the legislature. This is the case of acts in the CFSP area, by which the EU defines its non-economic policy towards third countries, of some acts in the field of police cooperation, as well as of acts concerning the working the Economic and Monetary Union, which aim at reacting to particular situations that are hardly liable to *ex ante* legislative regulation. This can be termed the 'autonomous' role of the Council acting as an 'executive' power. That includes operational activities that are given a certain pride of place in the new treaty.

[78] See, for specific examples of this phenomenon, D Curtin and IF Dekker (1999).

[79] J-P Jacqué (2007), 'Introduction: Pouvoir législatif et pouvoir exécutif dans l'Union européenne' in J-B Auby and J Dutheil de la Rochere (eds), *Droit administrative européen* (Brussels: Bruylant), pp 25–48.

[80] See further D Curtin (2004b), *Mind the Gap: The evolving EU executive and the Constitution* (Groningen: Europa Law Publishing) on the precursor of the Lisbon Treaty, the defunct Treaty establishing a Constitution for Europe.

[81] See, in general terms, JG Marsh and JP Olsen (1989), *Rediscovering Institutions* (New York: Free Press).

[82] H Sjursen (2007), 'Integration without democracy: Three conceptions of European security policy in transformation', RECON Online Working Paper 2007/19, available at <http://www.reconproject.eu/main.php/RECON_wp_0719.pdf?fileitem=5456242>.

The Final Report of the European Convention's Working Party on Justice and Home Affairs[83] underscored the need for a clearer distinction between the Council acting in its legislative capacity and the Council exercising specific executive functions that turns on what is termed 'operational collaboration'. This brought with it the creation of a more efficient structure for the coordination of operational cooperation at high technical level within the Council, namely the merging of various existing working groups and redefining the mission of the so-called 'Article 36 Committee', so that it would in the future focus on coordinating operational cooperation rather than becoming involved in the Council's legislative work.[84] The idea that this reformed structure would focus on the coordination and oversight of the entire spectrum of operational activity in police and security matters (inter alia police cooperation, fact-finding missions, facilitation of cooperation between Europol and Eurojust, peer review, civil protection) took root in the subsequent treaty. But as the Committee of Independent Experts put it in their second report: 'the distinction between formulating and implementing policy, namely between policy and operational matters is a falsely rigid one, difficult to define in principle and even more difficult to apply in practice'. The risk is that it leads to even more power being exercised in the shade of the formal powers.

4.3.4 COREPER, Council, high-level committees, and working parties

In order to prepare the decisions at the ministerial level, a great number of committees and working parties have been established in which all Member States and the Commission are represented. Traditionally, at the apex of this hierarchy is COREPER, the committee for the permanent representatives or the EU ambassadors of the Member States, which was established in 1958. It is generally considered highly influential in 'brokering' deals on difficult issues that have not been resolved at the more technical lower level of committees and working parties (populated by lower-level national civil servants). Many of the Council working parties and committees, including COREPER seem to govern 'in the shadow' in the sense that little is known about how such institutions work in practice and indeed the scholarly literature and empirical study is sparse—although this situation may well be changing thanks in no small measure to the information now available via the Internet (see Chapter 8 below).[85]

[83] European Convention, Final Report of Working Group X, 'Freedom, Security and Justice', 2 December 2002, available at <http://register.consilium.eu.int/pdf/en/02/cv00/00426en2.pdf>.

[84] This became Art 71 TFEU pursuant to the Treaty of Lisbon.

[85] See, for example, J Lempp and J Altenschmidt (2008), 'The prevention of deadlock through informal processes of "supranationalization": The case of COREPER', *European Integration*, 30/4, pp 511–26; A Juncos and C Reynolds (2007), 'The Political and Social Security Committee: Governing in the shadow', *European Foreign Affairs Review*, 12/2, pp 127–47.

Empirical research had shown some time ago that a very large proportion indeed of decisions pass through the upper ministerial and sectoral levels as 'A' points on the agenda.[86] An 'A' point implies that the issue has been settled at a lower level, and it will usually be passed as a matter of course at the higher level with no further discussion required. Ministers, when meeting in the Council, will therefore concentrate on the B points of the agenda, indicating the—much smaller—number of items on which officials or permanent representatives have not been able to reach agreement in their preparatory meetings. This means that the decisions (taken by the lower echelons in the hierarchy) are approved as such without any substantive negotiation or even discussion. In effect, it follows that a large proportion of Council decisions are being taken by either the lower-level civil servants sitting in working parties or the higher-level national civil servants sitting in committees. The high number of legal acts passed in the so-called 'A-point' procedure thus shows the importance of COREPER as well as the whole committee system behind it for the ability of the Council to actually take decisions.[87]

Available figures differ as to the exact percentage of 'decisions' that are fully worked out in advance of Council meetings. For example, in the field of CFSP it has been claimed that up to 90% of the issues have been solved before they reach the Council level; and 70% even at the lower administrative levels including, in particular, by the approximately 36 working parties playing a role in the preparation of CFSP decisions.[88] According to Hayes-Renshaw and Wallace, ministers are only involved in 10 to 15% of all Council decisions.[89] More recent research carried out with the benefit of a more liberal transparency policy strongly challenges the view that ministers are hardly involved in Council decision-making and reveals that almost 50% of all legislative decisions under the 'Community' pillar are discussed by ministers in the course of Council negotiations.[90] A more refined policy specific approach may therefore be necessary.

One rather hybrid actor to come more to the fore in recent years is the Political and Security Committee (PSC) that enjoys a role that is rather wide and has been entrenched at treaty level.[91] The predecessor of the PSC, the Political Committee was established in the beginning of the 1970s as part of the

[86] MPCM van Schendelen (1996), '"The Council decides": Does the Council decide?', *Journal of Common Market Studies*, 33/4, pp 531–48.

[87] See further J Lempp and J Altenschmidt (2008).

[88] RA Wessel (2009), 'The constitutional unity of the European Union: The increasing irrelevance of the pillar structure?' in J Wouters, L Verhey, and P Kiiver (eds), *European Constitutionalism beyond the EU Constitution* (Antwerpen: Intersentia), pp 283–306, (forthcoming).

[89] F Hayes-Renshaw and H Wallace (1997), pp 40, 78

[90] F Hage (2008), 'Who decides in the Council of the European Union?', *Journal of Common Market Studies*, 46/3, pp 533–58.

[91] A Juncos and C Reynolds (2007).

European Political Cooperation (EPC).[92] Its *esprit de corps* resulted in a 'consultation reflex' that formed the basis for the EPC and later CFSP.[93] An intensification of this cooperation clearly formed the rationale behind the creation of the Political and Security Committee that succeeded the Political Committee in the year 2000 as a standing committee based at the Council's premises in Brussels and meeting twice a week.

Unlike other Council high-level committees, Member States are in principle represented in this Committee at ambassadorial level, a fact that has occasioned conflict with COREPER in the past.[94] It also consists of one Commission member and four Council Secretariat members. The Council decision setting up the Political and Security Committee formally in January 2001 already listed an impressive range of tasks, including taking 'responsibility for the political direction of the development of military capacities'.[95] The PSC and its extensive range of working groups have seen its role expanded with every new mission and new policy: it now covers virtually every aspect of foreign policy.[96] Its preparatory bodies include the Committee for Civilian Crisis Management. It is closely related to the EU Military Committee[97] who reports to it and is composed of the Member States' Chiefs of Defence, represented by their military representatives. This Committee has its own Council working groups and is assisted by an EU Military Staff (EUMS) composed of around 150 officials who are seconded from the Member States to the Council General Secretariat (see further below).[98]

The EUMS is a Council Secretariat department directly attached to the High Representative/Secretary General. These new and permanent political and military bodies are designed to 'enable the EU assume its responsibilities for the full range of conflict prevention and crisis management tasks defined in the EU Treaty, the Petersburg tasks'.[99] These tasks include the operational functions of early warning, situation assessment, and strategic planning.[100] Subsequently the PSC also got tasks of 'political supervision' over the activities of for example

[92] See, for instance, ME Smith (2004), *Europe's Foreign and Security Policy: The institutionalisation of cooperation* (Cambridge: Cambridge University Press), pp 77–84.

[93] SJ Nuttall (1992), *European Political Cooperation* (Oxford: Oxford University Press). He defined the 'consultation reflex' as an 'automatic reflex of consultation brought about by frequent personal contacts with opposite numbers from the other Member States' (p 312). See also P de Schoutheete (1980), *La coopération politique européenne* (Paris: Nathan).

[94] See further S Duke and S Vanhoonacker (2006), 'Administrative governance in the CFSP: Development and practice', *European Foreign Affairs Review*, 11/2, pp 163–82, p 173.

[95] OJ L 27/1 (30 January 2001), Annex, 1(j).

[96] See further A Juncos and C Reynolds (2007).

[97] Council Decision of 22 January 2001 setting up the Military Committee of the EU, OJ L 27/4 (30 January 2001).

[98] Council Decision of 22 January 2001 on the establishment of the Military Staff of the EU, OJ L 27/7 (30 January 2001).

[99] Council Decision of 22 January, ibid, Annex, point 1, OJ L 27/8.

[100] Council Decision of 22 January, ibid, Annex, point 1, OJ L 27/4.

the legally independent European Union Satellite Centre[101] and the European Union Institute for Security Studies.[102] In other words the institutional map of the EU's foreign and security policy[103] is almost a paradigm case of what has been aptly termed 'complex interdependence embedded in a multilevel governance configuration'.[104]. Sjursen has drawn a map in intricate detail that makes the point of almost frightening complexity and executive expansion.[105]

National civil servants may indeed have to work within the confines of a politically circumscribed negotiating space but within these limits there is also some empirical evidence of a potential for collegiality and group dynamics, including the more—supranational—possibility that individual participants may be able to influence the proceedings 'based on their knowledge, the strength of their argument or negotiating skills rather than purely on the political weight of their member state'.[106] More recent case study research findings have shown that even low-level 'working groups' do not operate solely on a 'technical' level but that the 'political' enters into the equation even at these low-level institutional arenas.[107] The same conclusion of informal processes of 'supranationalization' seems to be possible, in certain instances, for COREPER itself.

One wonders to what extent a similar trend towards rather autonomous consensus-building and problem-solving holds true (or may do so over time) for other high-level Council bodies such as the new Standing Committee on Operational Cooperation on Internal Security (COSI is the French acronym) in the Lisbon Treaty performing specific executive functions.[108] This new committee is meant to provide a more 'efficient' structure for the coordination of operational cooperation at high technical level within the Council, namely the merging of various existing working groups and redefining the mission of the pre-existing 'Article 36 Committee', so that it would in the future focus on coordinating operational cooperation rather than becoming involved in the Council's legislative work.[109]

[101] Council Joint Action of 20 July 2001 on the establishment of a European Union Satellite Centre, OJ L 200/5, 25 July 2001.

[102] Council Joint Action of 20 July 2001 on the establishment of a European Union Institute for Security Studies, OJ L 200/1, 25 July 2001.

[103] For a complete list of all Council preparatory bodies see, most recently, <http://register.consilium.europa.eu/pdf/en/08/st05/st05525.en08.pdf>

[104] EO Eriksen and JE Fossum (2007), 'Europe in transformation: How to reconstitute democracy', RECON Online Working Paper 2007/01, available at <http://www.reconproject.eu/main.php/RECON_wp_0701.pdf?fileitem=5456091>.

[105] See the fascinating 'institutional map' of CFSP in Sjursen (2007).

[106] J Lewis (1998), 'Is the hard bargaining image of the Council misleading? The Committee of Permanent Representatives and the Local Election Directive', *Journal of Common Market Studies*, 36/4, pp 469–504.

[107] E Fouilleux, J de Maillard, and A Smith (2005), 'Technical or political? The working groups of the EU Council of Ministers', *Journal of European Public Policy*, 12/4, pp 609–23.

[108] Art 71 TFEU. This committee has been criticized by civil-rights campaigners concerned by the scope of its activities and the potential accountability vacuum within which it will operate.

[109] A precursor was also the Police Chiefs Operational Task Force established after the 1999 Tampere European Council that carried out both strategic and the planning and coordination of

This reformed structure will focus on the coordination and oversight of the entire spectrum of operational activity in police and security matters (inter alia, police cooperation, fact-finding missions, facilitation of cooperation between Europol and Eurojust, peer review, civil protection, etc). How it will work in practice remains for the moment shrouded in mystery. The terms 'internal security' can however be regarded as including all matters referring to the maintenance of law and public order as well as civilian-military capabilities.[110]

4.4 The European Commission: A 'normalized' executive

4.4.1 The core executive

The European Commission is generally regarded as the 'core executive' of the Community/Union[111] in the sense that its tasks gel remarkably well with what can be described as the central executive tasks in any political system. The Commission initiates legislation and thus up until relatively recently was the main agenda-setter in the EU context; it is the most important executive actor when it comes to implementation of legislation and delegated rule-making; it has a leading role in external economic relations and is responsible for drawing up and accounting for the Union budget.[112] But unlike national administrations it is not in the business of service delivery and it only has a limited 'direct administration' (for example, in the fields of competition policy); much of its focus is on policymaking and regulation. It depends heavily on national administrations in respect of service delivery and enforcement. In the words of one scholar 'The European Commission is one of the most unusual administrations ever created. It was born as a body that would perform both mundane administrative and overtly political tasks. It has always found it difficult to perform them simultaneously and well.'[113]

Not only does the Commission operate in practice as an autonomous institution subject to certain institutional and legal constraints that cannot be assigned back to the Member States, collectively or individually; its role and tasks have evolved considerably in recent years. This has led to a process of the Commission

operational tasks. In 2004 it was proposed to strengthen the EU operational police cooperation by linking the Police Chiefs Task Force with Europol. See further, Council of EU, 'Strengthening the EU Operational Police Cooperation', 13075/04, 27 October 2004.

110 T Bunyan (2008b), 'EU: Cementing the European State: New emphasis on internal security and operational cooperation at EU level', available at <http://www.statewatch.org/news/2008/feb/07lisbon-european-state.htm>.

111 S Hix (2005) *The Political System of the European Union*, 2nd edn, The European Union Series (Basingstoke: Palgrave Macmillan), p 32.

112 P Craig (2004b).

113 J Peterson (1999), 'The Santer era: The European Commission in normative, historical and theoretical perspective', *Journal of European Public Policy*, 6/1, pp 46–65, p 60.

reframing its own role in the integration process in recent years[114] in a manner that cannot readily be regarded as involving delegated functions from the Member States subject to control mechanisms. Instead, it involves a considerable element of the Commission as what one might term an 'autonomous' actor working out what its role is in a rapidly changing economic, political, and global context.[115]

Such autonomous powers are an intrinsic part of the distinctive 'Community method' of adopting decisions at the European level. The 'Community method' of integration is, by its very nature, a very legal method of integration. It is premised upon the Commission's exclusive right of legislative initiative and the legislative (and budgetary) powers of the Council of Ministers (and progressively those of the European Parliament), implementation by the Commission (and the Member States), as well as the adjudicatory role of the Court of Justice.[116] Over the course of time the so-called 'Community method' has come under challenge: both in the context of formal treaty-reform provisions and processes as well as in the more informal circuit where increasing reliance is placed on 'soft law' and newer methods of governance (open method of coordination and others).[117]

4.4.2 The president (and the commissioners)

Over the years it is clear that the role and position of the Commission president have been enhanced considerably and largely due to an incremental series of treaty provisions. The most important of these related to the relationship with fellow commissioners and especially his role in their appointment and even latterly selection. A clear distinction is made between the president and the other members of the Commission as to the appointment procedure. Before the Treaty of Nice entered into force the governments of the Member States appointed the Commission president by common accord. The Treaty of Nice introduced qualified majority decision-making, which is a significant step forward, removing effectively the right of veto by any single Member State and mandating in practice a more cooperative discussion. The new procedure post-Nice described in Art 214(2) TEC provides that the Council, meeting in the composition of Heads of

[114] European Commission, White Paper on Governance, COM (2001) 428 final, available at <http://ec.europa.eu/governance/white_paper/index_en.htm>.

[115] See too N Lebessis and J Paterson (1997), 'Evolution in governance: What lessons for the Commission? A first assessment', Working Paper, European Commission Forward Studies Unit, available at <http://ec.europa.eu/comm/cdp/working-paper/evolution_in_governance.pdf>.

[116] European Commission, COM (2001) 428 final (see n 114 above).

[117] See, for example, concerns expressed by the European Parliament in its 'Report on the Institutional and Legal Implications of the Use of "Soft law" Instruments', FINAL, A6–0259/2007. See too C Joerges (2007), 'Integration through de-legalisation? An irritated heckler', European Governance Papers No. N-07-03, available at <http://www.connex-network.org/eurogov/pdf/egp-newgov-N-07-03.pdf>.

State or Government and acting by a qualified majority, nominates the person it intends to appoint as president of the Commission. The nomination must subsequently be approved by the European Parliament.

The European Parliament has exercised this right of approval quite actively in recent years in particular, holding hearings and debates prior to its decision. The result has been the further politicization of the Commission. The fact that it is now in a certain sense (co-)'elected' by a parliament rather than simply only appointed by government representatives enhances claims of more democratic legitimacy (see Chapter 10 below). This has been due in no small part to the manner in which the European Parliament has in recent years given substance to its role as a constitutional agenda-setter.[118]

The new provision in the Treaty of Lisbon provides that account will be taken of the results of the elections to the European Parliament by the (European) Council prior to submission to the European Parliament of its candidate.[119] But this could also be done even if the Treaty of Lisbon were not to enter into force. The candidate is 'elected' by a majority of the component members of the European Parliament. If a majority is not obtained then the European Council has to begin the procedure all over again (within one month of the vote) with a new candidate.[120] In the words of one commentator: 'although the reform treaty might not change much in formal power relations, the new provision may allow the election procedure to gain more visibility in the broader public. If political parties decide to give support to a certain candidate of their political camp even before, the European election campaign could become a lot more personalized and tangible for many voters.'[121]

A candidate Commission president will necessarily have a political platform and party and political agenda in all likelihood. The choice by the European Parliament of a Commission president that is ideologically more in line with the 'winner' in European-wide elections will inevitably lead to enhanced 'politicization' in line with direct election outcomes and perhaps more left–right contestation in the choice of Commission president. At the same time the Member States did not give up their own powers completely even if they have seen them gradually watered down. But we are still quite far away from the situation of a direct election in some form of the Commission president by the peoples of Europe with a possibility to throw out one they are dissatisfied with over time.[122]

[118] S Hix (2002a), 'Constitutional agenda-setting through discretion in rule interpretation: Why the European Parliament won at Amsterdam', *British Journal of Political Science*, 32/2, pp 259–80. See too, in general, B Rittberger (2007a), 'Constructing Parliamentary democracy in the European Union: How did it happen?' in B Kohler-Koch and B Rittberger (eds), *Debating the Democratic Legitimacy of the European Union* (Plymouth: Rowman and Littlefield), pp 111–37.

[119] Art 17(7) TEU, Lisbon. [120] Art 17(7) TEU, Lisbon.

[121] Joint Study EPC, EGMONT and CEPS (2007), p 26.

[122] See, in particular, the proposal by S Hix (2002b), 'Why the EU should have a single president and how she should be elected', Paper for the Working Group on Democracy in the EU for the

The separate procedure followed for the appointment of the other members of the Commission has also changed over the course of recent years but not yet in the sense that the respective members are subject to 'election' by the European Parliament.[123] Initially the situation was that each Member State proposes one candidate and this was, in effect, rubber-stamped by the collectivity of Member states acting unanimously. Since the Treaty of Nice the situation is that the Member States draw up a list of the other persons whom it intends to appoint as Members of the Commission, and the Council, acting by a qualified majority and by common accord with the nominee for president, adopts this list. The College is then subject *as a body to* a vote of approval by the European Parliament. After approval by Parliament, the president and the other members of the Commission are formally appointed by the Council, which acts by a qualified majority. As we saw in recent years with the vote (by a parliamentary committee, not in plenary session) against the nomination of designate Commission member Rocco Buttiglione, the European Parliament takes this newly acquired role seriously.

The College of Commissioners as a whole once appointed works under the political guidance of the president.[124] The new Art 217 inserted by of the Treaty of Nice further strengthens the role of the president. It is now up to the president to decide on the internal organization of the Commission in order to ensure that it acts consistently, efficiently and on the basis of collegiality. The president appoints the vice presidents from among the members of the College.[125] The principle of collective accountability was thus formally included in the Treaties for the first time. The president allocates responsibilities to the members of the Commission and may reshuffle the allocation of those responsibilities during the Commission's term of office.

The Commission president also acquires the final say in how portfolios are allocated and even the right to reshuffle the team during the five-year term of office by redistributing dossiers, thus making it difficult for governments to attach particular national flags to particular portfolios. The president has also been given the authority to dismiss individual commissioners.[126] Concerning the cabinets, there must now be three nationalities in any cabinet, gender balance and three posts reserved for Commission officials rather than outsiders brought in by the commissioners or foreign ministries. 'The resulting changes produced *cabinet* constellations which would be unrecognisable to old Commission hands.'[127] Given that the average size of an 'ordinary' (not vice president/

British Cabinet Office, available at <http://personal.lse.ac.uk/hix/Working_Papers>.

[123] See, however, the far-reaching proposal made by C Grant (2007) that all commissioners should be directly elected by citizens in the Member States for a non-renewable term, in 'The view from 2027', Opinion paper (London: Centre for European Reform).

[124] Art 217 TEC. [125] Art 17(6)(c) TEU, Lisbon.

[126] Ibid.

[127] D Spence (2006), 'The President, the College and the Cabinets' in D Spence and G Edwards (eds), *The European Commission* (London: John Harper Publishing), p 72.

president) commissioner's cabinet seems to be seven members, such a composition has probably changed the role of entities previously portrayed as *national* enclaves[128] and as being apparently sensitive to national interests.[129]

A crucial issue for the manner in which executive power will be led is how the relationship between the president of the Commission and the president of the European Council will be given shape and substance in the light of the nature of their respective powers. With regard to the Commission the position is continued that the Commission President is *ex officio* a member of the European Council. One effect of the General Secretariat's traditional role in preparing European Councils was the establishment of direct contacts with the president of the European Commission.[130] In fact the Commission and the Council Secretariat cooperate on a regular basis in policymaking and in the preparation and running of the multitude of meetings within the Council structure, sharing an interest in the smooth running of the overall policy process.[131] In the field of external relations, given the overlap in responsibilities, there is however more scope for competition than cooperation in the management of the EU's external relations. The appointment of Javier Solana and the changes in the Council Secretariat that went with it have 'rather ruffled feathers in the Council Secretariat as well as in the Commission'.[132]

Further, there will be a special new relationship between the Commission and the European Council by virtue of the 'two hats' worn by the new High Representative of the Union for Foreign Affairs and Security Policy (see below) but this is in a specific policy field. Much will depend on the manner in which this relationship is implemented in practice, for example in the new rules of procedure of the European Council (to be adopted by simple majority[133]) and the revised ones of the Commission—to be adopted once the Treaty of Lisbon has entered into force.

4.4.3 Number of commissioners

There has been considerable debate in recent years on the overall size of the Commission. For many it was clear that the traditional principle of one national from each Member State and not more than two nationals from the same Member State (for certain larger states) could not be maintained in the light of enlargement to 27 members and beyond. In the IGC leading to the Nice Treaty, opinion

[128] HJ Michelmann (1978), 'Multinational staffing and organizational functioning in the Commission of the European Communities', *International Organization*, 32/2, pp 477–96.

[129] M Cini (1996), *The European Commission: Leadership, Organisation and Culture in the EU Administration* (Manchester: Manchester University Press), pp 111–15.

[130] See M Mangenot (2002).

[131] See further T Christiansen (2001b), 'Intra-institutional politics and inter-institutional relations in the EU: Towards coherent governance?', *Journal of European Public Policy*, 8/5, pp 747–69.

[132] Ibid, p 762.

[133] Art 235(3) TFEU.

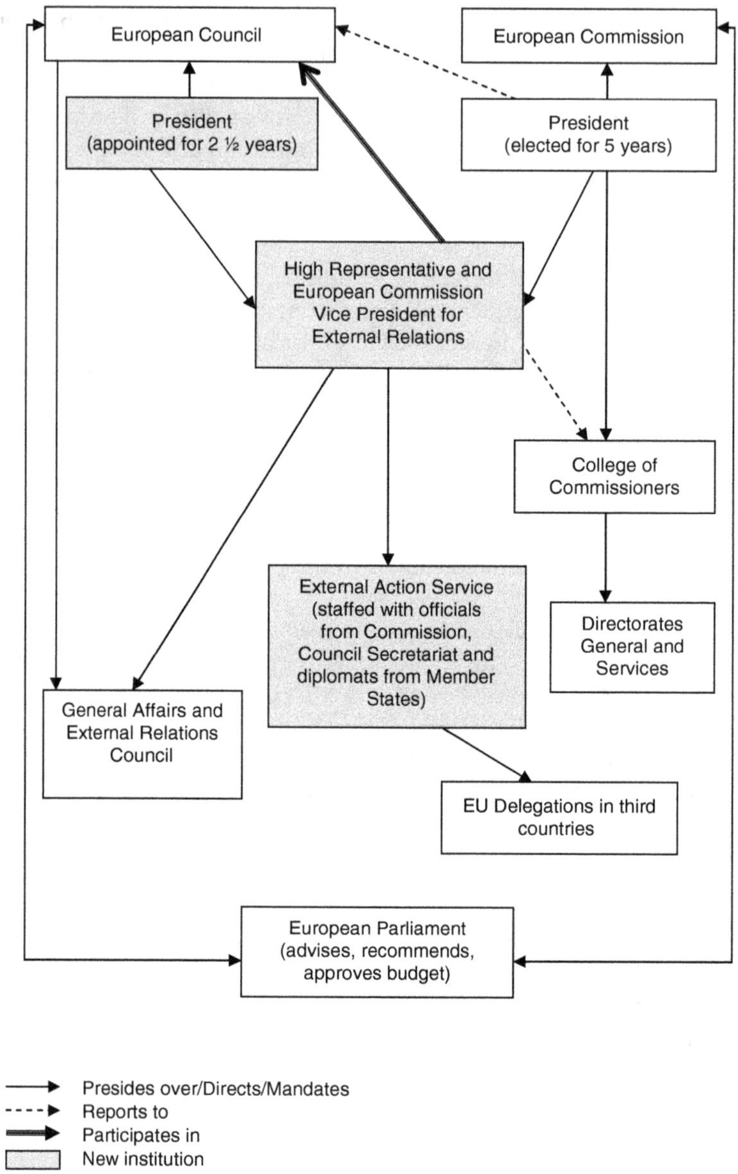

Fig 4.1 Commission's role in EU external action under the Lisbon Treaty

Source: Chart adapted from Annex I (iii), Commission Role in EU External Action under the European Constitution in D Spence (ed) (2006), *The European Commission* (John Harper Publishing, London), at p 555.

was divided as to whether there should continue to be one commissioner from each state, or whether there should be an upper limit combined with a system of rotation. The issue of decreasing the number of commissioners to below the number of Member States was extremely sensitive from a political point of view even if its salience was obvious from the point of view of efficiency and effectiveness. Traditionally, each Member State has had its 'own' commissioner even if they were constitutionally independent and bound to act in the interest of the Community/Union as a whole and not those of particular national interest. In the Nice Treaty an elaborate and complex compromise was found providing that from 1 January 2005 the Commission would consist of one national from each Member State.[134] When the Union had 27 Member States the Treaty would be further modified such that the number of commissioners would be less than the number of Member States.[135] The Council would further adopt a system of rotation and would decide on the number of commissioners—these changes never came into force because of ongoing discussions in the context of treaty revisions, first in the Constitutional Treaty and later in the Treaty of Lisbon.

A radically different system to that of the Nice Treaty was opted for in the Convention that proposed a draft text of the Constitutional Treaty. This devised an elaborate system of voting and non-voting commissioners. A rotation system of 13 full voting commissioners would be established by the Council following two guiding principles; first, the state equality principle and, secondly, the demographic and geographic principle.[136] Once the Member States were selected, the respective Member States would produce a list (in which both genders are represented) of three persons whom it considers qualified to be a European commissioner. The president then subsequently chooses one person from each of these lists on the basis of his or her competence, commitment, and independence, thereby selecting a 'cabinet' of 13 commissioners. The full Cabinet is then collectively subject to a vote of approval by the European Parliament. In this system the Commission president would appoint the non-voting commissioners chosen according to the same criteria as those applying to the members of the College as such. The powers of the president were thus considerably enhanced but in a manner likely to produce tensions not only between voting and non-voting commissioners but also between large and small Member States.[137]

At the insistence of most of the smaller countries (but excluding the Benelux three), this distinction between voting and non-voting members was thrown overboard in the Lisbon Treaty—to the relief of many. The Commission itself

[134] Protocol (No 10) on the Enlargement of the European Union (2001).

[135] Art 213(1) TEC.

[136] See further, with details, P Craig (2004a), 'European governance: Executive and administrative powers under the new constitutional settlement' in JHH Weiler and CL Eisgruber (eds), *Altneuland: The EU Constitution in a contextual perspective*, Jean Monnet Working Paper 5/04, available at <http://jeanmonnetprogram.org/papers/04/040501-12.html>.

[137] See further the criticisms expressed by P Craig (2004a), p 14.

described the relevant provisions of the Treaty establishing a Constitution for Europe as 'complicated, muddled and inoperable'.[138] In the Lisbon Treaty a further compromise was reached. Until 31 October 2014 each Member State was to have one commissioner;[139] thereafter, the number of commissioners would be reduced to two-thirds of the number of Member States, on the basis of a system of equal rotation among the Member States, 'unless the European Council, acting unanimously, decides to alter this number'.[140]

The fact however is that the risk of Member States not having their national present in the College led to considerable controversy and diminished support from in any event the voting Irish citizens. In effect, under pressure from the Irish government and the need for a second referendum to be held in Ireland in the autumn of 2009, this seems to have been pre-emptively ruled out even before the Treaty of Lisbon had entered into force![141] It now seems that not only will there not be, formally at any rate, two tiers between voting and non-voting commissioners, the numbers will not be reduced, and each Member State will retain its commissioner for the foreseeable future, with no explicit timetable as to when this could change. This is not to deny, legally at any rate, that this is:

> quite a tortured interpretation of Article 4(2) of the Protocol on Enlargement, but may not be entirely excluded by its text. It can only be noted in passing that the complications that will be caused... by the procedures for the appointment of the President of the Commission, followed by the selection of the other Members of the Commission, which is also quite different under Nice (Art 214(2) EC) and under Lisbon (Art 17(7) TEU), are likely to be also considerable, depending on if and when Lisbon enters into force, during this procedure.[142]

4.4.4 A normalized executive

The long-term aim of the Commission has been to obtain recognition as the single and unique executive power in the EU with effectively its normal role to play also in those more politically sensitive and newer policy areas of the European integration process. Thus, during the Constitutional Convention and the subsequent IGC that agreed the final text of the European Constitutional Treaty, the Commission put forward on a number of different occasions arguments and draft provisions to that effect.[143] The battle was not won in the kind of unequivocal fashion that the Commission would clearly have liked to see.

[138] Communication from the Commission, 'A Constitution for the Union: Opinion of the Commission pursuant to Article 48 of the Treaty on the European Union, on the conference of representatives of the Member States' governments convened to revise the treaties', COM (2003) 548 final, p 5.

[139] Art 17(4) TEU, Lisbon.

[140] Art 17(5) TEU, Lisbon.

[141] Conclusions of European Council, 12–13 December 2008.

[142] Editorial Comment (2009), 'The second second Irish referendum: Finally a fair choice', Legal Issues European Economic Integration, 36/2, pp 101–4.

[143] Communication from the Commission, 'A Constitution for the Union: Opinion of the Commission, pursuant to Article 48 of the Treaty on European Union, on the conference of

Nonetheless over the course of the past decade the European Commission has undergone significant modernization, the most far-reaching changes since its inception.[144] The aim of the modernization measures was to bring about a more efficient and well-managed bureaucracy that could improve the Commission's standing (see Chapter 5 below). In the words of Wille: 'The idea was to bring Weber back in the organization—merit based, detached from national differences and expressing a common European interest—and to move away from practices with national quotas and responsive to national interests.'[145]

The Commission clearly wanted to change its image and 'aim[ed] to be a world-class public administration' as stated on the European website at the start of the reform process.[146] At the same time the Commission struggled with its two tiers and hybrid political-administrative status. The ambitious process of administrative reform is nonetheless considered to have turned the Commission into a high performance, policy focused and 'one of the world's most well managed international organizations'.[147] New structures and rules with a range of *ex ante* constraints and *ex post* incentives combined to provide for a system with more control in and over a 'reinvented' Commission.[148]

Like national experts in the Commission services, commissioners have the Commission as their primary organizational affiliation, they are on medium-term 'contracts', and they might return to posts in their home government. These features could make them somewhat more susceptible to the wishes of their respective home governments compared to those on long-term contracts. Some work hints that the careful selection process at the national level of candidates for a commissioner post results in a close relationship between a commissioner and his or her home government but no data is presented substantiating this conclusion.[149] But in general, as regards the political leadership of the Commission, the picture emerging over time is of increasing autonomy vis-à-vis national governments.

representatives of the Member States' governments convened to revise the treaties', COM (2003) 548, 17 September 2003; see also CIG Doc 35/03 'Reply from the Commission to the questionnaire of the Legislative Functions, the Formations of the Council and the Presidency of the Council of Ministers (doc CIG 9/03)' of 15 October 2003, available at <http://ue.eu.int/igcpdf/en/03/cg00/cg00035.en03.pdf>.

144 A Wille (2007b), 'Senior officials in a reforming European Commission: Transforming the top?' in MW Bauer and C Knill (eds), *Management Reforms in International Organizations* (Baden-Baden: Nomos), pp 37–50, p 37.

145 Ibid, pp 39–40.

146 E Schön-Quinlavin (2007), 'Administrative reform in the European Commission: From rhetoric to re-legitimatization', *EU-Consent—Constructing Europe Network, Project No 513416*, p 28, available at <http://www.eu-consent.net/library/deliverables/D17_Team7_Schon2.pdf>.

147 A Wille (2007b).

148 J Peterson (2006), 'Where does the Commission stand today?' in D Spence (ed), *The European Commission* (London: John Harper Publishing), pp 502–19.

149 See, for example, A Wonka (2007), 'Technocratic and independent? The appointment of European Commissioners and its policy implications', *Journal of European Public Policy*, 14/2, pp 169–89.

The functioning—and autonomy—of the Commission itself is increasingly compared with a national government. This is so despite the fact that it is not directly elected and that it can still today be considered profoundly 'non-majoritarian'. Yet in the words of Egeberg: 'The Commission consists of a series of executive politicians who are in charge of various administrative services. Similar to national executives the Commission is authorized to initiate and formulate policy proposals and to implement policies, or more commonly, to monitor their implementation.'[150] However the Commission, as we have already seen in Chapter 3, cannot be considered as a kind of *parliamentary* government, even if there are clear signs that the College of Commissioners is gradually becoming more and more dependent on the European Parliament. This is especially the case with regard to new provisions providing for the election of the Commission president by the European Parliament. These new provisions rather stem from an effort to enhance the democratic legitimacy of the Commission in particular—the belief is that increasing the 'politicization' of the Commission in this manner will attenuate, in one respect at any rate, the 'democratic deficit' of the Union.

4.5 Double-hatted 'Minister for Foreign Affairs'

The function of High Representative of CFSP was introduced in the Treaty of Amsterdam. This was as a response to the realization that the external representation of the Union required considerably more focus and involvement than could be expected from the rotating Council presidency. The Treaty of Amsterdam basically 'beefed-up' the role of the Secretary General of the Council by introducing the function of High Representative of the CFSP with the intention that the High Representative would assist the presidency in its external representation role.[151] The function was originally conceived as an administrative function rather than a political function. In practice however, the High Representative 'is much more than an EU ambassador and the political nature of the function is hard to deny. This is partly the personal achievement of Javier Solana who has been extraordinarily agile in making the most of his role within a web of often-conflicting pressures.'[152]

The agenda-setting role of the High Representative CFSP is quite overtly political and up-front. Formally the High Representative has no right of initiative,

[150] M Egeberg (2002), 'The European Commission: The evolving EU executive', ARENA Working Papers, WP 02/30, available at <http://www.arena.uio.no/publications/wp02_30.htm>.

[151] W Coussins and B Crum (2003), 'Towards effective and accountable leadership of the Union: Options and guidelines for reform', EPIN Working Paper No 3, available at <www.ceps.be>. See too PJ Kuijper (2008), 'Of "mixity" and "double-hatting": External relations of the European Union explained', Inaugural Address, University of Amsterdam, 23 March 2008.

[152] W Coussins and B Crum (2003), p 3.

but by launching policy papers and bringing problem areas to attention, he has a certain leeway to influence the agenda and to steer the debates in a certain direction.[153] It is the staff of the Council policy unit who provides him with the background documents required to fulfil this agenda-setting function. Indeed it is precisely in this regard that it has been claimed that the Council Secretariat steps 'out of the shadows'.[154] It is safe to say that the High Representative CFSP in the person of Javier Solana has developed his own position significantly and forced the pace of change both as a constitutional and institutional agenda-setter. The fact that this position evolved considerably from the early years where he was kept on a tight rein by the Member States to the contemporary position has a lot to do with the first occupant's own vision of his role as a *political* executive and policy entrepreneur. At the same time as having being conferred with CFSP tasks by the Treaty of Maastricht as subsequently amended the previous High Representative was Secretary General of the Council. His role and status acquired a considerable shot in the arm from the provisions of the Treaty of Lisbon. Upon entry into force of the Lisbon Treaty the EU will acquire a reinforced and more autonomous High Representative CFSP (basically the same function was called the EU Foreign Minister in the Treaty establishing a Constitution for Europe). This new-style High Representative will take over where Javier Solana as High Representative left off and will go further.

The new High Representative will be appointed by the European Council, with the agreement of the Commission president,[155] with the task to 'conduct the Union's common foreign and security policy' and to preside over the Foreign Affairs Council.[156] The level of autonomy and status implied by this presidential function is reinforced by the provisions that imply a relatively autonomous policymaking role, also with regard to common security and defence policy.[157] These policies must, in the final analysis, be 'mandated by the Council', presumably the Foreign Affairs Council.[158] At the same time the High Representative takes part in the work of the European Council itself, not it seems as a fully-fledged member but as a participant.[159]

Whether this difference in status will have any practical consequences (voting?) will become clear only when further implementation has taken place in practice (for example in the rules of procedure that the European Council will adopt upon entry into force of the Treaty of Lisbon, in line with all the other institutions of the EU). In the person of the High Representative therefore there is a close linking between the European Council and the Foreign Affairs Council, as well as (doubly) with the Commission. The High Representative is

[153] See too T Christiansen and S Vanhoonacker (2008).

[154] T Christiansen (2006), 'Out of the shadows: The General Secretariat of the Council of Ministers', Journal of Legislative Studies, 8/4, pp 80–97.

[155] Art 18(1) TEU, Lisbon.

[156] Art 18(2)–(3) TEU, Lisbon.

[157] Art 18(2) TEU, Lisbon.

[158] Art 18(2) TEU, Lisbon.

[159] See the wording of Art 15(2) TEU, Lisbon.

not only Council chair and participant in the European Council but will also be one of the vice presidents of the Commission.[160] At the same time his position as a member of the Commission differs from the other members in three respects: he is appointed according to a different procedure; he cannot be dismissed by the Commission president as the decision in this regard is taken by the European Council;[161] and, in his tasks as agent of the Council, he is not bound by Commission procedures.[162] His task of ensuring the 'consistency of the Union's external action' also has an *internal* Commission component of ensuring such consistency within the Commission. This Janus-faced figure, a *novum* in the EU constitutional system, is both embedded and tasked within the Council of Ministers (and appointed and dismissed by the European Council) and within the European Commission. The 'double hatting' inherent in this post personifies the sharing of executive power between the European Council/ Council of Ministers axis and the Commission. It will involve much coordination between this new, rather schizophrenic actor and the Commission president, the rotating Council presidency, and the new president of the European Council. Here too, one can sense that the level of inter-institutional coordination and even agreement may be particularly crucial.

The split personality of the new actor, the High Representative, is still largely embedded within the putatively intergovernmental sphere; that of the European Council and the Council of Ministers, at least when it comes to his core functions in the fields of foreign policy, defence, and security, all of which are still steered and implemented by this joint axis. Yet his relationship with both these institutions is also a complicated one. He is in any event not a member of the Council of Ministers as such;[163] he merely chairs the Foreign Affairs Council.[164] He has the right to 'make proposals' to the Council on the Union's CFSP and common security and defence policy, and implements policy as the mandated 'agent' of the Council.[165] Finally he represents the Union externally, for matters relating to the CFSP.[166] At the same time, he participates in the work of the European Council but is not a member as such.[167]

As we have seen, the relationship of the High Representative with the Commission is equally aberrant. Despite the putative collegiality of the Commission, it appears that the High Representative may submit on his or her own, without the Commission's support, an initiative or proposal relating to the CFSP.[168] At the same time the view may be taken that the creation of this new

[160] Art 18(4) TEU, Lisbon. [161] Art 17(6), last alinea TEU, Lisbon.

[162] Art 18(4) TEU, Lisbon. See too R Barents (2008), pp 297–98.

[163] Art 16(2) TEU, Lisbon. [164] Art 18(3) TEU, Lisbon.

[165] Art 18(2) TEU, Lisbon.

[166] Art 27(2) TEU, Lisbon. In this he is not alone: Art 15(6) TEU, Lisbon foresees a role for the president of the European Council 'at his level'. See further JQTh Rood (2008), 'De EU na het Verdrag van Lissabon: Naar een Nieuw Politiek en Institutioneel Evenwicht?', *Sociaal-Economische Wetgeving*, 56/4, pp 132–5.

[167] Art 15(2) TEU, Lisbon. [168] Art 30(1) TEU, Lisbon.

High Representative may de facto enhance the power of the Commission. In the words of Paul Craig:

> The EU' s foreign policy work, as currently undertaken by the Commissioner for External Relations, covers a very wide range of important initiatives, as a bare glance at the web-site will confirm. The fact that the [High Representative] will be responsible for these matters, and that he will have a central place within the Council and the European Council is likely to increase and not decrease the Commission's overall influence in this area. This is so notwithstanding the fact that formal decision-making powers remain within the European Council and the Council.[169]

4.6 EU Plate Tectonics

A first decision of the drafters of the Lisbon Treaty (and the Constitutional Treaty before it) was to leave in place the three executive institutions (the European Council, the Council of Ministers, and the Commission) in name and in general profile. They renamed many things but not the institutions themselves. This strategy 'capitalizes on the benefits of public familiarity with the institutions as such'.[170] What they did do, however, was to somewhat 'slim down', for example, the Commission, given the risk of dysfunctionality of 27 members steadily increasing with new rounds of enlargement pending—an issue that played out very negatively in the subsequent Irish referendum process.[171] Finally, there was a move across all three institutions to enhance *leadership* by changing and reinforcing, in some respects, the role of the (various) presidents. Here too, complex provisions keep in place a complex and plural division of executive powers across policy areas. Only with regard to the area of external relations was there an effort made to ensure that there would be 'a visible face and a single audible voice' on the world scene;[172] even here, compromises and an inability to make clear unitary choices resulted in complex double-hats being worn at various times.

The tides of treaty reform culminating in the Treaty of Lisbon can nonetheless arguably be considered to lead to 'a certain restructuring of the tectonic plates and it does open up new faults or make old ones visible'.[173] In terms of the emerging 'executive order' introduced in Chapter 2, a number of points can be outlined from the discussion that has taken place in this chapter in terms of the ongoing narrative of reinforcement and expansion of executive power in the EU political

[169] P Craig (2004), p 35.

[170] G Bermann (2005), 'Executive power in the new European Constitution', Int'l J of Constitutional L, 3/2–3, pp 440–7.

[171] Ibid. [172] Ibid, p 442.

[173] This is the language used by HCH Hofmann (2003), 'A critical analysis of the new typology of acts in the Draft Treaty Establishing a Constitution for Europe', *European Integration Online Papers*, 7/9, at p 24, with regard to the Constitutional Treaty; it is equally apposite in broad lines to the changes effectuated by the Treaty of Lisbon even if in some respects these are less overt.

system. First, the previously existing situation of a shared or plural executive power at the level of the EU political system itself has been further reinforced and indeed expanded. Not only has the domain of executive power been marked off more clearly than hitherto from that of the legislative power, it has emerged quite clearly that, despite its own wishes to the contrary, the Commission is not the unique locus of executive power in the EU system. Alongside it are other more putatively intergovernmental actors: the Council of Ministers, the European Council including its enhanced president, and the new High Representative. All of these executive actors can at first glance be considered to have a predominantly 'political' role and image. Moreover the changes brought about in the latest treaty-reform processes, in particular the creation of a new semi-permanent actor, the president of the European Council, cannot but affect the existing 'institutional balance' in the Union political system. The expectation is that it will develop into more than a purely formal chairing role—indeed the foundations for a more substantive role are laid down in the provisions of the Lisbon Treaty itself with a substantive back-up in administrative and support terms of the General Secretariat of the Council of Ministers. If so, this will contribute both to further processes of weakening the role of the Commission as such as well as that of the Council of Ministers.

Secondly, examination of how these core executive actors have evolved in recent years may, however, reveal a more nuanced picture and also reveal the more 'administrative' side of executive power. The latter, in particular, is often less visible in 'high' constitutional provisions and must instead be unearthed from lower-level legal provisions and practices. This is the purpose of Chapter 5 of this book—to hold a magnifying glass to, respectively, the Commission, the Council of Ministers and, in Chapter 6, what I term 'satellite actors' in orbit around one or more of the main institutional actors, in particular EU-level agencies as well as some 'networks'.

Thirdly, these multiple executive actors are embedded within a constitutional framing of one kind or another. This is not only as a result of explicit-and-new provisions of the Treaty of Lisbon itself but also of other ongoing processes of constitutionalization by other actors, in particular the Court of Justice but also the European Parliament and other actors. The fact is that via the interpretation of norms the Court, in particular, contributes to fine-pointing the constitutional executive order of the EU. This is a gradual and ongoing process that involves much self-reflection not only as to its own role in the wider constitutional and political context but also as to the underlying core values of the European integration process in the early decades of the 21st century. Further reflections on the interface between the two will be given in Part III of this book.

5

Administrative Executive Power

5.1 Tides of 'Eurocrats'

In the popular view of the EU, its civil servants are often seen as the epitome of the stereotype of a bureaucrat—namely a rigid and inflexible person working for his bureau rather than its clients or society at large.[1] These bureaucrats, in the Weberian sense, are also referred to as 'technocrats' suggesting, 'technically trained experts' who 'rule by virtue of their specialized knowledge and position'.[2] The implication is that a technocratic system promotes technical solutions to political problems.[3] EU bureaucrats are moreover frequently associated with forming useless, interventionist policies, such as prescribing the size of a strawberry or the curve of a banana.[4] A more subtle understanding may, however, be called for as the various roles shift and may become blurred over time.

Who are these 'Eurocrats', what do they do, and where do they work? The administration of the EU is not only complex, drawing upon many varied traditions, but it is organized within a convoluted institutional geometry. European-level civil servants are often termed 'Eurocrats' who come from one of the Member States but become 'socialized' into the services and culture of the Union administration.[5] At the same time, the Union administration employs an increasing number of so-called 'national experts' seconded from the Member States.[6] This chapter seeks to sketch what can be considered as the core of the EU administrative executive, closely associated with—or part of—one or other of the institutions of the political executive (mainly the Commission and Council). Where do we find EU civil servants and where do we find national civil servants?

[1] M Herzfeld (1992), *The Social Production of Indifference: Exploring the symbolic roots of Western bureaucracy* (London: The University of Chicago Press).

[2] See, in general terms, F Fischer (1990), *Technocracy and the Politics of Expertise* (London: Sage), p 17.

[3] Ibid, p 18.

[4] R Thedvall (2007), 'The EU's nomads: National Eurocrats in European policymaking', Paper to be presented at the 10th EUSA Conference 17–19 May, 2007 in Montreal, Canada, available at <http://aei.pitt.edu/8046/01/thedvall-r-08j.pdf>.

[5] See, in general terms, A Stevens (2001), *Brussels Bureaucrats? The administration of the European Union* (Basingstoke: Palgrave Macmillan).

[6] See further A Trondal (2006a), 'Governing at the frontier of the European Commission: The case of seconded national experts', *West European Politics*, 29/1, pp 147–60.

How can we best qualify and understand them? What functions of administration and rule-making are being carried out and where?

5.2 The EU Administrative Executive

5.2.1 'Core' Eurocrats

In the first place, the EU has its own civil servants located predominantly in the Commission, both its policy Directorate Generals and its General Secretariat, in the Council General Secretariat (including its policy Directorate Generals), and other institutions (European Parliament, Economic and Social Committee, and the Committee of the Regions). In the *General Budget for the EU for the Financial Year 2009* the budget for administration grows to EUR 7.7 billion.[7] The Commission represents 46.4% of the total budget under the heading (EU) administration; 'other institutions' form together 36.0%. The Commission has by far the most administrative posts of all the institutions: 26,209 multinational European career civil servants, responsible for public administration in 2009 (as compared to 26,020 in 2008).

The next 'biggest' institutions are the European Parliament with 6,081 in 2009 and the Council with 3,512 equivalent posts.[8] The over 30 agencies (including 4 'executive agencies') is one of the clear growth areas in recent years; 4,537 administrative posts are assigned to these bodies in the 2009 budget.[9] Moreover, if one compares the cumulative figure for agencies' staff to the number of posts created within the Commission since 1992, we see that over a third of the executive positions created during that period have been assigned to regulatory agencies.[10]

The overall size of the Council Secretariat has increased steadily over the years as a result of the gradual expansion of the Council's areas of activity and successive enlargements (see Table 5.1).[11] New Directorate Generals were created and the numbers of 'A' (AD) officials have increased very steadily from a tiny beginning: from 5 in 1953, 161 in 1975[12], 1,448 in 2008. The total number of staff expanded from 30 in 1953, 1,475 in 1975, and to more than 3,500 in 2009,

7 <http://ec.europa.eu/budget/library/publications/budget_in_fig/syntchif_2009_en.pdf>.

8 OJ L 69, 13 March 2009, Annual Budget for 2009, p 1–1720, Annex Part C.

9 OJ L 69, 13 March 2009, Annual Budget for 2009, Annex Part C.

10 This point is made by R Dehousse (2008) on the basis of the figures from the 2007 Annual Budget: see 'Delegation of powers in the European Union: the need for a multi-principals model', *West European Politics*, 31/4, pp 789–805, at p 789–90.

11 F Hayes-Renshaw and H Wallace (2005), *The Council of Ministers*, 2nd edn (Basingstoke: Palgrave Macmillan), p 103.

12 M Mangenot (2002), 'L'affirmation du Secrétariat du Conseil de l'Union Européenne: Les transformations du rôle d'une institution non codifiée', Paper presented at the 'VIIe congrès de l'Association française de science politique', Lille, 18–21 September 2002.

Table 5.1 Growth in staff in Council General Secretariat

Year	Total	Of which A Grade officials
1970	569	95
1975	1481	165
1980	1547	179
1985	1792	191
1990	2184	219
1995	2379	274
2000	2659	343
2005	3280	525
2009	3512	702

Source: Council General Secretariat. Authorized permanent/temporary staff, situation as of January 2009, including Secretary General(s).

including translators and administrators.[13] The integration of the Schengen Secretariat following on the Treaty of Amsterdam, as well as the establishment of military staff, led to a significant increase in personnel numbers as well as the need to lease additional buildings (with special security requirements).

5.2.2 Seconded national experts

In addition to its own full time professional public administration the EU has in addition what has been termed the 'new Eurocrats' meaning national civil servants involved in EU policymaking as such.[14] Such national Eurocrats are engaged in a wide variety of decision-making processes at the EU level as well as at the purely national level and are, of course, funded within the national system. The Commission has in recent years become more and more dependent on what has been termed the 'new Eurocrats' including staff seconded for short periods from national administrations and on short-term contracts with a wide variety of 'experts'.[15] Such seconded national experts (SNE's) 'do build bridges between the EU and the member state via their roles in forming and sometimes maintaining policy networks in EU governance.'[16]

[13] See, for the most recent (2009) figures, *Final Adoption of the General Budget of the European Union for the Financial Year 2008*, OJ L 69/I, 13 March 2009.

[14] See further KP Geuijen et al (2008), *The New Eurocrats: National civil servants in EU policy-making* (Amsterdam: Amsterdam University Press), p 15.

[15] See, in general, European Commission, *Reforming the Commission: A White Paper.* Part 1, 5 April 2000, available at <http://europa.eu/documents/comm/white_papers/reform/com2000_200_part1_en.pdf>. See further S Suvarierol and C van den Berg (2008), 'Bridge builders or bridgeheads in Brussels? The world of seconded national experts' in KP Geuijen et al, *The New Eurocrats: National civil servants in EU policy-making* (Amsterdam: Amsterdam University Press), pp 103–27.

[16] S Suvarierol and C van den Berg (2008).

The approximately 900 national experts who are seconded by national administrations to the Commission for a maximum of four years represent an interesting category since they work full-time within the Commission's administrative hierarchy while at the same time are paid by their home government with a return to former positions in domestic ministries or agencies usually foreseen. However, even under these conditions, their primary structure (ie Commission affiliation) seems to be most important. A survey study of 71 national experts showed that they overwhelmingly identify with their respective DGs/Units or an independent-expert role rather than with their respective national governments. Accordingly, in their daily work they pay strong attention to signals from their directors in the Commission and very little attention to signals from their home governments.[17] Suvarierol, in a study of 'task-related informal networks' (for information and advice) of Commission officials found that nationality is not even a factor shaping these informal (information and advice) networks that are not hierarchically predefined.[18]

Just as is the case with regard to the Commission the staff in the General Secretariat of the Council are not all European civil servants—rather there is a significant proportion of national civil servants on secondment to the various departments of the Secretariat. The highest proportion of these are to be found among the military staff which to a large extent populates the Policy Planning and Early Warning Unit as well as the Joint Situation Centre of the EU (SITCEN), Communication Centre (COMCEN), all housed within the Secretariat itself. Of 152 EU military staff in the Secretariat, 136 are on secondment from the Member States. Special rules are formulated by the Council applicable to national military staff on secondment to the Secretariat.[19]

What does this mean in terms of the manner in which the 'European' tasks are being carried out? Little empirical work has been carried out in this regard yet, although there are probably comparisons and analogies that can be made with the secondment of staff on a temporary basis to the European Commission.[20] There is, in any event, hardly any empirical data on the interaction between the Secretariat's traditional civil servants who have passed the *concours* and are 'socialized' and the seconded national staff. What is known is that in the early 1990s when the CFSP unit was staffed with a mixture of seconded and Secretariat officials, the process of

[17] J Trondal (2006a).

[18] S Suvarierol (2008), 'Beyond the myth of nationality: Analysing networks within the European Commission', *West European Politics*, 31/4, pp 701–24. See too her doctoral thesis, S Suvarierol (2007), *Beyond the Myth of Nationality: A study on the networks of European Commission officials* (Delft: Eburon).

[19] See, most recently, Council Decision 2007/829/EC of 5 December 2007 concerning the rules applicable to national experts and military staff on secondment to the General Secretariat of the Council OJ L 327, 13 December 2007, p 10.

[20] See further J Trondal (2006a); J Trondal (2006b), 'An institutional perspective on representation: Ambiguous representation in the European Commission', *European Integration Online Papers*, 10/4, available at <http://eiop.or.at/eiop/texte/2006–004a.htm>.

integration took time, and was not without problems.[21] It seems clear however, in addition, that the fact that the military staffs consist not of normal civil servants but rather personnel from various ranks of the armies in various Member states—that cooperate closely with NATO—introduces a novel dynamic into the equation with regard to the security and protection of confidential information. This had structural and even physical consequences. It followed from the fact that the normal security arrangements for personnel and documents of the Council as a whole (including those of the other DG's in the Secretariat itself) were considered insufficient for the needs and requirements of the military staff, so that they were housed in a separate building from the rest in order to be able to implement what they considered adequate security vetting of staff and adequate security arrangements for their documents. The *Justius Lipsius* building failed the security test, and all ESDP-related departments are housed in a separate building in the *Avenue de Cortenberg*. Moreover, these documents have, virtually from the very beginning, been subject to special arrangements compared to the normal rules for access to information that prevails more generally in the EU as a whole (see Chapter 8).

This symbolizes very well the differences between the two worlds in which the officials from the Secretariat operate: the staff working in the non-military and security issues still primarily fulfilling the traditional administrative and advisory role, while those in CSDP performing more overtly executive tasks and functions.[22] The Council can thus, in some sense, be imagined as a Russian doll, housing within it several layers of, at times, quite separate actors or groups of actors. The general 'cultural' differences between civilian and military staff lead to visible and palpable differences between a 'transparency culture' and a 'security culture'.

5.2.3 National civil servants and (scientific) experts

EU committees encompass an array of bodies that vary considerably in what they do, how they are organized, what role they play in EU policymaking, and to which EU institution they are anchored.[23] In very general terms, they can be considered a response to the functional demands of the EU institutions for technical information and (scientific) expertise throughout the formal decision-making process. In various guises they are active at every stage of the EU decision-making process, from the expert groups of the Commission and the working groups of the Council to the comitology committees at the implementation phase.

[21] See further D Dinan (1999), *Ever Closer Union: An introduction to European integration* (New York: Palgrave); SJ Nuttall (2000), *European Foreign Policy* (Oxford: Oxford University Press).

[22] T Christiansen and S Vanhoonacker (2008), 'At a critical juncture? Change and continuity in the institutional development of the Council Secretariat', *West European Politics*, 31/4, pp 751–70. See, in general terms, Council of the EU, *Report on the Management of the General Secretariat*, 12860/04, 1 October 2004, available at <http://register.consilium.europa.eu/pdf/en/04/st12/st12860.en04.pdf>.

[23] A Gornitzka and U Sverdrup (2008), 'Who consults? The configuration of expert groups in the European Union?', *West European Politics*, 31/4, pp 725–50.

Expert groups attached to the Commission will provide input often *before* a legislative proposal is made.[24] The use of expert groups 'has developed into a routinised practice of the European Commission in order for it to connect to its environment and bring together state and societal actors'.[25] Recent empirical research has shown that the density and durability of these expert groups vary considerably between different Commission services and policy areas.[26] Within the Commission we also find a very special genus of committee—the so-called 'comitology' committees, the very name conjuring up images of secretive bureaucracy and opaque procedures. They 'assist' the Commission[27] by 'advising' or deciding the content of detailed measures of implementation, and a window on both their input and their output is provided by a specific Commission database with a register of all such committees.[28]

The activities of such comitology committees cover a wide variety of subject matter: from the Community's cereals regime and plant propagation to the technical standards for cableways and data protection. One of their most defining features for a long time was that comitology committees existed and functioned as a 'unseen hand'[29] of European integration, shrouded in a great deal of mystery. As recently as a decade ago, a Select Committee of the House of Lords reported that *no list* of comitology committees was 'publicly available nor is there an authoritative account of what each does'.[30] It was only with the advent of a new (general) comitology decision that the Commission was placed under a legal obligation to publish, from 2000, onwards an annual report on the working of committees.[31] This provides a public window on, at the very least, the numbers of such committees in existence at a given time as well as the types of procedures followed, the numbers of meetings held, etc. The Commission for the past seven years has systematically produced this report and it is a valuable source of general information that can be tracked on an annual basis.

As the seven years of Commission reporting show us the numbers of committees active in a given year do vary somewhat although they tend in recent years to be on and around the 250 mark.[32] For example, in the latest report, 2008,

[24] See, for details, the data in the Commission Register of Expert Groups, available at <http://ec.europa.eu/transparency/regexpert/index.cfm?lang=EN>.

[25] A Gornitzka and U Sverdrup (2008).

[26] Ibid.

[27] These are its own words; see for the list of comitology committees 'assisting' it, <http://ec.europa.eu/transparency/regcomitology/include/comitology_committees_EN.pdf >.

[28] Ibid.

[29] This section draws on GJ Brandsma, D Curtin, and A Meijer (2008), 'How transparent are EU comitology committees?', European LJ, 14/6, pp 819–38.

[30] House of Lords, Select Committee on European Communities, *Delegation of Powers to the Commission: Reforming comitology,* Third Report, 2 February 1999.

[31] Art 7(4) of Council decision of 28 June 1999 laying down the procedure for the exercise of implementing powers conferred on the Commission. The Commission had in fact prepared a prior report on the 'work of the committees in 1995' drafted at the specific request of the European Parliament and sent to the European Parliament on 24 July 1996 (SEC (96) 1498).

[32] See further GJ Brandsma, D Curtin, and A Meijer (2008).

Table 5.2 Number of comitology committees and their opinions

	2005	2006	2007
Number of comitology committees reported by Commission	250	279	269
Sections and configurations acting as comitology committees*	43	40	39
Inactive comitology committees	68	75	79
Total number of active comitology committees	225	244	229

* Some 'comitology' committees do not meet in their usual form, but work as 'sections' instead that look like a committee, act like a committee, and in fact are just committees (e.g. in 2008, all former 20-something management committees of the CAP were merged into one single committee for the CAP, with 20 odd different sections).

Source: Commission Staff Working Documents accompanying the Reports from the Commission on the working of committees during 2005, 2006 and 2007 (European Commission 2006, 2007, 2008). The figures for 2008 were not fully available at the time of going to press.

there were a total of 269 committees in 2007.[33] As might be expected certain directorates general dominate. For example, the DG's of Agriculture, Environment, Transport and Energy, and Health and Consumer Protection, together account for approximately 45 per cent of all committees, while 18 other DGs host the remaining approximately 55 per cent. It has been estimated by a Commission insider that the Commission has adopted in total approximately 80,000 executive rule-making measures since the early 1960's, of which approximately 12,000 are still in force.[34] As an outsider it is difficult to obtain information other than through a sustained dialogue with Commission services. It seems from the following overview that the average number of opinions issued every year is well over 2000. It must be noted that there may be conflicting sources as to numbers of measures adopted with so-called 'light type acts' adopted but not published in the Official Journal.

What is often underestimated in considering the Council is the important role played by the permanent officials and by the national civil servants who staff the Council's gamut of working parties and coordinating committees in driving forward specific measures within the broad parameters of policy set by the Member State holding the presidency. The Council in fact consists of a hierarchy of committees in which the participants negotiate and bargain

[33] Report from the Commission on the working of committees during 2007, COM (2008) 844 final, Brussels.

[34] P Ponzano (2009), 'Comitologie: Un point de vue de la Commission', *Revue du droit de l'UE*, 2/2009.

within and between different sectoral arenas, at the levels of (national) civil servants and only later diplomats (COREPER) and (if at all) ministers. The Council's decision-making can, to a high degree, be considered a 'clearing system'.[35] It works bottom-up from the working groups, followed by the committees, such as the Political and Security Committee, Economic and Financial Committee, Employment Committee, European Union Military Committee and the Strategic Committee on Immigration, Frontiers and Asylum, followed, in principle, by COREPER, followed by the general or sectoral (ministerial) councils.

In the case of the Council, however, the function of the high-level committees (about 13) is to oversee the work of a large number of specialized working parties, all made up of what are also termed 'new Eurocrats', national civil servants, involved in the various stages of Council decision-making.[36] There are about 140 working parties at the bottom of the hierarchy that deal with the day-to-day work of the Council and form the backbone of the organization.[37] A list published in (June) 2008 contained a total of 300 distinct bodies covering all areas of the Council's work.[38]

Council working parties and committees integrate *national civil servants* into EU decision-making processes. In the words of Trondal, 'EU committees represent underused laboratories for studying what happens when contrasting decision-making dynamics meet because such committees embody civil servants from different layers of government'.[39] At the same time empirical work by political scientists has shown that some 'socialization' takes place and that 'the attention, energy, contacts, coordination behaviour and loyalties of national civil servants are to a considerable extent directed towards the Brussels committee system'.[40] The shared culture, embedded in informal practices, as well as rooted in formal procedures, is reinforced by processes of socialization and *engrenage*, much on the lines identified long ago by the neofunctionalists.[41] However when it comes specifically to Council committees some of the more

[35] The term is of MPCM van Schendelen (1996), '"The Council decides": Does the Council decide?', *Journal of Common Market Studies*, 33/4, pp 531–48.

[36] The empirical work that has taken place points to weak 'socialization' into a supranational outlook and subject to scope conditions that are related to domestic level factors. See J Beyers (2005), 'Multiple embeddedness and socialization in Europe: The case of Council officials', *International Organizations*, 59/4, pp 899–936.

[37] See further M Westlake and D Galloway (2004), *The Council of the European Union* (London: John Harper Publishing), pp 217–22.

[38] See Council document number 5433/09 with the most recent list of Council preparatory bodies, available at <http://register.consilium.europa.eu/pdf/en/09/st05/st05433.en09.pdf>.

[39] J Trondal (2006c), 'EU Committee governance and the multilevel community administration' in H Hofmann and A Türk, *EU Administrative Governance* (Cheltenham: Edward Elgar), pp 391–416, p 391.

[40] See, for example, ibid.

[41] F Hayes-Renshaw and H Wallace (1995), 'Executive power in the European Union: The functions and limits of the Council of Ministers', *Journal of European Public Policy*, 2/4, pp 559–82, and references cited.

recent empirical research points towards an understanding as 'intergovernmental arenas in the sense that participants primarily seem to behave as representatives of their home governments'.[42] Officials attending Council working parties and committee meetings are, from some countries at any rate, more likely to participate in committee meetings with clearly coordinated positions from their respective national governments.[43] However, it appears too that 'negotiators, rather than receiving orders from the national capital as to what position they *should* take, end up telling their masters what position in a shifting debate they *can* take'.[44]

5.3 Executive Rule-making and Autonomy

5.3.1 The Commission's evolution as an autonomous actor

The aim of the White Paper on Administrative Reform presented in the beginning of 2000 was to modernize the Commission's administration.[45] The reform programme was highly inspired by the New Public Management movement with a strong emphasis on performance-oriented working methods.[46] The strategy focused on three main objectives: improving the effectiveness of the whole organization through better priority setting and matching of tasks with resources (activity-based management); maximizing staff performance through considerable changes in human-resource management and staff policy; and an overhaul of financial management, on the basis of a precise definition of the responsibilities of each actor. A key aspect of the Commission's reform was to shift away from simply following the rules towards a more proactive approach, ie delivering outputs and results. Its key feature lay in the planning of the Commission's activities. The use of its resources would be much more policy-driven than in the past due to the system of activity-based management, the setting up of the Strategic Planning and Programming (SPP) function, located within the

[42] M Egeberg, G Schaefer, and J Trondal (2003), 'The many faces of EU committee governance', *West European Politics*, 26/3, pp 19–40, p 20.

[43] See, for example, J Trondal (2000), 'Multiple institutional embeddedness in Europe: The case of Danish, Norwegian and Swedish government officials', *Scandinavian Political Studies*, 23/4, pp 311–41. See, however, J Beyers and G Dierickx (1998), 'The working groups of the Council of the EU: Supranational or intergovernmental negotiations', *Journal of Common Market Studies*, 36/3, pp 289–317.

[44] See further T Christiansen (2001a), 'The Council of Ministers: The politics of institutionalised intergovernmentalism' in J Richardson (ed), *European Union: Power and policy-making* (London: Routledge), pp 135–54, p 148.

[45] See, in general, European Commission, *Reforming the Commission: A White Paper*, Part 1, 5 April 2000, available at: <http://europa.eu/documents/comm/white_papers/reform/com2000_200_part1_en.pdf> and Action Plan, available at: <http://europa.eu/documents/comm/white_papers/reform/com2000_200_part2_en.pdf>.

[46] See further MW Bauer (2009), *Reforming the European Commission* (Milton Park: Routledge).

Secretariat-General under the authority of the Commission president.[47] Indeed from this time approximately one can discern a move from a sectoral approach to a more horizontal approach, led in many ways from within a more prominent Secretariat General (see further below).

Empirical work carried out by political scientists seems to show that the Commission has over time increased its actual autonomy in relation to national governments.[48] The growing 'internalization' (into the services) of professionalized recruitment and appointment processes is also highly indicative of the development of more autonomy. The process of appointing top officials has been described as having become 'objectivized'; meaning that a transparent procedure and clearly specified requirements have been adopted. Staff resources have been allocated to the process, and career officials dominate the selection committee, which presents the shortlist of candidates to the commissioners. Normally, the recruiting commissioner seems to accept the candidates recommended by this committee.[49] Thus, the internalization of appointment processes means that the highly contentious practice of attaching national flags to particular posts in the various directorates general (DGs) has been considerably reduced.[50] It seems that the Commission administration, as regards the degree of politicization of the higher management and the degree of openness of the career system has, over time, moved away from its Continental origin and instead moved closer to a British or Scandinavian model, ie in crucial respects a more *independent service*.[51]

5.3.2 The evolving role of the Commission Secretariat General

Another aspect of the evolution of the Commission as an autonomous administration over the years that has tended to get overlooked in the scholarly discussions so far is the expanding role of its Secretariat General (SG).[52] Given the

[47] See further E Schön-Quinlivan (2007), 'Administrative reform in the European Commission: From rhetoric to re-legitimatization', *EU-Consent–Constructing Europe Network, Project No 513416*, available at <http://www.eu-consent.net/library/deliverables/D17_Team7_Schon2.pdf>.

[48] This section draws on D Curtin and M Egeberg (2008), 'Tradition and innovation: Europe's accumulated executive order' in D Curtin and M Egeberg (eds), *Towards a New Executive Order in Europe?, Western European politics*, 31/4, pp 639–61; and on M Egeberg (2006b), 'Europe's executive branch of government in the melting pot: An overview' in M Egeberg (ed), *Multilevel Union Administration: The transformation of executive politics in Europe* (Basingstoke: Palgrave Macmillan).

[49] M Egeberg (2006a), 'Balancing autonomy and accountability: Enduring tensions in the European Commission's development' in M Egeberg (ed), *Multilevel Union Administration: The transformation of executive politics in Europe* (Basingstoke: Palgrave Macmillan).

[50] A Wille (2007b), 'Senior officials in a reforming European Commission: Transforming the top?' in MW Bauer and C Knill (eds) *Management Reforms in International Organizations* (Baden-Baden: Nomos), pp 37–50.

[51] T Balint, MW Bauer, and C Knill (2008), 'Bureaucratic change in the European administrative space: The case of the European Commission', *West European Politics*, 31/4, pp 677–700.

[52] See, however, the work done by H Kassim (2004), 'The Secretariat General of the European Commission, 1958–2003: A singular institution' in A Smith (eds), *Politics and the European*

attention that has been paid in recent years to the at times high-profile role and practice of the SG of the Council of Ministers (see below) it is appropriate to briefly consider the sister institution, even if the correct analogy is between the Council General Secretariat as a whole and the Commission administration as a whole. The SG of the Commission occupies a more defined role than its Council counterpart. Nonetheless it has increasingly come to occupy a pivotal and horizontal role within the total administration of the Commission, both upwards and downwards, providing administrative support to the College on a day-to-day basis and overseeing interdepartmental coordination and ensuring coherence overall as well as performing tasks of a more routine administrative nature.[53] In its own words, it ensures 'the overall coherence of the Commission's work—both in shaping new policies, and in steering them through the other EU institutions.'[54] Catherine Day, the current Secretary General to the Commission, compares the SG with an 'enzyme. It causes the chemical reaction but is consumed in the process.'[55]

The modernization programme of far-reaching administrative reforms foresaw a key role for the Secretariat General—the elite staff in the Commission under the direction of the Commission president—in a reformed Commission. In particular, systematic use is made of the SG in order to introduce modern management techniques into the Commission such as policy evaluations and impact studies. Integrated Impact Assessment (IIA)—the *ex ante* examination of potential social, economic and environmental impacts—lies, for example, at the heart of the European Commission's Better Regulation programme. By making a commitment to systematically consider the potential consequences of its major legislative and policy-defining proposals, the European Commission has put itself at the forefront of a wider move towards evidence-based policy-making.[56] Impact assessment is a process aimed at structuring and supporting the development of policies horizontally within the Commission; it is designed as an aid to political decision, not a substitute for it and is steered and guided from within a (specialized) unit of the Commission's SG.[57]

Commission (London: Routledge), pp 47–66; and (2006), 'The Secretariat General of the European Commission' in D Spence and G Edwards (eds), *The European Commission*, 3rd edn (London: John Harper Publishing), pp 75–94.

[53] H Kassim (2006).

[54] See its web site, <http://ec.europa.eu/dgs/secretariat_general/index_en.htm>. See too, Art 20 of the Commission Decision of 15 November 2005 amending its Rules of Procedure, OJ L 347/83 (30 December 2005) on the specific role of the 'Secretary General'.

[55] Interview with author, March 2009.

[56] See too C Robertson (2008), 'Impact assessment in the European Union', *EIPA Scope*, 2008/2, pp 17–20, available at <http://www.eipa.eu/files/repository/eipascope/20080905132533_SCOPE2008-2_3_CraigRobertson.pdf>.

[57] See further, European Commission, 'Impact Assessment Guidelines', 15 June 2005, SEC (2005) 791, available at <http://ec.europa.eu/governance/impact/docs/key_docs/sec_2005_0791_en.pdf>. These guidelines explicitly give the SG an important role in several key areas.

At the same time there is an increasing tendency to confer upon the SG new and horizontal tasks that affect the Commission administration as a whole. Indeed the Commission's Rules of Procedure specifically provide that the SG is to be consulted on all initiatives which 'a) are of political importance; or b) are part of the Commission's annual work programme or the programming instrument in force; or c) concern institutional issues; or d) are subject to impact assessment or public consultation'.[58] Thus the SG prepares the Commission's input into treaty negotiations, assumes responsibilities for competencies new to the Commission and, in the words of the web site,[59] 'helps Commission departments in their contacts with civil society[60] and support the President in leading on key policies such as... partnership for growth and jobs,[61] sustainable development and the debate on the future of Europe.'[62] It takes charge of complex, sensitive, or controversial policy dossiers. Examples of the latter would include the exercise of administrative reform, the preparation and discussions surrounding the White Paper on governance, reflections on the role of 'civil society' input into Commission policy processes in general, as well as general work on fostering further transparency and on devising an inter-institutional approach to 'European Regulatory Agencies'. Many of these dossiers span a time frame of several years and require quite some administrative leadership and horizontal coordination. All of these tasks support the view that the SG is the central node in a complex policy network throughout the Commission.[63] Moreover its function seems to pervade the process of policymaking throughout the Commission and it exercises important tasks of coordination and oversight.[64]

The ambitions of the SG for the future are to foster its 'special role' within the Commission and to work on ensuring outward looking dynamic policies, in touch with the key 'governance' issues of the times, in a manner that ensures effectiveness and coherence. In the area of external EU relations and as a repository of institutional memory and technical expertise, it is subject to rivalry from the greatly enhanced role of the Council SG (see below).[65] Unlike the latter, it remains a 'modest, back-stage actor' and is not 'powerful in a political sense'.[66]

[58] Art 23(5) of Commission Decision of 15 November 2005 amending its Rules of Procedure, OJ L 347/83, 30 December 2005.

[59] <http://ec.europa.eu/dgs/secretariat_general/index_en.htm>.

[60] <http://ec.europa.eu/civil_society/index_en.htm>.

[61] <http://ec.europa.eu/growthandjobs/index_en.htm>.

[62] <http://europa.eu/institutional_reform/index_en.htm>.

[63] See too PL Lindseth, AC Aman, and AC Raul (2008), 'Oversight' in G Bermann, C Koch, and JT O'Reilly (eds), *Administrative Law of the European Union* (Chicago, IL: ABA, Section of Administrative Law and Regulatory Practice), p 51.

[64] These tasks are conferred in various Articles of the Commission's Rules of Procedure, Commission Decision of 15 November 2005 amending its Rules of Procedure (2005/960/EC, Euratom), OJ 2005 L 347.

[65] H Kassim (2006).

[66] Ibid.

5.3.3 The Commission and rule-making with comitology committees

As we have seen in earlier chapters, there is in the EU political system a plural executive: the Council is the original executive power and the Commission exercises executive (implementing) power when the Council delegates that power to it. One can understand the Commission as, in this sense, the 'agent' of the Council, and in this perspective it is not so surprising that the Council as traditionally the primary lawmaker in the EU has devised a number of procedural strategies to 'rein-in' the Commission in the manner it could exercise its (delegated) executive power. Very early on in the history of European integration (1962) the expansion of the Common Agricultural Policy (CAP) led the Council of Ministers to entrust the Commission with a growing volume of executive duties. Even though the Commission was responsible for implementation of general rules in principle, the Council felt that it should not have too much freedom in doing so. The Commission sought to establish purely *advisory* committees but the Member States in Council turned this initial proposal by the Commission into something quite unknown from their own national legal and political systems: a system of more binding (non-parliamentary) 'control' of the Commission by 'committees'.[67] Eventually so-called 'management committees' were established by the Council with formal powers. These were composed of representatives of the Member States who were empowered to advise in detail on specific implementation proposals made by the Commission.[68]

Such management committees are still with us today, and are mainly used for managing European funds and the Common Agricultural Policy. It is now known as the *management procedure*. If a committee objects to a Commission proposal by means of a qualified majority vote, the matter is forwarded to the Council. In the absence of such a qualified majority against its proposal the Commission can go ahead with implementation. The *regulatory procedure* is much more constraining and is the procedure that the Commission objects to most.[69] If the regulatory procedure is imposed in secondary legislation for a specific (sub-)sector then the comitology committee has to first approve the draft measure by a qualified majority of its members before the Commission can go ahead. If a qualified majority of the committee is not in favour, then the matter must be forwarded to the Council as well.[70] It has been shown that it is in fact

[67] See further J Blom-Hansen (2008), 'The origins of the EU comitology system: A case of informal agenda-setting by the Commission', *Journal of European Public Policy*, 15/2, pp 208–26.

[68] See further CF Bergström (2005), *Comitology: Delegation of powers in the European Union and the committee system* (Oxford: Oxford University Press), p 285.

[69] See the Commission's *White Paper on Governance*, COM (2001) 428, final, 25 July 2001.

[70] Council Decision 1999/468/EC, OJ L 184/23 (17 July 1999). There is one other procedure known as the *safeguard procedure* that gives every single member of the committee the right to bypass the Commission and go directly to the Council—but it is very rarely used in practice.

the *management procedure* that restricts the Commission the least.[71] Under this procedure the Commission has the most power in setting detailed rules of implementation of legislation.

According to the Court, delegated regulations discussed in such 'comitology' committees, as they became known generically, may only amend or supplement 'certain non-essential elements of the law or framework law' not covering 'essential elements of an area'. This is an attempt to limit the remit of the tasks they carry out and to ensure that the underlying legislation (framework law) will guide the exercise of delegated power by the Commission and the comitology committees. The latter does not amount to a non-delegation doctrine such as that existing in the US where the courts can strike down delegations where the primary law is insufficiently precise in various respects. Rather, the opposite is true in the EU where the essential elements that must be specified in the primary law are traditionally defined quite loosely by the ECJ with the result that implementing regulations can legally have a rather broad remit.[72]

The involvement of the Council has been obligatory under specific circumstances since comitology committees were established. The current management-committee procedure states that, if a comitology committee gives a negative opinion, the proposal can be passed on to the Council that can then take a decision by qualified majority. The same holds true for the regulatory procedure: if a regulatory committee gives a negative opinion—or does not give any opinion, the proposal has to be referred to the Council which will then take a decision by qualified majority. The Commission can then amend the proposal, resubmit the same proposal, or refer the matter back to the legislative process. As a matter of practice, it appears that comitology committees rarely exercise their formal powers with the result that it is rather uncommon for a draft implementing regulation to be sent back to the Council.[73] Indeed it seems that such drafts have been sent back to the Council in less than 1 per cent of all cases.[74] The fact remains, however, that discussions in comitology committees will take place in the shadow of the formal powers vested in the Council and that this will almost inevitably also influence the Commission's behaviour in trying to ensure a positive opinion on its draft decision when it is finally submitted to the comitology procedure. This can lead to a strengthening in practice of the position and semi-autonomous role of comitology committees.

In 2006 the basic comitology regulation was amended so as to add a new procedure, known as the 'regulatory procedure with scrutiny' (also known by its

[71] See the game theory analysis to back this up: B Steunenberg, C Koboldt, and D Schmidtchen (1996), 'Policymaking, comitology and the balance of power in the European Union', International Review of Law and Economics, 16/3, pp 329–44, p 341.

[72] KStC Bradley (2006), 'Comitology and the courts: Tales of the unexpected' in H Hofmann and A Türk (eds), *EU Administrative Governance* (Cheltenham: Edward Elgar), pp 417–47.

[73] See, for examples, Commission Staff Working Document accompanying the report from the Commission on the Working of Committees during 2007, SEC (2008) 3018.

[74] P Ponzano (2007).

French acronym 'PRAC'). The main aim of this new procedure was to give the European Parliament, for the first time, a significant role in the supervision of the content of what might be called quasi-legislative acts. Quasi-legislative acts involve actual ('technical') changes by the executive to existing EU legislation.[75] This does not amount to a general right to supervise the Commission's exercise of its powers of implementation, rather a highly specific one limited to the implementation of acts adopted under co-decision designed 'to amend non-essential elements of' a basic act. At the same time, even this modest result provoked much resistance by the Member States, in particular the Council who resented, it seems, the possibility of *democratic* supervision by a parliament (even if fairly circumscribed and proceduralized).[76]

Comitology committees are in any event Janus-faced as to where, in institutional terms, they belong: they are established by the Council and populated by national civil servants and, sometimes, scientific experts, but their task is to assist the Commission in performing its executive/rule-making tasks. In formal terms they (only) deliver 'opinions' on a draft decision of the Commission and it is the Commission that formally adopts the subsequent instruments (legal acts and administrative decisions). It can be argued therefore that comitology committees do not act independently and with unqualified discretion as they only advise on a decision of another actor and they are not delegated powers as such by the Commission. This is, however, a rather formal and legalistic view of the empirical realities.[77] Very often in practice, in order to ensure that the Commission can adopt the draft implementing measure, it engages in a process of discussion and debate as to the precise provisions of its final draft implementing measures with the committee.[78] This informal process gives committee members more power than they might formally appear to have. In practice it appears that the Commission almost never differs from the opinion of the committee.[79] Moreover the issue is also whether they are in a position to substitute the opinions reached by expert scientists in highly technical policy areas. The complexity of the institutional and multilevel positioning of comitology committees in structural terms is represented by the following multilevel model.

The shift that seems to have been effectuated is from their initial role as a 'control' device—the eye and mouth of national governments, the primary task of which was to supervise the executive tasks of the Commission—to

[75] Council Decision 2006/512 amending Decision 1999/468, of 17 July 2006, OJ 2006, L 200/11.

[76] See, for details, KStC Bradley (2008), 'Halfway house: The 2006 comitology reforms and the European Parliament: A view from the ground floor', *West European Politics*, 31/4, pp 837–54.

[77] For such a view see BJ Drijber (2006), 'Europese integratie: bottom up of top down?', *Nederlands Juristen Blad*, 81/26, pp 1418–22.

[78] C Joerges and J Neyer (1997), 'From intergovernmental bargaining to deliberative political processes: The constitutionalization of comitology', European LJ, 3/3, pp 273–99.

[79] See, for example, European Commission, *Report from the Commission on the Working of Committees during 2005*, SEC (2006) 1065, 9 August 2006.

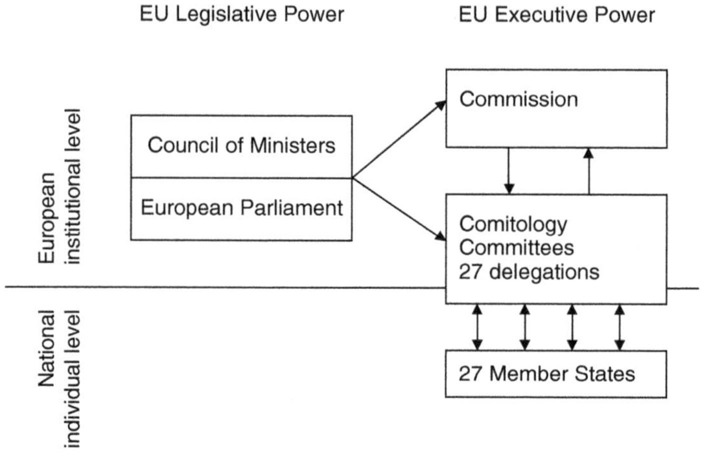

Fig 5.1 Multilevel comitology governance

Source: GJ Brandsma (2007), 'Accountability deficits in European "Comitology" decision-making', *European Integration Online Papers* 11.

much more 'autonomous' entities with (at times at least) a consensual style of decision-making rather than diplomatic negotiations among 'representatives' of the Member States.[80] The argument is made that over time committee members become socialized into inter-administrative discourse patterns within the various committees and 'deliberate' among one another, ultimately producing an epistemically good result.[81] In any event, ongoing empirical work (both quantitative and qualitative) by a political scientist, Brandsma, shows that comitology committee members tend to be fully autonomous in organizing their own work in Brussels.[82]

This de facto 'autonomy' of many comitology committees in terms of the substance of the decision-making and the expertise possessed by the (national) scientific experts is often ignored by lawyers on the basis that the formal position is that their decisions are 'adopted' in the formal sense by the Commission.[83] For this reason too the Court of Justice has been able to judicially review comitology Commission 'decisions' although not the procedures themselves.[84] But it ignores the more sociological and political reality that such committees are de

[80] R Dehousse (2003), 'Comitology: Who watches the watchmen?', *Journal of European Public Policy*, 10/5, pp 798–813, p 799.

[81] C Joerges and J Neyer (1997).

[82] See further GJ Brandsma (2008), 'Making comitology accountable', Paper presented at the Dutch and Flemish Political Science Associations Annual Conference, Nijmegen, 29–30 May 2008.

[83] See, for example, BJ Drijber (2006).

[84] See further KStC Bradley (2006).

facto exercising, at times, quite real powers in a manner that cannot be directly and explicitly controlled.

Comitology is a very important part of the executive process (or delegated legislative process since the formulation of such detailed rules can often be regarded as the equivalent of what would be known in the Member States as 'delegated legislation). In the year 2006 alone about 64 per cent of all the delegated rules legislation that was eventually adopted by the Commission was passed through the committees first.[85] The remainder mainly consisted of acts that applied existing legislation to new Member States, acts that distributed fishing quotas and legislation directed against specific international suspects of terrorism. Such committees include experts employed by national or local governments, non-governmental research organizations, private enterprises, universities etc, alongside national civil servants.[86]

5.3.4 The Commission and 'delegated legislation' post-Lisbon

One of the problems of the existing EU legal system was the difficulty of differentiating between acts of a legislative and of a non-legislative character. The instruments traditionally provided for (regulations, directives, and decisions) are used for both legislation and implementation. The hierarchical relationship between these two norms of secondary legislation can, in principle, only be identified by analysing the legal basis of the respective act—a time-consuming, technical and structurally intransparent way of understanding how the hierarchy of norms is organized and given effect in the context of the EU. The Treaty establishing a Constitution for Europe introduced an entire new terminology in this context (with a clear hierarchy of norms), namely the new instruments of 'laws' and 'framework laws'.[87] The latter would have replaced regulations and directives having a legislative character, if the treaty had entered into force.[88] The idea was to use this new typology for legislative acts (laws and framework laws) and a different typology (for example, European implementing regulation or decision) for the so-called non-legislative acts thereby making the hierarchical relationship more visible and formal. In the transition to the Lisbon Treaty, the idea of a new and clearly identifiable typology of acts was not pursued. Instead the European Council of June 2007 which initiated the process leading to the Lisbon Treaty

[85] This was calculated by Gijs Jan Brandsma by retrieving in September 2007 all Commission legislative output for the year 2006 through EUR-LEX and counting how many times an opinion of a comitology committee was referred to in the preamble under 'whereas'. See further, G Brandsma, D Curtin and A Meijer (2008).

[86] See S Smismans (2004), *Law, Legitimacy and European Governance: Functional participation in social regulation* (Oxford: Oxford University Press).

[87] Arts I-33–9 of the Treaty establishing a Constitution for Europe.

[88] See further B de Witte (2008a), 'Legal instruments and law-making in the Lisbon Treaty' in S Griller and J Ziller (eds), *The Lisbon Treaty: EU constitutionalism without a Constitutional Treaty?* (Vienna: Springer), pp 79–108.

decided that the new terminology of law and framework law be dropped as indicating a 'constitutional character'.[89] Instead we find in the new Art 288 TFEU the same three types of binding legal instruments as are currently listed in Art 249 TEC, namely regulations, directives, and decisions. However each of these instruments will, in the future, be available at three different levels of lawmaking: for 'real' legislation, for the adoption of (a new category of acts) 'delegated acts' (pre-Lisbon covered in effect by the 'PRAC'), and for the adoption of 'implementing acts' (via, for example, normal comitology procedures).

In other words, a version of the hierarchy of norms is preserved in the Lisbon Treaty that distinguishes between legislative acts, quasi-legislative acts of general application, and implementing acts.[90] Article 289 TFEU defines a legislative act as one adopted in accordance with a legislative procedure, either the so-called 'ordinary' legislative procedure (the Council in co-decision with the European Parliament) or a 'special' legislative procedure (generally only involving the Council as legislator). Secondly, the power to adopt quasi-legislative acts of general application may be given to the Commission by a legislative act (Art 290 TFEU). Thirdly, so-called 'implementing acts' may be provided for implementing legally binding Union acts and may be conferred by the Commission, or in certain cases the Council (Art 291 TFEU).

In effect, once the Treaty of Lisbon enters into force there will be two types of non-legislative 'executive' measures: first, *delegated acts* and, secondly, *implementing acts*. This can be considered a confusing use of terminology as up until now the case has been that delegated acts were precisely implementing acts![91] Nevertheless the provisions of the Treaty of Lisbon did attempt to distinguish them on the following grounds: delegated acts are acts that expand on elements of the legislative act within the framework worked out by the latter. In other words, these can perhaps be understood most easily as *delegated legislative acts*, working out the detail of legislation—the idea presumably being that this will ensure that the legislature does not have to spend valuable time on the specifics of legislation but can 'delegate' that task to the executive (the Commission) with more time and resources at its disposition. The powers delegated may range from rules on the technical and detailed elements that develop a legislative act, to the subsequent amendment of certain aspects of the legislative act.[92] The fact that legislative acts, by whatever procedure they are adopted, can be taken to mean rules of general scope determining at least the *essential elements* of a given policy

[89] Brussels European Council, 21–2 June 2007, Annex 1, para 3.

[90] See too P Craig (2008), 'The role of the European Parliament under the Lisbon Treaty' in S Griller and J Ziller (eds), *The Lisbon Treaty: EU constitutionalism without a Constitutional Treaty?* (Vienna: Springer), pp 109–35.

[91] See further, on the distinction between the two, H Hofmann (2009), 'Legislation, delegation and implementation under the Treaty of Lisbon: Typology meets reality', European LJ, 15/4, pp 482–505.

[92] Final Report of Working Group IX on Simplification, 29 November 2002, available at <http://register.consilium.eu.int/pdf/en/02/cv00/00424en2.pdf>, p 10.

area means that it is up to the legislator to determine the degree of detail required for the essential elements in a specific area and to what extent (the limits) those elements should be expanded on by 'delegated' acts.

The 'delegated act' procedure is not a genuinely novel one in the sense that it covers the same scope of application covered by the pre-existing PRAC, the difference lying in the conditions to which delegated acts will be subject. For example, it seems from the wording of the treaty provisions that the Council and the European Parliament are placed on an *equal* footing (this is not the case under PRAC) with a right of call back or opposition. It is not explicitly foreseen that regulatory or other committees will be involved (this is obviously a big difference with PRAC) in how the Commission exercises its executive power in this regard. This does not mean that the Commission cannot consult an advisory committee of experts before it adopts a delegated act or sends the European Parliament draft measures, as is currently the case with PRAC. It is, moreover, perfectly open to the institutions concerned (the Commission, the Council, and the European Parliament) to agree among themselves more far-reaching conditions to apply to any basic act after the entry into force of the Treaty of Lisbon. There is thus scope for considerable and salient detail to be 'filled in' at the level of an inter-institutional agreement and subject to a process of behind-closed-doors institutional negotiations and horse-trading. The institutions may also choose to apply these provisions in a consistent and holistic fashion to, for example, what will still be known as a 'binding framework act' in the future.

The other 'executive' instruments mentioned in the Treaty of Lisbon are called 'implementing acts' which are more in line with what we have known up until now in the Union legal system, namely a rule-making measure that implements the legislative or delegated act in the sense of adopting the necessary rules to apply it (rules which correspond to the level of regulations at national level) or actually applying it to specific cases (individual decisions). Such implementation will be carried out mainly by the Commission, 'reined in' it seems by the comitology procedure that lays down the rules and general principles concerning mechanisms of control by Member States of the Commission's exercise of implementing powers. The existing 'acquis' will at the same time presumably remain in force as no provision is made to the contrary and all existing committees can continue to work on the basis of the last comitology decision amended in 2006.

The assumption may be made however that for the future, once the Treaty of Lisbon enters into force, a new comitology regulation may be required. The major change in this regard will be that where there is a disagreement between the Commission and the comitology committee under management and regulatory procedures no referral will be made any longer to the Council. Rather it will only be the Member States (explicitly mentioned in the text of Art 291(3) TFEU) as such that retain the power to control the Commission (and not the Council), in line with the provisions of the Treaty of Lisbon. How this should be implemented in practice (again by inter-institutional agreement of some form it seems) remains a subject for speculation but some kind of appeal will probably have to be provided for. If no decision is taken by the Member States in some institutional form or other then the Commission may presumably adopt the draft implementing procedure but is not obliged to do so. Alternatively will the comitology committees be able to block the measures proposed by the Commission? Only time will tell how these provisions will be implemented in practice. With regard to the role the European Parliament will play in this context, it is by no means clear that it will be the current far-reaching one of information and scrutiny under the PRAC procedure. Yet the fact that an inter-institutional dialogue will clearly be needed also with the European Parliament makes it likely that the status quo will be maintained.

The question arises as to why there should be the parallel possibility of detailed legislation in the form of a 'delegated regulation' by the Commission and the Commission issuing an 'implementation' regulation. In the view of Hofmann 'even within the legal system the distinction between delegated and implementing regulations is regarded as unintelligible for the Courts'.[93] And in the view of Commission insiders what should happen over time is that the comitology system should be dropped completely as an anomaly, with the possibility (only) of legislative delegation remaining.[94] That could help a further weakening of the institutional position of the Commission by restricting its autonomy when proposing legislation.[95]

Delegated legislation and implementing regulations do not in any event constitute an exhaustive description of the broad category of 'non-legislation'. Other special categories of legal acts that have existed under the EU and EC Treaties, at all levels of the hierarchy, will continue to exist under the changes introduced by the Treaty of Lisbon. Examples of binding non-legislation include, in any event, inter-institutional agreements (a widespread phenomenon referred to in the Treaty of Lisbon[96]) as well as the legally binding acts of the common foreign and security policy (CFSP) (for example the binding 'decision').[97] *Ipso facto* binding 'decisions' adopted by the European Council are non-legislative given the specific provisions of Art 15(1) TEU, Lisbon.

[93] H Hofmann (2003), 'A critical analysis of the new typology of acts in the draft Treaty Establishing a Constitution for Europe', *European Integration Online Papers*, 7/9, p 13.

[94] P Ponzano (2008), '"Executive" and "delegated" acts: The situation after the Lisbon Treaty' in S Griller and J Ziller (eds), *The Lisbon Treaty: EU constitutionalism without a Constitutional Treaty?* (Vienna: Springer), pp 135–41.

[95] R Barents (2008), *Het Verdrag van Lissabon: Achtergronden en Commentaar* (Deventer: Kluwer), p 461.

[96] See the very brief mention of the Commission's specific role in Art 17(1) TEU, Lisbon and also in the new Art 295 TFEU.

[97] See, for example, Arts 25 and 26 TEU, Lisbon.

5.3.5 Executive tasks and the Council General Secretariat's internal structures

In terms of formal legal provision, the Council General Secretariat was not mentioned in the founding treaties and was only formally introduced in a treaty Article (alongside COREPER) in the Maastricht Treaty in 1992. Article 151 of the then EEC Treaty provided the initial indirect legal basis for the SG but said very little other than that the Council would be assisted by a general secretariat under the direction of the Secretary General. But the General Secretariat has, however, always been referred to, albeit in cursory fashion, in the Council's own internal rules of procedure, and the changes over the years made to these internal rules reflect the gradually growing significance the Secretariat has had for the operation of the Council over the years.[98] The fact, however, that this institution was initially set up without a clear set of formal rules governing its activities meant that the foundation was laid for 'unwritten rules, existing practices and bureaucratic reflexes to fill the normative vacuum'.[99] In other words the formal legal rules traditionally tell little about the manner in which this institution has evolved in practice or its significance on a day-to-day basis across a wide range of policy fields.

In the early years of the EU and its predecessors the general secretariats of both the Commission and the Council fulfilled primarily an organizational and administrative function in the classic way that the secretariats of international organizations do, as a low-key, back-up to effective political decision-making. The Council General Secretariat was in charge of organizing meetings, preparing agendas, translating and distributing documents, and drafting minutes. Its main task was to create the conditions for a smooth running of the Council machinery. A development that strengthened the position of the Council Secretariat was the creation of the European Council in 1974. From the very early days the Council Secretariat was involved in helping to prepare a meeting of the European Council with primarily administrative and logistical support, although depending on the size and experience of the Member State in office; the support could also be 'substantive or even political'.[100] Up until recently it was not a very visible actor in the EU institutional landscape.[101]

Due to the regular rotation of the presidency, the Secretariat developed into the Council's institutional memory and also functioned as a bridge between various chairs. Its officials do not only support the Council in all its formations but also its preparatory bodies such as the Committee of Permanent Representatives (COREPER) and the various working groups. As a result, the Secretariat also

[98] See further T Christiansen and S Vanhoonacker (2008). [99] Ibid.

[100] F Hayes-Renshaw and H Wallace (1997), *The Council of Ministers*, 1st edn (Basingstoke: Palgrave Macmillan), p 170.

[101] T Christiansen (2006), 'Out of the shadows: The General Secretariat of the Council of Ministers', Journal of Legislative Studies, 8/4, pp 80–97.

becomes a source of coordination, coherence, and continuity in the Council's work.[102] The Council decision of 1980, appointing the third Secretary General, explicitly refers to these tasks.[103] From 1982 onwards the General Secretariat started to play a key role in the preparation of the draft presidency conclusions.[104] As a result of this role at a high political level, the position of the Secretary General grows in importance and is reflected on the Secretariat as a whole. This political status increased with the advent of the common foreign security policy and the fact that, after the entry into force of the Treaty of Maastricht and subsequent treaties, the European Council acquired an incrementally more important role in deciding on common strategies and taking decisions in that regard.

What is interesting is that already, in a relatively early period, the Secretariat follows dossiers through the legislative process and makes available, inter alia, legal and procedural expertise when advising the chair on possible compromises between various national positions. Moreover the Secretary General of the Council attends meetings of the European Council, along with a number of Secretariat officials, who take a note of the meeting and provide legal and procedural advice if required. In the aftermath of the meeting the Secretariat is responsible for ensuring that where necessary the issues discussed at the European Council are placed on the agendas of the relevant subsequent meetings of the Council. The General Secretariat of the Council has thus evolved significantly during this time frame from having a passive notary/registrar role to a much more active role in assisting the presidency:

> not only in the application of procedures, but also in preparing for substantive negotiations; at the same time, the role of the Legal Service has become established and has developed to encompass intergovernmental conferences; in general, the six-monthly rotating Presidency with its increased role has made it more and more necessary to call upon the General Secretariat's assistance in ensuring continuity and efficiency of work by giving successive Presidencies the benefit of the experience it has accumulated over the years.[105]

It seems that it played a pivotal role in behind-the-scenes outcomes and even, on a number of occasions, has shifted outcomes closer to its own vision of the manner in which the EU should evolve.[106]

In the words of Christiansen and Vanhoonacker, during this period 'increasingly the Presidency relies on the Secretariat for the drafting of text proposals or

[102] See too T Christiansen and S Vanhoonacker (2008).

[103] Council Decision of 26 September 1980 appointing the Secretary General of the Council of the European Communities (80/918/EEC, Euratom, ECSC), in OJ L 261 (4 October 1980), p 16.

[104] See further J Werts (2008), *The European Council* (London: John Harper Publishing); M Mangenot (2002).

[105] 'Trumpf/Piris Report' (10.03.1999), Report by the working party set up by the Secretary-General of the Council, 'Operation of the Council with an enlarged Union in prospect'.

[106] T Christiansen (2006); D Beach (2004) 'The unseen hand in treaty reform negotiations: The role and impact of the Council Secretariat, *Journal of European Public Policy*, 11/3, pp 408–39.

the provision of tactical advice. This does not imply, however, that the Secretariat can articulate its own position. The norm is that its civil servants are impartial.' But it does play a central role in the presidency's gathering of information and works side by side with the presidency throughout negotiations. Through long-term involvement in a dossier and informal communication with government representatives, the Secretariat gains an in-depth and horizontal picture of state preferences. At the same time, there may well be powerful self-referential concepts at work—the idea that the Council General Secretariat considers its role as being one of an 'honest broker' may heavily influence how the actor and those working for it operate in practice.[107]

In general terms, the Council Secretariat has seen the scope of its activities and even its role increase on several occasions in line with the growing powers of its political masters the Council, and also the European Council. Thus, with the introduction of the co-decision procedure in the Maastricht Treaty, the Council and the European Parliament became co-legislators with a shared interest in agreeing on legislation. The increased institutional interaction considerably intensified the Secretariat's contacts with the European Parliament in a relatively novel fashion. In the words of Christiansen and Vanhoonacker:

> As most dossiers span more than one Presidency, the Secretariat fulfils an important bridging function, providing an element of continuity between the rotating chairs. In contrast to the country at the helm, its civil servants are well versed in this complex decision-making procedure and its many informal 'do's and don'ts'. The chair is assisted by the responsible Directorate General as well as by a special co-decision unit known as the '*dorsale*' or 'backbone'. The officials in the *dorsale* follow all legislative acts falling under the co-decision procedure and closely cooperate with their counterparts in the European Parliament and the Commission.[108]

This underlines the importance of fostering inter-institutional contacts also at the level of the Secretariat, a level that is not so visible to outsiders.

From the 1990s the continuous process of treaty reform creates new opportunities for the General Secretariat in terms of participation in IGC conference secretariats and intensified contact with both the European Parliament (as a result of co-decision) and the Commission. One effect of the Secretariat's role in preparing European Councils is the establishment of direct contacts with the president of the European Commission.[109] In fact the Commission and the Council Secretariat cooperate on a regular basis in policymaking in the preparation and running of the multitude of meetings within the Council structure, sharing an

[107] J Talberg (2006), 'The power of the chair: Formal leadership in international cooperation', Paper presented at the Third Pan-European Conference in EU Politics, Istanbul, 21–3 September 2006, p 45, quoted by T Christiansen and S Vanhoonacker (2008).

[108] T Christiansen and S Vanhoonacker (2008).

[109] M Mangenot (2002).

interest in the smooth running of the overall policy process.[110] In the field of external relations, given the overlap in responsibilities, there is more scope for competition than cooperation in the management of the EU's external relations. The appointment of Javier Solana and the changes in the Council Secretariat that went with it have 'rather ruffled feathers in the Council Secretariat as well as in the Commission'.[111]

But also ongoing enlargements with new Member States have brought new changes—and solutions.[112] The absorption of large numbers of new staff required adaptations of working practices and even internal reform processes. This was also prompted by the need for inter-institutional and administrative cooperation and the large-scale and fundamental administrative reform process initiated by the Commission in preceding years. In 2002 the Council Secretariat embarked on its own process of administrative modernization, 'aimed at introducing modern management methods throughout the Council in order to ensure that it remains efficient in an increasingly complex environment'.[113] This included an Action Plan for Modernising the Administration adopted in 2002.[114] This ultimately led to a newly created Department for General Administrative Questions within the Secretariat. In addition, the new financial regulation governing the general budget of the EU prompted the Secretariat to reform its financial function. This included the implementation of a new model of financial management based on attribution of responsibility to the authorizing officer and on internal management rules applying to all the financial players.[115]

At the same time, the fact that the Treaty of Maastricht started the process of conferring powers on the Council (and not the Commission) in the fields of CFSP and CJHA has significant implications for the tasking and role of the Council Secretariat. Because the Member States were afraid of losing sovereignty to the supranational Commission they instead delegated authority to the Council Secretariat in these policy areas. Yet it is clear that the acquisition by the Council of new powers in the fields of justice and home affairs and especially foreign and security policy 'have turned the Secretariat into a sizeable, executive agency in

[110] See further T Christiansen (2001b), 'Intra-institutional politics and inter-institutional relations in the EU: Towards coherent governance?', *Journal of European Public Policy*, 8/5, pp 747–69.

[111] Ibid, p 762.

[112] See further *Report on the Administrative Consequences for the General Secretariat of the Council of the Enlargement of the European Union*, 12 March 2002, prepared by the Task Force on Enlargement under the authority of the Deputy Secretary General, available at <http://register.consilium.europa.eu/pdf/en/02/st07/07301en2.pdf>.

[113] General Secretariat of the Council, 'Preparation of the Budget Guidelines for 2004—Points Concerning the Needs of the General Secretariat of the Council', 8 April 2003, available at <http://register.consilium.europa.eu/pdf/en/03/st08/st08265en03.pdf>.

[114] For some implementation details, see Council of the EU, Report on the Management of the General Secretariat, 12869/04, 1 October 2004, p 7, available at <http://register.consilium.europa.eu/pdf/en/04/st12/st12860.en04.pdf>.

[115] See further General Secretariat of the Council (n 113 above).

its own right'.[116] It is not easy to pinpoint, however, empirical evidence that the Secretariat has as such driven a specific agenda itself in terms of proposals or draft legislation as opposed to exercising influence over the details of measures that are already on the agenda. Yet in both of the newer policy fields of CJHA and CFSP there is some more concrete evidence available of a 'steering' and even agenda-setting role by the Council Secretariat. This is tied up also with the limits of the presidency role and especially the fact that presidencies rotate every six months and moreover do not start from scratch: they 'inherit' a lot of ongoing business, especially in the fields of CJHA and CFSP.[117]

The manner in which the Secretariat managed quietly, and from a basis of apparent institutional weakness, to give substance to various policy aspects within the broad and new policy field of justice and home affairs is cited as an example of effective *political* dynamism.[118] Since 1994 the Council Secretariat has had a separate Directorate General (DG H) and has built up high-quality (bureaucratic) expertise in this time frame.[119] The fact that the Commission did not have a general power of initiative (and only acquired some role in 1999) in this area meant that there was a vacuum to be filled in institutional terms—and the obvious candidate to fill it was the Council Secretariat given that the formal right of initiative was dispersed among (at that time) 15 Member States. According to Mangenot, the French political sociologist who studied these processes empirically, the reason why the Secretariat could conceive, draft, and 'sell' their draft initiatives to the various presidencies in this time frame was the accumulated trust in the functioning of the Secretariat as such in the preceding years as well as the organizational flexibility of the administrative structure.[120] In a sense, this reached a certain climax with the European Council held in Tampere in October 1999 that saw the adoption of Eurojust (a rival project to the European public prosecutor defended by the Commission). Eurojust, it has been argued, represents the culmination of a process of agenda-setting 'in the shadows' by the Secretariat.[121] The reliance on this type of instrument (the Tampere Action Plan) is arguably closely linked to the emergence of a more autonomous or distinct role for the Council Secretariat. Thus the Secretariat has been charged with the task of implementing various recommendations contained in the High Level Report and can take initiatives independently of the Member States themselves.

[116] T Christiansen and S Vanhoonacker (2008).

[117] See further on CFSP, S Duke and S Vanhoonacker (2006), 'Administrative governance in the CFSP: Development and practice', *European Foreign Affairs Review*, 11, pp 163–82, p 167.

[118] See further M Mangenot (2003), 'Une "chancellerie du Prince": Le Secretariat général du Conseil dans le processus de decision bruxellois', *Politique Européenne*, 11, p 123–42.

[119] The Commission only acquired a separate DG quite a bit later in 2000.

[120] M Mangenot (2003), p 133.

[121] See further M.Mangenot (2009), 'European Games and institutional innovation: The making of Eurojust (1996–2004)' Working Paper, Centre for European Political Sociology, University of Strasbourg, <http://prisme.u-strasbg.fr/workingpapers/WPMangenot.pdf>.

The agenda-setting role of the High Representative CFSP is more overtly political and up-front. New structures and their rapid expansions have much to do with the fact that as and from the Cologne European Summit in 1999 the amalgamation of the office of Secretary General of the Council with the newly created position of High Representative in the person of a high-profile politician: the first incumbent was the former Spanish Minister of Foreign Affairs, Javier Solana. Formally, the High Representative has no right of initiative but, by launching policy papers and bringing problem areas to the attention of the Council and the European Council, he has a certain leeway to influence the agenda and to steer the debates in a certain direction.[122] It is the staff of the policy unit who provide him with the background documents required to fulfil this agenda-setting function. Indeed it is precisely in this regard that it has been claimed that the Council Secretariat steps 'out of the shadows'.

The tasks of the Secretariat include agenda-setting, and policy formulation and implementation, especially in the fields of internal and external security. In addition, various external secretariats were effectively integrated into the Council Secretariat—that of the European Political Cooperation (EPC), the Schengen Convention, and the West European Union (WEU)—with a resulting considerable expansion of tasks and responsibilities. The growth was not only in terms of the numbers of staff working in the Council Secretariat (external staffs largely ingested) but also much greater diversity than hitherto in terms of the sectoral policies covered and expertise provided. Also, the relative autonomy with which the Council Secretariat exercises its new found functions is illustrated, for example, by the fact that a member of the General Secretariat actually holds the chair of a number of preparatory bodies of the Council (including the Security Committee and a number of working parties).[123]

Entrusted with the broad task of assisting the presidency with the formulation, preparation, and implementation of CFSP (Art 26 TEU) it was clear that the head of the General Secretariat was responsible for a vast array of executive-type tasks. This was particularly striking with what is now termed European Security and Defence Policy (ESDP). The governance structure of ESDP was established during the Nice European Council[124] and has become operational through a range of civilian, military, and civil-military crisis-management instruments and missions. The Secretariat plays an important and influential role in the preparation and implementation of civilian and military missions.[125] It draws up

122 See too T Christiansen and S Vanhoonacker (2008).

123 See list included in the latest list of Council preparatory bodies (January 2009), available at <http://register.consilium.europa.eu/pdf/en/09/st05/st05433.en09.pdf>, at pp 13 (Annex II).

124 See, in general, S Duke and S Vanhoonacker (2006).

125 See further, in detail, H Dijkstra (2008), 'The Council Secretariat's role in the common foreign and security policy', *European Foreign Affairs Review*, 13, pp 149–66.

background documents and draft joint actions. Once the Member States have agreed upon the launching of a civilian or military operation, it prepares an operational plan, in cooperation with the Commission and the presidency. Also during missions it fulfils certain implementing tasks. Through the so-called Athena mechanism, for instance, it administers the financing of the common costs of military operations.[126]

The Council's General Secretariat became rather hybrid in its composition with certain policy divisions (especially those relating to defence) being almost entirely composed of national civil servants and seconded national military officers (the European Union Military Staff[127]). A combined civilian-military approach has been pursued in the planning and conduct of crisis management and, so far at least, 15 civilian and military ESDP operations have been conducted.[128] It combines military officers, diplomats, civilian experts, and Council and Commission Officials in an integrated setting. Since 1 January 2007 the Council Secretariat even has its own independent civilian–military EU Operations Centre. This Operations Centre—with its own premises, equipment and core staff—can be transformed at short notice into a fully fledged (predominantly military) operations centre for the conduct of specific autonomous operations.[129] In the words of the Council web site:

> In the case of a predominantly military operation, a total of 89 officers and civilians will be able to start planning after five days following Ministers' decision, and will achieve its full capability to command the operation not later than after 20 days. The staff of the EU Operations Centre will be composed of the permanent Key Nucleus double-hatted personnel from the EU Military Staff and other parts of the Council General Secretariat, as well as further reinforcements from Member States' parent-HQs. The Council will also appoint the commander for the specific operation.[130]

The most recent and far-reaching changes are brought about by the Treaty of Lisbon. The relevant changes include not only the altered and widened co-decision panorama in terms of policy and issue areas but also the range of non-legislative powers of the Council in one or other of its permutations. In addition, the Treaty of Lisbon mentions explicitly the General Secretariat of the Council twice: first with regard to providing support for the Council of Ministers and,

[126] A Missiroli (2003), 'Euros for ESDP: Financing EU operations', *Occasional Paper 45*, (Paris: EU Institute for Security Studies).

[127] For an organigram of EUMS see, <http://consilium.europa.eu/uedocs/cmsUpload/Organigrammepressephotos071029.pdf>.

[128] See further Presidency Report on ESDP, 10 December 2007, available at <http://register.consilium.europa.eu/pdf/en/07/st16/st16426.en07.pdf>.

[129] The Council in its conclusions on ESDP, adopted on 19 November 2007, noted that it had been activated once (June 2007). See, Council Conclusions on ESDP, available at <http://register.consilium.europa.eu/pdf/en/07/st15/st15417.en07.pdf>.

[130] See further <http://consilium.europa.eu/uedocs/cmsUpload/070228-EU_OpsCentre.pdf>.

Secretary-General/High Representative

Deputy Secretary General

Private Office
Civilian Planning and Conduct Capability
Joint Situation Centre of the EU/Military Staff
Policy Unit

Private Office
Directorate General Political Questions/Data Protection/Infosec
Internal Audit/Prevention Service/Security Office

	DG A	DG B	DG C	DG E	DG F	DG G	DG H	DG I
LEGAL SERVICE	**Personnel and Administration**	**Agriculture and Fisheries**	**Competitiveness, Innovation and Research, Industry and Information Society, Internal Market, Competition and Customs, Transport, Energy**	**External and Politico-Military Affairs**	**Press, Communication and Protocol**	**Economic and Social Affairs**	**Justice and Home Affairs**	**Environment, Health, Consumers, Foodstuffs, Education, Youth, Culture, Audiovisual**
Directorate 1A Internal Market, Environment, Transports, Co-decision	Directorate 1A Human Resources	Directorate 1 Market Organisations, Veterinary and Zootechnical Questions, including International Aspects	Directorate 1 Internal Market, Competition, Customs Union	Directorate for Development, ACP, Multilateral Economic Affairs and non-EU Western Europe	Unit 1 Press Service	Directorate 1 Economic and Regional Affairs	Directorate 1 Asylum, Visas, Immigration, Borders	Directorate 1 Environment
Directorate 1B Social, Energy, Research, Telecom	Directorate1B Personnel administration	Directorate 2 Agricultural Structures, Rural Development, Agromonetary and Agrofinancial Questions, Plant Health, Organic Products, Food Quality, GMOs, Codex Alimentarius, Plant Protection	Directorate 2 Competitiveness, Lisbon Strategy, Industry, Research, Information Society and Electronic Communications	Directorate for the Americas, UN and Counter-terrorism	Unit 2 Communication	Directorate 2 Budget and Financial Regulations	Directorate 2 Judicial Cooperation in Civil and Criminal Matters	Directorate 2 Health, Consumers, Foodstuffs, Education, Yourth, Culture, Audiovisual
Directorate 2 Ecofin, Agriculture and Fisheries	Directorate 2 Conferences, Organisation, Infrastructure	Directorate 3 Fisheries including External Relations	Directorate 3 Transport Policy	Directorate for the Western Balkans, Eastern Europe and Central Asia	Unit 3 Transparency, Archives, Libraries and Official Journal		Directorate 3 Police and Customs Coooperation, Schengen	
Directorate 3 External Relations	Directorate 3 Translation and Document Production			Directorate for Defence Issues			Directorate 4 Civil Protection	
Directorate 4 Institutional Questions, Budget and Staff Regulations	Directorate 4 Finance			Directorate for Civilian Crisis Management				
Directorate 5 Justice and Home Affairs	Directorate 5 Information and Communication Systems			Directorate for Non-proliferation of Weapons of Mass Destruction				
Directorate 6 Inter-institutional Relations				- Coordination Unit - Enlargement Unit - Middle East/Mediterranean Region/ Gulf - Africa Unit - Asia and Oceania Unit - Human Rights Unit				
Directorate 7 Quality of Legislation				- New York Liaison Office - Geneva Liasion Office				

Fig 5.2 Structure of the Council General Secretariat

secondly, with regard to providing support for the European Council.[131] This exercise of formal 'catch-up' with what has long been reality in practice does not necessarily give an adequate picture of the manner in which, bit by bit and often quite invisibly, the position and tasks and ultimately influence of the General Secretariat have incrementally increased. At the same time it is also very much tied into the increase or alteration in the powers and practices of the Council itself as well as all its supporting instances and of course, increasingly, that of the European Council. The role of the Council Secretariat is frequently underestimated if not completely ignored (by lawyers in any event). Besides its traditional supporting role there is an emerging political function.[132] This relatively new role began with the creation of the position of the High Representative and the Policy Unit and the fact that they have a voice of their own in order to do their own agenda-setting. It is likely that this more political role will only increase with the implementation of the Lisbon Treaty, even though there is more counterbalance with the Commission than hitherto, both in certain aspects of CFSP and with regard to PJCC.

The General Secretariat of the Council initially in the early years after the Maastricht Treaty assumed a role that parallels that played by the Commission administration in other (EC) policy areas. In particular, the Council of Ministers largely assumed responsibility for implementation of legislation and delegated rule-making in the newer policy fields (CFSP and security policy and justice and home affairs) in a manner which it never did in the traditional Community system (under the so-called 'Community method') where the Council simply had some reserve powers of execution (in addition to control over the Commission for the manner of its execution of Community legislation). The Council of Ministers, as an institution, initially exercised its newfound powers in a manner that largely excluded the Commission, thereby ensuring the marginalization of the Commission's position in these newer policy fields. In practice however, in more recent years, the Commission has been delegated some implementing powers by the Council, in particular with regard to measures whose legal basis is to be found in Title IV of the EC Treaty.[133] However, the Commission was denied—notably—implementing powers with regard to the amendment/development of the Common Consular Instructions and External Border manual.[134]

[131] See Arts 240(2) and 235(4) TFEU, respectively.

[132] See too S Duke and S Vanhoonacker (2006).

[133] See further S Peers (2006), *EU Justice and Home Affairs Law* (Oxford: Oxford University Press).

[134] See Case C-257/01 *Commission v Council* [2005] ECR I-345. Advocate General Leger had opined (opinion of 27 April 2004) to the contrary in that case that the Council's decision to reserve to itself the implementing powers in the contested regulations infringed the principle of institutional balance since it failed to establish the specificity of the situation in which the implementation powers are to be reserved. He found that it was 'incompatible with the very requirement of specificity for an entire area to be covered by a reservation of powers' (paras 68–70).

5.4 Integration by Stealth?

European integration rests upon the Monnet method, 'integration by stealth' as it has been called.[135] Government by committee[136] enabled national administrators to work within the permissive limits of political consensus for many decades. Monnet's hope was indeed that, as he put it in his memoirs, a few hundred European civil servants would be enough to put thousands of national experts to work.[137] The figures have grown considerably—as might be expected—in the interim decades but the idea remains largely the same and salient. Recent tides of treaty reform seem to ensure some continued existence of comitology for the future (but maybe according to altered conditions) but, at the same time, have introduced a new and convoluted notion of 'delegated legislation' all implying a reform of the institutional balance of powers between the legislative and executive powers carried out by the EU institutions. Particularly in the latter regard, the Commission's role as executive power is confirmed and strengthened, especially as it may be assumed that once the Treaty of Lisbon enters into force this will constitute the primary way in which legislative acts will be implemented and that the traditional comitology procedures may be assigned to the back seat and used only for the very technical 'implementing 'provisions. The next chapter, Chapter 6, details the so-called 'satellite' actors delegated putatively administrative or managerial powers by political institutions seeking to cordon off the political—and non technical—nature of their role and functions. This description implicates both the Council of Ministers and the Commission although much more systematically the latter rather than the former.

[135] See, for example, G Majone (2005), *Dilemmas of European Integration: The ambiguities and pitfalls of integration by stealth* (Oxford: Oxford University Press).

[136] A Weale (2000), 'Government by committee: Three principles of evaluation' in T Christiansen and E Kirchener (eds), *Committee Governance in the European Union* (Manchester: Manchester University Press), pp 161–70.

[137] J Monnet (1978), *Memoirs* (Garden City: Doubleday), p 373.

6

Satellite Executive Power

6.1 The Unseen Hands

Over the course of the past decade and more, actors other than the formal EU institutions and their administrations as described in Chapters 4 and 5 have emerged on the EU level. They often have not insignificant administrative–executive powers (not always entirely 'insulated' from political questions) but without necessarily a clear or explicit place in the EU constitutional system.[1] These 'unseen hands'[2] include a great number of 'fringe bodies', extra-governmental organizations, independent non-majoritarian institutions, and quasi-autonomous non-governmental organizations that form 'a significant and administratively dense component of modern governance structures'.[3] In recent years the empirical range of such unelected or 'non-majoritarian' actors has increased considerably as has the type of tasks that are conferred or delegated by the EU institutions and by the EU Member States. Organs such as the European Central Bank (ECB), Europol, and a wide array of regulatory and even operational EU-level committees and agencies, privilege expert and scientific expertise and deliberately exclude parties and political competition.

Such bodies congregate not only around the Commission as a core executive actor in the EU political system but also around the Council of Ministers in recent years. In that context it is generally assumed that it is necessary that they are enabled to operate independently from their political masters but they are nonetheless subject to a number of procedural and substantive constraints. These 'satellites' are not at the heart of the 'community method' as such but in orbit around it, with differing ties back to the core political actors and the formal decision-making processes depending on the actor involved. But they have on

[1] D Curtin (2005b), 'Mind the gap: The evolving EU executive and the constitution', Third Walter van Gerven Public Lecture, University of Leuven (Groningen: Europa Law Publishing). See too G de Búrca (1999), 'The institutional development of the European Union: A constitutional analysis' in P Craig and G de Búrca (eds), *The Evolution of EU Law* (Oxford: Oxford University Press), pp 52–82.

[2] MPCM van Schendelen and R Scully (eds) (2003), *The Unseen Hand: Unelected EU legislators* (London: Frank Cass Publishers) who use the term more specifically to refer to 'unelected EU legislators'.

[3] M Flinders (2004), 'Distributed public governance in the European Union', *Journal of European Public Policy*, 11/3, pp 520–44.

the whole become more 'visible' in recent years thanks to extensive information made available on the Internet both passively and actively.[4]

The purpose of this chapter is not to provide a comprehensive analysis of the changing nature of public governance also in the context of the EU. This has been done much more extensively elsewhere.[5] Rather it will focus on a number of significant examples of 'satellite' actors that operate in and around the formal decision-making structures of the EU, all having grown extensively in recent years as a matter of legal and institutional 'practice'.[6]

How must we further understand these different phenomena: EU 'non-majoritarian agencies', EU networks of national actors and 'double-hatted' national authorities? What is their role in the perspective of the exercise of executive power at the EU level? Do they have autonomy or discretion in the day-to-day exercise of their tasks and are they subject to some mechanisms of (*ex ante*) control (as opposed to *ex post* accountability mechanisms that are the subject of Chapter 9 below)?

6.2 The 'Independent' European Bank

The ECB is without question a core non-majoritarian institution of the EU. On a par with the European Court of Justice it is accorded the constitutional status of 'independence' from the whims and wishes of the political masters. Both sets of institutions, although different in nature, have nonetheless many similarities. Neither is elected (and hence are intrinsically and fundamentally non-majoritarian) and both perform functions (judicial and price stability and monetary policy) that are regarded as core functions of any polity. Both allocate values. Both have been delegated (politically sensitive) powers by political masters (for both, the political principal is the Member States in the final analysis). In that sense, there are probably more points of comparison between them than with the host of other non-majoritarian 'agencies' that have, mainly in recent years come into existence under the auspices of the EC/EU. The latter can to a large extent be considered lower-level entities that have been delegated powers by the political and decision-making institutions operating at the level of the EU political system itself. Moreover they often are delegated discrete powers in functional areas and the discourse is not that of 'independence' rather (often) of control by and accountability to the political masters.

[4] See further, G de Búrca (1999); P Craig (2006), *EU Administrative Law* (Oxford: Oxford University Press).

[5] CF Sabel and J Zeitlin (2008), 'Learning from difference: The new architecture of experimentalist governance in the EU', European LJ, 14/3, pp 271–327 and references cited.

[6] The agencies as such are not mentioned in the treaty texts (although this changes with the Treaty of Lisbon) but the parameters of institutions such as the ECB clearly are regulated by explicit treaty provisions.

Unlike the ECB, the Court of Justice does not perform an executive function. When the drafters of the Treaty of Maastricht set out the structure and operations of the ECB, they did not formally add it to the list of Community institutions in Art 7 TEC alongside the European Parliament, Council, Commission, ECJ, and the Court of Auditors. Yet it can be regarded, in terms of the importance of its operational role and the executive functions it exercises in the highly salient field of monetary policy, as being comparable in substance to a Union 'institution'—a point acknowledged in the text of the Lisbon Treaty.[7] The Governing Council of the ECB totally controls the monetary policy of the Member States currently in the Euro-zone and regulates the use of the single currency, the Euro, within those Member States. Moreover the General Council of the ECB, which includes national central bank governors from all the Member States of the EU, helps coordinate monetary policy throughout all these states.

One of the unique features of the manner in which the institutional position and role of the ECB is regulated in the treaties is by 'constitutionalizing' its independence. This principle is such a salient part of its own image that it has led to the argument that it is in fact (and unlike any other EU 'institution') entirely *autonomous* from the Community framework. In other words the debate about the constitutional nature and autonomy of the ECB has become intertwined, at least at the level of legal and constitutional debate, with the appraisal of its level of independence. This materialized in a recent ECJ case that has now definitively ruled on the constitutional nature of the ECB and the scope of its 'independence'.

The ECB was granted institutional independence with legal personality distinct from that of the Community.[8] Moreover, EC Treaty Art 108 states the central principle that the ECB and the European System of Central Banks (ESCB) shall have *total independence* in their monetary policy operations. The ECB and its individual members are categorically forbidden to take instructions either from Community institutions or from Member States or from any other body.[9] The national central banks, which, together with the ECB, also implement monetary policy within the ESCB, are likewise to enjoy full independence from their respective governments. It follows from these provisions that no political instructions can be given for example by the European Council to the ECB: the ECB has totally autonomous regulatory and decision-making powers within the monetary policy field. The reason for copper-fastening the principle of independence in this fashion was to ensure that the ECB enjoys full autonomy in its control of monetary policy in order to achieve its 'primary objective' stated in Art 105 TEC, namely the maintenance of 'price stability'. The text on the independence of the ECB was modelled upon that contained in Art 213 concerning the independence of the Commission and its members. At the same time it reflects more

[7] The text of the Lisbon Treaty designates ECB as a Union 'institution' in Art 13 TEU, Lisbon.

[8] Art 107(2) TEC and Art 9.1 of the Statute.

[9] Art 108 TEC.

generally what has been termed a 'widespread...shift' to granting central banks operational independence.[10]

In addition to operational independence, a high degree of personal independence was granted to the members of the ECB. Thus, the decision to give the Executive Board members a non-renewable, but relatively long, eight-year term can be viewed as fostering their independence. Moreover, Art 11.4 of the Protocol on the Statute of the ECB and the ECSB further ring-fences ECB Board members by providing that Executive Board members can only be removed from office for incapacity or 'serious misconduct' through legal proceedings before the Court of Justice, ensuring a judicial rather than a political decision. Governors can be removed in national proceedings only under 'equally strict conditions'.

There are other factors promoting the independence of the ECB, including the fact that it is not in any way financially dependent on the Community's political institutions (including the EP).[11] From the very beginning this decision to strongly affirm the independence of the ECB has on the whole been applauded by policy-makers and scientific commentators alike.[12]

The fact that the principle of independence was incorporated into the EC Treaty itself as a constitutional principle gives it a very high status indeed, arguably giving the ECB greater independence than the banks of the other G7 countries which are not part of the euro-zone: the US Federal Reserve Board, the Bank of England, the Bank of Japan, the Bank of Canada,[13] and virtually all central banks prior to the advent of Monetary Union.[14] In fact, it has been claimed: 'the ECB reigns as the most politically independent central bank in the world'.[15] At the same time, some provision was made for example for the president of the Council and a Commission member to participate without vote in Governing Council and General Council sessions.[16] According to Advocate General Jacobs,

[10] CAE Goodhart (2003), 'The constitutional position of an independent central bank', *Government and Opposition*, 37/2, pp 190–210.

[11] Art 28 of the Protocol on the Statute of the ESCB and ECB provides that only the national central banks subscribe to its capital.

[12] See, for example, Committee for the Study of Economic and Monetary Union (1989), *Report on Economic and Monetary Union in the European Community* (the Delors Report). See too, R Smits (1997), *The European Central Bank Institutional Aspects* (New York: Aspen Publishers); RM Lastra (1992), 'The independence of the European system of central banks', Harvard Int'l LJ, 33/2, p 475–519. See however, contra, J de Haan and L Gormley (1997), 'Independence and accountability of the European Central Bank' in M Andenas, L Gormley, C Hadjiemmanuil, and I Harden (eds), *European Economic and Monetary Union: The institutional framework* (Dordrecht: Kluwer Academic Publishing), pp 333–53.

[13] See too J de Haan and SCW Eijffinger (2000), 'The democratic accountability of the European Central Bank: A comment on two fairy-tales', *Journal of Common Market Studies*, 38/3, pp 393–407, p 396.

[14] F Snyder (1994), 'EMU: Metaphor for European Union? Institutions, rules and types of regulation' in R Dehousse et al (eds), *Europe After Maastricht: An ever closer union?* (Munich: Law Books in Europe), pp 63–78.

[15] K McNamara (2002), 'Rational fictions: Central Bank independence and the social logic of delegation', *West European Politics*, 25/1, pp 47–76, p 66.

[16] Art 123 TEC.

'it seems clear that their status is not limited to that of mere observers. They presumably have the right to speak in order to influence, within reasonable limits, the decision-making of the ECB.'[17]

Some years after the ECB came into being and started functioning, a variant on the independence argument was forcefully made. In legal and constitutional terms it was argued that the ECB constituted an 'independent specialized organization of Community law', one that is 'from a functional perspective . . . a new Community within the European Union's central pillar which stands on equal footing with the original three Communities', namely the EC, the ECSC, and the European Atomic Energy Community (Euratom).[18] In other words the argument was basically that the ECB constituted a type of new international organization not subsumed completely within the EC. This constituted a 'rather absolutist theory of ECB autonomy and independence'[19] designed to ensure that the ECB could never be subject legally to the political institutions of the EC. At the same time it was not denied that the primacy of Community law applied fully to the ECB and its decisions nor the jurisdiction as such of the ECJ.

Similar legal arguments were put to the Court of Justice in the *OLAF* case by the ECB. Both the Advocate General's opinion in this case as well as the (less detailed) Court judgment provides a definitive legal assessment of the ECB, as well as its level of independence. At its core this case raised the issue of whether the ECB was subject to the general jurisdiction of the European Anti-fraud Office (OLAF) to conduct anti-fraud investigations or whether its independent (and autonomous) status meant that it could adopt its own distinct internal rules in this regard.[20] The ECB believed that its autonomous status and operational independence might be jeopardized if it subjected itself to OLAF investigations. The Commission challenged this view before the ECJ on the basis that the ECB fell within the scope of application of OLAF's constitutive regulation that could exercise its investigative powers 'within the institutions, bodies, offices and agencies established by, or on the basis of, the Treaties'.[21] In its defence the ECB argues that its treaty-guaranteed status, in particular its guarantee of independence, insulated it from the jurisdiction of OLAF. It maintained, in effect, that the EC Treaty granted the ECB a legally autonomous status quite distinct from

[17] Opinion of Advocate General Jacobs of 3 October 2002 in Case C-11/00 *Commission v European Central Bank* [2003] ECR I-7147 para 156 (the OLAF case).

[18] C Zilioli and M Selmayr (2000), 'The European Central Bank: An independent specialized organization of Community law', Common Market L Rev, 37, p 591.

[19] RG Goebel (2006), 'Court of Justice oversight over the European central ban: Delimiting the ECB's constitutional autonomy and independence in the OLAF judgment', Fordham International LJ, 29, pp 610–24. This theory was the subject of much criticism: see, for example, R Torrent (1999), 'Whom is the European Central Bank the central bank of?, Reaction to Zilioli and Selmayr', Common Market L Rev, 36, p 1229.

[20] In fact, the ECB did adopt its own rules creating internal procedures to combat fraud: ECB Decision 1999/726/EC, OJ 1999 L 291/36/ and the legality of this measure was the subject of the Court proceedings.

[21] Council Regulation, No 1073/1999, OJ 1999 L 136/1, p 3, Art 1(3).

a Community agency or body and that its budget, revenues and financial operations were quite separate and distinct from those of the Community, so that the OLAF Regulation in question simply did not apply to it.

The Court and its Advocate General rejected in no uncertain terms the arguments of the ECB based on its putative autonomy and complete independence from the wider Community/Union framework. Rather, the ECB's constitutional nature had to be understood as a Community organ or body within the EC structure, not some sort of autonomous supranational organization. The treaty's grant of independence covers only the ECB's conduct of monetary policy and does not preclude the ECB's subjection to general Community rules to combat fraud. In other words the very fact that the ECB is operationally and functionally independent of the political institutions does not preclude its subjection to other accountability forums laid down in the treaties: on the contrary, it would seem. This is an important conclusion with more general implications as to the scope of the relationship between the principles of independence and the principles of accountability applying to the ECB in particular.

This general point of the relationship between even fully 'independent' organs and institutions of the EU and a more general accountability framework is highly salient and of more general relevance than just with regard to the ECB. Indeed the Commission is also in certain respects constitutionally 'independent' from instructions by politicians (the Member States, the European Council, or the Council of Ministers). Nonetheless the Commission is embedded in a web of accountability arrangements, both *ex ante* and *ex post*, arrangements that have increased in intensity and significance in recent years (see further Chapter 9 below).

6.3 The Commission Sheds Layers

6.3.1 Delegation to private actors

In the original conception there was never meant to be a strong or extensive executive apparatus at the central EU level; at most the Commission would function as a public administration but with largely managerial functions in the context of the 'direct administration' of the EC. Those managerial functions consisted of a wide range of management tasks which could and did include tasks as diverse as managing a large number of undertakings, managing specific policy projects in very diverse fields (eg tourism, cooperation with non member countries of the Southern Mediterranean), the financial and administrative management of policy programmes. As the number and scope of EC (EU) policies steadily expanded, the tasks of the Commission increased to the point that at a certain point it felt obliged to 'contract-out' such tasks on the grounds of efficiency, expediency, and cost. It sought to free its limited resources by outsourcing or informally delegating away some of what it perceived to be its more lower-level purely managerial tasks to outside bodies and contractors.

The mechanism of 'contracting out' tasks to independent contractors from the private sector was used by the Commission in a rather unstructured and *ad hoc* fashion without embedding the delegation of its public functions in a system of contracting out. The medium used was largely that of so-called TAO's (technical assistance offices). Initially it did so in an informal fashion to these private third parties and did not institute a system of control of the powers thus 'delegated'.[22]

Problems arose over time from the rather haphazard and uncontrolled manner in which the Commission organized a system of delegation of putatively managerial tasks to outside contractors but failed to monitor or control the manner in which its contractual 'agents' performed their management tasks. The fact that such tasks are carried out in such close proximity to the Commission's activities as a public authority, and the major likelihood that conflicts of interest could occur, would have justified the performance of very careful checks on the subcontracts concluded. This did not happen in practice. The mismanagement of these external contracts in particular and its failure to exercise control over the tasks it delegated in this fashion in an adequate fashion led to crisis (the resignation of the Santer Commission) and renewal (a rather rigorous reform programme of the Commission administration). A special committee appointed by the European Parliament was established to explore what had gone wrong—the 'Committee of Independent Experts' (CIE).[23]

The difficulties of maintaining control when work is contracted out were, for example, apparent in the context of ECHO, the European Community Humanitarian Assistance Office. It was established on 1 March 1992 to give the EC a more effective means for providing aid in emergency relief situations. The demands upon it grew exponentially in the years immediately following its establishment, but there was no corresponding increase in the staff available to it. Nor were there well-recognized financial or organizational procedures in place to regulate its activities. The Committee of Experts found that budgetary appropriations were used in an irregular manner: money intended to be used for operations was used to finance staffing.

One of the main criticisms of the Committee concerns the issue of staffing. One of the common themes in the various programmes studied (tourism, the MED programmes, etc) was the need to contract out because of inadequacies in the staffing levels within the Commission. The Committee was not, on the whole, unsympathetic with this rationale but felt that this did not excuse

[22] Committee of Independent Experts (1999), Second Report on 'Reform of the Commission: Analysis of current practice and proposals for tackling mismanagement, irregularities and fraud', vol I, para 2.1.37, available at <http://www.europarl.eu.int/experts/pdf/rep2–1en.pdf>.

[23] For its two reports see <http://www.europarl.eu.int/experts>.

delegation to the private sector without a sufficient control structure. In its view, the Commission should never have taken on policies when it lacked proper resources to do so. For example, with regard to the MED programmes, the Committee stated that the 'Commission as a whole deserves serious criticism for launching a new, politically important, and highly expensive programme without having the resources—especially staff—to do so'. Moreover, the Commission should have calculated the overall demands on its resources better and the College of Commissioners should have drawn up a list of priorities.

The Commission's subsequent internal response to many of its problems was to engage in a serious process of internal administrative reform at the same time as it tried to refocus its activities and tasks on what it perceived to be its 'core tasks', defined in terms of their *political* significance. The Commission in its White Paper on Administrative Reform[24] recognized the force in these management- and staffing-related points made by the CIE in its reports and sought to concentrate more on core functions such as policy conception, political initiative and enforcing Community law as a manner of overcoming it. In the Committee's words, 'it goes without saying that the Commission must have the means to carry out its duties'.

In the intervening years the Commission has carried through a series of internal administrative reforms on a rather large scale in order to redress some of these weaknesses (described in Chapter 5 above). Because of severe criticisms by the European Parliament-established Committee of Independent Experts as to the nature of the tasks being delegated to private companies, the Commission established a new type of implementing agency (executive agency) that was, in effect, designed as an extension of the Commission itself. At the same time the Commission continues its standard practice of delegating to approved intermediaries within the Member States the performance of tasks which go far beyond pure management, but are in line with criteria laid down by a council regulation.[25] This can, in practice, include delegation (via the Member States) to (national) private bodies. This is, in principle, in line with Art 54 of the Financial Regulation applicable to the general budget of the European Communities, which allows the Commission to entrust tasks of public authority to inter alia (a) executive agencies and (b) national public-sector bodies 'or bodies governed by private law with a public sector mission (under certain circumstances)'.[26]

[24] European Commission, 'Reforming the Commission: A White Paper, Part 1', COM 2000/0200 final and European Commission, 'Reforming the European Commission: A White paper, Part II: Action Plan', COM/2000/0200 final.

[25] See, for details, X Yataganas (2001), 'Delegation of regulatory authority in the EU: The relevance of the American model of independent agencies', Jean Monnet Working Paper 3/01, available at <http://www.jeanmonnetprogram.org/papers/01/010301.html>.

[26] Council Regulation 1605/2002 of 25 June 2002, OJ L 248, 16 September 2002.

6.3.2 Internal delegation to executive agencies

The main objective underlying the creation of so-called 'Executive Agencies' is to empower structures with their own legal personality distinct from a Commission department with the execution of management tasks (inter alia implementation of a Community programme) that are not directly linked to 'tasks requiring discretionary powers in translating political choices into actions'[27] that the Commission wants to keep under its direct control (for example, its role as guardian of the treaties or its right of initiative). Executive agencies are termed by the Commission as 'Community bodies' and are considered bodies exercising limited discretion.[28] In fact the term 'Community bodies' is considered a misnomer, the term 'Commission bodies' being more accurate given the fact that they are exercising specific tasks of implementation and administration directly delegated by the Commission itself to them without intervention of any outside body.[29] Obviously such executive agencies are designed to have no real zone of discretion and the thinking is that they will not fall foul of the criteria laid down by the Court of Justice in the *Meroni* case (see Chapter 3 above). They do however make the real operational choices in terms of grants, awards, or funding, albeit within the broad structure laid down in the relevant empowering legislation.

Executive agencies were not meant to be permanent but rather were set up for the duration of a specific project and do not contain Member States representatives. The idea was also that such agencies facilitate the working together of Commission officials seconded to the agency, with staff from the private sector that have responsibility for particular aspects of the Community programme.[30] On this new approach the Commission seeks to effectively 'delegate' away internally within the Commission itself some technical and administrative tasks that do not (apparently) engage its political responsibility. At the same time, working arrangements to govern executive agencies were agreed with the European Parliament Committee on Budgets.[31] Their

27 Council Regulation (EC) No 58/2003 of 19 December 2002 laying down the statute for executive agencies to be entrusted with certain tasks in the management of Community programmes, OJ L 11/1, 16 January 2003, Art 6(1).

28 Council Regulation (EC) No 58/2003, ibid, Preamble (7).

29 In legal terms a framework regulation based on Art 308 of the Treaty was adopted by the Council in 2002 Council Regulation (EC) No 58/2003. The Commission resorts to it on a case-by-case basis and establishes specific Executive Agencies by Commission decision. There are currently six such executive agencies: the Education, Audiovisual and Culture Executive Agency; the Executive Agency for Competitiveness and Innovation; the Research Executive Agency; the Trans-European Transport Network Executive Agency; the European Research Council Executive Agency; and the Executive Agency for Health and Consumers: <http://europa.eu/agencies/executive_agencies/index_en.htm>. See too, European Commission (2008), *General Report on the Activities of the European Union* (Luxembourg: Office for Official Publications of the European Communities), p 252.

30 P Craig (2006), p 25.

31 See details, Commission, 'European agencies: The way forward', COM (2008) 135 final, p 3.

annual activity reports are annexed to the report from their parent Directorate General. The standard financial regulation adopted by the Commission governing the establishment and implementation of the budget applies to all executive agencies.[32]

6.3.3 The Commission and the 'auxiliary' agencies

Over time the Commission has repeatedly stressed the necessity to preserve 'the unity and integrity of the executive function' to ensure 'that it continues to be vested in the chief of the Commission if the latter is to have the required responsibility of vis-à-vis Europe's citizens, the Member States and the other institutions'.[33] In the 2005 draft Inter-institutional Agreement, agencies are described as mere auxiliaries of the Commission. They must 'provide the Commission, in particular, with the experience and expertise it needs so that it can fully meet its responsibilities as the Community executive'. From this viewpoint, agencies are only supposed 'to help regulate a particular sector at European level and to help implement a particular Community policy'.[34] The 'Penelope project', the Commission contribution to the Convention on the Future of Europe in 2002/3, included Art 71 on agencies. This explicitly stated that 'In the exercise of its executive function, the Commission may be *assisted* by agencies.'[35] Most recently the Commission opined 'they *help the Commission* to focus on core tasks, making it possible to devolve certain *operational functions* to outside bodies'.[36]

The agencies that exist at the European level to date can largely be viewed as a compromise between the Commission's wish to pull *more powers* towards the EU level and expectations by the Member States that they would be able to control their policies better by delegation to agencies and not to the Commission.[37] Yet their considerable growth in recent years also points to the fact that the core executives (primarily the Commission but also in certain respects the Council)

[32] Council Regulation (EC, Euratom) No 1605/2002 of 25 June 2002 on the Financial Regulation applicable to the general budget of the European Communities, Official Journal L 248, 16/09/2002, pp 0001–48.

[33] See, for example, Commission, 'Communication on the operating framework for the European regulatory agencies', COM (2002) 718 final, 11 December 2002, p 1

[34] See, Council Opinion 7861/05 of the Legal Service on the Draft Inter-institutional Agreement on the operating framework for the European regulatory agencies—choice of legal act and legal basis, 6 April 2005 (08.04), p 5, quoted by R Dehousse (2008), 'Delegation of powers in the European Union: The need for a multi-principals model', *West European Politics*, 31/4, pp 789–805.

[35] European Commission, Working Document, Contribution to a Preliminary Draft Constitution of the European Union, Report of 4 December 2002, available at <http://www.kent.ac.uk/kcfe/euconstitutions/penelope.pdf>. Author's emphasis.

[36] Commission, Communication to the European Parliament and Council, *European Agencies: The Way Forward*, SEC (2008) 323, p 2. Author's emphasis.

[37] See further D Keleman (2002), 'The politics of Eurocratic structure and new European agencies', *West European Politics*, 25/4, pp 93–118.

are engaged in a process of respectively either delegating down executive-type powers to lower-level actors ('agents') in the EU political and administrative system or of creating new executive and operational tasks at the EU level and tasking newly created actors in that regard.[38]

In various position papers, the Commission has presented itself as the principal that must evaluate the possibility of delegating a share of its powers to autonomous bodies, which will assist in completing its tasks and operating the internal market.[39] The idea that they are helpers or auxiliaries and not autonomous bodies with salient discretionary powers is often justified by legal constraints, in particular the *Meroni* line of case law limiting institutional choice within the EC (EU). From a legal point of view the legal problems in setting up European agencies have remained considerable.[40] The Commission cannot be openly seen to delegate the discretionary powers conferred on it by the treaties—only those concerning implementing powers clearly defined and adequately controlled or supervised.

It follows from the need to respect the principle of institutional balance (laid down in *Meroni*: see Chapter 3 above) that delegation (by the Commission or indeed other institution) to (quasi-)autonomous agencies is not permitted either of the power to adopt secondary legislation nor the power to formulate rules for implementing legislation. This is why some European agencies (for example, the European Agency for the Evaluation of Medicinal Products) do not themselves adopt decisions but prepare opinions (on product authorizations for example) that are subsequently formally adopted by the Commission itself. Other agencies have been given the power to themselves adopt decisions applying the rules of secondary legislation to specific cases. The thinking seems to be that the latter is permissible once it involves a margin of technical appraisal related to precise objectives and not a 'broad margin of appraisal in a complex economic field or a decision with political implications'.[41] But there is definitely a tension between the Commission's recent administrative reform strategy (back to the core political functions) and long established legal doctrine in a very different legal and political context.

What is in any event not permissible, it has been assumed until now, is the full-scale delegation by the Commission of its own discretionary decision-making power, for example with regard to competition policy to a (new) European

[38] D Curtin (2007), 'Holding (quasi-)autonomous EU administrative actors to public account', European LJ, 13/4, pp 523–41.

[39] See, for example, European Commission White Paper, *Reforming the Commission*, March 2000. See, in general, R Dehousse, (2008), p 792.

[40] See, for further details, D Curtin (2005), 'Delegation to EU non-majoritarian agencies and emerging practices of public accountability' in D Gerardin et al, *Regulation through Agencies in the EU: A new paradigm of European governance* (Cheltenham: Edward Elgar), pp 88–119.

[41] Delegations of power have in some instances been upheld by the Courts but only if compatible with the so-called *Meroni principle*: see the various cases discussed at length by P Craig (2006), Ch 5.

Competition Agency.[42] In other words, the delegation by the Commission of its treaty-based powers in relation to competition policy to a 'EU Competition Agency' with power to enact regulatory instruments subject to certain conditions governing their operation and supervision would clearly go way beyond what *Meroni* permits. A clear breach of *Meroni* in this manner does not, in my view, exist yet in the existing topography of EU agencies. Yet what remains problematic—at the very least constitutionally fuzzy—is the continued creation and operation of agencies that are not formally 'delegated' existing treaty-based powers as such by a specific EU institution but rather by the Union legislator, including powers previously held by the Member States. Let us now looker closer at the scope of the phenomenon in terms of legal and institutional 'facts' in order to assess where problems may lie.

6.4 The Institutionalization of (Quasi-)Independent 'Agencies'

6.4.1 The internal acceleration of agency construction

The creation of an autonomous (regulatory) agency structure at the level of the EU and its predecessors is one of topsy-turvy-like growth (see Fig 6.1). The result has been variously described as leading to an 'epidemic of agency fever',[43] an 'explosion of agencies',[44] and as a 'maze'.[45] Both the Commission and the Council have had established under their auspices—in one form or another—a whole series of EC/EU-level agencies, some of which have executive, regulatory, and management tasks and are composed of both European civil servants—and some nationals on secondment.[46] An overview is given of this accelerated growth in Fig 6.1.

In 2000 only 12 agencies existed plus the anomalous Europol. Only nine years later—2009—this number has more than doubled to over 30, with several more in the pipeline.[47] Twenty-seven of these have been created over the course of the past 15 years and 13 over the course of the past 6 years. This figure includes the various organizations established under the label of decentralized

[42] See, for example, CD Ehlermann (1995), 'Reflections on a European Cartel Office', Common Market L Rev, 32/2, pp 471–86.

[43] T Christiansen and P Lægreid (2005), 'Agencification and regulatory reform', Paper prepared for the CSANCOR/SOG workshop on 'Autonomization of the State: From integrated administrative models to single purpose organization', Stanford University, 1–2 April 2005.

[44] E Chiti (2000), 'The emergence of a community administration: The case of European agencies', Common Market L Rev, 37/2, pp 309–43.

[45] J Pollak and S Puntscher Riekmann (2008), 'European administration: Centralisation and fragmentation as means of polity-building', *West European Politics*, 31/4, pp 771–88.

[46] See further D Curtin (2005); J Pollak and S Puntscher Riekmann (2008).

[47] This figure includes both what the Commission home page describes as 'Commission Agencies' (24) and Common Foreign and Security Policy Agencies (3) and Police and Judicial Cooperation in Criminal Matters Agencies (3). See further <http://europa.eu/agencies/community_agencies/index_en.htm>.

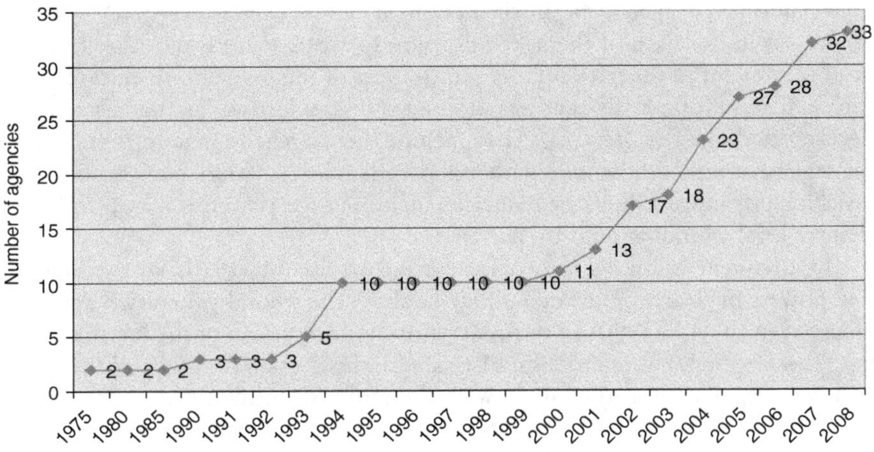

Fig 6.1 Number of EU-level agencies, 1975–2008

Source: M Egeberg, M Martens, and J Trondal (2008), 'Building executive power at the European level: Some preliminary findings on the role of EU-Level agencies', Paper presented of the UACES Conference, Edinburgh, 1–3 September 2008.

'Community agencies', as well as the 'Union agencies' set up in the second and third pillars, such as the Institute for Security Studies, EUROPOL or EUROJUST. In budgetary terms and compared to the overall size of the 'core Commission executive[48] these agencies take up a sizeable portion of the EU budget—in excess of 4,250 posts expected in 2009 with a total budget in excess of 1.2 billion euros.[49] Moreover, it appears that during the past 15 years, if one compares the cumulative figure for agencies staff to the number of posts created within the Commission since 1992, over a third of the executive positions created during that period have been assigned to regulatory agencies.[50] Dehousse describes this growth as follows: 'Eight autonomous agencies were established during the Delors years, while another ten were created by the Prodi Commission. During the same period (2001–2005), five agencies were created in the second and third pillars of the EU. As noted in a 2005 report by the French Senate, more autonomous organs had been created by the EU in the previous 50 months than in the preceding 50 years.[51]

A piecemeal logic appears to dominate at the European level, making it extremely difficult to define a clear typology for the classification of each

[48] OJ L 69, 13 March 2009, Annual Budget for 2009.

[49] This represents a 7% increase compared to 2008. See further, European Parliament, Policy Department on Budgetary Affairs, Meeting with the decentralized agencies, 28 May 2008, Background document, <http://www.europarl.europa.eu/meetdocs/2004_2009/documents/dv/200/200805/20080528_background_en.pdf>.

[50] R Dehousse (2008).

[51] R Dehousse (2008), p 789.

non-majoritarian agency or institution in a homogenous category.[52] As one report put it, 'for each of them, the decision to create them is motivated by the need to respond to the particular circumstances of the moment. In certain cases the occurrence of a crisis that has aroused public sensitivity is the basis of the decision to create the agency.'[53] They include those agencies that perform purely management tasks, those who gather and collate information, and those whose tasks include more regulatory-like tasks including the power to adopt decisions that are legally binding on third parties.

The first-generation agencies were created in the mid-1970s with very limited powers in clearly delineated policy fields.[54] The second-generation agencies emerged in the mid-1990s in the context of the completion of the internal market. These agencies were more sophisticated in institutional/management terms and were entrusted on the whole with tasks of a scientific/technical nature.[55] What can be termed the third wave, or generation, of agencies were those established since the early 2000s with more overtly regulatory and far-reaching tasks in many instances.[56] It is particularly in recent years that acceleration in the numbers of agencies being constructed has taken place.

In addition to what the *Europa* website calls 'Community agencies', there are Union agencies with the Council of Ministers in the steering seat. In recent years a number of new agencies have been created and powers delegated to them.[57] Here too one can refer to an 'acceleration' in recent years of processes of polity-building by the EU.[58] Accelerating agencification in the EU has created a complex administrative space characterized by simultaneous centralization and fragmentation. The administrative space in question is moreover multiple: part of it is centred around the Commission (Community agencies) and the other—a not insignificant part—is centred around the more intergovernmental Council of Ministers and the Member States (Union agencies).

Europol is probably the best-known example of an independent organ set up by the Member States with links to the Council, whose tasks have been incrementally expanded to cover those of a more operational nature such as its participation

[52] Report by the Working Group 'Establishing a framework for decision-making regulatory agencies' (Group 3a), Preparation of Commission White Paper on Governance, para 8, available at <http://ec.europa.eu/governance/areas/group6/report_en.pdf>.

[53] See further Report by the Working Group 'Establishing a Framework for Decision-Making Regulatory Agencies' (Group 3a), Preparation of Commission White paper on Governance, available at <http://ec.europa.eu/governance/areas/group6/report_en.pdf>.

[54] These were the Centre for Development of Vocational Training (CEDEFOB) and the European Foundation for the Improvement of Living and Working Conditions (EUROFOUND).

[55] Examples include the European Environment Agency, the European Agency for the Evaluation of Medicinal Products, the European Agency for Health and Safety at Work, and the Office for Harmonization of the Internal Market.

[56] Examples include the European Food Safety Authority, the European Aviation Safety Authority, and the European Agency for the Management of Operational Cooperation at the External Borders (FRONTEX).

[57] See further D Curtin (2005a).

[58] J Pollak and S Puntscher Riekmann (2008).

in so-called 'Joint investigation teams'.[59] It was provided for in the Maastricht Treaty (1992), established by multilateral convention in 1995[60] and entered into force—after lengthy national ratification processes—in 1999. Barely a decade later, it was integrated fully into the EU as an EU-level 'agency', funded from the general EC budget and subject to the general EU rules and procedures.[61] Eurojust was set up in 2002 and was established by Council decision, not requiring Member State ratification, precisely so its powers and tasks could be amended more easily with the passage of time.[62]

The European Defence Agency was created to help those EU Member States who join[63] 'develop their defence capabilities for crisis-management operations under the European Security and Defence Policy'.[64] It was established by a measure of secondary legislation by the Council, at the time known as a 'joint action' in the field of common foreign and security policy (CFSP) and is given a formal legal basis in the Lisbon Treaty.[65] Like all the other agencies, it has its own legal personality and a certain financial autonomy (although unlike the Community agencies, it is not financed fully out of the Community budget but out of contributions by the Member States[66]). The leading role played by the Secretary General/High Representative in the Agency structure (formally the 'head of the agency')[67] is intended to provide the 'essential link' between the Agency and the Council of Ministers.[68] The former operates under 'the authority and the political supervision' of the Council in various ways (see also Chapter 9 below).[69]

The common thread among all these agencies is that, depending on the policy area and applicable legal basis, they are established either by secondary legislation in one form or another or by an international agreement among Member States. The constituent legal instruments vary from Council Regulation to Council and European Parliament Regulation to Council decision (or joint action) to

[59] For its website see <http://www.europol.europa.eu/>. For further detailed (secondary- and tertiary-level) rules governing analysis files, liaison officers, confidentiality, budget, external relations, etc see details at <http://www.europol.europa.eu/index.asp?page=legal_other>

[60] OJ C 316, 27 November 1995, p 1.

[61] Council Decision establishing the European Police Office (Europol) of 6 April 2009, OJ L 121, 6 April 2009, p 37.

[62] Council Decision of 28 February 2002 setting up Eurojust with a view to reinforcing the fight against serious crime, OJ L 63/1, 6 March 2002. See further, Council Decision 2009/426/JHA of 16 December 2008 on the strengthening of Eurojust and amending Decision 2002/187/JHA, OJ L 138, 4 June 2009, p 14. See in general on Eurojust: <http://www.eurojust.europa.eu/>.

[63] There are currently 26 members, all Member States of the EU with the exception of Denmark. See the website of the European Defence Agency: <http://www.eda.europa.eu/genericitem.aspx?area=Background&id=79>.

[64] See Art 2 of Council Joint Action 2004/551/CFSP of 12 July 2004 on the establishment of the European Defence Agency, OJ L 245/17, 17 July 2004. See further, <http://www.eda.europa.eu/>.

[65] See Council Joint Action 2004/551/CFSP (n 64 above). See too Art 42(3) TEU, Lisbon.

[66] Arts 16 and 22 of Council Joint Action 2004/551/CFSP of 12 July 2004 (n 64 above).

[67] Art 7 of Council Joint Action 2004/551/CFSP of 12 July 2004 (n 64 above).

[68] Recital 9 of Council Joint Action 2004/551/CFSP of 12 July 2004 (n 64 above).

[69] See further ML Sanchez Barrueco (2008), 'L'Agence européenne de défense: un organe intergouvernemental au service d'une institution communautaire?', *Revue du Droit de l'Union Européenne*, 3, pp 507–42.

Convention of the Member States. The tasks that they are to carry out are specified in the constituent instrument. They have their own legal personality, their own management structure, their own technical or scientific committees, and they are often expressly and formally endorsed as 'autonomous' actors. In this context it is relevant to explore further two issues: (a) the manner in which the constituent text is drawn up and the participants in that process (in particular the growing voice and role of the European Parliament), and (b) the meaning of institutional 'autonomy' in practice.

6.4.2 The European Parliament struggles for voice

The fact that the EU political system knows of a multiplicity of principals at the level of the EU political system itself has largely shaped the politics of agency creation and contract design. The Commission proposes the establishment of the vast majority of agencies, greatly shapes their structure and powers, and often provides them with their first director. In more recent times, however, the European Parliament's influence significantly shaped the politics of agency design.[70] As the European Parliament's legislative power increased it asserted a more powerful role in the oversight of existing agencies and in the design of new ones—with the exception it seems of those constructed in the field of CFSP.[71]

The institutional design of the agency and the inclusion or otherwise of 'public' moments of accountability for the exercise of future discretion will, to a significant extent, depend on *who* is taking the decision and according to what *procedure*. The dominant issue at the level of contract design is that of the legal basis in the treaties. Depending on which legal basis is used, the process will be more or less open or more or less closed. In the case of a so-called 'Community' agency then the Commission will, in principle, makes a proposal and a decision will be taken by the legislator, either the Council or in some cases in recent years the Council and the European Parliament jointly. It follows that the discussion on the institutional design features of the proposed agency on the whole takes place on the basis of a publicly available proposal. This has been quite different with regard to agencies that have been proposed and adopted by the Council of Ministers in the newer policy areas of police cooperation and defence policy. For example, the European Parliament was not consulted at all on the initial Europol Convention nor on any subsequent changes made to that Convention (by means of protocols). Europol was originally established by means of an international Convention ratified by all the Member States as distinct from secondary EC or EU measures. That meant that amendments to the Convention had to be ratified by the Member States in the same way as the original Convention but the Council also enjoyed various quite far-reaching powers,

[70] D Keleman (2002).

[71] For example, with regard to the European Defence Agency, no role is made for—nor even mention made of—the European Parliament. See further M Sanchez Barrueco (2008).

acting unanimously, to extend Europol's competences further and to modify the definitions of crime in the Annex to the Convention.[72] It was only with the Treaty of Amsterdam that provision was made that the European Parliament had to be consulted on (future) Conventions and, by implication, all amendments to existing Conventions and all measures implementing Conventions. This means in practice that the various references in the Europol Convention to the Council's power to adopt implementing measures henceforth entail an obligation to consult the Parliament before those measures can be adopted. This was considered as a significant broadening of the Parliament's right to at the very least express an opinion in public on the basis of public drafts before the Council formally adopted an implementing measure.[73]

When the legal basis of Europol was changed from that of a Convention among Member States to that of a Council decision (anticipating the provisions of the Treaty of Lisbon in this regard[74]) in 2008, the Commission drafted the proposal and the European Parliament was fully consulted. This procedural 'opening up' had salient implications from the point of view of *ex post* accountability (see Chapter 9).

Another important issue of contract design is the *ex ante* selection of the members of the Management Board as well as the executive director of the agency in question. Initially, the tendency was for those agencies with the Commission as effective principal that the executive director be appointed by the Management Board 'on a proposal by the Commission' for a limited period (for example, five years).[75] In such circumstances it is the Commission itself that will undertake its own screening and selection processes and no further details or requirements are laid down. In the very early days of agency design it was, in fact, the other way around: the Management Board had to submit a 'list of candidates' to the Commission who would then select and appoint the executive director.[76]

A more recent example is provided in the terms of the European Aviation Safety Agency that provides a different model of agency design.[77] Here it is

[72] See further, for chapter and verse, S Peers (2004), 'Governance and the third pillar: The accountability of Europol' in DM Curtin and RA Wessel (eds), *Good Governance and the European Union: Concept, implications and applications* (Antwerpen: Intersentia), pp 253–76.

[73] In practice, however, it appears that the Parliament has not been systematically consulted on all measures: on one calculation some years ago this happened in only 12 of the 17 relevant implementing measures. See S Peers (2004).

[74] Art 88(2) TFEU.

[75] See, for example, with regard to the European Environment Agency that so provides in Art 9 of Council Regulation (EEC) 1210/90 of 7 May 1990 on the establishment of the European Environment Agency and the European environment information and observation network, OJ L 120, 11 April 1990.

[76] See, for example, Art 6 of Regulation (EEC) No 337/75 of the Council of 10 February 1975 establishing a European Centre for the Development of Vocational Training, OJ L 039, 13 February 1975.

[77] See, in general, A Schout (2008), 'Agencies and inspection powers: The case of EASA as new or more of the same?' in E Vos (ed), *European Risk Governance: Its science, its inclusiveness and its effectiveness* (Connex Book Series: Mannheim: Mannheim University Press), pp 257–89.

provided that the executive director of the agency 'shall be appointed on grounds of merit and documented competence and experience relevant for civil aviation' by the Management Board on the proposal of the Commission.[78] Some criteria of competence and experience were thus laid down on the basis of which a name should be proposed to the Management Board that then acts as the formal appointing authority.[79]

With regard to the European Food Safety Authority (EFSA) established in 2002, provision was made for a 'list of candidates' to be forwarded to the Management Board which then would be able to choose and appoint a specific candidate. The list of candidates was to be drawn up by the Commission on the basis of an open competition 'following publication in the Official Journal and elsewhere of a call for expressions of interest'.[80] Moreover, before the Management Board could appoint a specific candidate, it is noteworthy that it is to 'be invited without delay to make a statement before the European Parliament and answer questions put by members of that institution'. With regard to the more recent European Agency for the Management of Operational Cooperation at the External Borders (FRONTEX) established in 2004, the European Parliament went further and requested, on analogy with the practice that has developed regarding commissioners-designate, to hear the designate executive director prior to his appointment and to issue an opinion.[81] Likewise in the new 'basic' regulation for European Civil Aviation Agency agreed in 2008, it was provided that 'before being appointed, the candidate selected by the Management Board may be asked to make a declaration before the competent committee or committees of the *European Parliament* and answer questions from its, or their, members'.[82]

[78] Art 30 of Regulation (EC) No 1592/2002 of the European Parliament and of the Council of 15 July 2002 on common rules in the field of civil aviation and establishing a Civil Aviation Safety Agency, OJ L 240/1, 7 September 2002. The executive director may be similarly dismissed by the Management Board on the proposal of the Commission. In virtually all the earlier agencies no provision was made for dismissal.

[79] This was not the first time: see Art 8(1) of Council Regulation (EC) No 1035/97 of 2 June 1997 establishing a European Monitoring Centre on Racism and Xenophobia, OJ L 151, 10 June 1997.

[80] See, Art 26 of Regulation (EC) No 178/2002 of the European Parliament and of the Council of 28 January 2002 laying down the general principles and requirements of food law, establishing the European Food Safety Authority and laying down procedures in matters of food safety, OJ L 31/1, 1 February 2002. For a similar approach see Art 30 of Council Regulation (EC) No 768/2005 of 26 April 2005 establishing a Community Fisheries Control Agency and amending Regulation (EC) No 2847/93 establishing a control system applicable to the Common Fisheries, OJ L 128/1, 21 May 2005.

[81] 'Report of 24 February 2004 drawn up on behalf of the Committee on Citizen's Freedom and Rights, Justice and Home Affairs on the Proposal of Council regulation establishing a European Agency for the Management of Operational Co-operation at the External Borders' (COM(2003)687-C5-0613/2003-2003/0273(CNS)), EP Doc A5-0093/2004 FINAL, Amendment 37.

[82] See Art 44 of Regulation (EC) No 216/2008 of the European Parliament and the Council of 20 February 2008 on common rules in the field of civil aviation and establishing a Civil Aviation Safety Agency, and repealing the earlier regulation, OJ L 79/1, 19 March 2008.

This involvement of the European Parliament in the selection and screening of candidates indicates a fairly recent trend to take account of the European Parliament's increased status as co-legislature in the EU. The hypothesis is moreover that mention and involvement of the European Parliament in the selection process is directly related to the intensity of its role in the contract design (as co-legislator and thus co-principal, or only in an advisory capacity to the Commission and the Council). Thus, with regard to the European Food Safety Authority and the European Aviation Safety Agency, with the European Parliament as co-legislator, we find rather advanced provisions (compared to earlier agency designs[83]) involving the European Parliament in selection and screening issues. But even the earlier European Environment Agency that was not adopted (in 1990) pursuant to co-decision by the European Parliament included a provision enabling the European Parliament 'to designate, as members of the management board, two scientific personalities particularly qualified in the field of environmental protection'.[84] In later agency designs the European Parliament has often fought for this right to designate members of the Management Boards, alongside the Member States and the other EU institutions (Council and or Commission), sometimes successfully,[85] other times not.[86] Very often it is, moreover, specified with regard to representatives of the European Parliament what specific expertise they must possess and the responsibilities they will exercise whereas for the other representatives (from the Member States and from the Commission) no such specification is necessarily made.

There is more recent indication that the European Parliament has changed its tactics in terms of its involvement in selection and screening mechanisms. Where it is involved in co-decision and the Agency is clearly being established according to the Community method with the Commission as effective principal, recent practice indicates that the European Parliament no longer insists on designating members to the Management Board. Where this is not the case, and where the agency is constructed in what it feels is a more intergovernmental fashion (with the Council more in steering position, albeit falling under Community competence

[83] See, for example, the agency design of the European Foundation for the Improvement of Living and Working Conditions, Regulation (EEC) No 1365/75 of the Council of 26 May 1975, OJ L 139, 30 May 1975, with the European Parliament only being mentioned in its budgetary capacity.

[84] For a similar provision with regard to the European Monitoring Centre for Drugs and Drug Addiction (EMCDDA), see Art 8 of Council Regulation (EEC) No 302/93 of 8 February 1993, OJ L 36, 12 February 2003.

[85] See, for example with regard to the European Agency for the Evaluation of Medicinal Products (EMEA), Art 56 of Council Regulation (EEC) No 2309/93 of 22 July 1993, OJ L 214, 24 August 2003. See too in the Agency for the Cooperation of Energy Regulators under construction, R Brunetta, Draft Report on the proposal for a regulation of the European Parliament and of the Council establishing an Agency for the Cooperation of Energy Regulators, 11 February 2008 (for the 'Administrative Board').

[86] For example, the Office for Harmonization in the Internal Market (Trade Marks and Designs), Council Regulation (EC) No 40/94 of 20 December 1993, OJ L 11, 14 January 2004.

as such) the European Parliament attempts to shift the balance of power more towards the Commission as principal. Thus, with regard to FRONTEX (2004) the European Parliament has for example very deliberately suggested that it not designate any members of the Management Board in favour of achieving a more central role for the Commission as opposed to the Council[87] in the overall agency design. This is a substantial change in approach, relying on the fact that the more overall involvement of the Commission, the more the European Parliament in any event exercises its general powers of political control over the actions and failure to act of the Commission.

This change in tactics by the European Parliament is in line with the sentiments expressed by the Commission to the effect that the European Parliament should not as co-legislature be 'represented' by members on the Management Board as this amounted to mixing up the legislative power with the executive power in an undesirable fashion; rather the European Parliament should see its powers of political control over agencies increased.[88] However the *quid pro quo*, in the Commission's view at any rate, is that the Commission should see its representation on the Boards considerably increased, to the point of parity with those of the Member States.[89]

When it comes to those EU agencies established by the Union (and with the Council more as principal with little to no involvement of either the Commission or the European Parliament) a quite different picture emerges. Thus in the original agency design of Europol for example, not only was the European Parliament not formally consulted but no role was envisaged for it (nor indeed the Commission) in the designation of members of the Management Board nor with regard to the appointment of the executive director. The director is appointed by the Council, acting unanimously and 'after obtaining the opinion of the Management Board'.[90] A similar pattern emerges with regard to the later Eurojust,[91] the EU

[87] Report of 24 February 2004 drawn on behalf of Committee on Citizens' Freedoms and Rights, Justice and Home Affairs on the proposal for a Council regulation establishing a European Agency for the Management of Operational Co-operation at the External Borders (n 82 above).

[88] Communication from the Commission, 'The operating framework for the European regulatory agencies', COM (2002) 718 final.

[89] Ibid, p 9. The European Parliament, in its report on the communication, sees this as one option but in fact comes down in favour more of the model already used in the European Food Safety Authority, namely 'to entrust the Commission with the task of drawing up a comprehensive list of candidates on which Parliament may express its opinion and on the basis of which the Council makes the appointments except for one members directly appointed by the Commission'. See Report of 4 December 2003 drawn up on behalf of the Committee of Constitutional Affairs on the communication from the Commission, 'The operating framework for the European regulatory agencies' (COM(2002)718–2003/2089(INI)), EP Doc A5-0471/2003 FINAL, para 17(d).

[90] Art 29(1) of Council Act of 26 July 1995 drawing up the Convention based on Art K.3 of the Treaty on European Union, on the establishment of a European Police Office (Europol Convention), OJ C 316, 27 November 1995, pp 0002–32.

[91] Council Decision 187/JHA of 28 February 2002 setting up Eurojust with a view to reinforcing the fight against serous crime, OJ L 63, 6 March 2002.

Satellite Centre,[92] and the EU Institute for Security Studies,[93] as well as the European Defence Agency.[94] With regard to the latter it is, for example, specifically stated that the agency will act 'under the Council's authority' and no provision whatsoever is made for any involvement by the European Parliament in the selection and screening mechanisms leading to the appointment of agency members and director. With the new Europol decision this has now changed for Europol with the Parliament acquiring the right to hear the director and other rights.[95]

6.4.3 EU agencies on a leash?

Many authors refer to agency 'independence' or 'autonomy' of Community agencies in particular as a 'fact' but they only look at the level of formal, legal independence.[96] Autonomy is used here to refer to institutional autonomy from a lead 'political' institutional (mainly either the Commission or the Council, depending on nature and contract design of the specific agency). Agencies were organizationally detached from the Commission and the Council and possessed their own internal management structure (their own executive director and management board). Many authors equated *this internal management structure* with the real degree of agency *independence*. A different and unrelated issue is that of the (relatively undisputed) autonomy of the scientific experts who often participate in the internal scientific or technical decision-making processes of agencies—such as, for example, the European Medicines Agency (EMEA), the European Fund Administration (EFA), etc. In the words of Shapiro writing more than a decade ago, 'in any event it is clear that EU independent agencies are independent in the sense of being relatively free of control by any of the other organs of the Community'.[97] But the argument is now increasingly being made, in particular by political scientists carrying out empirical work with regard to specific agencies, that it is necessary to move beyond a purely legal and formal analysis to take into account those aspects of institutional life that involve both formal and informal processes.[98]

[92] Council Joint Action 555/CFSP of 20 July 2001 on the Establishment of a European Union Satellite Centre, OJ L 200, 25 July 2001.

[93] Council Joint Action 554/CFSP of 20 July 2001 on the Establishment of a European Union Institute for Security Studies, OJ L 200, 25 July 2001.

[94] Council Joint Action 551/CFSP of 12 July 2004 on the Establishment of the European Defence Agency, OJ L 245, 17 July 2004.

[95] Art 48, Council Decision establishing the European Police Office (Europol) of April 2009, <http://register.consilium.europa.eu/pdf/en/09/st08/st08142.en09.pdf>.

[96] See further M Szapiro (2005), 'The framework for European regulatory agencies: A balance between accountability and autonomy', Paper presented on the 3rd ECPR Conference; and references cited in M Busuioc (2009).

[97] M Shapiro (1997), 'The problems of independent agencies in the United States and the European Union', *Journal of European Public Policy*, 4/2, pp 276–91, p 289.

[98] See, for example, M Martens (2008), 'Voice or loyalty? The evolution of the European Environmental Agency (EEA)', Paper presented to ECPR Standing Group on Regulatory Governance, 5–7 June, Utrecht.

An underlying assumption in a significant part of the agency literature is thus that because agencies are set up as entities formally separated from their 'parent bodies' they automatically benefit from a considerable autonomy in the use of their decision-making competencies and, implicitly, independence post-establishment.[99] Recent empirical political-science work has however shown that the formal *de jure* situation does not mean that in practice agencies really enjoy post-delegation autonomy from their primary political 'principal'—at least not in terms of management and priority setting.[100] While European agencies are indeed legally separate institutions from the Council and the Commission it does not necessarily follow that agencies are de facto independent from these bodies and able to exercise decision-making autonomy within their mandate.[101] In fact, the empirical evidence that has been gathered indicates that in some cases the opposite is true and the real decisional powers of some European agencies are below the formal scope of delegated authority. The reason lies in ongoing controls exercised by one (or other) of the principals. It appears in particular that what is called ongoing/simultaneous control during the management process is the most salient. This is not the same as saying that there is control over the (technical) substance of the actual decisions taken or rules promulgated (by the scientific experts). For example, with regard to the European Environment Agency (EEA), it has been explicitly found that there have been incidents in the past where DG Environment in the Commission has tried to influence the running of the EEA on matters that 'have gone well beyond legitimate differences of view as to the EEA's priorities and the way it interprets its mission'.[102] Moreover, it appears that DG Environment has even raised the prospect of EEA budget reductions in order to exert pressure on the agency to follow the Commission point of view on various matters.[103]

This is a clear example of not only tensions in the relationship of the Commission and the Agency in particular but also of the Commission clearly trying to 'control' the Agency and steer it in certain respects. This will clearly not always be the case and there is certainly variation among agencies. Whereas no agency appears to be fully autonomous from the Commission or the Member States, some may achieve a level of actual autonomy above their formal autonomy while some may achieve less actual autonomy. Groenleer in his empirical research

[99] See further M Busuioc (2009), 'Accountability, control and independence: The case of European agencies', European LJ, 15/5, pp 599–615.

[100] See too M Groenleer (2008), 'Building autonomous European Union agencies? Identity, legitimacy and leadership in a comparative perspective', Paper presented at the 3rd UACES Annual Conference, 1–3 September, Edinburgh, paper on file with author.

[101] M Busuioc (2009).

[102] Institute of European Environmental Policy and European Institute of Public Administration (2003), *Evaluation of the European Environment Agency: An IEEP/EIPA study. A final report to DG Environment* (August 2003), para 4.6.2 , available at <http://ec.europa.eu/environment/pubs/pdf/eea_a_en.pdf>.

[103] Ibid, para 4.6.2 (Main Report).

links this to particular conditions such as legitimacy, control over information, and the role of leaders.[104]

Ongoing control is, in Busuioc's formulation, an informal type of direct control exercised by a principal vis-à-vis an agent in which the agent's (future) actions are steered and/or determined by the principal resulting in a decrease in the original mandated discretion of the agent to accomplish the delegated tasks and implicitly, its decision-making autonomy. Ongoing control restricts or nullifies the original, formal level of mandated discretion and implicitly the agent's decision-making autonomy, through the direct interference of the principal. In the words of Busuioc: 'Ongoing control brings the principal in through the back door. It amounts to a reversal of the original delegation. In this situation, the agency is controlled and by default also *under control* given its decreased decision-making autonomy and independence.'[105]

Available empirical information in the form of interviews conducted with practitioners shows that ongoing (management) control by the Commission and the Council does occur and is manifested through interference in the agency decision-making at two stages: informally (in preparatory meetings) or formally (in the Management Board meetings), being equally binding in both cases. This type of non-mandated control does not appear to be exclusively encountered in the case of the EC agencies; some instances have also been reported in justice and home affairs. For example, the Management Board of Europol has made an unprecedented formal complaint to the Art 36 Committee concerning informal requests to Europol by the Council working groups, outside the text of Europol's legislative framework. The Management Board of Europol expressed the 'growing concern ... that the legislative framework applicable to Europol and its work was not always applied. In particular, on several occasions Council working groups have asked Europol to carry out tasks originally not foreseen by its yearly work programmes and budgets, which are approved by the Council upon the recommendation of the Management Board.'[106] According to Statewatch, the 'Council Working Parties have by-passed the Council of Ministers and the Europol Management Board and sent requests for action directly to Europol itself, not once but on several occasions[107] which were both irregular and unconstitutional.'[108]

[104] M Groenleer (2008). See too M Groenleer (2009), *The Autonomy of European Agencies. A Comparative Study of Institutional Development*, forthcoming.

[105] M Busuioc (2009).

[106] Letter from the Chairman of the Management Board to Article 36 Committee, 12838/03, Brussels, 30 September 2003. See further M Busuioc (2009).

[107] Statewatch, 'Unprecedented complaint by the Europol Management Board about informal requests for action by Council working parties by-passing legislative process', available at <http://www.statewatch.org/news/2003/oct/03europol.htm>.

[108] Ibid.

6.4.4 Internal agencies with external powers

At the same time, some autonomy is almost inevitably given to the agencies. For example, the head of an agency, such as the director of Europol, is given the power to negotiate 'administrative arrangements' with third countries and other organizations. As a Council Act from 1998 provides, 'Europol may conclude agreements with third States and non-European Union related bodies.'[109] However, it is for the Council to determine 'the third States or non-European Union related bodies' the agreements shall be negotiated with.[110] The Council has authorized negotiations with regard to a number of third countries and other international organizations.[111] The Management Board defines 'the prioritization of the negotiations, taking account of the Council's declaration on Article 42 of the Europol Convention'.[112]

In this context, the director of Europol has a pivotal role concerning the negotiations of international agreements for Europol. He coordinates the negotiations 'after consulting the Management Board and after authorization by the Council'. The Council may, however, stipulate certain conditions which have to be taken into account by the director when negotiating. Also, an agreement can only be concluded after the authorization by the Council.[113]

The director of Europol has in fact quite extensively exercised the power to negotiate and conclude international agreements with third countries and other international organizations,[114] most controversially with the United States on the exchange of personal information. The 'political control' in such case is provided by the Council of Ministers which must authorize the director of Europol to conduct negotiations with the country or organization in question; the results of such negotiations are then presented back to the Council and the director of Europol is 'authorized' by the Council—behind closed doors—to proceed to signing the agreement as negotiated.[115] The understanding from interviews conducted with

[109] Art 2(1) Council Act of 3 November 1998 laying down rules governing Europol's external relations with third states and non-European Union related bodies, OJ C 026, 30 January 1999, pp 19–20.

[110] Ibid, Art 2(2).

[111] See Art 1 Council Decision of 27 March 2000 authorizing the director of Europol to enter into negotiations on agreements with third states and non-EU related bodies. A more detailed account of this practice is given below.

[112] Art 1(3) Council Act of 3 November 1998 laying down rules governing Europol's external relations with third states and non-European Union related bodies, OJ C 026, 30 January 1999, p 19–20.

[113] Art 2(3) Council Act of 3 November 1998 laying down rules governing Europol's external relations with third States and non-European Union related bodies, OJ C 026, 30 January 1999, p 19–20.

[114] See the rules laid down by the Management Board of Europol of 15 October 1998 laying down the rules governing Europol's external relations with European Union related bodies, OJ C 26/89, 30 January 1999.

[115] Council of the European Union, 2002.

Council practitioners on this point is that the Council is liaising quite closely with Europol in advance of decisions being taken.

A distinction is made between 'operational agreements' and 'strategic agreements'. The main difference between these types of agreements is that the latter usually refer to the exchange of technical and strategic information, but do not include the exchange of information on an 'identified individual or identifiable individuals'.[116] These agreements do thus not allow for the exchange of any person-related data.[117]

As far as operational agreements are concerned, special precautions have to be taken concerning the transmission of personal data. In this context, the Project Team of Europol will prepare a comprehensive report on the existing legislation on data protection and data confidentiality. This report will be submitted to the Management Board and the Joint Supervisory Body and, provided they approve it, to the Council that shall consult the national parliaments.[118] Further negotiations on this issue may only be initiated 'once the Council is satisfied that there are no obstacles to the start of such negotiations, taking account of the laws and administrative practice in the field of data protection in the third State or non-European Union-related body concerned'.[119] If the Council gives its consent, the negotiations are initiated. Hereby, Europol frequently uses a draft agreement that provides it with a relatively strong position in the negotiations.[120] In case an agreement between both parties is reached, it has to be approved in accordance with the procedure described above.

According to the website of Europol, to date, 15 agreements have been concluded with non-EU states, both operational and strategic agreements.[121] Operational agreements have been concluded with Australia, Canada, Croatia, Iceland, Norway, Switzerland, as well as with the United States.[122] Strategic Agreements have been concluded with Albania, Bosnia and Herzigovina, Colombia, Former Yugoslav Republic of Macedonia, Moldova, Russia,

[116] A clause clarifying this point is included into all strategic agreements: see, for example, the Agreement on Cooperation between the European Police Office and the Republic of Turkey concluded on 27 March 2000, OJ 2000/C106/01.

[117] C Rijken (2001), 'Legal and technical aspects of cooperation between Europol, thirds states and Interpol' in V Kronenburger (ed), *The European Union and the International Legal Order: Discord or harmony* (The Hague: TMC Asser Instituut Press), pp 577–603, p 588.

[118] Ibid, p 590 *et seq*.

[119] Recital 5 Council Decision of 27 March 2000 authorizing the director of Europol to enter into negotiations on agreements with third states and non-EU-related bodies.

[120] Draft Model Agreement on Cooperation with Third States, The Hague, 15 October 1999, for internal use only: see C Rijken (2001), p 593 *et seq*.

[121] The full text of these agreements can be found at <http://www.europol.europa.eu/index.asp?page=agreements>.

[122] See <http://www.europol.europa.eu/index.asp?page=agreements>. Europol has concluded two agreements with the United States, such as the Agreement between the USA and the European Police Office and the Supplemental Agreement between Europol and the USA on Exchange of Personal Data and Related Information.

and Turkey. Furthermore, Europol concluded one operational agreement with Interpol[123] and two strategic agreements, with the World Customs Organization[124] and the United Nations Office on Drugs and Crime.[125]

A similar procedure with a similar role of the director of Europol is provided for the negotiation of agreements with EU bodies.[126] As far as EU bodies are concerned, an operational agreement has been concluded with Eurojust and strategic agreements have been concluded with the ECB, the European Commission, the European Monitoring Centre for Drugs and Drug Addiction, OLAF, and Frontex.[127]

In conclusion, it seems that the discretionary (and at times far from 'intergovernmental') power enjoyed by the director of Europol in such circumstances appears to be far-reaching, despite the existence of formal moments of Council authorization and control. It is not excluded that in some instances directors of EU agencies may to some extent be considered as wielding some de facto 'supranational power'.[128] Just like the Commission with regard to the content of the draft decisions agreed upon by committees of scientific experts with the explicit and detailed technical expertise in a given area (for example in the context of the EMEA),[129] one cannot easily imagine that the Council is in a position to second-guess or change the content of detailed and specific negotiations with a third state. So the formal Council 'control' can be analysed in terms of a formal rubber-stamping exercise so that the Council's responsibility is not completely shifted to an organ that has to date operated outside the formal framework of the treaties as such (recalling the *Meroni* case law).

6.4.5 What's in a name? 'European regulatory agencies'

The Commission has already been advocating for some years now the further intensification—and expansion—of what it terms 'European regulatory agencies' in the not-so-distant future.[130] Yet there is no evidence to date that despite

[123] Agreement between Interpol and Europol concluded 5 November 2001, see <http://www.europol.europa.eu/legal/agreements/Agreements/8890.pdf>.

[124] Cooperation Agreement between the World Customs Organization (WCO) and the European Police Office (EUROPOL), 13 June 2002, OJ 2000/C106/01.

[125] Cooperation Agreement between the United Nations Office on Drugs and Crime and the European Police Office, concluded 16 March 2004.

[126] Act of the Management Board of Europol of 15 October 1998 laying down the rules governing Europol's external relations with European Union-related bodies, OJ C 026 (30 January 1999) p 89–90.

[127] The full text of all agreements mentioned is available at: <http://www.europol.europa.eu/index.asp?page=agreements>.

[128] See further M Busuioc and M Groenleer (2008), 'Wielders of supranational power? The administrative behaviour of the heads of European Union agencies', Paper presented at the ECPR Standing Group on Regulatory Governance, 5–7 June Utrecht.

[129] See, for example, Joined Cases T-74, 76, 83, 85, 132, 137, 141/00, *Artegodan GmBH v Commission* [2002] ECR II-4945.

[130] See communication of 12 December 2002, 'The operating framework for the European regulatory agencies', COM (2002) 718 final.

the name the Commission envisages the creation of real regulatory agencies US-style. Rather, there still seems to be fuzzy thinking on what is exactly the nature and purpose of the so-called EU 'regulatory agencies'.[131] They are sometimes called 'traditional agencies', because of their long-standing nature and, sometimes, 'decentralized agencies' because they are spread around Europe. They are independent bodies with their own legal personality. Most are funded by the EU budget—as well as, in some cases, by the direct receipt of fees or payments.

In its White Paper on Governance in 2001 the Commission flagged the fact that in its view there was (in addition) a need for more independent and autonomous structures in the form of European regulatory agencies that would be delegated with certain specific (discretionary) regulatory functions.[132] In this context, the use of the term 'regulatory' is to denote activities that 'do not necessarily involve the adoption of legal acts. They may also involve measures of a more incentive nature, such as co-regulation, self-regulation, recommendations, referral to the scientific authority, networking and pooling good practice, evaluating the application and implementation of rules etc.'[133] Regulatory agencies in the US, on the other hand, may have (much) more far-reaching powers in relation to specific sectors.[134] Yet in 2002 in a 'communication', the Commission defined (EU) 'regulatory agencies' as 'actively involved in exercising the executive function by enacting instruments which contribute to regulating a specific sector'.[135]

One wonders whether the Commission is being disingenuous. Some agencies—in any event the European Aviation Safety Agency (EASA), the Office for Harmonization in the Internal Market (OHIM), and the Community Plant Variety Office (CPVO)—were from the relatively early days given the power to themselves adopt binding legal acts without any involvement by the Commission (rubber-stamping or otherwise).[136] More recently the EMEA joined the ranks of

[131] Communication from the Commission to the Council and the European Parliament, 'European agencies: The way forward', COM (2008) 135, 11 March 2008. See too the 'Draft inter-institutional agreement on the operating framework for the European regulatory agencies', COM (2005) 59, final. See further, as to the terminological used, CA Stephanou, (2006), 'La nouvelle gouvernance Européenne: bilan et perspectives', *Cahiers de droit Européen* (No 1–2), pp 581–627, p 620.

[132] 'The White Paper on European Governance of 25 July 2001', COM (2001) 428 final, p 24.

[133] Commission, 'Draft inter-institutional agreement on the operating framework for the European regulatory agencies', COM (2005) 59 final, 25 February 2005, para 7.1.

[134] D Gerardin (2004), 'The development of European regulatory agencies: What the EU should learn from American experience', Columbia J of European L, 11, pp 1–52, p 39.

[135] COM (2002) 718 final, 11 December 2002.

[136] I am grateful to Madalina Busuioc for drawing these examples to my attention. See further her forthcoming book (2010), *The Accountability of EU Agencies. Legal Provisions and Ongoing Practices*, forthcoming. It concerns in particular what are known as 'non-validations', the final act of procedure prior to a decision and entailing no role for the Commission. These were challenged in two cases before the CFI: Case T-123/00 *Thomae v Commission* [2002] ECR II-5193 and Case T-133/03 *Schering–Plough v Commission and the EMEA*, order of 5 December 2007, nyr. In both cases the Court adopted the subterfuge that the decision in question (the so-called non-validation) was adopted by the Commission despite the fact that this was patently not the case, as

these 'regulatory' agencies (to use the Commission's rather specific terminology). Does the fact of transfer of decision-making authority to these agencies mean that the *Meroni* line of case law is breached? On the one hand, this very delegation of powers has been explicitly approved by the legislator and is not a question of internal delegation by the Commission itself, so on this ground the facts can be distinguished with *Meroni* albeit not from two other cases: *Romano*[137] and *Alliance for Natural Health*.[138]

The fact remains that an actual transfer of responsibility might be considered to have taken place, de facto, from the Commission to the agencies in question, albeit with the explicit approval of the EU legislator.[139] The result is nonetheless that such agencies (unlike what would have been the case with regard to the Commission) are, in theory at any rate, simply not subject to the constraints and protections offered in the treaties. There is, prima facie, no direct remedy and no access to justice for individuals to challenge the decisions of such agencies that they are unhappy with because they are 'not one of the bodies referred to in Article 230 EC, whose acts may be challenged'.[140] Of course, if the Treaty of Lisbon enters into force this significant and salient treaty lacuna will be filled.[141] In the meantime and pending this constitutional tidying-up exercise the Court of First Instance (CFI) has ruled to largely the same effect, at least where the delegated power enables an agency (not envisaged in the treaty) to adopt measures with legal effects on third parties.[142] This judgment rather radically alters the prospects for individuals affected by decisions of agencies. In one fell swoop (if upheld by the Court of Justice) they are granted a judicial remedy and access to justice. The CFI held that an action for annulment brought on the basis of the fourth paragraph of Art 230 TEC against an act of the European Agency for Reconstruction (not mentioned in Art 230 TEC) was admissible. It took this rather radical, and certainly 'activist', step to fill what otherwise would have been

otherwise there would have been no judicial remedy and the decision would fall through the rule of law sieve. This approach changed rather radically with the CFI's more recent judgment in Case T-411/06 *Sogelma v European Agency for Reconstruction (EAR)*, judgment of 8 October 2008. Here the CFI held that the action was admissible as an action for annulment brought on the basis of the fourth paragraph of Art 230 EC against an act of the EAR (not mentioned in Art 230 EC). It took this rather radical and certainly 'activist' step to fill what otherwise would have been a 'legal vacuum'. Under the motto that any act of a Community body intended to produce legal effects vis-à-vis third parties had to be open to judicial review, despite any delegation of powers that had de facto taken place. It remains to be seen what happens on appeal.

[137] Case 98/80 *Giuseppe Romano v Institut national d'assurance maladie-invalidite* [1981] ECR 1241.

[138] Cases C-154–155/04 *The Queen, on the application of Alliance for Natural Health and Nutri-link Ltd v Secretary of State for Health* [2005] ECR I -6541, para 90.

[139] See further on this point, S Griller and A Orator (2007) '*Meroni* revisited: Empowering European agencies between efficiency and legitimacy', *NewGov-4/D40*, available at <http://www.eu-newgov.org/database/DELIV/D04D40_WP_Meroni_Revisited.pdf>.

[140] Case T-133/03 *Schering–Plough v Commission and the EMEA* (n 138 above), para 16.

[141] See Art 263 TFEU.

[142] Case T-411/06 *Sogelma v European Agency for Reconstruction (EAR)*, judgment of 8 October 2008.

a 'legal vacuum'. Under the motto that any act of a Community body intended to produce legal effects vis-à-vis third parties had to be open to judicial review, despite any delegation of powers that had de facto taken place. In other words, on my reading, the Court is giving a new twist to the *Meroni* line of case law by taking a stance of legal realism in the sense that it recognizes what is happening in practice and refuses to accept that the result can deprive individuals affected of their right to a judicial remedy. Perhaps it contains the seed of the *sotto voce* recognition that the principle of institutional balance may be evolving in ways that were inconceivable back in 1958 and that the Court (the CFI at any rate) would act so as to address the underlying concerns behind the Court's classic jurisprudence.

6.4.6 Powers of European regulatory agencies

According to the Commission, regulatory agencies 'are required to be actively involved in the executive function by enacting instruments which help to regulate a specific sector'.[143] The intention is that regulatory agencies will enact regulatory instruments subject to a general framework of conditions governing their creation, operation, and supervision.[144] The specific intention is that certain of these regulatory agencies will be empowered to adopt individual decisions binding on third parties in the specified policy area. The Commission in fact acknowledges this in its definition 'European Regulatory Agencies' as it envisages they already exist.[145] Among existing agencies we find some that are empowered to adopt individual decisions that are legally binding on third parties (for example, the Office for Harmonization in the Internal Market, Community Plant Variety Office, the European Aviation Safety Agency, the European Agency for Reconstruction, and the European Chemicals Agency, in addition to the Agency for the Cooperation of Energy Regulators under construction) as well as those that primarily provide assistance in the form of opinions and recommendations, which give the technical and scientific basis for the Commission's decisions (for example, the European Agency for the Evaluation of Medicinal Products and the European Food Safety Authority).[146] In other words, new-style 'regulatory agencies' as conceptualized by the Commission already exist: at least four decision-making agencies and six agencies performing operational tasks.[147]

[143] Commission Communication of 12 December 2002, 'The operating framework for the European regulatory agencies', COM (2002) 718 final, p 4.

[144] See further Communication from the Commission to the European Parliament and the Council, 'European agencies: The way forward', COM (2008) 135 final, 11 March 2008.

[145] See further Report by the Working Group 'Establishing a framework for decision-making regulatory agencies' (Group 3a). Preparation of Commission White Paper on Governance, available at <http://ec.europa.eu/governance/areas/group6/report_en.pdf>.

[146] See further F Comte (2008), 'Agences européennes: relance d'une réflexion interinstitutionelle européenne', *Revue du Droit de l'Union Européenne*, 3, pp 461–506.

[147] Ibid, p 477, for overview.

Within all these agencies, of whatever kind and generation, there are often (considerable) differences as to their internal structures and their relations with the Commission in particular. According to the Commission 'agencies have proved particularly relevant in the field of shared competences when the implementation of new policies at Community level needs to be accompanied by close cooperation between the Member States and the EU. The establishment of agencies can make possible a pooling of powers to EU level which would be resisted if centred on the institutions themselves.'[148] For example, prior to the establishment of EMEA or OHIM, marketing authorizations for medicinal products were delivered and trademarks were registered by national bodies rather than the Commission.[149] To the extent that there is a delegation, it involves a vertical transfer of powers (from the national to the EU level) rather than a horizontal one (from Community institutions to specialized agencies). Another example is provided by the Community Fisheries Control Agency.[150] According to its website, it is 'a new European Union body established in 2005 to organize operational coordination of fisheries control and inspection activities by the Member States and to assist them to cooperate so as to comply with the rules of the Common EU Fisheries Policy in order to ensure its effective and uniform application'.[151]

In the case of the European Agency for the Management of Operational Cooperation at the External Borders (FRONTEX)[152] it can be argued that the Council did not delegate its own existing executive powers but rather that the tasks in question had been largely exercised by the Member States and not the Council (or the Commission). At the same time the agency replaces, in a sense, much of the fragmentary and opaque structures that were attached to the Council in one form or another, for example the Common Unit for external border practitioners (SCIFA) that was a Council working party.[153] Perhaps it is the latter fact that explains why, despite being proposed by the Commission, the institutional design of the agency is very much leaning towards the Council as principal. In any event, it is rather clear that the agency has been given (delegated) quite far-reaching powers, including operational powers and in the future 'tasking the Agency with the carrying out of inspections at external borders and the facilitation of operational cooperation with

[148] Communication from the Commission to the European Parliament and the Council, 'European agencies: The way forward', COM (2008) 135 final, 11 March 2008, p 5.

[149] These examples are cited by R Dehousse (2008).

[150] Council Regulation (EC) No 768/2005 of 26 April 2005 establishing a Community Fisheries Control Agency and amending Regulation (EEC) No 2847/93 establishing a control system applicable to the common fisheries policy, OJ L 128 (21 May 2005), p 0001–14.

[151] <http://ec.europa.eu/cfca/index_en.htm>.

[152] Council Regulation (EC) No 2007/2004 of 26 October 2004 establishing a European Agency for the Management of Operational Cooperation at the External Borders of the Member States of the European Union, OJ L 349, 25 November 2004.

[153] See further S Peers (2006), *EU Justice and Home Affairs Law* (Oxford: Oxford University Press).

relevant third countries and international organizations' is explicitly envisaged (recital 19).[154]

What seems to be involved in the construction of such control agencies is the 'Europeanization' of the functions of the administrations of the Member States rather than the delegation of the powers of the Commission authorities as such.[155] In that sense, such agencies go considerably further that the mandate given by the Financial Regulation[156] to the Commission to entrust tasks, when it shares administration, to national public-sector bodies, to bodies governed by private law with a public-service mission guaranteed by the State,[157] as well as to purely private-sector entities with tasks involving technical expertise and administrative, preparatory, or ancillary tasks involving neither the exercise of public authority nor the use of discretionary judgment.[158]

6.4.7 Full speed ahead

The European Parliament supports the Commission's call for specific new inter-institutional initiatives (no formal inter-institutional agreement but an inter-institutional 'declaration' with a similar 'horizontal' ambition) and indeed an inter-institutional working party seems to have been set up and a new 'meta-evaluation' planned of the agency system.[159] Despite so much evaluation in progress the march towards new agencies apparently continues unabated: at least four more are in the pipeline. These seem to include, in any event, the following 'regulatory'-type agencies, with the power in some instances to take binding decisions: an Agency for the Cooperation of Energy Regulators[160] and the European Electronic Communications Market Authority.[161] In addition it

[154] See, in general on FRONTEX, <http://www.frontex.europa.eu>.

[155] See, for example, G Majone and M Everson (2001), 'Institutional reform: Independent agencies, oversight, coordination and procedural control' in O de Schutter, N Lebessis, and J Paterson (eds), *Governance in the European Union* (Luxembourg: Office for Official Publications of the European Union), pp 129–68.

[156] Council Regulation (EC, Euratom) No 1605/2002 of 25 June 2002 on the Financial Regulation applicable to the general budget of the European Communities, OJ L 248, 16 September 2002, vol 45, pp 0001–48. See further P Craig (2003), 'The constitutionalisation of Community administration', European L Rev, 28, pp 840–64.

[157] Council Regulation 1605/2002 (n 158 above), Art 54(2c).

[158] Council Regulation 1605/2002 (n 158 above), Art 57(2).

[159] A first meta-evaluation on the Community Agency system was published in September 2003 by the Budget Directorate General of the Commission, <http://ec.europa.eu/budget/library/documents/evaluation/eval_review/meta_eval_agencies_en.pdf>. This meta-evaluation focused only on the so-called Community agencies; the forthcoming second meta-evaluation forthcoming in 2009–10 will presumably provide horizontal examination of all the agencies (including Union agencies). See further F Comte (2001), p 491.

[160] COM (2007) 530 final, <http://eur-lex.europa.eu/LexUriServ/LexUriServ.do?uri=COM:2007:0530:FIN:EN:PDF>. See Council Common Position of 15 December 2008, <http://register.consilium.europa.eu/pdf/en/08/st14/st14541.en08.pdf>.

[161] COM (2007) 699 final, <http://ec.europa.eu/prelex/detail_dossier_real.cfm?CL=en&DosId=196420>.

seems that the Commission is planning further agencies in the field of justice and home affairs, in particular an agency with operational tasks on SIS II (Schengen Information System[162]) and other linked systems.[163] An Asylum Support 'Office' is in the offing.[164] There does not therefore seem to be any deceleration in the ongoing ad hoc process of ever-more EU-level agencies—including the category that can take decisions intended to produce legal effects vis-à-vis third parties. Quite the contrary—one can detect both institutional acceleration and intensity in terms of the types of functions envisaged as well as the powers granted (or in the process of being granted). This is particularly the case it seems with regard to the Commission proposals for what can be termed the 'European Regulatory Network Agencies'.[165] It seems in this context that the 'voice' of the European Parliament is getting louder with its substantial amendments of the energy agency in particular amounting to a not inconsiderable expansion of powers (including the power putatively to adopt general binding measures).[166] This is evidence of the further, incremental growth of the largely unseen hands of European integration in processes that are not terribly visible or coherent from an overall constitutional perspective.

6.5 Satellite Networks of Actors

6.5.1 Shared administration with 'double-hatted' national partners

Traditionally, administrative action is associated with implementation of policies defined in legislation and in the context of the EU this involves actors (public administrations) both at the central EU level and at the de-central Member

162 Council Decision 2008/839/JHA of 24 October 2008 on migration from the Schengen Information System (SIS 1+) to the second generation Schengen Information System (SIS II), OJ L 299/43 (8 November 2008). See further, European Commission (2006b), Communication from the Commission to the European Parliament and the Council, 'An area of freedom, security and justice serving the citizen', COM (2009) 262/4, para 4.2.3.2.

163 F Comte, (2008) p 492

164 See further Council of Justice and Home Affairs, 18 April 2008, that explicitly 'invite[s] the Commission to come forward in the near future with proposals to provide adequate support for practical cooperation activities between Member States, including the creation of an Asylum Support Office which would provide for adequate structural and financial backing in order to guarantee the level of ambition necessary to complete the Common European Asylum System': <http://europa.eu/rapid/pressReleasesAction.do?reference=IP/08/607&format=HTML&aged=0&language=EN&guiLanguage=en>.

165 See further S Lavrijssen and L Hancher (2008) ' Networks on track: From European regulatory networks to European regulatory "network agencies" ', Legal Issues of Economic Integration, 34/1, pp 23–55.

166 European Parliament, Committee on Industry, Research and Energy, on the proposal for a regulation of the European Parliament and of the Council establishing an Agency for the Cooperation of Energy Regulators, of 11 February 2008, PE400.717v01–00. See too, European Commission, 'Communication from the Commission to the European Parliament concerning the common position of the Council on the adoption of a Regulation of the European Parliament and of the Council establishing an Agency for the Cooperation of Energy Regulators', COM (2008) 908 final.

State level. Indirect implementation portrays the Union as a system in which the constituent states are integrated into a larger whole as coherent entities. Such administration has in particular been central to the implementation of such areas as the Common Agricultural Policy (the CAP) and the Structural Funds where the sums involved may be considerable. In the definition provided by the Committee of Independent Experts, shared management is the 'management of those Community programmes where the Commission and the Member States have distinct administrative tasks which are inter-dependent and set down in legislation and where both the Commission and the national administrations need to discharge their respective tasks for the Community policy to be implemented successfully'. This is quite a traditional view of the applicable model as being that of 'executive federalism', which in the view of some authors needs modification on several counts in the reality of today's EU political system.[167]

In the reality of today's EU system of administrative governance there is, however, intensive cooperation of administration in all phases of the policy cycle from agenda-setting over decision-making to implementation of policies.[168] In some instances this has led to what is termed 'integrated administration' encompassing both the European and national levels and suggesting that there is no rigid separation anymore between these levels.[169] The term 'Europe's integrated administration' takes on board the situation where in contemporary European integration processes the traditional distinction of direct and indirect administration has become blurred with the levels being interwoven to form a more unitary pattern of 'integrated administration'.[170] The factual integration of European and national administrations is in any event occurring with a level of intensity not necessarily recognized in administrative law and public administration/political science literature on the subject.

The EU level is also involved in implementing activities undertaken by member state authorities, while Member States' administrations are involved in creating EU legislation and implementing acts.[171] Case studies within five different policy fields (competition, telecoms, food safety, environment, and statistics) have shown that national agencies in fact seem to act in a 'double-hatted' manner; constituting parts of national administrations while at the same time becoming parts of a multilevel Union administration in which the Commission in

[167] H Hofmann and A Türk (2007), 'The development of integrated administration in the EU and its consequences', European LJ, 13/2, pp 253–71.

[168] See further T Gross (2005), 'Die Kooperation zwischen europäischen Agenturen und nationalen Behörden', *Europarecht*, 1, pp 54–68.

[169] See further H Hofmann and A Turk (2006), *EU Administrative Governance* (Cheltenham: Edgar Elgar).

[170] See further, ibid.

[171] This section draws on D Curtin and M Egeberg (2008) 'Tradition and innovation: Europe's accumulated executive order', *West European Politics*, 31/4, pp 639–61.

particular forms the 'hub'.[172] As parts of national administrations, serving their respective ministerial departments, agency officials seem to play a crucial role in transposition of EU legislation as well as in Council working parties and comitology committees. However, when it comes to the application of EU legislation in particular, agencies also cooperate rather closely with their respective directorates in the Commission, often by-passing their ministerial departments.[173] Not surprisingly, in this situation agencies may face competing policy expectations from two 'masters' that may be hard to reconcile. 'Double-hattedness' entails new patterns of cooperation and conflict in executive politics, evoking conflicts that cut across national boundaries as well. It could also be expected to lead to more even implementation across countries compared to indirect implementation, although not as even as if the Commission had its own agencies or if the application of EU law was in the hands of EU-level bodies.

There are varying degrees of formality in the different types of networks incorporating 'double-hatted' agents of one kind or another. Even rather informal networks can lead to more homogenous implementation but at the same time can challenge institutional balance at the EU level.[174] This is part of a wider trend towards developing networked administrative structures in which national and European level institutions create closer cooperative arrangements.[175] It seems that even informal and weak institutionalization can have effects on actors' behaviours (and dilemmas).[176]

An example of a rather institutionalized form of 'double-hatting' is the role of national competition authorities in applying the EU rules on competition 'in close cooperation' with the Commission.[177] The European Competition Network (ECN) has been established in Regulation 1/2003 and provides for rather detailed cooperation among the national authorities in the exercise of their duties under the EU competition rules.[178] This network includes among its members also those national competition authorities that enjoy quasi-judicial

172 See further M Egeberg (2008), 'European government(s): Executive politics in transition?, *West European Politics*, 31/4, pp 235–57, p 247.

173 M Egeberg and J Trondal (2007), 'National agencies in the European administrative space: Government driven, commission driven or networked?', in M Egeberg (ed), *Institutional Dynamics and the Transformation of Executive Politics in Europe* (Mannheim: CONNEX Report Series No 3).

174 See further M Martens, 'Double-hatted agencies on the European scene? A case study of the IMPEL network', ARENA Working Paper 05/12.

175 See too HP Graver (2002), 'National implementation of EU law and the shaping of European administrative policy', ARENA Working Paper 02/17.

176 This fits in with the findings from 'institutionalist' literature. See, in general, J March and JP Olsen (1989), *Rediscovering Institutions: The organizational basis of politics* (New York: Free Press).

177 See, for further details, the European Commission site on the European Competition Network, <http://ec.europa.eu/comm/competition/ecn/index_en.html>.

178 See further Council Regulation (EC) No 1/2003 of 16 December 2002 on the implementation of the rules on competition laid down in Arts 81–2 of the Treaty, OJ L 1, 4 January 2003, p 1–25.

functions in the enforcement of competition law giving rise to a distinctive kind of 'double-hatting'. In addition to formal consultations in individual cases pursuant to the terms of Regulation 1/2003[179] the ECN also seeks to encourage a regular exchange of views between the national competition authorities among themselves and between them and the Commission.[180]

The role played by the Commission in this new decentralized system of competition law enforcement is still that of the predominant actor in the system with the national authorities 'obliged' to, inter alia, provide certain types of information to the Commission and with certain 'surveillance' type rights. Brammer highlights in her detailed work on the subject the fact that 'Regulation 1/2003 marks a new form of administrative execution (*Verwaltungsvollzug*) in which a Community institution (the Commission) and Member States authorities (the national competition authorities) fully share the responsibility to enforce primary Community law (Articles 81 and 82 EC)'.[181] At the same time the national competition authorities exercise their duties and tasks under national competition legislation and by virtue of the rules and procedures laid down in the national legal context. The ECN is an elaborate, interactive and intensive form of administrative cooperation both horizontally (among the national authorities themselves) and vertically (with the Commission) taking place on the basis of detailed rules in a highly institutionalized manner.[182] It would be hard to dispute the assessment that such networks are properly regarded as one part of shared administration in the EU.[183]

6.5.2 EU networks of actors

Networked implementation means that vertical relationships between, on the one hand, national agencies and, on the other hand, ministerial departments, Commission directorates or EU-level agencies are complemented by horizontal relationships among 'sister agencies' in various countries. A national agency may see itself as part of a transnational network of institutions pursuing similar objectives and facing analogous problems.[184] Thus, the actual amount of discretion that national agencies exercise when implementing EU legislation might be circumscribed in practice through information exchange and consultation among 'sister agencies' rather than through 'steering dialogues' with 'superior' bodies. In this sense, strong agency networks could challenge the authority of

[179] Arts 11(3)–(4) and 12 of Regulation 1/2003.

[180] See further S Brammer (2009), *Co-operation between National Competition Agencies in the Enforcement of EC Competition Law* (Oxford: Hart Publishing). See too, M d Visser (2008), *Network-based Governance in EC Law. The example of EC competition law and EC communications law* (Nijmegen: Wolf Legal Publishers).

[181] Ibid, p 462. [182] Ibid.

[183] See, more generally, P Craig, (2009) 'Shared administration and networks: Global and EU perspectives' in G Anthony, J-B Auby, J Morison and T Zwart (eds), *Values in Global Administrative Law*, forthcoming.

[184] G Majone (1996), *Regulating Europe* (London: Routledge); A-M Slaughter (2004), *A New World Order* (Princeton: Princeton University Press).

national governments as well as that of EU-level bodies. It follows that such networks might enhance implementation uniformity across member states, however not necessarily in accordance with the intentions of the politically superior institutions.

In order to enhance its control, the Commission has itself initiated the creation of such networks in some instances, as in the telecom sector,[185] with regard to competition[186] or in the education area.[187] It is, in practice, very often what Craig terms the 'institutional orchestrator' behind the establishment of many of the EU networks.[188] However, the EU executive has also successfully linked into already-existing networks that have been relatively independent in the past[189] but for which it has gradually taken over the coordinating functions, as seems to be the case for the implementation network of pollution authorities.[190] Thatcher and Coen observed that, over time, networks have become gradually more institutionalized and centralized around EU-level bodies, in particular the Commission.[191]

There are other networks that operate in areas where the EU does not have well defined or only (very) reduced competences, some of which do in fact enjoy (formal) rule-making powers. This is the case of the Committee of European Securities Regulators (CESR) that operates in the area of financial securities.[192] This committee advises the Commission and is responsible for convergence. This enables the Commission to directly participate in the coordination of national regulators without the mediation of Member States' governments.[193] The sheer scale of CESR's influence over EC financial market regulation is only now becoming apparent.[194] CESR's advice is heavily influential on the shape of

[185] GH Nørgård (2006), 'National limits to transnational networking? The case of the Danish IT and Telecom Agency' in M Egeberg (ed), *Multilevel Union Administration: The transformation of executive politics in Europe* (Basingstoke: Palgrave Macmillan).

[186] On the European Competition Network in general, see JS Venit (2003), 'Brave New World: The modernization and decentralization of enforcement under Articles 81 and 82 of the EC Treaty', Common Market L Rev, 40/3, pp 545–80.

[187] A Gornitzka (2008), 'Networking administration in areas of national sensitivity: The Commission and European higher education' in A Amaral et al (eds), *European Integration and the Governance of Higher Education and Research* (Dordrecht: Springer).

[188] P Craig (2009).

[189] B Eberlein and G Grande (2005), 'Beyond delegation: Transnational regulatory regimes and the EU regulatory state', *Journal of European Public Policy*, 12, pp 89–112, pp 101–2.

[190] M Martens (2006), 'National regulators between Union and governments: A Study of the EU's environmental policy network IMPEL' in M Egeberg (ed), *Multilevel Union Administration: The transformation of executive politics in Europe* (Basingstoke: Palgrave Macmillan), pp 124–42.

[191] M Thatcher and D Coen (2008), 'Reshaping European regulatory space: An evolutionary analysis', *West European Politics*, 31/4, pp 806–36.

[192] See further W Van Gerven (2005), *The European Union: A polity of states and peoples* (Oxford: Hart Publishing).

[193] See further C de Visscher, O Maiscocq, and F Varone (2008), 'The Lamfalussy Reform in the EU securities markets: Fiduciary relationships, policy effectiveness and balance of power', *Journal of Public Policy*, 28/1, pp 19–47.

[194] See further N Molony (2007), 'The view from the financial markets: Institutional risks to law-making for the EC financial market in the post-FSAP environment', Paper presented at the Irish European Law Forum, 19 January 2007.

measures being adopted by the Commission. Even more significantly (in what is known in the field as level 3) CESR is increasingly exercising direct influence over the financial markets without the filter of Commission and Parliament oversight, as its powers are considered non-binding. This is not the place for a detailed description, merely a marker as to how entities like this grow incrementally and acquire real influence and powers, albeit putatively in a non-binding (soft) fashion. CESR's range of activities is becoming formidable as its 2005 annual report makes clear: it notes that 2006 'would witness CESR's metamorphosis from being primarily a regulatory advisory body to becoming a body which is well on its way to becoming an operational network of supervisors'.[195] This—independent[196]—body is created by and given functions in the context of the core of the EC internal financial market and there are huge rule of law— and democratic— implications here.[197]

The same phenomenon seems to be emerging more widely also in the context of for example police cooperation and law enforcement. In this latter context it is more the Council that has a steering role by drafting EU legal instruments to impose obligations on (specific) national regulatory and other authorities so that they can cooperate together more closely and exchange information more readily and adopt rules or enforce rules, as the case may be, according to the needs of specific policy fields. The EU thus embraces enforcement networks of parts of national administrations that are formally empowered at the EU level to carry out certain tasks or to exchange information. For example, the network of law enforcement authorities of the Member States are in the process of being formally empowered in the equivalent of a 'directive' (a Council framework decision) to exchange information and intelligence between them under certain conditions. In other words, we are seeing the nascent beginnings of a process of 'disaggregating' the various Member State functions–legislative, adjudicative, and executive—and a joining-up of disaggregated counterparts at the transnational level in close partnership with the supranational institutions (both the Commission and the Council, as the case may be). This is now being carried a step further with the new 'Lamfalussy'-type agencies, currently under construction, the so-called network agencies.[198]

Finally, cooperative and informal networks may be set up bottom-up by various national actors themselves. A good example is the network of national

[195] CESR Annual Report (2005), foreword by Chairman.

[196] The CESR Annual Report (2004) describes CESR as 'an independent Committee of European Securities Regulators'. The foundation decision establishing CESR simply requires CESR to present an annual report to the Commission and to maintain close operational links with the Commission and the ESC.

[197] See too W van Gerven (2006), 'Closing the accountability gap: And the rule of law', unpublished manuscript on file with author. See too KU Schmolle (2006), 'Die Einbeziehung des Komitologieverfahrens in den Lamfalussy-Prozess: Zur Forderung des Europäischen Parlaments nach mehr Entscheidungsteilhabe', *Europarecht*, 3, pp 432–48.

[198] S Lavrijssen and L Hancher (2008).

parliaments both grouped in COSAC and outside of that context.[199] In the abeyance of the Lisbon Treaty and the formal legal framework that it provided empowering national parliaments to (quasi-collectively) produce a 'yellow card' or 'early warning' that planned EU legislation might breach the subsidiarity principle, the network of national parliaments is planning to, in practice and informally, do more or less the same anyway and thus bring considerable political pressure to bear on the Commission.[200] There are (information and enforcement) networks that, in principle, have a clear legal basis in the EU legal system such as the European Competition Network (ECN)[201] referred to above although it is clearly not an organ or agency of the EU (EC) as such.

Political scientists argue that no centre of decision-making can be located in a network; power is dispersed among more or less autonomous actors, decision-making is a negotiating process and 'government does not have enough power to exert its will on other actors'.[202] Lawyers have difficulty in coming to grips with their fluidity and lack of procedures and 'hard' (enforceable) results. Many European lawyers rather instinctively believe that European integration requires clear guidance, uniform treatment, sanctions to deter non-compliance, and justiciability and thus can only come about through hard treaty law and regulations and directives. Those who see merit in new governance and soft law question however the utility of traditional forms of hard law in the context of many of the issues confronting the EU today.[203] They prefer to provide a soft framework that accommodates diversity, facilitates mutual learning, spreads good practices, and fosters convergence towards EU goals.[204]

6.6 The Shadow of Hierarchy

It is well known from national political systems that the basic tenets of representative democracy are not (always) up to the range and complexity of tasks that modern governments now have to perform. This may be for a wide range of reasons including lack of time and lack of technical expertise. From a comparative

[199] See further P Kiiver (2005), *The National Parliaments in the European Union: A critical view on constitution-building* (Maastricht: Maastricht University).

[200] 'National parliaments to show Commission yellow card', 18 November 2005, <http://www.euobserver.com>.

[201] In general see JS Venit (2003).

[202] See further W Kickert (1993), 'Complexity, governance and dynamics: Conceptual explorations of network management' in J Kooiman (ed), *Modern Governance: New government–society interactions* (London: Sage), p 275. See also C Harlow and R Rawlings (2007), 'Promoting accountability in multilevel governance: A network approach', European LJ, 13/4, pp 542–62.

[203] CF Sabel and J Zeitlin (2008), 'Learning from difference: The new architecture of experimentalist governance in the EU', European LJ, 14/3, pp 271–327.

[204] See, for example, K Jacobsson and H Schmidt (2003), 'The European employment strategy at the crossroads: Contribution to the evaluation' in D Folden and L Magnusson (eds), *Five Years Experience of the Luxembourg Employment Strategy* (Brussels, ETUI).

perspective it is not surprising that the Commission has come to share executive functions with an increasing number of EU-level agencies since 'agencification' has taken place all over the Western world during the last couple of decades.[205] Of course the parallel with agencies in other jurisdictions should not be taken too far, especially with the powerful and genuinely 'regulatory' agencies that operate in, for example, the United States. This is not what we have in the context of the EU.

There may be some difficulty in relating the institutional practice that has evolved with regard to EC and EU agencies, particularly in recent years with what is still regarded as a foundation stone of the EU political and legal systems, the principle of 'institutional balance' emanating from the *Meroni* judgment in 1958. One has the impression from the Commission's to date rather futile attempts to 'order' more rationally the messy EU landscape and to exert some more structured means of control that the Commission feels that it is de facto losing influence. As we have seen from the results of the empirical work that has been undertaken to date, there is no coherent picture in this regard. In some cases some of the agencies may in certain regards be 'out of control'. Ultimately it will be up to the Court to decide this matter and possibly redefine the thrust of *Meroni* to fit with modern-day realities. It may have to do this sooner rather than later given the fact that the CFI has recently assumed jurisdiction where the legal acts of an Agency has effects on third parties even though this was not part of the original institutional design or intention.[206]

Is the *Meroni* line of case law being dismantled from within, invisibly, through empirical practice? Some legal scholars clearly think so.[207] However, the argument can also be made that *Meroni* is still good law[208] on the ground that the manner of construction of some of the newer agencies by the legislature is qualitatively different to the factual context of *Meroni*.[209] In the *Meroni* case the delegation was by the High Authority (the precursor of the Commission) of a treaty-based competence to two *private bodies*. In the contemporary EU landscape there is the construction (and not so much the 'delegation' in any strict sense) of public agencies of one kind or another but some with autonomous and discretionary 'decision-making' powers possessed by them alone (not formally rubber-stamped by the Commission or other 'principal'). The extent to which powers are being

[205] See further T Christiansen and P Lægreid (eds) (2006), *Autonomy and Regulation: Coping with agencies in the modern state* (Cheltenham: Edward Elgar).

[206] Case T-411/06 *Sogelma v European Agency for Reconstruction (EAR)*, judgment of 8 October 2008. See, too the pending case of Case T-264/07 *CSL Behring v Commission and EMEA*, action brought on 18 July 2007, OJ C 235, 6 October 2007, p 12.

[207] See too M Wittinger (2008), '"Europäische Satellitenen": Anmerkungen zum europäischen Agentur(un)wesen und zur Vereinbarkeit europäischer Agenturen mit dem Gemeinschaftsrecht', *Europarecht*, 5, pp 609–26, p 617.

[208] See, for example, S Griller and A Orator (2007).

[209] See too J Dutheil de la Rochere (2009), 'EU regulatory agencies: What future do they have?' in M Bulterman et al (eds) *Views of European Law from the Mountain*, (The Hague: Kluwer), pp 355–66, p 364.

'delegated' (or given) is coupled with 'a freedom to make assessments implying a wide discretionary power' may prove to be the crucial point.[210] Is the power of the existing 'regulatory' agencies to be considered as 'wide discretionary power' or not? This will depend on a factual analysis but with regard to EMEA, for example, the power of non-committal clearly implies discretionary power of some kind. It seems that it is the nature of the discretionary power that brings about 'an actual transfer of responsibility' which takes its exercise outside the context of the general treaty conditions (which do not apply to the agencies but only to the mentioned institutions and organs). But *whose* responsibility is the complex issue: is it that of the Commission, of the Council, of the EU legislator or of the Member States acting collectively? The many hands contribute to the confusion of the lines of responsibility for outcomes. And were the powers 'delegated' (or simply 'given') more extensive than those originally possessed? If these questions were answered positively then the spectre of 'integration by stealth' would be hard to avoid.[211] This would also be the case with regard to the external relations powers conferred on the directors of some EU agencies (in particular Europol).

With regard to new-style networks of actors it is clear that they are an important feature by now of the broader administrative landscape in the EU. They can be considered part of the shared or composite administration of the EU and the Member States: they too are 'betwixt and between'. Concerns can and are raised as to their overall structural visibility in the system as a whole. In particular their links with the normal (European or national) democratic circuit may be considered weak. Yet even in the context of a more general debate on accountability of global (and European) networks, this is considered the crucial challenge: to engage in a process of more loose (and institutionally innovative) coupling of such networks and what can be referred to as the normal democratic circuit.[212] The shadow of hierarchy and of central political actors cannot, it seems, be factored out of the equation with regard to a range of 'satellite' actors in orbit around the more central parts of the political and administrative process.[213] Chapter 10 will return more explicitly to the theme of democratic legitimacy by way of offering some concluding reflections.

[210] Cases T-369/94 and 85/95 *DIR International Film Srl and others v Commission,* [1998] ECR II-357, para 52.

[211] G Majone (2005), *Dilemmas of European Integration: The ambiguities and pitfalls of integration by stealth* (Oxford: Oxford University Press).

[212] See further, Y Papadopoulos (2007), 'Problems of Democratic Accountability in Network and Multilevel Governance', *European Law Journal,* 13 (4), pp 469–486.

[213] See, in general, A Héritier and D. Lemkuhl (2008), 'Introduction: The Shadow of Hierarchy and New Modes of Governance', *Journal of Public Policy,* (28) 1, pp 1–17.

PART III

A LIVING EU CONSTITUTION

7

Unitary Executive Power

7.1 Framing the Living Executive

In Chapter 1 the metaphor of geology, and more particularly of sedimentation, was used to describe a process of an accumulation of layers of 'deposits' being piled upon one another and involving the settling of solid particles from fluids. A very clear example of this phenomenon is provided by the manner in which the Court of Justice has in particular built upon the bare provisions of the Treaty of the EU and the pillarization explicitly laid down since the Treaty of Maastricht in order to construct what may be termed a principle of legal unity across the spectrum of the EU as a whole. This principle has both normative and institutional elements and applies above all in the context of the structurally fragmentary executive power that was put in place in the EU (in particular that of the Council and the Commission) in the aftermath of the Treaty of Maastricht. The term 'unitary' is not used in the sense of one executive power for the EU as a whole: we have seen from Part II of this book that the EU clearly has multiple sources and manifestations of executive power. Rather, the term 'unitary' refers above all to the construction by the Court of Justice in a line of case law of some general elements of normative unity stretching across the manner in which power was exercised across the various pillars. This is not only a linear development; there are also certainly examples where the Court felt that it could not construct a unitary narrative given the explicit wording of the treaties in particular.

The significance of the application of a unitary principle to the exercise of executive power in the current context is that in this way the Court also ensured that the primarily executive activities of the various institutions were subject to some balancing and checking possible under the modus of judicial review. That the originally loose construction of the EU did not evolve as a legal construct into a Europe of 'bits and pieces'[1] can, with the benefit of hindsight, be largely attributed to the role the Court of Justice has chosen to proactively play. Indeed its vision of a relatively unitary EU founded on a European notion of the 'rule of law' is acquiring rather specific content over the years, in particular in recent

[1] D Curtin (1993), 'The constitutional structure of the Union: A Europe of bits and pieces', Common Market L Rev, 30/1, pp 17–69.

cases. Fifteen years after the Maastricht Treaty declared that the pillars would be separate, the Lisbon Treaty in its Art 1 ordains that the Union 'shall replace and succeed the European Community'.[2] Legal unity is, it seems, the order of the day. In one fell swoop the systemic visibility and structural clarity of European integration processes is improved. At the same time, this catches up with social reality and the perception of citizens and third states already from the early days that the EU constitutes an organizational and legal unity.[3]

Article 1 of the Lisbon Treaty does not come out of the blue. On the contrary, a wide variety of legal and institutional 'practices' have over the course of the past 15 years knitted the putatively separate parts (pillars) of the legal and political systems of the EU much closer together. Processes of institutional isomorphism have, step by step, enabled various actors to put more supranational (*communautaire*) flesh and blood on what were certainly drafted as largely intergovernmental cooperation.[4] In some respects one could already speak for some years now of unity as the guiding *leitmotif* of an emerging EU legal system and EU political system. In a series of scholarly writings written largely towards the end of the 1990s the concept of legal unity was introduced and defined and the argument made already a decade ago that over and above the formal treaty provisions (and the various linkages therein) legal and institutional 'practices' at that time tended towards (more and more) 'unity', albeit largely 'in disguise' as it was called at that time.[5] Since then, such practices have become much more visible—both individually and structurally—largely thanks to the case law of the Court of Justice in that regard.

Through the medium of its case law, both in the generic field of 'justice and home affairs' (the so-called 'third pillar') and of security and defence issues (the so-called 'second pillar') the Court has breathed life into the living and evolving constitution, in a manner that some may well consider was explicitly not the intention of the treaty framers at the time.[6] Indeed the spectre of 'contamination' over and across these quite distinct issue areas was precisely what the lawyers and

[2] Art 1 TEU.

[3] See further D Curtin and IF Dekker, (1999) 'The EU as a "layered" international organization: Institutional unity in disguise?' in P Craig and G De Búrca (eds), *The Evolution of EU Law* (Oxford: Oxford University Press), pp 83–137.

[4] RA Wessel (2009), 'The constitutional unity of the European Union: The irrelevance of the pillar structure?' in J Wouters, L Verhey, and P Kiiver (eds), *European Constitutionalism Beyond the EU Constitution* (Antwerpen: Intersentia), pp 283–306.

[5] See, for early references, D Curtin and IF Dekker (1999). See too RA Wessel (1999), *The European Union's Foreign and Security Policy: A legal institutional perspective* (The Hague: Kluwer Law International); A von Bogdandy (1999), 'The legal case for unity: The European Union as a single organization with a single legal system', Common Market L Rev, 36/5, pp 887–910. For more recent work see S Lucarelli (2007), 'The EU in the eyes of others: Towards filling a gap in the literature', *European Foreign Affairs Review*, 12/2, pp 249–70.

[6] For example, in Case C-14/08 *Roda Golf and Beach Resort SL*, Opinion of Advocate General Ruiz-Jatabo Colomer of 5 March 2009, nyr, where he opined that restrictions under Art 68 EC (different speed references for preliminary rulings in the area of justice and home affairs) 'may be relaxed when they are interpreted in the light of the principle of effective legal protection'.

politicians had sought to avoid. To put it in broad terms relating to the subject matter of this book, namely the executive power of the EU, the Court constructed interlocking branches between the different policy areas as well as overarching limitations that applied to the manner in which, above all, the executive power was exercised, pillar by pillar.

In adopting an approach that goes at times quite far beyond a literal and formal interpretation of the text of the treaties themselves, the Court seems to be inspired and motivated by its own fundamental points of self-reference: the need to ensure that law in the EU is capable of being interpreted and applied as much as possible across the wide spectrum of the (legislative, executive, and other) activities of the EU and that individuals enjoy access to justice (right to effective legal protection). In this manner the Court has fostered the construction of what can be termed a unitary executive power, a power that first emerged in the various legal and institutional practices of some of the key institutions, in particular the Commission and the Council and their evolving interrelationship and struggles as to their respective roles in the various 'pillars'. This more 'political' dimension has emerged in earlier chapters in particular in the context of the 'administrative' executive power in Chapter 5. But it must also be noted that 'legal' unity and more 'political' unity are almost inevitably communicating vessels: legal unity as it has evolved is not static but takes into account changing context and practices that make it easier for the Court to breathe life into the living executive and the living overarching constitution. And the manner in which the Court has imposed rules of 'higher law' on the EU executive power, in particular the Council of Ministers in the *Kadi* case, certainly reveals that the Court does not shy away from more political overtones to its legal findings. In this sense too, it is difficult to separate out the evolving legal system and the evolving political system. They are interrelated and interconnected in an almost symbiotic way.

7.2 The Court of Justice Uncovers Normative Unity

7.2.1 Depillarization through judicial review

As is well known, two different policy-making processes have coexisted within the outer layer of the EU from the very beginning. The more 'supranational' Community method predominated in the first pillar and the more 'intergovernmental' in the second and third pillars. These are characterized in broad lines by different legislative procedures and by distinctiveness in the role of the institutions, the typology of the instruments adopted, and their implementation and enforcement.[7] Looking back, some 15 years after its creation it was possible to draw this rather broad and generic distinction, although up until relatively

[7] See further RA Wessel (2009a).

recently it was more customary to isolate the hard-core EC as such and each of its flanking pillars quite separately. It is probably fair to say that the third pillar, with its focus on justice and home affairs and subsequently police and judicial cooperation, always occupied the middle ground (with more explicitly binding legal instruments, more judicial control, and explicit *passerelles* to the EC Treaty)[8] and the second pillar (common foreign and security policy, hereafter CFSP) was always the 'outlier'. With the Lisbon Treaty, the third pillar was absorbed more or less completely and the second pillar moved to the vacated 'middle ground'.[9] In the second pillar there will still be different legal instruments in the future to the normal or usual legal instruments in all other policy areas (regulations, directives, decisions). The Lisbon Treaty will rename joint actions and common positions as 'decisions'[10] and some authors argue that this is merely a change of title.[11] However, it must be noted that the specific use of the term 'decision' also in the CFSP context may potentially contribute to further unity and may be a reason for the Court to take them into account in future cases more often. After all, it can be assumed that all 'decisions' post entry into force of the Lisbon Treaty will have the same legal effect as they are based on the same treaty article, irrespective of their specific locus.[12] Given that what was previously the policy area 'police and judicial cooperation in criminal matters' (PJCC) will be more or less fully integrated with the Court's normal role once the Treaty of Lisbon enters into force,[13] the Court's 'unity' case law is unlikely to continue to remain salient in this regard.

In formal legal terms, the role of the Court was excluded completely only with regard to the subject matter of CFSP.[14] Even in that regard however the argument can be made that the Court of First Instance (CFI) has, in a number of relatively recent cases, interpreted the relevant (non-legislative) common positions adopted by the Council in detail in order to see whether the EU's autonomous

[8] For details see, for example, C Ladenburger (2008) 'Police and criminal law in the Treaty of Lisbon: A new dimension for the Community method', European Constitutional L Rev, 4/1, pp 20–40.

[9] JP Terhechte points out that the CFSP will thus be 'the Union's last policy area with a strong intergovernmental impetus' ('Die GASP wird damit zum letzten stark intergouvernemental geprägten Politikbereich'): JP Terhechte (2009), 'Artikel 11 EUV' in J Schwarze (ed), *EU-Kommentar*, 2nd edn (Baden-Baden: Nomos), pp 110–17, p 112.

[10] Art 25 TEU, Lisbon.

[11] See, for example, RA Wessel (2009b), 'The dynamics of the European Union legal order. An increasingly coherent framework of action and interpretation', European Constitutional L Rev, 1, pp 117–42.

[12] This argument that not only the title has changed is supported by the clause in the transitional protocol stating that all the existing second pillar measures remain valid until amended or repealed.

[13] There will still be a small distinction as regards the Court's police/criminal law jurisdiction. The Court will not be competent to review the proportionality of operations of the 'police or other law enforcement services' taken in order to maintain 'law and order' and the internal security: Art 276 TFEU. A transitional regime will also apply: see Art 10, Protocol 36, regarding transitional measures of the Treaty of Lisbon.

[14] Art 46 TEU.

antiterrorist lists are valid (see below).[15] This can be argued to imply a kind of implicit or indirect jurisdiction over second-pillar acts and provides an indication of the impact that second-pillar measures can have in judicial proceedings as regards the position of individuals.[16] The Court of Justice recently assumed a similar kind of implied or indirect jurisdiction over the acts of agencies with effects on third parties where there constitutive instrument has not done so-and irrespective of the fact that the treaty currently gives the Court no explicit jurisdiction in this regard.[17] It seems to be the fact that measures can have effects on or impose obligations on individuals that is a key element in the rather active assumption of jurisdiction over the behaviour of executive actors.[18] Both lines of case law provide interesting examples of the Court of Justice and the CFI filling in the lacuna in terms of the legal protection of individuals. In the *Segi* case the Court of Justice ruled similarly that third pillar 'common positions could not validly bind individuals and if they occasioned legal effects for third parties they would have to be the subject of judicial review by the Court', despite explicit treaty wording to the contrary.[19] On the contrary, the right to make a reference to the Court of Justice for a preliminary ruling 'must therefore exist in respect of all measures adopted by the Council, whatever their nature or form, which are intended to have legal effects in relation to third parties'.[20] In other words, the very fact that a legal instrument (*in casu* a common position) has a scope going beyond what was permissible meant that it had to be subjected to judicial review.

The Lisbon Treaty still provides that the Court of Justice does not have jurisdiction on CFSP matters and the only obligation in future is, in parallel with the previously existing Art 47 TEU, to ensure that the *acquis comunautaire* is maintained.[21] With regard to what for a long time was known generically as justice and home affairs, the situation has always been more nuanced with the Court's jurisdiction limited to direct actions by Member States and the Commission against legal acts adopted by the Council. No actions for infringement can be brought by the Commission and preliminary rulings from national courts are only possible if the Member State in question had 'opted-in' to this jurisdiction of the Court.[22] Under the Lisbon Treaty this situation will be continued for

[15] See further Cases T-228/02 *Organisation des Modjahedines du peuple d'Iran v Council and UK*, [2006] ECR II-4665 and T-256/07 *People's Mojahedin Organization of Iran v Council*, judgment of 23 October 2008, nyr. See too T-284/08 *People's Mojahedin Organization of Iran v Council*, judgment of 4 December 2008, nyr.

[16] I am grateful to Steve Peers for having drawn my attention to this argument.

[17] Case T-411/06 *Sogelma v European Agency for Reconstruction (EAR)*, judgment of the Court of First Instance of 8 October 2008, nyr.

[18] This issue of legal effect on individuals emerges as a key element also from the Court of Justice' s judgment in Case C-345/06 *Gottfried Heinrich*, judgment of 10 March 2009, nyr.

[19] Case C-355/04 P *Segi v Council*, [2007] ECR I-1657.

[20] Ibid, para 53. [21] Art 275, second alinea, TFEU*.

[22] See further S Peers (2007a), 'The jurisdiction of the Court of Justice over EC immigration and asylum law: Time for a change? in H Toner, E Guild, and A Baldaccini (eds), *EU Immigration and Asylum Law and Policy* (Oxford: Hart), pp 85–108.

measures adopted under the prior Nice Treaty—thanks to the insistence of the UK in this regard—for a further transitional period of five years after the entry into force of the Treaty of Lisbon.[23] Despite this different legal environment from what prevailed with regard to the original EC communities ('first pillar') of full and original jurisdiction, the Court has displayed creativity and ingenuity in applying some of the classic Community principles potentially across the broad reach of Union-wide policy and irrespective of the absence of explicit jurisdiction over (all) Union policies as such.

The starting point in terms of judicial reasoning has been Art 47 TEU, which states the general principle of the preservation of the *acquis communautaire*,[24] by providing that 'nothing in this Treaty shall affect the Treaties establishing the European Communities or the subsequent Treaties and Acts modifying and supplementing them'. Evidently the function of Art 47 TEU is to preserve the integrity of the legal order that was brought into being by the EC Treaty, in the face of the new competences conferred upon the Union by the new treaty.[25] Even before the establishment of the Union, the Court applied this principle to the external competences of Member States. It held that these external competences 'must be exercised in a manner consistent with Community law'.[26] This was later confirmed by the Court and applied in the context of justice and home affairs policies in the *Airport Transit Visa* case,[27] in which the Commission challenged a Council act adopted under Title VI of the EU Treaty (third pillar) with the argument that a Community legal basis in Title IV of the EC Treaty (first pillar) should have been used. The logic of Art 47 TEU may also work the other way around[28] and this has been made explicit in Art 40 TEU upon entry into force of the Treaty of Lisbon. This provides that the implementation of the CFSP policies shall not affect the application of the procedures and the extent of the powers of the institutions laid down by the treaties for the exercise of the Union competences in the other policy areas.[29]

In the *Airport Transit Visa* case however the Court held that it could exercise its powers under Art 47 TEU 'to ensure that acts which, according to the Council,

[23] Art 10 Protocol 36 regarding transitional measures.

[24] Art 2 EU. On the interpretation and content of the *acquis communautaire*, see further S Weatherill (1998), 'Safeguarding the *acquis communautaire*' in T Heukels, N Blokker, and M Brus (eds), *The European Union after Amsterdam: A legal analysis* (The Hague: Kluwer, Law International), pp 153–78, p 153; GC Gialdino (1995), 'Some reflections on the acquis communautaire', Common Market L Rev, 32/5, pp 1089–121, p 1089.

[25] A Dashwood (2008), 'Article 47 TEU and the relationship between first and second pillar competences' in M Cremona and B de Witte (eds), *EU Foreign Relations Law: Constitutional fundamentals*, (Oxford: Hart Publishing), pp 53–78. See also HH Herrnfeld (2009), 'Artikel 47 EUV' in J Schwarze (ed), *EU-Kommentar*, 2nd edn (Baden-Baden: Nomos), pp 230–6, p 234.

[26] Case C-124/95 *Centro-Com* [1997] ECR I-81, para 41.

[27] Case C-170/96 *Commission v Council* [1998] ECR I-2763, paras 15–16.

[28] For example, in the so-called *Passenger Name Record* case, Joined Cases C-317/04 and C-318/04 *Parliament v Council* [2006] ECR I-4721 a Community Directive was annulled as the correct legal basis would have been a framework decision under Art 24 and 38 TEU.

[29] Art 275 TFEU grants the Court jurisdiction on this matter.

fall within the scope of [Title VI] of the Treaty on EU do not encroach upon the powers conferred by the EC Treaty on the Community'.[30] The Court ruled that if the subject matter of the contested 'joint action' fell within the scope of Community competence then it would have jurisdiction to annul the measure in question.[31] In the event, the Court dismissed the action on its merits and there was no reason to annul the act in question. The Council was justified in choosing Title VI EU as the relevant legal basis for adopting the measure under review, since the situation governed by the joint action did not entail the crossing of Member States' external borders by third-country nationals, a domain that is covered by Community competence. In a subsequent case the Court did, however, annul a CFSP decision implementing a joint action (see further below).[32]

The Court was involved in a number of subsequent actions that sought to challenge third-pillar measures that putatively encroached upon powers conferred upon the Community as such and with an alternative legal basis within the EC Treaties. A rather dramatic example is provided by what is often termed the *Environmental Penalties* cases.[33] In this case the Court annulled a Council framework decision laying down environmental offences, in respect of which the Member States were required to lay down criminal penalties. The Court found that 'on account of both their aim and their content, Articles 1 to 7 of the framework decision have as their main purpose the protection of the environment and they could have been properly adopted on the basis of Article 175 EC'. Since the framework decision encroached upon powers conferred upon the Community, it infringed Art 47 TEC and was therefore annulled. This reasoning was confirmed in a decision in 2007, which dealt with Framework Decision 2005/667/JHA—Enforcement of the law against ship-source pollution. Also in this case the Court held that the respective legal act could have been adopted under EC law, in this case Art 80(2) EC, and therefore contravened Art 47 TEU.[34]

In none of the cases that came before the Court did it have to take (or consider whether it could take) the next logical step of actually annulling the non-Community acts adopted under the specific CFSP legal provisions. Indeed, 'it remains doubtful whether the combined effect of Article 46(e) and 47 EU may result in the conferral upon the ECJ, in respect of provisions of Title V of the EU Treaty, of the same powers of judicial review which it enjoys under the

[30] Case C-170/96 *Commission v Council* [1998] ECR 1–2763, 12 May 1998. This approach was more recently confirmed in Case C-176/03 *Commission v Council* [2005] ECR I-7879, 13 September 2005 and in Case C-440/05 *Commission v Council*, 23 October 2007 (see below).

[31] Case C-170/96 *Commission v Council* [1998] ECR I-2763.

[32] Case C-91/05 *Commission v Council* [2008] ECR I-3651.

[33] Case C-176/03 *Commission v Council* [2005] ECR I-7879; Case C-440/05 *Commission v Council*, 23 October [2007] ECR I-9097.

[34] Case C-440/05 *Commission v Council* [2007] ECR I-9097, para 52 *et seq*. For more information see IE Fromm (2008), 'Rahmenbeschluss 2005/667/JI des Rates vom 12.7.2005 zur Verstärkung des strafrechtlichen Rahmens zur Bekämpfung der Verschmutzung durch Schiffe ist nichtig', *Zeitschrift für internationale Strafrechtsdogmatik*, 3/1, pp 168–77, at p 170 *et seq*.

Community Treaty'.[35] Recent case law on sanctions against individuals in the fight against terrorism seems rather to confirm the absence of a competence of the Court to annul CFSP common positions. In *Segi*, for example, the CFI could merely annul the Community decision, but not the common position on which this decision was based.[36] On appeal the Court merely stated that the appellants had not come up with new arguments and it did not therefore pronounce on the correct legal basis for the common position in question.[37] In the OMPI line of case law a particular common position (re autonomous anti-terrorist financial sanctions) was interpreted in some detail—the Council's long line of defeats stem essentially from its failure to apply the precise obligations under the common position properly—the rationale of the CFI is that the relevant regulation refers to the common position and is thus open to interpretation (see above).

7.2.2 The evolving nature of EU legal instruments

We have seen a gradual process of assimilation of CFSP instruments with the other legal instruments (both first and third pillar) and the discourse has become more normalized (less specific) in this regard. While the binding nature of common positions, joint actions, or other decisions is only marginally dealt with in the treaty,[38] the language used by the relevant treaty provisions nonetheless suggests that those CFSP acts, once adopted,[39] limit the freedom of Member States in their individual policies.[40] In particular, joint actions 'shall commit the Member States in the positions they adopt and in the conduct of their activity'

[35] MG Garbagnati Ketvel (2006), 'The jurisdiction of the European Court of Justice in respect of the common foreign and security policy', Int'l and Comp LQ, 55/1, pp 77–120, p 90. See also R Baratta (2002), 'Overlaps between European Community Competence and European Union foreign policy activity' in E Cannizzaro (ed), *The European Union as an Actor in International Relations* (The Hague: Kluwer Law International), pp 51–75, p 51, who suggested that the Court could also rule on the 'irrelevance or inefficacy of such an act in the Community order'.

[36] Case C-355/04 P *Segi v Council*, [2007] ECR I-1657.

[37] Ibid, para 21. See further S Peers (2007b), 'Salvation outside the church: Judicial protection in the third pillar after the *Pupino* and *Segi* judgments', Common Market L Rev, 44/4, pp 883–929.

[38] No interpretation may be expected from the Court of Justice given that Art 46 TEU excludes Title V from its jurisdiction; as confirmed by eg Case T-201/99 *Royal Olympic Cruises Ltd and others v Council and Commission* [2000] ECR II-4005; Case T-228/02 *Organisation des Modjahedines du peuple d'Iran* [2006] ECR I-4665, para 49; C-354/04 P *Gestoras Pro Amnistía and Others v Council* [2007] ECR I-1579, para 50. The situation is different only with regard to the largely similarly worded instruments of Title VI EU (justice and home affairs).

[39] The publication in the Official Journal of CFSP autonomous acts is decided, on a case-by-case basis, by unanimous decision of the Council or the COREPER: see Art 17, para 3 of the Council Rules of Procedure; OJ 2004 L 206, 15 April 2004.

[40] On CFSP joint actions specifically, see A Dashwood (2007); F Dehousse (2005), 'Les caractéristiques fondamentales de la politique étrangère et de securité commune' in JV Louis and M Dony (eds), *Relations Extérieures: Commentaire J Mégret: Le droit de la CE et de l'Union européenne* (Bruxelles: Institut d'Etudes Europénnes), pp 441–62, p 475; P Koutrakos (2006), *EU International Relations Law* (Oxford: Hart Publishing), p 399; L Münch (1997), *Die gemeinsame Aktion als Mittel der Gemeinsamen Aussen- und Sicherheitspolitik* (Berlin: Duncker & Humblot).

(Art 14, para 3 TEU) and 'Member States shall ensure that their national policies conform to the common positions' (Art 15 TEU).[41] Hence, Member States are not allowed to adopt positions or otherwise to act contrary to joint actions.

In fact in February 2007, the Court confirmed for the first time the binding nature of common positions in the *Segi* case:

> A common position requires the compliance of the Member States by virtue of the principle of the duty to cooperate in good faith, which means in particular that Member States are to take all appropriate measures, whether general or particular to ensure fulfilment of their obligations under European Union law.[42]

This interpretation certainly confirms the constitutional nature of the non-Community parts of Union law. The case primarily concerned the third pillar, but it is tempting, though not perhaps entirely justified, to transpose the above findings to the second pillar. After all, the common position in question could also be regarded as a CFSP decision since it was equally based on both Art 15 (CFSP) and Art 34 (PJCC) EU. Indeed, as suggested by previous practice, the subject matter—economic and financial sanctions against groups and individuals—is primarily a second-pillar issue, and in that capacity closely linked to the Community legal order. In this way one sees the evolution of a principle of legal unity applying across the board to the EU executive power, in its various institutional forms, irrespective to some extent of the niceties of the specific—and different—policy areas. At the same time there is some case law, especially in the field of police and judicial cooperation (the so-called 'third pillar') where the Court has come up against clear limits to its ability to read the EU/EC through the unitary lens.[43]

[41] In the same vein, EU common strategies, envisaged in Art 13 TEU, bind not only the EU institutions but also the Member States. For instance, the European Council 1999 Common Strategy on Ukraine provided that the Council, the Commission and Member States shall review, according to their powers and capacities, existing actions, programmes, instruments, and policies to ensure their consistency with that common strategy; see pt 41, Common Strategy on Ukraine, OJ 1999 L 331/1.

[42] See Case C-355/04 P *Segi v Council* [2007] ECR I-1657, para 52. It can be noted that in addition in the PMOI cases the CFI seems to assume that common positions are binding upon institutions.

[43] See, by way of example, Case C-354/04 P *Gestoras Pro Amnistia v Council of the EU* [2007] ECR I-1579, where the (Grand Chamber of the) Court of Justice ruled that damages could not be claimed by the appellants being included in the list of persons, groups or entities referred to in Art 1 of Council Common Position 2001/931/CFSP of 27 December 2001 on the application of specific measures to combat terrorism (OJ 2001 L 344, p 93), in Art 1 of Council Common Position 2002/340/CFSP of 2 May 2002 updating Common Position 2001/931 (OJ 2002 L 116, p 75), and in Art 1 of Council Common Position 2002/462/CFSP of 17 June 2002 updating Common Position 2001/931 and repealing Common Position 2002/340 (OJ 2002 L 160, p 32). Loss suffered as a result of measures adopted under the third pillar (Title VI) could not be claimed in damages against the EU simply because Art 35 TEU conferred no equivalent jurisdiction on the ECJ equivalent to the action of damages of Art 288(2) EC. Another example is provided by the inability of the Commission to get the Member States to accept that the preliminary ruling mechanism applying in the context of Title VI should be brought into line with the normal (and more extensive) preliminary ruling mechanism applying in the Community context. But it

The Lisbon Treaty explicitly stresses the binding nature of CFSP provisions by strengthening the loyalty obligation in Art 11, para 2 (new 3): 'The Member States shall support the CFSP actively and unreservedly in a spirit of loyalty and mutual solidarity and shall comply with the Union's action in this area.' In addition, the Council will not be alone in its responsibility to 'ensure that these principles are complied with'; the Lisbon Treaty also entrusts this task to the High Representative. On the other hand, a clear distinction with other policy areas will be maintained, as (new) Art 24 excludes 'the adoption of legislative acts', which in turn excludes the use of the legislative procedures (the 'Community method').[44] Apart from the (continued) exclusion of the European Parliament and the Commission in the decision-making phase, as well as the almost complete exclusion of the jurisdiction of the Court, this does not settle the issue of the binding nature of CFSP decisions in national legal orders.

The *Segi* judgment only partly helps in answering the question of the binding nature of CFSP instruments. As the Court's jurisdiction on CFSP provisions remains limited in the Lisbon Treaty, and given the ambiguity of the possible application of the principles of primacy and direct effect to CFSP,[45] a relationship with either Community law or the third pillar will continue to be helpful to interpret the scope of the CFSP legal restraints. This, however, is exactly what the Court confirmed in some recent cases, in which the connection between the pillars proved to be crucial for the interpretation (see below).

One example is the fact that it now seems to be more accepted that CFSP 'joint actions' might be in some respects the equivalent of EC 'regulations'; in any event according to the Commission (and others) they can constitute acts 'of a general legislative nature'.[46] The implication would seem clearly to be that CFSP acts may in general constitute such general legislative acts—at least in the opinion of one of the major institutional players and legislative partner. This reading would seem to be confirmed by Advocate General Mengozzi who

seems that there may be some judicial impetus possible in this context: see Case C-14/08 *Roda Golf and Beach Resort SL*, Opinion of Advocate General Ruiz-Jatabo Colomer of 5 March 2009, nyr, where he opined that restrictions under Art 68 TEC (different speed references for preliminary rulings in the area of justice and home affairs) 'may be relaxed when they are interpreted in the light of the principle of effective legal protection'.

44 See Art 249a TFEU. See on this JP Terhechte (2009), p 112.

45 Most commentators have argued that there are many reasons (including the special nature of CFSP, the general absence of ECJ jurisdiction, the relation with established case law, and the probable absence of direct effect) not to apply the principle of primacy to CFSP. See in particular A Dashwood (2004), 'The relationship between the Member States and the European Union/ European Community', Common Market L Rev, 41/2, pp 355–81, pp 363 and 379; as well as his (2005) 'The EU Constitution: What will really change?', Cambridge Yearbook of European Legal Studies, 7/1, pp 33–56, p 34. See also the Editorial Comment (2005), 'The CFSP under the EU Constitutional Treaty: Issues of depillarization, Common Market L Rev, 42/2, pp 325–9, p 327. In this respect, see the Declaration on Primacy envisaged in footnote 1 of the 2007 'Draft IGC Mandate annexed to the Presidency Conclusions', 21–2 June 2007.

46 OJ C 115/10, 14 May 2005. See, contra, R Gosalbo Bono (2006), 'Some reflections on the CFSP legal order', Common Market L Rev, 43/2, pp 337–94, p 364.

implicitly accepts the applicability of the plea of illegality to joint actions in parallel to regulations 'of a legislative nature'.[47] Regulations 'of a legislative nature' are clearly something very different from 'international law decisions' binding Member States only as to the positions they adopt. Moreover, recent practice (especially the use of so-called 'smart sanctions') has shown that CFSP measures are not only directed at Member States but may even directly affect the rights and interests of individual citizens. They may not be formally 'self-executing' or 'directly effective', in the language of EC law, yet they are affecting directly or indirectly individual citizens.[48] This has been enough for the Court to assume jurisdiction to interpret.

It has been argued that the Community principles of primacy and of direct effect are not completely alien to the CFSP legal order. Gosalbo Bono, for example, put it in these terms:

> As regards to the principle of direct effect, the practice has started, especially in the EU's fight against terrorism, to insert unconditional obligations in common positions which relate to physical and legal persons as opposed to governments...As regards the principle of primacy, joint actions and common positions are legally binding upon Member States which are under a duty to abide by them 'actively' and 'unreservedly' (Art. 11(2) EU...[49]

Indeed, both the legal nature and the content of CFSP decisions may form a good reason for Member States to allow for direct effect and primacy in their national legal order. The ECJ has, however, thus far refrained from turning this into an obligation. The provision of the Constitutional Treaty concerning the primacy of (all) EU law (Art I-6) was not inserted into the EU Treaty by the Lisbon Treaty. A (non-binding) 'declaration' on primacy referring to the previous case law of the Court on this point was included in the Lisbon Treaty, but this obviously does not refer in this respect to CFSP as this was never part of the *acquis communautaire*.

7.3 The Court of Justice as Constitutional Geologist

7.3.1 Judicial tunnels

From the above discussion it is already clear that the Council of Ministers composed of national ministers (and civil servants) is adopting the equivalent of

[47] Case C-91/05 *Commission v Council*, Opinion of Advocate General Mengozzi, 19 September 2007, [2008] ECR I-3651, paras 62–72.

[48] For an argument to the effect that Union law is in principle 'directly applicable' in the national legal orders of the Member States see D Curtin and IF Dekker (2002), 'The constitutional structure of the European Union: Some reflections on vertical unity-in-diversity' in N Walker et al (eds), *Convergence and Divergence in European Public Law*, (Oxford: Hart), pp 59–78. See too K Lenaerts and T Corthaut, (2006) 'Of birds and hedges: The role of primacy in invoking norms of EU law', European L Rev, 31, pp 287–315.

[49] R Gosalbo Bono (2006), p 378.

general legislative acts within the framework of CFSP as well as measures that affect directly the rights and interests of individuals and that may be more executive in nature. The fact that such measures can, and are, being adopted without anything resembling co-decision with the European Parliament, indeed still only with the weakest obligation to inform the European Parliament in the Lisbon Treaty, makes it all the more important that they are subject to judicial review just as all acts of the Council in all other policy areas post-Lisbon will fall under the full jurisdiction of the Court. This is precisely what is *not* changed in the Treaty of Lisbon (see below). In this context a case brought by the Commission against two CFSP decisions adopted by the Council concerning, inter alia, the EU contribution to the West African organization ECOWAS[50] is very interesting.[51]

The facts of this ECOWAS case were, briefly, as follows. In 2005 the Commission challenged the legality of two acts which the Council had adopted in the context of Title V TEU, namely a CFSP joint action 'on the EU's contribution to combating the destabilizing accumulation and spread of small arms and light weapons' and the implementing decision 'with a view to a EU contribution to ECOWAS in the framework of the Moratorium on Small Arms and Light Weapons'.[52] Although the Commission did not protest at the time the joint action was adopted by the Council in 2002, the subsequent Council decision relating specifically to ECOWAS went too far in stepping on the Commission's own competences and planned proposals to be easily tolerated.

The idea of a 'fixed' boundary between the Community (the Commission) and the EU (the Council) acting in the framework of CFSP means that the latter can potentially encroach on the former (Community competence) and this must be subject to judicial review via Art 47 TEU. In this sense the Union acting with regard to CFSP under Title V of the EU Treaty is something more than the collectivity of Member States exercising concurrent competences. In the recent judgment in the ECOWAS case[53] much is clarified regarding the structure of the Union Treaty and the position of CFSP within that overall structure. In the words of the Advocate General in his opinion in that same case:[54] 'Article 47 EU ... appears to rest on the presumption that all the competences given to the Community, irrespective of the distribution that exists between the Community and the Member States, deserve to be protected against any encroachment on

[50] Case C-91/05 *Commission v Council* judgment of 20 May 2008, nyr.

[51] In Cases T-349/99 *Miskovic* and T-350/99 *Karic*, the CFI was deprived of the opportunity when the Council amended the decision challenged by two individuals who had been refused visas on the basis of a CFSP act and both cases were removed from the register.

[52] Council Joint Action 2002/589/CFSP of 12 July 2002 on the European Union's contribution to combating the destabilizing accumulation and spread of small arms and light weapons, OJ 2002 L 191, p 1, and Council Decision 2004/833/CFSP of 2 December 2004 implementing Joint Action 2002/589/CFSP with a view to a EU contribution to ECOWAS in the framework of the Moratorium on Small Arms and Light Weapons, OJ 2004 L 359, p 65

[53] Case C-91/05 *Commission v Council*, [2008] ECR I-3651.

[54] Opinion of Advocate General Mengozzi, 19 September 2007.

the part of the European Union by adopting a measure based on Titles V and/or VI of the EU Treaty.'[55] Reliance was placed on earlier case law[56] in reaching this conclusion that the nature of the competence given to the Community and the distribution of the competences between it and the Member States are immaterial for the purpose of applying Art 47 TEU, provided that competence exists. This also applied where competences are concurrent as specifically was the case with regard to development cooperation: Member States were free to act but action of the EU under Titles V and VI 'is in principle excluded because adequate competences are provided for by the EC Treaty, irrespective of the nature of those competences (exclusive, shared or concurrent) assigned to the Community'.[57]

In other words the Advocate General did not delimit the scope of Art 47 TEU according to the distribution of competences between the Community and the Member States, but quite irrespective of that distribution. In very general terms, the aim of Art 47 TEU is 'to keep watertight, so to speak, the primacy of Community action under the EC Treaty over actions undertaken on the basis of Title V and/or Title VI of the EU Treaty, so that if action could be undertaken on the basis of the EC Treaty, it must be undertaken by virtue of that Treaty'.[58] What emerges in general terms from the Advocate General's reading is indeed the sense that a holistic reading of the entire EU Treaty is called for and not one that views the special CFSP in isolation from all the rest. Indeed he specifically states that the provisions of Title V of the EU Treaty 'cannot be read in isolation, but must be interpreted in the light of the common and final provisions of that Treaty, which refer to the EU as a "facade" of the three pillars'.[59]

In virtually every respect, the approach he took in his opinion (interpreting the plea of illegality, types of Union/Community competence and their inter-relationship with the second pillar, the principle of pre-emption and the function of Art 47 TEU) was one of assimilation to a considerable extent of the second pillar, both with the provisions of the first pillar and by analogy also with the provisions of the third pillar. Considerable emphasis was, in addition, placed on ensuring the 'overall coherence of the provisions of the EU Treaty'[60] read holistically. It followed that Art 47 TEU was not breached in this case by the contested decisions and there was no need to consider whether the contested decisions could in fact have been annulled (if they were found to have been in breach). But the Advocate General's opinion is resolute that there can only be a 'substitution effect' in the interaction between first and second pillar competences and never 'overlap'.[61]

[55] Para 98.

[56] See, in particular, Case C-170/96 *Commission v Council* and Case C-176/03, *Commission v Council*, op. cit.

[57] Para 111.

[58] This language of the Advocate General echoes that of P Eeckhout (2004), *External Relations of the European Union: Legal and constitutional foundations* (Oxford: Oxford University Press), p 146.

[59] Para 119. [60] Para 122

[61] See, contra, A Dashwood (2004).

The Court however interpreted the decision differently—more expansively than its Advocate General—and concluded that 'taking account of its aim and its content, the contested decision contains two components, neither of which can be considered to be incidental to the other, one falling within Community development cooperation policy and the other within the CFSP'.[62] The Court was therefore of the view that Art 47 TEU was violated and the Council, in adopting the CFSP decision in question, had trespassed (at least in part) on Community competence in a manner that a legal basis in the EC Treaty should have been used. If an EC competence exists then the decision in question cannot be based on the second (or third pillar): 'Since Article 47 EU precludes the Union from adopting, on the basis of the EU Treaty, a measure which could properly be adopted on the basis of the EC Treaty, the Union cannot have recourse to a legal basis falling within the CFSP in order to adopt provisions which also fall within a competence conferred by the EC Treaty on the Community.'[63]

In this case, the Court confirmed its constitutional role also with regard to the relationship with the second pillar. Indeed the Treaty of Lisbon will codify the Court's ruling in ECOWAS with respect to its jurisdiction.[64] It is curious that the Court explicitly pointed out that CFSP joint actions may (or even must) be implemented not only by means of other CFSP decisions but also by Community decisions. The contested decision was based on a CFSP joint action and the Court concluded in this regard that: 'The conclusion that the objectives of the contested joint action can be implemented both by the Union, under Title V of the EU Treaty, and by the Community, under its development cooperation policy, corresponds, in the end, to the approach advocated by the Union's institutions and by the European Council in numerous documents.'[65] The link between the pillars is thus very explicit and direct. In this sense too the judgment can be read as a victory for the more holistic vision of the Commission compared to that defended vigorously by the United Kingdom of the specificity of CFSP provisions entirely separate from Community law as such.

The interpretation of the CFSP common position and of other CFSP decisions plays an important part in the Court's judgments. The Court can only come to a final judgment when it takes the second pillar measures into account. Irrespective of the formal exclusion of the Court in CFSP matters, it cannot—and indeed does not—ignore what has been decided in the non-Community pillars. For example, in the *Yusuf* and *Kadi* cases, the CFI not only addressed the vertical hierarchy between the national, EU, and UN legal order, but also 'the constitutional architecture of the pillars'. That constitutional architecture involved the coexistence of

[62] Para 108. [63] Para 77.

[64] Art 275 of the TFEU. See too, R van Ooik (2008), 'Cross-pillar litigation before the ECJ: Demarcation of Community and Union competences', European Constitutional L Rev, 4/3, pp 399–419.

[65] Para 88.

Union and Community as integrated but separate legal orders.[66] At least in relation to the imposition of economic and financial sanctions to individuals (which is not covered by Arts 60 and 301 TEC), the CFI held that the Union's objectives could only be attained by making use of Community competences and that '[u]nder Articles 60 EC and 301 EC, action by the Community is therefore in actual fact action by the Union, the implementation of which finds its footing on the Community pillar after the Council has adopted a common position or a joint action under the CFSP'.[67]

This is a clear example of an explicit subordination of the Community to CFSP decision-making and an indication that the 'unity' of the Union's legal order cannot be neglected by the Courts.[68] At the same time, however, it still merely reflects the *indirect* adjudication on CFSP provisions. We know also from a case such as *Hautala* that the CFI argued that it could adjudicate on the legality of a Council decision on the public access to documents even if this decision extended to CFSP documents.[69] This applied an earlier ruling to the same effect with regard to third-pillar measures and public access to justice and home affairs documents.[70]

While the case law thus reveals a certain willingness of the Courts to at least not ignore CFSP measures when there is a relation with Community law, it does not enable us to definitively answer the question to what extent it is competent to judge actions by Member States once these conflict with established Union policies.[71] So far, we have only seen examples of direct judicial review actions based on Art 230 TEC. This leaves open the question whether national courts have complete discretion to decide on the validity of a CFSP act in the event that the legal basis of a national implementation act is challenged. It seems relatively clear that they have no duty to refrain from annulling EU decisions as the relevant line of Court of Justice case law (*Foto-Frost*) only relates to *Community* law as such and not *Union* law where the jurisdiction of the Court of Justice is explicitly excluded.[72] In that respect, the judgment by the Court in *Segi* is arguably quite

66 Cases T-306/01 *Ahmed Ali Yusuf and Al Barakaat International Foundation v Council and Commission*; and T-315/01 *Yassin Abdullah Kadi v Council and Commission*, 21 September 2005, (para 156 *Yusuf* case) [2005] ECR II-3533.

67 Ibid, para 161 *Yusuf* case.

68 See more extensively on this issue D Curtin and IF Dekker (1999); RA Wessel (2000), 'The inside looking out: Consistency and delimitation in EU external relations', Common Market L Rev, 37/5, pp 1135–71; D Curtin and IF Dekker (2002); RA Wessel (2004), 'Fragmentation in the governance of EU external relations: Legal institutional dilemmas and the new constitution for Europe' in J de Zwaan et al (eds), *The European Union: An ongoing process of integration. Liber Amicorum Fred Kellermann* (Cambridge: Cambridge University Press), pp 123–40.

69 Case T-14/98 *Hautala v Council* [1999] ECR II-2489, paras 41–2.

70 See Case T-174/95 *Svenska Journalistförbundet* [1998] ECR II-2289.

71 See too D Curtin and R Wessel (2008).

72 Case 314/85 [1987] ECR 4199. Advocate General Mengozzi also considers that the *Fotofrost* doctrine is not applicable to measures adopted in accordance with Title VI of the EU Treaty: see Cases C-355/04 P *Segi v Council* and C-354/04 P *Gestoras Pro Amnistía and Others v Council*, Opinion of Advocate General Mengozzi, of 26 October 2006, para 121 *et seq*. See, however, for

revealing. This judgment concerns an appeal by *Segi* (and in a similar case by another Basque organization, *Gestoras Pro Amnistía*) to set aside an earlier order of the CFI.[73] The legal instrument being challenged in this case was Common Position 2001/931/CFSP with a dual legal basis in both the second (Art 15 TEU) and the third pillar (Art 34 TEU). Although Art 35(1) EU does not enable national courts to refer a question to the Court for a preliminary ruling on a common position, the relevant question according to the Court is whether or not the decision produces legal effects in relation to third parties (individuals or entities). In this case the two organizations were placed on a list with terrorist organizations that was annexed to Common Position 2001/931/CFSP that led the Court to conclude that this particular common position had produced legal effects in relation to the two organizations. The Court continued:

> As a result, it had to be possible to make subject to review by the Court a common position which, because of its content, has a scope going beyond that assigned by the EU Treaty to that kind of act. Therefore, a national court hearing a dispute which indirectly raises the issue of the validity or interpretation of a common position adopted on the basis of Article 34 EU... and which has serious doubt whether that common position is really intended to produce legal effects in relation to third parties, would be able, subject to the conditions fixed by Article 35 EU, to ask the Court to give a preliminary ruling... The Court would also have jurisdiction to review the lawfulness of such acts when an action has been brought by a Member State or the Commission under the conditions fixed by Article 35(6) EU.[74]

One could argue that this reasoning should also be maintained when a common position would only have a CFSP legal basis. After all, there is no difference in principle between the different types of common position if they produce legal effects in relation to individuals. On the other hand, the only reason why the Court rules on the issue of a legal remedy in this case seems to be the presence of a judicial competence in the third pillar in relation to other instruments (decisions and framework decisions).[75] There is no comparable role for the Court in relation to acts with only a CFSP legal basis. This may not however be the end of the matter. As illustrated by the earlier *Pupino* judgment, the Court may seek inspiration from its interpretation of EC provisions when called upon to interpret similar EU provisions.[76] Not only has the Court made an explicit comparison

arguments to apply the *Foto-Frost* reasoning to Union law: DM Curtin and IF Dekker (1999), p 123. See for this question, and others in relation to the impact of the 2004 Constitutional Treaty, Editorial Comment (2005).

[73] See Cases C-355/04 P *Segi v Council* and C-354/04 P *Gestoras Pro Amnistía and Others v Council*, judgments of 27 February 2007, op. cit.

[74] Case C-355/04 P *Segi v Council*, paras 54–5.

[75] This does seem to be rather important and in the view of at least some authors enables in principle third pillar measures to take precedence over national law in certain circumstances (even if there is no 'direct effect' as such. See further R Barents (2006).

[76] Case C-105/03 *Pupino* [2005] ECR I-5285, paras 19, 21, and 28 (similarity between the system established by Art 234 TEC and that of Art 35 TEU); paras 33–4 (similarity in the wording of Arts 249 TEC and 34(2)(b)) TEU.

between third-pillar framework decisions and Community Directives in terms of their legal effects, it also suggests that Community principles—in this case the principle of loyal cooperation, expressed particularly in Art 10 TEC—may have a cross-pillar application. In particular, the Court held that:

> [i]t would be difficult for the Union to carry out its task effectively if the principle of loyal cooperation, requiring in particular that Member States take all appropriate measures, whether general or particular, to ensure fulfilment of their obligations under European Union law, were not also binding in the area of police and judicial cooperation in criminal matters, which is moreover entirely based on cooperation between the Member States and the institutions.[77]

Unconvinced by the Italian and United Kingdom governments' argument that the EU Treaty contains no obligation similar to that laid down in Art 10 EC, the Court held that the principle of loyal cooperation binds the Member States in relation to the Union, 'in order to contribute effectively to the pursuit of the Union's objectives'.[78] The Court thereby suggested that the principle of loyalty has a cross-pillar definition and application.[79] Even the lack of direct effect of framework decisions proved to be irrelevant and did not stop the Court from extending the principle of indirect effect to the third pillar legislation.[80] It should, however, be kept in mind that the Court reached this conclusion by looking at the similarities between framework decisions and directives. Such a comparison would be more difficult with regard to CFSP instruments. Moreover, unlike in the second pillar, in the third pillar the jurisdiction of the Court is not completely excluded.

Nevertheless, it has been argued that *Yusuf* and *Kadi*, as well as the subsequent cases, show a paradigm shift by which the Court (of First Instance) forces itself to follow UN obligations and pay allegiance to its own principles at the same time.[81] The fact is that in the recent cases—from *Pupino*, via *Yusuf/Kadi* to *Segi*—the Courts are confronted with the question of the protection of human rights of individuals in Union pillars that do not provide for the same legal protection as the Community. In all cases the solution seems the same: the Court either interprets the non-Community (Union) provisions in the light of overall Union law (*Yusuf/Kadi*), or it uses Community analogy to establish the outcome it considers necessary from a constitutional point of view (*Pupino/Segi).* Thus, the Court has

[77] Ibid, para 42.

[78] Ibid, para 39. Lebeck speaks of an 'indirect direct effect of framework decisions': see C Lebeck (2008), 'Sliding towards supranationalism? The constitutional status of EU framework decisions after *Pupino*', German L Rev, 8/5, pp 501–32, p 520.

[79] Further on the *Pupino* ruling, E Spaventa (2007), 'Opening Pandora's Box: Some reflections on the constitutional effects of the decision in *Pupino*', European Constitutional L Rev, 3/1, pp 5–24.

[80] See B Kurcz and A Lazowski (2007), 'Two sides of the same coin? Framework decisions and directives compared' in P Eeckhout and T Tridimas (eds), *Yearbook of European Law 2006* (Oxford: Oxford University Press), pp 177–203, p 179;

[81] M Nettesheim (2007), 'UN sanctions against individuals: A challenge to the architecture of European Union governance', Common Market L Rev, 44/3, pp 567–600.

turned itself into a constitutional Court of the EU as a whole and does not shy away from combining different Union norms to reach a preferred outcome.[82]

7.3.2 Defending internal constitutionalism from external challenges

The Court of Justice is not only busy performing, potentially at any rate, a role as a constitutional geologist linking different layers of sedimentation in the EU context; at the same time it may be engaged in what Maduro once called more 'defensive constitutionalism'.[83] This involves the defence of certain core principles of the EC (EU) constitutional legal order against attack—or 'shafting'—from the outside. This phenomenon is well illustrated by the recent judgment (and Advocate General's opinion) in the *Kadi/Yusuf* cases. *Kadi* is an example of dynamic, albeit perhaps 'defensive', constitutionalism. From the perspective of a relatively autonomous and dynamic legal order with a sophisticated relationship with national legal orders the ECJ established a clear borderline between the European and the UN level of governance.

The Court of Justice in Luxembourg, with a relatively broad mandate, is precisely what distinguishes the EU from other international organizations such as the UN. As is well known, the Court transformed the original EC treaties governed by the rules of international law into what it calls a 'constitutional charter'. A constitutional charter aims to ensure that the exercise of power by the Union is subject to effective constitutional constraints and the rule of law.[84] In this perspective the Courts in Luxembourg are engaged in an ongoing process of settling constitutional space and the content of the 'rule of law' in practice, even in the absence of formal treaty provisions.

A striking example of the above phenomenon is formed by the Court's case law on the so-called 'terrorist blacklists' adopted by the Security Council of the United Nations. In the aftermath of the dreadful events of 11 September 2001 a set of resolutions were adopted by the Security Council of the UN blacklisting certain terrorist organizations as well as individuals with the consequence that their bank accounts and other assets are to be frozen.[85] Counterterrorism policy

[82] R Barents (2006), 'Case annotation of C-105/03, *Pupino*', *SEW – Tijdschrift voor Europees en Economisch Recht*, 1/2, pp 74–8, who compared the impact of the reasoning in *Pupino* to the one in *Van Gend & Loos*. See too, with regard to earlier case law, D Curtin and RH van Ooik (1999), 'Een Hof van Justitie van de Europese Unie?', *Sociaal Economische Wetgeving*, 47/1, pp 24–38.

[83] M Maduro (2000), 'Europe and the Constitution: What if this is as good as it gets?' in JHH Weiler and M Wind (eds), *Rethinking European Constitutionalism*, (Cambridge: Cambridge University Press), pp 74–102.

[84] See, for example, FG Jacobs, (2007), *The Sovereignty of Law: The European way*, The Hamlyn Lectures 2006, (Cambridge University Press), in particular Ch 4.

[85] The interaction among various resolutions is quite complex but need not concern us unduly here. See further JE Alvarez (2003), 'The UN's "war" on terrorism', International Journal of Legal Information, 31/2, pp 238–50; M Happold (2003), 'Security Council Resolution 1373 and the Constitution of the United Nations', Leiden J of Int'l L, 16/3, pp 593–610; N Krisch, (2003), 'The

requires a delicate balance between important interests representing fundamental values of liberal democracies. This substantive issue however is preceded by the question of who the final authority should be to decide where the tipping line of this balance is to be placed. What is the role of courts in finding this balance, and which decisions should be reserved for the executive?[86] The *Kadi* case is a particularly illustrative example of this expanding executive power because it combines the substantive area of counterterrorism policy—an area in which executive powers have most prominently increased in recent years—with the formal context of externalization and Europeanization of this policy area. This situation facilitates political actors in exercising real powers in a constitutional 'vacuum' since their decisions are adopted outside of the domestic legal framework and with no forum able to hold them to account *ex post* for their actions.[87]

The Security Council of the UN is not normally regarded as being a lawmaker in the sense we know from our constitutional states. It is an intergovernmental organ, composed of representatives of 15 member states; its decisions are however binding on all 192 members. As an intergovernmental organization, it is not meant to affect the rights and interests of individuals directly. Yet it is seemingly increasingly adopting normative rules that are 'legislative' and executive in their effects.[88] These Security Council rules are binding but require further implementation by the members of that organization. The EU seems to have taken the view that although the EC was not as such a member of the United Nations, it was required to act in such a way as to facilitate the obligations of all its Member States towards the UN. The Community was regarded, for all practical purposes, as being in the same position as the members of the UN.[89]

In a series of legislative and executive decisions the Council of Ministers incorporated the UN blacklisting laws into the European legal order.[90] This is usually

rise and fall of collective security: Terrorism, US hegemony and the plight of the Security Council' in C Walter et al (eds), *Terrorism as a Challenge for National and International Law: Security versus liberty?* (Springer), pp 879–908; P Fratangelo (2006), 'L'Union européenne face à la lutte contre le financement du terrorisme', *Revue du Droit de l'Union Européenne*, 4, pp 815–41, p 822 *et seq*.

[86] See further D Curtin and C Eckes (2008), 'Kadi: Mapping the boundaries between the executive and the judiciary in Europe', International Organizations L Rev, 5/2, pp 365–9.

[87] See further ibid.

[88] See further S Talmon (2005), 'The Security Council as world legislature', The American J of Int'l L, 99/1, pp 175–93; C Ohler (2006), 'Die Verhängung von "smart sanctions" durch den UN-Sicherheitsrat: Eine Herausforderung für das Gemeinschaftsrecht', *Europarecht*, 6, pp 848–65.

[89] W Vlcek (2006), 'Acts to combat the financing of terrorism: Common foreign and security policy at the European Court of Justice', *European Foreign Affairs Review*, 11/4, pp 491–507, p 499.

[90] See, for example, Council Common Position 1999/727/CFSP concerning restrictive measures against the Taliban (OJ 1999 L 294, p 1); Council Common Position 2001/154/CFSP concerning additional restrictive measures against the Taliban and amending Common Position 96/746/CFSP (OJ 2001 L 57, p 1); Council Regulation (EC) No 467/2001 prohibiting the export of certain goods and services to Afghanistan, strengthening the flight ban and extending the freeze of funds and other financial resources in respect of the Taliban of Afghanistan, and repealing Regulation No 337/2000 (OJ 2001 L 67, p 1). In Commission Regulation (EC) No 2062/2001 of 19 October

done by a CFSP Council common position and a Council regulation, which implements the latter.

In fact, the EU adopted two different types of individual sanctions: those reproducing the UN lists and those drawn up autonomously, reflecting the different types of UN Security Council resolutions.[91] The competent national authorities in the Member States then subsequently froze the bank accounts and other assets of the named individuals on the authority of the EU regulations and decisions.[92]

The problem is that individuals whose rights and interests are affected cannot defend themselves in any way against Security Council action. At the level of the United Nations there is simply no court that can hear actions from individuals or organizations challenging the legality of UN laws. There is a reporting obligation and a monitoring committee (the Counter-Terrorism Committee) with, inter alia, competence to review the reports submitted. The guarantees that citizens enjoy in terms of criminal procedure and even human rights at the national level can thus be 'hollowed out' from above in a manner that is neither visible nor accountable.[93] A series of challenges brought by individuals named and shamed on UN (EU) terrorist blacklists before the CFI were already successful in having decisions overturned.[94] The Court was in particular concerned about lack of respect

2001 amending, for the third time, Regulation No 467/2001 (OJ 2001 L 277, p 25), Mr Kadi's name was added, with others, to Annex I. By Commission Regulation (EC) No 2199/2001 of 12 November 2001 amending, for the fourth time, Regulation No 467/2001 (OJ 2001 L 295, p 16), the name Al Barakaat was added, with others, to Annex I; Common Position 2002/402/CFSP concerning restrictive measures against Osama bin Laden, members of the Al-Qaeda organization, and the Taliban and other individuals, groups, undertakings, and entities associated with them and repealing Common Positions 96/746, 1999/727, 2001/154 and 2001/771/CFSP (OJ 2002 L 139, p 4); Common Position 2003/140/CFSP concerning exceptions to the restrictive measures imposed by Common Position 2002/402 (OJ 2003 L 53, p 62); Council Regulation (EC) No 561/2003 amending, as regards exceptions to the freezing of funds and economic resources, Regulation (EC) No 881/2002 (OJ 2003 L 82, p 1). See too Council Common Position 2001/154/CFSP of 26 February 2001 concerning additional restrictive measures against the Taliban and amending Common Position 96/746/CFSP and Council Regulation (EC) No 2580/2001 of 27 December 2001 on specific restrictive measures directed against certain persons and entities with a view to combating terrorism which implements this Council common position. See on this <http://europa.eu/scadplus/leg/en/lvb/l33208.htm>. See in addition Council Common Position 2001/154/CFSP of 26 February 2001 concerning additional restrictive measures against the Taliban and amending Common Position 96/746/CFSP and Council Regulation (EC) No 2580/2001 of 27 December 2001 on specific restrictive measures directed against certain persons and entities with a view to combating terrorism that implements this Council Common Position. See on this <http://europa.eu/scadplus/leg/en/lvb/l33208.htm>.

[91] See further C Eckes (2008), 'Sanctions against individuals: Fighting terrorism within the European legal order', European Constitutional L Rev, 4, pp 205–24, p 208.

[92] See further M Nettesheim (2007).

[93] It is not clear whether the committee will use the material submitted to it as the basis for addressing recommendations or orders under Chapter VII to particular states to take legislative or administrative measures. See further I Cameron (2003), 'UN targeted sanctions, legal safeguards and the European Convention on Human Rights', Nordic J of Int'l L, 72/2, pp 159–214, p 164.

[94] See further B Hayes (2007), '"Terrorist lists" still above the law', *Statewatch analysis*, available at <http://www.statewatch.org/news/2007/aug/proscription.pdf>.

for fundamental rights and due process. One case in particular prompted a full review of the proscription regime by the EU. This resulted in some—limited—changes to the existing regime providing some reasoning and information and a procedure for de-listing.[95] In yet other cases the Court ruled that it could not override UN law nor review it.

In the *Kadi* case the applicant challenged the various legal regulations that led to his assets being frozen as a suspected terrorist and brought his case before the CFI in Luxembourg some years ago. This court dismissed his case on the grounds that the EU regulations were based on Security Council rules. The latter had a type of 'supra-constitutional' effect in the European legal order and could not be challenged by individuals.[96] In other words the CFI ruled that no judicial remedy was available for Mr Kadi because the UN system did not provide any and it was not up to the EU system to fill the gaps in that regard. On appeal to the Court of Justice, Advocate General Maduro's opinion to the ECJ[97] was diametrically opposite to the lower court. He found that the EU measures necessary for the implementation of resolutions adopted by the Security Council are not exempted from the constitutional principles set by EU law. It was precisely the absence of judicial control by an independent tribunal at the level of the United Nations that gave the EU the obligation to fill the gaps in its own legal system. Those EU constitutional principles include the rule of law and the right to judicial review. Since the UN Security Council instruments on which the EU rules

[95] For the current practice of providing limited information on the grounds of the listing and the possibility to comment on these grounds see the 5th Recital of Commission Regulation (EC) No 1109/2008 of 6 November 2008 amending for the 100th time Council Regulation (EC) No 881/2002 imposing certain specific restrictive measures directed against certain persons and entities associated with Osama Bin Laden, the Al-Qaida network, and the Taliban. In some other cases the problem arose that the UN did not provide the current addresses of the individuals concerned. The Commission published, therefore, a note in the Official Journal so that the victims could contact the Commission in order to receive the grounds of their being blacklisted in order to comment and reply on the validity of these grounds. See the fifth Recital of Commission Regulation No 1330/2008 of 22 December 2008 amending for the 103rd time Council Regulation (EC) No 881/2002 imposing certain specific restrictive measures directed against certain persons and entities associated with Osama bin Laden, the Al-Qaida network, and the Taliban. See, Commission Regulation (EC) No 1190/2008 of 28 November 2008 amending for the 101st time Council Regulation (EC) No 881/2002 imposing certain specific restrictive measures directed against certain persons and entities associated with Osama bin Laden, the Al-Qaida network and the Taliban. As appears from the recitals of this regulation, the individuals concerned, who were the applicants of the *Kadi* case before the ECJ, were provided with a statement containing (limited) information on the grounds for their listing. It was also mentioned that the individuals were given the possibility to comment on the grounds and that the Commission took the comments into account. However, the individuals were nonetheless included in the blacklist (see the Annex of this regulation).

[96] Case T-315/01 *Yassin Abdullah Kadi v Council of the European Union and Commission of the European Communities* [2005] ECR II-3649.

[97] Advocate General Maduro's Opinion of 16 January 2008 in Case C-402/05, *Yassin Abdullah Kadi v Council of the European Union and Commission of the European Communities*, nyr.

were based offended the rule of law, the EU rules based on the Security Council instruments should be annulled.

The *Kadi* case[98] confronted the ECJ with several difficult choices, including the question whether the EU courts have jurisdiction[99] to rule on the validity of legal instruments adopted within the European legal order to give effect to United Nations (UN) Resolutions. The ECJ gave a ruling of principle. It accepted full jurisdiction to review the contested regulation irrespective of its 'UN origin' and applied what it identified as 'higher law', arguing that 'the principles of liberty, democracy, and respect for human rights and fundamental freedoms enshrined in Article 6(1) EU as a foundation of the Union' could not be derogated from.[100] In essence, the ECJ used the 'rule of law' as a defensive mechanism protecting certain core principles of the EU constitutional legal order against attack—or 'shafting'—from the outside. Implicitly the ECJ rejected herewith the CFI's suggestion of a 'European political question doctrine'[101] and established clear limits for the external exercise of executive power.

In parallel with this process of establishing the Union's autonomy from pressures by the Member States from within the European legal order, the ECJ defended in *Kadi* the Union's autonomy against external pressure created by Member States cooperating with third states in the UN. At the same time, the ECJ rejected the UN's claim to independent normative authority. *Kadi* is an example of decisions adopted by the UN Security Council that directly affect individuals and hence the accumulation of executive power at the international level becomes more of a human-rights concern. The downside of the judgment however is, as Blokker rightly puts it, 'the undermining of the legal supremacy and the underlying political authority of the UN Security Council and its resolutions'.[102] This is not a small—or one presumes unintended—side effect.

It could be said that the absence of 'a genuine and effective mechanism of judicial control by an independent tribunal at the level of the United Nations' and hence the absence of a constitutionalized international legal order meant that the EU had the obligation to provide for judicial control of implementing measures that apply within its own legal order. Since EU instruments giving effect to UN Security Council resolutions offended the rule of law, they were annulled. This means Union measures necessary for the implementation of resolutions adopted

[98] C-402/05 P *Kadi v Council and Commission*, and C-415/05 P *Al Barakaat International Foundation v Council and Commission*, judgments of 3 September 2008, nyr.

[99] The CFI had denied its own competence to review: see its judgment of 21 September 2005, T-315/01 *Kadi v Council*, 2005 ECR II-3649.

[100] C-402/05 P *Kadi*, paras 302–3; see more generally, on 'higher law', T Koopmans (2006), 'De herontdekking van "hoger recht"', *Tijdschrift voor Privaatrecht*, 43/4, pp 1747–61.

[101] See discussion by AG Maduro, C-402/05 P *Kadi*, para 33 *et seq*.

[102] N Blokker (2009), 'Reviewing the review: Did the European Court of Justice in *Kadi* indirectly review Security Council resolutions? On the downside of a courageous judgment' in M Bulterman et al (eds), *Views of European Law from the Mountain* (The Hague: Kluwer), pp 315–26, p 325.

by the Security Council are *not* exempted from the constitutional principles set by Union law. However as Halberstam and Stein point out, the Court could also have gone further and engaged in a dialogue with the United Nations and provided 'a model for how domestic courts should interact responsibly with the international legal order...engaging productively with international law and developing human rights as a fundamental part of the international rule of law is a critical task that should not be ignored'.[103] Now it just threw down the gauntlet and left it at that.

In line with the traditionally strong position of the ECJ in ensuring that the rule of law is respected internally and that the institutional balance is maintained within the European legal order, the ECJ offered in the *Kadi* appeal a clear vision of the role of courts in ensuring boundaries of externalized executive power. The ECJ's *Kadi* judgment is a landmark case both in institutional terms and for the protection of fundamental rights. Taking a (purely) domestic European perspective from which the EU Courts have a relatively broad mandate,[104] the ECJ continued to build the equivalent of the national *Rechtsstaat* at the European level[105] and as a consequence to reinforce the features that distinguish the EU from other international organizations such as the UN. The 'rule of law' applied as a concept of EU constitutional discourse seems to be developing along the lines of what can be called the substantive-ideal-type rule of law aligned with norms of substantive justice (in particular the right to a legal remedy).[106]

In a core sense 'the rule of law reflects history of efforts to restrain sovereign power that continue in many States today, including some established liberal democracies confronting what the modern sovereign claims are emergencies requiring ever-greater claims to executive authority'.[107] The ECJ's ruling in *Kadi* is an attempt to stop the executive from hollowing out the rule of law from above, but the struggle between the Court and the executive to find the right balance in the fight against terrorism will go on.[108] The Court's role is traditionally a reactive one; they judge, from an *ex post* perspective, what is lawful and what is not. Hence, more challenges to the Court of Justice's vision of the 'Union of law'

[103] D Halberstam and E Stein (2009), 'The United Nations, the European Union and the King of Sweden: Economic sanctions and individual rights in a plural world order', Common Market L Rev, 46/1, pp 13–72, p 68.

[104] Art 220 TEC. [105] See too FG Jacobs (2007).

[106] See further the analysis by RH Fallon (1997), 'The "rule of law" as a concept in constitutional discourse', Columbia L Rev, 97/1, pp 1–56.

[107] S Chesterman (2008), 'An international rule of law?', American J of Comparative L, 56/2, pp 331–61, pp 360–1.

[108] Parallel developments can be witnessed with regard to restrictive measures adopted by the European Union in an autonomous (not directly UN related) procedure: see Cases T-228/02 *Organisation des Modjahedines du peuple d'Iran v Council and UK* [2006] ECR II-4665 and T-256/07 *People's Mojahedin Organization of Iran v Council*, judgment of 23 October 2008, nyr. See too T-284/08 *People's Mojahedin Organization of Iran v Council,* judgment of 4 December 2008, nyr; C Eckes (2008); J Hoffmann (2008), 'Terrorism blacklisting: Putting European human rights guarantees to the test', *Constellations*, 15/4, pp 543–60, p 551 *et seq*.

can be expected. Protecting liberty has been a particular challenge in the area of counter-terrorism policy, and the Court's strict stance can be contrasted with several recent decisions of regional and national courts in which the latter showed a high level of deference to externalized executive decisions intended to maintain peace and security.[109]

In terms of a response from the EU executive to the Court's judgment in Kadi the Commission has proposed an amendment to the relevant EU regulation in order to codify certain procedural requirements to be applied systematically to individuals and entities newly listed by the UN.[110] These amount to three separate stages. Upon notification by the UN Sanctions Committee of a new listing decision and the statement of reasons, the Commission will take a provisional decision to freeze the funds and economic resources of the individual or entity concerned. In parallel the Commission will send the statement of reasons to the individual or entity concerned without delay, in order to give him, her or it an opportunity to express his, her or its views. The Commission will then examine these views and consult an advisory committee of experts of the Member States before taking the final decision. In addition it is proposed that a review will take place of all names on the existing UN list in order to consider according to the same criteria whether their name should be maintained on the list or delisted. This newly proposed procedure applied to the UN lists would introduce the equivalent listing and delisting procedures for those followed for the EU's own terrorist list since the Court judgment in the *PMOI* case. According to the Commission such a procedure ensures that the fundamental rights of defence and in particular the right to be heard are respected also for those on the UN, at least in the EU context. Others insist that this represents the absolute minimum of an EU executive response to the Court ruling in *Kadi* and copper fastens the bizarre situation in which entities and individuals included on the UN list will have more rights in practice than those outside the EU.[111] In any event it seems that the authoritarian temptation hovers above the (secret) activities of and information released by both the UN sanctions committee and the secret EU

[109] ECtHR 2 May 2007, Application Nos 71412/01 and 78166/01, *Behrami v France; Saramati v France, Germany and Norway*. For a discussion on the cases see A Sari (2008), 'Jurisdiction and international responsibility in peace support operations: The *Behrami* and *Saramati* cases', Human Rights L Rev, 8/1, pp 151–70; see also the line of cases dismissed by the ECtHR after *Behrami*: *Beric and others v Bosnia and Herzegovina*. See further on these cases and the relevant cases of national courts, C Eckes (2009), *EU Counter-Terrorist Policies and Fundamental Rights: The case of individual sanctions* (Oxford: Oxford University Press), Ch 5, forthcoming. It is interesting that the judgment of the Swiss Federal Tribunal more or less adopted the same approach as the CFI: *'Nada gegen seco, Staatssekretariat für Wirtschaft, sowie Eidgenössisches Volkswirtschaftsdepartement'*, BGE 133 II 450, available at <http://www.bger.ch/index/juridiction/jurisdiction-inherit-template/jurisdiction-recht/jurisdiction-recht-urteile2000.htm>.

[110] See further, European Commission (2009), Proposal for a Council Regulation amending Regulation (EC) No 881/2002 imposing certain specific restrictive measures directed against certain persons and entities associated with Usama bin Laden, the Al-Qaida network and the Taliban Brussels, 22 April 2009, COM(2009) 187 final.

[111] Statewatch, <www.statewatch.org>.

Committee that will assist the Commission in preparing its decisions. To date there is little evidence that challenges to the statement of reasons provided are taken seriously (and perhaps the EU executive is in the difficult position that they may simply often not have the information available to them on which the UN statement of reasons is based), the courts in Luxembourg are likely to continue to assume a very pivotal role in the coming years.[112] Indeed already we have the imminent follow up to the *Sison* judgment and the relisting by him by the EU. *Sison* challenges the accuracy and legitimacy of the 'statement of reasons' upon which the Council based its listing decision.[113]

7.4 Internal and External Autonomy

The Court of Justice has in recent case law furthered its own thinking on the nature of 'autonomous legal order' as originally defined in cases such as *van Gend en Loos* and *Costa v Enel* in the early 1960s.[114] In so doing, it did not follow its CFI in giving Security Council resolutions a type of supra-constitutional status within the EU legal order, capable of justifying departure from primary European law including 'higher law' fundamental rights by its own executive power.[115] The Court of Justice took a firm stand in favour of the internal autonomy of the Union (Community) legal order vis-à-vis the UN Charter and the (executive-type) activities of the UN Security Council. In the words of Eckes, this 'was the right choice not only from an *effet utile* perspective of European law, but it is also justifiable in a normative dimension. The most laudable outcome of the ECJ's ruling in *Kadi* is that it ensures that member states cannot use European legal instruments in order to circumvent national constitutional guarantees.'[116]

The Court of Justice has, in fact, not only constructed an internal and reasonably unitary legal system but also in external terms, in particular in terms of its relationship with public international law, it has further delimited the nature of the autonomous legal order as a 'municipal' legal order, using the classic international law term hitherto reserved for a state domestic legal system.[117] In other words, the distinction between the autonomous nature of the (EU) legal order and that of public international law could not be greater: this adds an important further refinement on autonomy *externally*. After the Treaty of Lisbon enters into

[112] There are a number of new pending cases at the EU courts: Case C-27/09 P, Appeal by France against judgment in Case T-284/08, (PMOI); Case T-85/09, *Kadi v Commission* and Case T-45/09, *Al Barakaat International Foundation v Commission*.

[113] Case T-341/07, *Sison v Council*, hearing before the CFI on 30 April 2009.

[114] See too R Barents (2006), 'Case annotation of C-105/03, *Pupino*', *SEW- Tijdschrift voor Europees en economisch recht*, 1/2, pp 74–8, p 77.

[115] T-315/01 *Kadi v Council*, 2005 ECR II-3649.

[116] C Eckes (2010).

[117] See too D Halberstam and E Stein (2009), p 47.

force all doubt must surely be removed that one must speak of the 'municipal legal order' that is the Union as a whole. That legal order for the EU as a whole applies to the EU executive power as a whole irrespective to a very great extent of the specifics of the separate pillars. This trajectory—one could almost say by stealth, certainly 'hidden' in overall structural terms—of ever-greater legal unity is one that became clearly visible at the level of primary treaty law with the Treaty of Lisbon. It is a vivid example of the phenomenon of 'catch-up', how treaty-reform processes are used to adjust the highest law in accordance with legal and institutional practices, in this instance very largely a series of judgments by the Court of Justice in Luxembourg over the course of a decade.

The question whether the Court of Justice has played a role in constructing an interpretative constitutional framework internally for the EU as a whole and not just for the Community legal system as such must, it seems, be answered in the affirmative but with some qualifications. After the failure of the Treaty on the establishment of a Constitution for Europe to come into force, one question was whether this implied a denial of the constitutional status of the Union's legal order. We have seen that the development of the Union over the past 15 years was more based on what Germans would refer to as *Eigendynamik*, rather than on deliberate choices made in treaties. Nonetheless, as Hermann argues, 'Given the deliberate placing of the second and third pillar outside the Community framework by the Member States, it would be difficult to argue in favour of an identical legal nature of the pillars only on the basis of a claimed unity.'[118] While this is a truism, it is also obvious that legal unity referred to in this chapter does not merely concern the application of the Community characteristics and principles (in particular direct effect, primacy and the 'community method' in decision-making)[119] to the non-Community pillars, but also to the effect of the integration in the Community on CFSP and on the impossibility of approaching this pillar in isolation. The main conclusion in this regard could be that the Union's pillars are still separate, but inseparable. This has continuing relevance even after the Lisbon Treaty enters into force—in particular with regard to CFSP.[120]

The fact that emerges from the analysis in this chapter is that it is the Court that has provided the only constitutional framework we formally have to date—that of 'constitutionalization' of the treaties (a 'constitutional charter') in various, often scattered, ways, with reference to the principles of 'higher law'. It is supported by activities and practices by other actors that can also be understood as 'constitutionalization'. This includes in particular some inter-institutional agreements that, step by step and from 'below' (by the institutional actors themselves), introduce elements into the decision-making process and institutional

[118] CW Hermann (2007), 'Much ado about Pluto? The "unity of the legal order of the European Union" revisited', EUI Working Paper RSCAS 2007/05, p 18.

[119] See, for the importance of the 'Community method' to constitutional unity also, J Bast (2005), 'The Constitutional Treaty as a reflexive constitution', German LJ, 6/11, pp 1433–52.

[120] See too D Curtin and R Wessel (2008).

inter-actions that may be important from a wider 'constitutional' perspective (more parliamentary accountability, for instance). This will be elaborated on further in Chapter 9 below. Another salient example is what Craig refers to as the 'constitutionalization' of the administration by the EU (including direct and shared management as discussed in Chapter 5 above) by horizontal and overarching legal regulation such as the Financial Regulation of 2002. Constitutionalization is used here to denote 'the emergence of overarching principles that frame the entirety of Community administration'.[121]

Such judicial and wider institutional practices arguably all form part of what can be termed a sedimentary constitution. This is not a democratic political constitution, nor even a formal constitution ratified as such by national political actors (parliaments or the peoples) but is part of a broader constitutional perspective on the manner in which both the political and legal systems are evolving and are intertwined in the perspective of some fundamental tenets of constitutionalism.

Within a very limited time frame the EU has not only developed its own legal order—distinct both from the international legal order and the national legal orders—but its political system has evolved too, as well as the tension between the two. The role of the Court has been primordial but as the recent debate on the adoption of a 'European Constitution' showed, the domain of the 'constitutional' is no longer controlled by the judges (and lawyers) only but also by politicians (European and national) and one would hope—ultimately—by the citizens. But as the next two chapters will show on the issue of 'transparency' (Chapter 8) and 'public accountability' (Chapter 9), the EU institutions more generally may also have a very important role to play in the incremental build-up of substantial legal and institutional practices in those regards that frame legal and institutional checks and balances, building intricate (and at times overlapping) interconnections among executive and non executive institutions and actors.

[121] P Craig (2003), 'The constitutionalisation of Community administration', European L Rev, 28/6, pp 840–64.

8

Transparent Executive Power

8.1 Lifting the Veil of Secrecy

The origins of the term from the Latin *transparere* suggest something appearing as a result of light shining through; as a result, the composition of the space in question can be seen and understood. The term 'transparency' evokes the image of a clear pane of glass through which the sunshine (or the light) can beam in an unrestrained fashion. Transparency can be said to refer to the 'constant visibility of information'.[1] General definitions of transparency include 'lifting the veil of secrecy'[2] or 'the ability to look clearly through the windows of an institution'.[3] The term 'public' and the principle of publicity are often subsumed under the concept of 'transparency' as it is used in the context of debates in the EU. *Brewer's Politics* even defines the term 'transparency' as 'the catch word for the openness of the operations of the European Community to the public gaze'.[4]

The aim of achieving more transparency in the functioning of public EU institutions is lauded by the European institutions themselves, the politicians and bureaucrats, members of the European Parliament, the judiciary, and civil society. All these actors expect beneficial effects of EU transparency. In the short time frame of its emergence as a fundamental guiding principle of the EU political system, it has been presented as a type of holistic medicine designed to remedy many of the ailments the body of the EU is perceived to have. Thus, we are told, it will increase the legitimacy of the EU, increase the citizens' understanding of what the EU is about, stimulate deliberation about policy matters,

[1] R Lastra and H Shams (2001), 'Public accountability in the financial sector' in E Ferran and C Goodhart (eds), *Regulating Financial Services and Markets in the 21st Century* (Oxford: Hart Publishing), pp 165–88, p 171. See, in general, C Hood and D Heald (eds) (2006), *Transparency: The key to better governance?* (Oxford University Press).

[2] See, J Davis (1998), 'Access to and Transmission of Information: Position of the Media', in V Deckmyn and I Thomson (eds), *Openness and Transparency in the European Union* (Maastricht: European Institute of Public Administration), pp 121–126, at p 121.

[3] M den Boer (1998), 'Steamy windows: Transparency and openness in justice and home affairs' in V Deckmyn and I Thomson (eds), *Openness and Transparency in the European Union*, (Maastricht: European Institute of Public Administration), pp 91–105.

[4] W Safire (1998), 'On language: Transparency totally', *The New York Times*, 4 January, p 4.

and enable participation by citizens and their representatives.[5] These may well be 'myths'.[6]

The concept of transparency captures, in any event, the accessibility and visibility of information. A transparent political system is one where it is possible for people on the outside to acquire the information they need to form opinions about actions and processes within the political and administrative institutions. Transparency refers not only to access to executive-held information by individuals and legislative assemblies (both the European Parliament and the national parliaments) but also, more widely, to 'open government' as such (the question of opening up meetings, rule-making proceedings and governmental deliberations to the public). The term is also used in the more structural sense of clarity of language as part of good administrative practice. This latter aspect is not considered further in this context.[7]

The purpose of this chapter is to explore within the framework of the evolving legal and political systems of the EU the manner in which a legal principle of transparency has been conceptualized and applied in practice. In addition the manner in which the different executive institutions and actors have given proactive content to the principle of openness as a matter of practice will be explored and analysed. In later chapters (respectively Chapters 9 and 10) a link will be made between the concept and practice of accountability and with normative conceptions of democratic legitimacy.

8.2 Conceptualizing the EU Principle of 'Transparency': Legal Constitutionalism

8.2.1 The veil of secrecy

The introduction of direct elections to the European Parliament in 1979 might have been expected to produce some effect on the traditional secrecy of the Council's legislative and executive roles but it did not.[8] As late as the early 1990s an insider observed: 'The cloak of secrecy was an essential part of the Council's methodology...'.[9] Explanations of what transpired at meetings of the Council of Ministers were given in 'off-the record' briefings to Brussels-based journalists.

[5] European Commission, 'European Transparency Initiative' COM (2006) 194 final, 3 May 2006, p 2; 'A partnership for European renewal: Prosperity, solidarity and security', Communication from the President in agreement with Vice President Wallström, COM (2005) 12 final, 26 January 2005, p 5.

[6] See, in this sense, D Curtin and A Meijer (2006), 'Does transparency strengthen legitimacy? A critical analysis of European Union policy documents', *Information Polity*, 11/2, pp 109–22.

[7] But see M Aziz (2004), 'Mainstreaming the duty of clarity and transparency as part of good administrative practice in the EU', European LJ, 10/3, pp 282–95.

[8] T Bunyan (2002), 'Secrecy and openness in the European Union: The ongoing struggle for freedom of information', available at <http://www.freedominfo.org/features/20020930-ch1.htm>.

[9] M Westlake (1995), *The Council of the European Union* (London: Catermill), p 145.

The political system of the EU is not, as a whole, known for its 'transparency' either in terms of its institutional design or in terms of the full range of its rule-making outputs. Change was 'kick-started' by a number of exogenous events.[10]

The first was the very first rejection of a EU Treaty by a national electorate—the Danes—in 1992. In an attempt to persuade the Danish electorate when they voted second time around on the Treaty of Maastricht, the adoption of a Code of Conduct by both the Commission and the Council 'concerning public access to Council and Commission documents'[11] marked a step forward. This attempted to give substance to Declaration no 17 of the Maastricht Treaty that 'transparency of the decision-making process strengthens the democratic nature of the institutions and the public's confidence in the administration'. From December 1993 the Council was forced to make a series of concessions when challenged by journalists and an MEP in the Court of First Instance (CFI) and via the European Ombudsman (see further below). EU Member States who had always favoured more openness, especially Denmark and Sweden (who joined the EU in 1995), and who were joined on different occasions by Finland, the Netherlands, and the UK, were able to build on these external challenges to Council secrecy.[12]

In recent years it has become especially clear that a secret administrative culture is at the heart of many of the EU's problems and exists right across the spectrum of its institutions and organs. The second exogenous event was the resignation of the Santer Commission in the aftermath of the publication of the First Report of the Committee of Independent Experts (CIE) in March 1999. The boils of secrecy and of lack of (collective) responsibility of the Commission were rather publicly lanced as a result. The gist of the general problem, according to the Committee, was openness and transparency, as linked with responsibility and accountability. In the CIE's view, these fundamental principles needed urgently to permeate the EU's political and administrative culture *in all areas and at all levels*. Transparency came to be regarded as a hallmark of good governance and, as such, as a value in itself. From that perspective, good government conforms to criteria such as responsiveness, accountability, effectiveness, transparency, and so forth.[13]

8.2.2 The general legal principle of reasoned administration

In 1998, the European Ombudsman, Jacob Söderman defined the term transparency in a rather descriptive and narrow fashion, as mandating that: 'the

[10] For an overview of the emergence of the EU transparency agenda see S Peers (2002), 'From Maastricht to Laeken: The political agenda of openness and transparency in the European Union' in V Deckmyn (ed), *Increasing Transparency in the European Union?* (Maastricht: European Institute of Public Administration), pp 7–32.

[11] OJ L 340, 31 December 1993, pp 41–2.

[12] T Bunyan (2002).

[13] See, for example, European Commission, White Paper on Governance, COM (2001) 428 final.

process through which public authorities make decisions should be understandable and open; the decisions themselves should be reasoned; as far as possible, the information on which the decisions are based should be available to the public'.[14] The emphasis in this definition clearly lies on the legal dimension in the sense of the formal manner in which decisions are reasoned as well as on the issue of public access to information.[15] According to Lord Nolan transparency is said to require that 'holders of public office should be as open as possible about all decisions and actions they take'.[16] They should, in his view, give reasons for their decisions and restrict information only when the wider public interest clearly so demands. It can be argued however that transparency not only incorporates the rather passive right of every citizen to have access to information (if they activate that formal legal right) but also the much broader and more pro-active duty of the administration itself to ensure that information about its policy and actions is provided in an accessible fashion.

The evolution of the concept of transparency in the context of the EU can be divided into two periods. The first—initial—period was dominated by a legal understanding and, in particular, a focus on the principle of *access to documents*. In the second—later—more *political* period of EU transparency, the Internet has played a much more important role and is the main medium for the EU to create transparency for the widely dispersed population of Europe. This later period was not dominated by the law and lawyers but rather by the institutions themselves and ongoing digitization processes (see further below) and represents a rather descriptive and empirical approach to the concept of transparency.

The legal approach is more normative and sought to build on existing EC case law on the right to be heard, the right to have reasoned decisions, and to have access to a file.[17] It gave further substance to the quite developed legal accountability mechanisms within the framework of the EU. It is based on the specific responsibilities of three decision-making institutions (the European Commission, the Council, and the European Parliament) that have now been laid down in increasingly 'hard' legal instruments and also the interpretation by the European Courts of legal standards laid down in such measures.

[14] J Söderman (1998), 'The citizen, the administration and community law', General Report for the XVIII Congress of FIDE (Fédération Internationale pour le Droit Européen), Stockholm, 3–6 June 1998.

[15] V Deckmyn (2002), *Increasing Transparency in the European Union?* (Maastricht: European Institute for Public Administration); B Vesterdorf (1999), 'Transparency: Not just a vogue word', Fordham International LJ, 22/3, pp 902–29, p 903.

[16] Lord Nolan (1995), *Standards in Public Life: First report of the Committee on Standards in Public Life* (London: HMSO), available at <http://www.archive.official-documents.co.uk/document/cm28/2850/285002.pdf>, p 14.

[17] See further H Ragnemaln (1999), 'The Community courts and openness within the European Union' in A Dashwood and A Ward (eds), Cambridge Yearbook of European Legal Studies, 2, pp 19–30; B Vesterdorf (1999); KStC Bradley (1999), 'La transparence de l'Union européenne: une évidence ou un trompe l'oeil?', *Cahiers de Droit Européenne*, 35 3–4, pp 283–362, p 283.

The EU transparency-related measures adopted prior to entry into force of the Treaty of Amsterdam in 1999 were largely inspired by two key considerations. First, they were motivated by the overall aim of increasing confidence in the administration itself, by making the institutions behave in accordance with the precepts of good administration. The CFI and the Court of Justice have been particularly insistent on this point, stressing that the function of the specific rules adopted by certain institutions under their rules of procedure has been 'to ensure that their internal operation is in conformity with the interests of good administration'.[18] What precisely we must understand by the use of this term in this context is less clear: for example, in his general study of the subject, Nehl stresses the caution of the court(s) over the years in imbuing this vague concept with substantive parameters in the EC context.[19] Considering the term 'good' administration as synonymous with the principle of 'sound' or 'proper' administration does not take us very far beyond the realm of a rhetorical phrase and does not necessarily imply a procedural standard. Article 41(2) of the Charter of Fundamental Rights includes specific procedural rights such as access to a person's own file as an individual manifestation of access to documents and as such part of the 'right to good administration'.[20] Prechal and de Leeuw include under this heading also such specific and 'established' procedural rights under EU law as the 'need to have clear procedures' and the duty of the administration to inform complainants of decisions and their consequences.[21]

One view is that reason-giving by political and administrative actors contributes not only to judicial review but also to the general transparency of official decision-making, thereby facilitating oversight and accountability to political actors and the general public and not just to the courts and litigants. European judges have tended not to require reasons for every detail but rather it is sufficient to show how the major issues of fact and law were resolved. This procedural rationality tends to demand more careful attention to the articulation of the bases for decisions precisely where they are most within the technical expertise of the administrative actors. It seems that in both the US and the European case law:

> the right to receive reasons is a sort of derivative right. It facilitates individual decision-making about whether to contest official decisions, protects rights to individualized adjudication, and promotes the monitoring activities of both political and legal institutions. And reasons in both systems have a special value in maintaining vigorous judicial review along the treacherous boundary between law and policy. From this perspective,

[18] Case C-58/94 *Netherlands v Council* [1996] ECR I-2169.

[19] HP Nehl (1999), *Principles of Administrative Procedure in EC Law* (Oxford: Hart Publishing), p 17.

[20] See, for an analysis of the structure and implications of this right, B Grzeszick (2006), 'Das Grundrecht auf eine gute Verwaltung: Strukturen und Perspektiven des Charta-Grundrechts auf eine gute Verwaltung', *Europarecht*, 2, pp 161–81; DU Galetta (2007), 'Inhalt und Bedeutung des europäischen Rechts auf eine gute Verwaltung', *Europarecht*, 1, pp 57–81.

[21] See further S Prechal and M de Leeuw (2007), 'Dimensions of transparency: The building blocks for a new legal principle?', Review of European Administrative Law, 0/1, pp 51–61.

the fundamental value of reason giving is political and legal accountability. The requirement that administrative officials give reasons is merely a crucially important means to that end.[22]

The argument is, however, also made that there is more to reason-giving as an aspect of good administration than this instrumental account. In particular, it can be argued that the right to reasoned administration might be available even where there is no right to (specific) judicial review of the decision's substance. In the light of the limited judicial review at EU level this view, grounded in a broad notion of *democratic* legitimacy, may be salient. The result is that the right to receive reasons is not only an enforceable right in court but may also be promoted through other non-legal means. Examples of the latter may include not only oversight exercised, for example, by the Ombudsman but also oversight by for example audit institutions such as the Court of Auditors attempting to ensure *responsible administration*. EU administration without reason-giving cannot meet the challenge of defending the democratic legitimacy either of the administrative executive or of the evolving polity as a whole.[23]

8.2.3 Proactive litigants and courts

Specific transparency-related measures adopted pre-Amsterdam have been viewed as a matter for the affected institutions themselves, to do with their internal functioning and hence falling under their respective rules of procedure. This essentially self-regulatory approach meant that initially the tendency was to view the principle of public access as, at most, a voluntarily assumed specific principle of administrative law that has gradually, through the medium of case law, acquired some *procedural* flesh and substance.[24] That case law is in line with more general procedural case law emphasized the nature of procedural discretion in balancing the various interests at stake. It was not considered a 'general principle' of European law but rather overlaps with certain other well-established general principles (such as the principle of legal certainty and the principle of non-discrimination) in areas of EU law other than specifically access to documents.[25] In the decade since the Treaty of Amsterdam included a specific treaty provision on openness and access to documents, it seems to now be acknowledged that there is a EU legal principle of the right to documents.

[22] See too J Mashaw (2007), 'Reasoned administration: The European Union, the United States and the project of democratic governance', George Washington L Rev, 76/2, pp 99–124, p 115.

[23] See too O Brouwer and D Curtin (2009), 'Why? The giving reasons requirement of EU administration' in MK Bulterman et al (eds), *Views of European Law from the Mountain* (Kluwer, The Hague), pp 133–41.

[24] On this case law see further D Curtin (2000), 'Citizens' fundamental right of access to information: An evolving digital passepartout?', Common Market L Rev, 37/1, pp 7–21.

[25] For a very general discussion see S Prechal and M de Leeuw (2007).

The focus in this first time period was on gradually constructing a right of access by the public to certain categories of document held by the three decision-making institutions. The European CFI and the Court of Justice played a crucial role. In a short period of time, they effectively built a body of case law that on the whole kept pressure on the institutions to behave fairly and to devise adequate systems of scrutiny. They tended rather generously to interpret the scope of the legal provisions so that, for example, specific institutional arrangements did not operate to reduce the reach of the access to documents provisions. Thus, in the very first case to reach the European Courts, the *Guardian* journalist, John Carvel, successfully challenged the Council's refusal to grant him the agendas and minutes of various Council meetings including those relating to policymaking in the new and sensitive area of justice and home affairs.[26] Later the Swedish Union of Journalists challenged the refusal of the Council to reveal documents relating to the establishment of Europol, using the more generous Swedish Freedom of Information Law to highlight the unnecessary degree of secrecy that prevailed at the European level.[27]

The technique of legal interpretation used by the Courts during this foundational period involved a type of teleological reasoning which placed the initial Code of Conduct adopted by two decision-making institutions in the context of its broader democratic purpose.[28] The Courts tended to emphasize the underlying purpose of access to documents, namely to provide the 'public', the citizens, with a means of controlling the abuse of power and corruption, as well as resting on general notions of public control of the activities of public institutions. Thus, the Courts developed what can be termed a constitutional perspective on access to documents provisions *avant la lettre*. Only later were these 'rights' given an explicitly constitutional foundation, first in the Treaty of Amsterdam, then in the Charter on Fundamental Rights and later in the Constitutional Treaty taken over in the Lisbon Treaty.

8.2.4 Union legislation consolidates

The specifically 'legal' phase culminated with the adoption of a new and binding legal instrument, Regulation 1049/2001 that entered into force on 3 December 2001.[29] This regulation introduced more transparency into the

[26] Case T-194/94 *Carvel and Guardian Newspapers v Council* [1995] ECR II-2765.

[27] Case T-174/95 *Svenska Journalistfo'rbundet (Swedish Union of Journalists) v Council* [1998] ECR II-2289.

[28] See further D Curtin (1996), 'Betwixt and between: Democracy and transparency in the governance of the EU' in JA Winter et al (eds), *Reforming the Treaty on European Union* (The Hague: Kluwer Law International), pp 95–121; D Curtin (1999), 'The fundamental principle of open decision-making and EU (political) citizenship' in D O'Keeffe and P Twomey (eds), *Legal Issues of the Amsterdam Treaty* (Oxford: Hart Publishing), pp 71–92.

[29] Regulation (EC) No 1049/2001 regarding public access to European Parliament, Council and Commission documents, OJ L 145, 31 May 2001, p 43.

work of the EU institutions.[30] EU level legislation granting a public right of access to the documents of certain EU institutions has given individual citizens and other actors the legal right to obtain a wide range of documents on request, without the need to provide any reasons.[31] This includes access to preparatory documents of the institutions themselves as well as documents from the many committees operating under the auspices of the three main lawmaking institutions (the Commission, the Council of Ministers, and the European Parliament).[32] A significant limitation is the fact that the right of access is limited to documents of these three named institutions in line with the specific text of Art 255 TEC. This however leaves out of account not only four other institutions named explicitly in the treaty, namely the Courts (of First Instance and of Justice), the Committee of the Regions, the ESC, and the Court of Auditors but also a whole host of other bodies and agencies (for example, Europol, the Trade Mark Agency etc).[33] What happens in practice is that they all (with the only exception of the Courts in Luxembourg) adopt parallel legal provisions via their own internal rules of procedure—prodded by an own investigation by the Ombudsman back in 1998.[34] This legislation has been applied voluntarily by a wide variety of other institutions and (quasi-) autonomous actors.[35] The Treaty of Lisbon in Art 15(3) TFEU consolidates this position in practice with the explicit treaty level provision that the right of access is to 'documents of the Union institutions, bodies, offices and agencies, whatever their medium'.

[30] European Commission (2003) 'Report from the Commission on the application in 2002 of Regulation (EC) No 1049/2001 of the European Parliament and the Council regarding public access to European Parliament, Council and Commission documents' (Brussels). For an overview of the legal characteristics of this regulation and perspectives for a possible revision, see M Maes (2007) 'L'accès du public aux documents des Institutions de la Communauté européenne: vers une révision du règlement (CE) 1049/2001', *Revue du Droit de l'Union Européenne,* pp 411–32, p 416 *et seq*.

[31] Regulation (EC) No 1049/2001 regarding public access to European Parliament, Council and Commission documents, OJ L 145, 31 May 2001, p 43. See further, European Commission, 'Green Paper: Public access to documents held by the institutions of the European Community. A review', COM (2007) 185 final, 18 May 2007. See too Commission Staff Working Document, Report on the Outcome of the Public Consultation on the Review of Regulation (EC) No 1049/2001 regarding public access to European Parliament, Council and Commission documents, SEC (2008) 29/2 (16 January 2008).

[32] S Bartelt and HE Zeitler (2003), 'Zugang zu Dokumenten der EU', *Europarecht,* 3, pp 487–503, p 491.

[33] Riemann points to the risk that the creation of autonomous agencies might be used to evade the access to documents regulation, see F Riemann (2004), *Die Transparenz der Europäischen Union: Das neue Recht auf Zugang zu Dokumenten von Parlament, Rat und Kommission* (Berlin: Duncker & Humblot), p 274 *et seq*.

[34] Draft recommendation by the Ombudsman to the European institutions, bodies and agencies in the own initiative inquiry OI/1/98/OV, available at <http://www.ombudsman.europa.eu/cases/draftrecommendation.faces/en/507/html.bookmark>.

[35] See further J Helliskoski and P Leino (2006), 'Darkness at the break of noon: The case law on Regulation No. 1049/2001 on Access to Documents', Common Market L Rev, 43/3, pp 735–82.

Regulation 1049/2001 is currently undergoing a revision process. Based on a Green Paper[36] and a public consultation,[37] the Commission adopted its proposal for a revision of the Regulation on 30 April 2008.[38] According to the Commission, the draft revised regulation took into account both the public consultation, the 'Cashman Resolution' of the European Parliament of 4 April 2006,[39] and the relevant case law of the European Courts.[40] However, the proposal was almost immediately subject to severe criticism by the European Ombudsman,[41] academics, and NGOs[42] who argue that the Commission's proposal actually provided not more but less protection than the current regulation. One of the main points of criticism regards the proposed new definition of a 'document'. Under the Commission's proposal, documents would be covered be the Access Regulation if they were 'formally transmitted to', 'registered, or received' by a Community institution.[43] It was argued that this definition would delay public access to documents and would in many cases completely exclude it where the document was simply not registered.[44] Doubts were also raised with respect to the compatibility of this proposed amendment with Art 255 TEC that constitutes the legal basis of the Access Regulation.[45] In February 2009 the Committee on Civil Liberties, Justice and Home Affairs of the European Parliament adopted the 'Cashman Report'.[46] This report proposed substantial changes to the Commission's

[36] COM (2007) 185 Green Paper of 18 April 2007, 'Public access to documents held by institutions of the European Community: A review', OJ C 181, 3 August 2007.

[37] SEC/2008/29 final, Commission staff working document of 11 January 2008—Report on the outcome of the public consultation on the review of Regulation (EC) No 1049/2001 regarding public access to European Parliament, Council and Commission documents.

[38] COM (2008) 229 final, Proposal of 30 April 2008 for a Regulation of the European Parliament and of the Council regarding public access to European Parliament, Council and Commission documents, <http://eur-lex.europa.eu/LexUriServ/LexUriServ.do?uri=COM:2008:0229:FIN:EN:PDF>.

[39] European Parliament Resolution of 4 April 2006 with recommendations to the Commission on access to the Institutions' texts, A6–0052/2006 / P6_TA-PROV(2006)0122.

[40] COM (2008) 229 final (n 38 above).

[41] European Ombudsman, Ombudsman warns that citizens' right of access to documents is at risk, Press release no 7/2008 of 2 June 2008, available at <http://www.ombudsman.europa.eu/press/release.faces/en/241/html.bookmark>.

[42] Statewatch analysis, The European Commission proposals to amend the Regulation on access to EU documents (1049/2001), Statewatch 2008, available at <http://www.statewatch.org/news/2008/apr/com-access-1049-statewatch-analysis-April.pdf>.

[43] COM (2008) 229 final (n 38 above), Amendments to Art 3(a).

[44] T Bunyan (2008a), 'Access to EU documents: When is a "document" not a "document"?', *Statewatch Analysis*, available at <http://www.statewatch.org/news/2008/sep/access-to-eu-docs-eu-what-is-a-document.pdf>, p 2; S Peers (2008), 'Proposal on access to documents: Article-by-article commentary', *Statewatch Analysis*, available at <http://www.statewatch.org/foi/sw-analysis-docs-june-2008.pdf>, p 5.

[45] S Peers (2008).

[46] European Parliament, Committee on Civil Liberties, Justice and Home Affairs Report of 19 February 2009 on the proposal for a regulation of the European Parliament and of the Council regarding public access to European Parliament, Council and Commission documents (recast) (COM (2008)0229–C6–0184/2008–2008/0090 (COD)) ('Cashman Report'). See also Committee on Civil Liberties, Justice and Home Affairs, Draft Report of 5 January 2009 on the

proposal, removing, among other things, the restrictive definition of 'document' put forward by the Commission.[47] On 11 March 2009 the European Parliament adopted on the first reading the Commission's proposal.[48] As the 'Cashman Report', it proposed numerous amendments, ranging from a broader definition of the term 'document',[49] to a provision enabling the European Ombudsman to give its view on the existence of a 'question of harm and/or overriding public interest' regarding disclosure of a document.[50] In a reaction to this vote, the European Ombudsman has welcomed the European Parliament's amendments.[51] In this manner we can observe how, through the normal co-decision legislative process, the European Parliament (and other actors) are able to engage in a constructive fashion in an inter-institutional dialogue with the aim of increasing, not decreasing openness in the manner that decisions are taken in the context of the EU.

8.2.5 The legal–constitutional approach

In conclusion, some ten years after its commencement, the legal–constitutional approach can be considered as solidly anchored in legal texts, including at the most fundamental level of the EU Treaty. The provisions on public access to documents clearly have caused changes by giving citizens a tool to obtain the documents they wish to obtain, albeit with a considerable time lag in practice. Access to documents has acquired the status of a rather fundamental norm in

proposal for a regulation of the European Parliament and of the Council regarding public access to European Parliament, Council and Commission documents (recast) (COM(2008)0229–C6-0184/2008–2008/0090 (COD)).

[47] Committee on Civil Liberties, Justice and Home Affairs Report of 19 February 2009 on the proposal for a regulation of the European Parliament and of the Council regarding public access to European Parliament, Council and Commission documents (recast) (COM (2008) 0229–C6-0184/2008–2008/0090 (COD)) ('Cashman Report'), Amendment 36.

[48] European Parliament, Draft Resolution of 11 March 2008, P6 TA-PROV (2009) 0114 Public access to European Parliament, Council and Commission documents (recast), Proposal for a regulation of the European Parliament and of the Council regarding public access to European Parliament, Council and Commission documents (recast) (COM (2008) 0229–C6-0184/2008–2008/0090 (COD)) (Co-decision procedure—first reading).

[49] European Parliament, Draft Resolution of 11 March 2008, P6 TA-PROV (2009) 0114 Public access to European Parliament, Council and Commission documents (recast), Proposal for a regulation of the European Parliament and of the Council regarding public access to European Parliament, Council and Commission documents (recast) (COM (2008) 0229–C6-0184/2008–2008/0090 (COD)) (Co-decision procedure—first reading), p 8, Amendments to Art 4.

[50] European Parliament, Draft Resolution of 11 March 2008, P6 TA-PROV (2009) 0114 Public access to European Parliament, Council and Commission documents (recast), Proposal for a regulation of the European Parliament and of the Council regarding public access to European Parliament, Council and Commission documents (recast) (COM (2008) 0229–C6-0184/2008–2008/0090 (COD)) (Co-decision procedure—first reading), p 8, Amendments to Art 17.

[51] European Ombudsman, Ombudsman welcomes European Parliament's suggestions to improve public access to EU documents, Press release no 6/2009 of 11 March 2009, available at: <http://www.ombudsman.europa.eu/press/release.faces/en/3838/html.bookmark>.

the EU legal and constitutional system. At the same time it has however also in recent years become highly 'legalized' with many of the most crucial issues as to the meaning of the exceptions, the relationship with national legal provisions and the relationship with other legal rights that also enjoy a fundamental status (eg privacy and data protection[52]). The Courts in Luxembourg who were once seen as the 'unsung heroes' of those seeking to open up the inner institutional workings of the EU have come under fire at times for what is perceived to be an unnecessarily generous interpretation of the scope and meaning of several key exceptions to the legal right.[53] This criticism is less salient in the light of more recent far-reaching judgments of the Court of Justice overturning the CFI, for instance in the *Turco* case. In that judgment, the Court did not fail to state the underlying principle at stake in very fundamental terms. Increased openness, in the view of the Court, 'enables citizens to participate more closely in the decision-making process and guarantees that the administration enjoys greater legitimacy and is more effective and more accountable to the citizen in a democratic system'.[54] Likewise it has rejected claims by the Commission in particular that what has been termed a 'general right to anonymous participation in public activities'[55] exists for (national) civil servants and experts in the context of EU decision-making.[56]

The Court's approach is underpinned by the complementary work of the Ombudsman who also adopts a rather legal approach in his work, although his emphasis is more on the structural aspects of the manner in which certain institutions, mainly the Council and the Commission, made information available or not.[57] Thus, the first Ombudsman tended to focus on substantiating what he termed 'good administrative behaviour', in a manner highly complementary to the more formal judicial interpretation of the Courts.[58] As arbiter of maladministration, the Ombudsman has an interest in transparency as good governance

[52] See further H Kranenborg (2007), *Toegang tot documenten en bescherming van persoonsgegevens in de Europese Unie: Over de openbaarheid van persoonsgegevens,* (The Hague: Kluwer Law International).

[53] See further J Helliskoski and P Leino (2006).

[54] Joined Cases C-39/05P and C-52/05P *Turco v Council of Ministers*, consideration 45, judgment of 1 July 2008, nyr.

[55] Letter of the European Ombudsman, Jacob Soderman of 30 September 2002, <www.ombudsman.europa.eu/letters/eu/default.htm>.

[56] See respectively the Court of First Instance's judgments in Case T-194/04, *Bavarian Lager Company Ltd v Commission* [2007] ECR II-4523 and Case T-121/05, *Borax Europe Ltd v Commission*, judgment of 11 March 2009, nyr. See further on the inter-relationship between access to documents and data protection in the EU, H Kranenborg (2008), 'Access to documents and data protection in the EU: On the public nature of personal data' 45 CML Rev, pp 1079–114.

[57] For an overview of the activities of the Ombudsman in this respect see I Harden (2002), 'The European Ombudsman's efforts to increase openness in the Union' in V Deckmyn (ed), *Increasing Transparency in the European Union* (Maastricht: European Institute of Public Administration), pp 123–45, p 130 *et seq*.

[58] P Magnette (2003), 'Between parliamentary control and the rule of law: The political role of the Ombudsman in the European Union', *Journal of European Public Policy*, 10/5, pp 677–94.

and his Code of Good Administrative Behaviour helps to promote transparency through the formulation of policies as rules and guidelines.[59] The code provides guidance to public servants on requests for access to information. Indeed, the work of the Ombudsman helps to move the understanding of transparency in the EU context away from an individual and passive focus on the legal right of every citizen to have access to certain documents to a much broader and proactive duty of the EU administration to ensure that information about its policies and actions are made genuinely accessible. The European Ombudsman's inquisitorial procedures, allow him to access administrative files and also to make files public during the proceedings and are perhaps the most potent machinery for opening windows on public information yet devised. They can also provide an alternative route for members of the public to access documents—and one that does not entail the costs involved in the more formal 'legal' route. Thus the office acts as an important catalyst for openness and transparency.[60] The work of the Ombudsman in this period facilitated the process of creating visible spaces around which the public could form.

The best way of understanding overall the legal contribution to the transparency discourse is that it has made some of the institutions more aware of how they can proactively make their own information widely available to the public using information and communication technologies. The Internet played a limited role in this early period since the EU did not actively create transparency. Documents were only provided to citizens when they specifically asked for them. It was only the implementation in practice of the obligation to make available and maintain a register of documents on each of the three main decision-making (legislative) institutions that has enabled the 'public' to know what sorts of documents they might want to have access to. In providing such a register the Internet does play an important role.

8.2.6 Comparing apples and oranges

Examining the data available from the Commission and Council in their annual reports on the subject, it is clear that there is a relatively sustained growth in the exercise of the right to access documents. For example, for the Council this figure grew from 431 documents requested in 1994 to 7,809 documents requested in 2007 (with 11,353 documents requested in 2006). In 2007 there were 1,964 actual requests from the public (2,224 requests in 2006), with a high

[59] European Ombudsman, *European Code of Good Administrative Behaviour*, available in the latest version at <http://www.euro-ombudsman.eu.int/>. For efforts to turn the code into a law, see his Annual Report for 2003, pp 27–8; Annual Report for 2004, p 20; and the introduction to the 2005 version of the Code.

[60] See too C Harlow (2009), 'Transparency in the European Union: Weighing the public and private interest' in J Wouters, L Verhey, and P Kiiver (eds), *European Constitutionalism beyond Lisbon* (Antwerp: Intersentia), pp 209–38.

proportion of success (approximately eight out of ten).[61] But as emerges from Fig 8.1, it is not always possible to compare even across institutions. From 1994, shortly after the access to documents policy was introduced, up to 2005 it was possible to compare the numbers of requests made for documents (taking into account that these often covered groups of documents and not just individual documents). Since its 2006 annual report on access to its documents the Commission stopped providing information on the numbers of requests as such and ordered its information differently (numbers of documents). This is why the figures in the graph below (Fig 8.1) include requests for multiple documents and after 2005 could not be compared for both Council and Commission on the basis of publicly available information. It can be seen from the graph that the number of requests peaked about 2004 for the Council, although the Commission figures continued to increase. It is not possible to explain on the basis of the respective annual reports why the variations in numbers occur. Despite the largely incremental increase, it is true that if the access request numbers are put in relation to the population of the EU then a very limited number of citizens overall have used that right to date.[62]

Comparing the formal access to document provisions with access to information on web pages is the equivalent of comparing apples to oranges. For example in the case of the Council of Ministers, the 'apples' are the 7,809 documents released as a result of formal requests; the 'oranges' are the 102,087 documents made directly available via the register as soon as they had been circulated in 2007. As of 31 December 2007 the register listed 1,010,217 documents (all languages together) of which 724,338 (71.7% of those registered) were public, ie either available in downloadable format (700,449 documents in PDF or HTML format) or on request (23,889 documents in other formats).[63] These latest figures represent an increase of 19% in the number of documents referred to in the register and an increase of 20% in the number of documents directly accessible via the register (as compared to only one year previously).[64]

With the implementation of online access to the Council Register in particular the number of downloads of the Council's documents multiplied however very considerably.[65] Moreover, if a rough estimate is made of users and the number of screens accessed, then online access is approximately 500 hundred times that of non-virtual access. In 2007 the total number of visits to the Council's public document register was 2,078,602 visits and 9,212,745 screens were consulted.[66]

[61] Council Annual Report on Access to Documents, 2007 (April 2008), <http://www.consilium.europa.eu/uedocs/cmsUpload/ACCESS_int.en08.pdf>.

[62] L Cotino (2006), 'Theory and reality of public access to EU information' in D Curtin, A Kellermann, and S Blockmans (eds), *The EU Constitution: The best way forward?* (The Hague: Kluwer), pp 233–44, 239, who refers to the exercise of formal accesss as 'practically anecdotal': in 2006 33,000 citizens had exercised that right.

[63] See further Council Annual Report on Access to Documents, 2007 (April 2008).

[64] Ibid. [65] See further L Cotino (2006).

[66] Council Annual Report on Access to Documents, 2007 (April 2008).

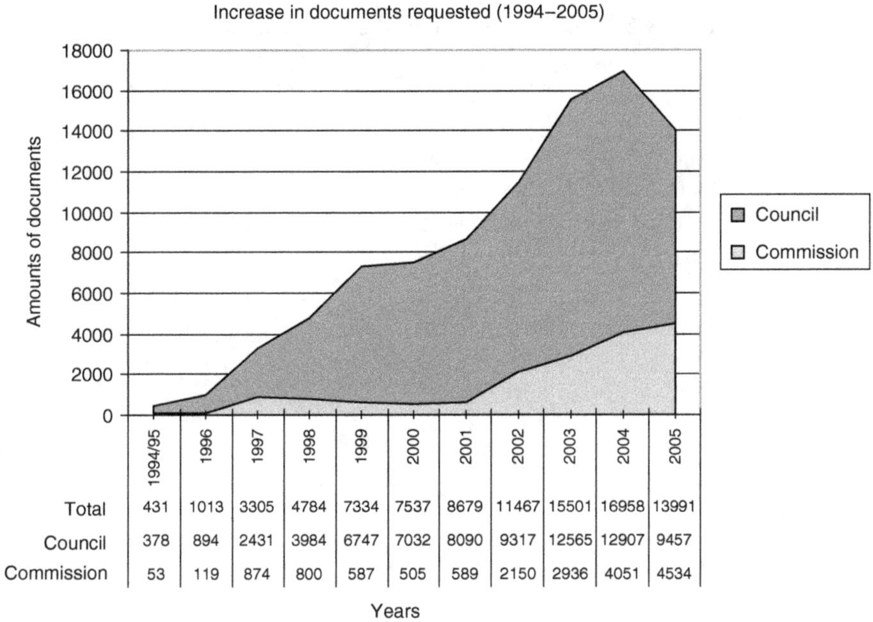

	1994/95	1996	1997	1998	1999	2000	2001	2002	2003	2004	2005
Total	431	1013	3305	4784	7334	7537	8679	11467	15501	16958	13991
Council	378	894	2431	3984	6747	7032	8090	9317	12565	12907	9457
Commission	53	119	874	800	587	505	589	2150	2936	4051	4534

Fig 8.1 Increase in documents requested (1994–2005)

Source: L Cotino (2006) for the figures until 2004. The figures for 2005 are drawn from *Reports on use Regulation* 1049/2001 of both the Council and Commission.

Table 8.1 Amount of documents in register of the Council and the Commission

	2001	2002	2003	2004	2005	2006	2007	Total
Commission	12,118	11,889	11,876	12,808	12,394	12,623	13,179	86,887
Council	-	-	448,236	569,372	691,410	727,685	1,010,217	3,446,920

This was the fifth successive annual increase and represents an increase of 21 per cent in one year in the number of visits. The number of individual users of the register increased moreover by 22.4 per cent during the reference period. These figures reveal just how central the digital highway and the proactive provision of documents have become in the six-plus years that it has been effective. But the crucial point is that despite the large and increasing numbers of 'oranges' the similarly increasing numbers of requests for 'apples' relate almost exclusively to documents that are listed but not directly accessible via the register.[67] This latter

[67] Ibid p 27.

Table 8.2 Visitors to the Europa site (www.europa.eu)

Year	Number of visitors	Increase in %
1998	80,000,000	-
1999	177,600,000	122
2000	318,300,000	79
2001	479,400,000	51
2002	612,800,000	28
2003	840,915,076	37
2004	1,060,181,999	26
2005	1,394,343,602	32
2006	1,394,684,283	0
2007	1,412,647,371	1
2008	1,746,496,079	24

Source: Cotino (2006) for 1998–2002 (figures used are rounded off). From 2003 onwards, <www.europa.eu> and reports on use Regulation 1049/2001 of both the Council and Commission.

figure accounts for 32.8 per cent of the Council documents produced in 2007 and listed on the Council register—some 52,778 documents.

8.3 Operationalizing the EU Principle of 'Transparency': Institutional Politics

8.3.1 The role of the Internet

As we have seen above the academic discussion on EU transparency has been overwhelmingly focused on the chapter and verse of the legal right of access to information. Just as critical, and in practice what it is all about, is the quality and scope and completeness of the information and documents that the institutions make available on the Internet, via either specific registers on their respective websites or via specific databases placed on the Internet. This is as far as most users get: either they get a 'hit' in terms of the document or information they are looking for or they do not. These 'passive' users as they might be termed will however benefit greatly from the front-running 'active'—and often highly critical—users who monitor the various registers and at times rather systematically request the institutions to put on the Internet those documents registered but not with availability via PDF file. The numbers of users seeking to access information and documents directly via the Internet and the respective EU linked websites is significantly larger than those who will follow the heavily procedural legal path.

European websites grant access to an enormous amount of information on European policymaking and policy execution. The increased development of Internet use and the growing transparency of the EU are indeed concurrent developments. Administrations worldwide use the Internet to enhance their transparency proactively. According to Moon, Welch, and Wong who have studied the effects of government websites on transparency, transparency refers to the availability of information for navigating a large-scale social system.[68] Transparency is about the magnitude of online information available on official government websites. Web-based transparency is measured using different elements of interactivity. Transparency can be regarded as a sort of layman's basic map of an organization and reveals the depth of access it allows, the depths of knowledge about processes it is willing to reveal, and the level of attention to citizen response it provides.[69] In a sense one can say the more transparent an organization is (via its website or otherwise), the more it is willing to allow citizens to monitor its performance and to participate in its policy processes.

Public administrations all over the world find it imperative to ensure that they are in a position to engage in social processes of collective learning as a means of harnessing collective intelligence as a source of continuous improvement as well as of information-sharing.[70] Information and communication technology (ICT) is at the same time responsible for a vast increase in the amount of information that is available both in a quantitative sense and in the manner in which it renders information accessible. ICT generates information about the underlying productive and administrative processes through which public administration accomplishes its tasks.[71]

Right from the start, literature on information processes has indicated that the use of ICTs increases transparency.[72] Using the work of Davenport, Meijer

[68] MJ Moon, EW Welch, and W Wong (2005), 'What drives global e-governance? An exploratory study at macro level', Proceedings of the 38th Hawaii International Conference on System Sciences.

[69] EW Welch and CC Hinnant (2003), 'Internet use, transparency, and interactivity effects on trust in government', Proceedings of the 36th Hawaii International Conference on System Sciences, available at <http://www2.computer.org/portal/web/csdl/doi/10.1109/HICSS.2003.1174323>, (last checked 7 Feb 2009) p 2

[70] N Lebessis and J Paterson (2000), 'Evolution in governance: what lessons for the commission? A first assessment', Working Paper European Commission Forward Studies Unit, available at <http://ec.europa.eu/comm/cdp/working-paper/evolution_in_governance.pdf>.

[71] See, in general, ITM Snellen and WHBJ van de Donk (eds) (1998), *Public Administration in an Information Age: A handbook* (Amsterdam: IOS Press).

[72] S Nora and A Minc (1980), *The Computerization of Society: A report to the president of France* (Cambridge: MIT press); V Bekkers (1993), *Nieuwe vormen van sturing en informatisering/New Forms of Steering and Informatization* (Delft: Eburon); PHA Frissen (1996), *De Virtuele Staat: Politiek, Bestuur, Technologie. Een Postmodern Verhaal* (Schoonhoven: Academic Service); CD Raab (1997), 'Electronic confidence: Trust, information and public administration' in ITM Snellen and WBHJ van de Donk (eds), *Public Administration in an Information Age* (Amsterdam: IOS Press), pp 113–33.

stresses that the use of ICTs especially strengthens the informational transparency of government—ie more data are registered—and the analytical transparency is increased—ie ICTs offer more opportunities to analyse data.[73] This impact of ICTs on government results in what he calls 'transparent government'. Welch and Wong emphasize the same effects but also indicate that many organizations are reluctant to use the Internet in order to increase transparency and therefore empirical practices may prove to be different from what organizations express in their policy documents.[74]

8.3.2 Digital registers and core executive institutions

The second phase in the debate on transparency has thus come from the institutions themselves albeit prompted, and at times pushed, by certain actors such as active members of the general public seeking to push back the frontiers of openness. As a response to the gradually changing culture shifting from 'secrecy' to (more) 'openness' there has been a proactive effort by the core (executive) institutions to make information on their decision-making committees and their wider information processes more easily accessible to the 'public' via the Internet in particular.

It is increasingly considered an obligation on the part of all executive and administrative and legislative (and even judicial) authorities within the EU to put on the Internet extensive information about their tasks, their organization structure, their activities, the agendas for their meetings as well as information on the most important documents under discussion in that context. On the whole the information placed on the web pages of the various institutions relates to documents that may already be considered as within the public domain. In other words the initial function of putting information on the Internet was simply to make such information more speedily available and more readily accessible to a wide range of users. Such material is subsequently published elsewhere (generally by the Official Publications Office of the EU and also by commercial publishers) and may be obtained on payment of often quite hefty sums of money. Other information is available via dedicated public websites such as *Pre-Lex*,[75] *Oeil*,[76] and *Eur-Lex*[77] as well as other specific Commission websites providing insight and an overview of information.[78]

[73] AJ Meijer (2003), 'Transparent government: Parliamentary and legal accountability in an information age', *Information Polity*, 8/1–2, pp 67–78.

[74] EW Welch and W Wong (2001), 'Global information technology pressure and government accountability: The mediating effect of domestic context on website openness', *Journal of Public Administration Research and Theory*, 11/4, pp 509–38.

[75] <http://ec.europa.eu/prelex/apcnet.cfm?CL=en>.

[76] See the Oeil database on inter-institutional decision-making procedures, <http://europa.eu/documents/oeil/index_en.htm>.

[77] <http://europa.eu/documents/eur-lex/index_en.htm>.

[78] <http://europa.eu/geninfo/info/index_en.htm>.

With the advent however of registers of documents in recent years, in particular those of the Council and of the Commission, more documents are being placed on the Internet at an earlier stage of the decision-making procedure and including documents that are not necessarily published elsewhere.[79] This has resulted in the relatively recent establishment of a number of general document registers of specific institutions (most impressively that of the traditionally highly secretive Council of Ministers).[80] The combined result of these two developments has, among other results, given researchers the tools to build up a picture of the inner workings of various (sub-)institutions based on a range of empirical data that is immediately accessible via the Internet.[81]

In recent years the Commission, in particular, has set up several different specific document registers. These include a very detailed 'comitology' register[82] and other specific websites by the various directorate generals as well as a specific register on expert groups. All of these specific registers and websites relate also to non-legislative policymaking and may include some documents of a more internal nature (for example minutes of committee meetings, meeting documents and minutes of meetings as well as draft decisions). The 'Register on Expert Groups'[83] aims to give an overview of the advisory bodies that assist the Commission and its services in preparing legislative proposals and policy initiatives. The register lists formal and informal advisory bodies established either by Commission decisions or created informally by the Commission services. It provides key information on those groups, such as the lead service in the Commission, the group's tasks as well as the category of participants. This register also contains direct links

[79] See further D Curtin (2003), 'Digital government in the European Union: Freedom of information trumped by "internal security"' in A Roberts (ed), *National Security and Open Government: Striking the right balance* (New York), pp 99–120.

[80] The three lawmaking institutions are under a legal obligation to establish such registers: see Art 11 of Regulation 1049/2001 (n 31 above). The register of the Commission and that of the European Parliament have both been the subject of critique from the non-governmental sector in particular as being incomplete and not easily accessible. Statewatch 'won' a complaint to the Ombudsman who ruled that the Commission is in breach of its legal obligations to provide a proper register of its documents. See further Press Release, <http://www.statewatch.org/news/2009/jan/eu-sw-ombudsman-complaint-com-register.pdf>. As a result of this complaint the Commission has introduced proposals to redefine what is meant by a document: <http://www.statewatch.org/news/2009/jan/07sw-ombs-com-register-complaint.htm>.

[81] See further D Naurin and H Wallace (eds) (2008), *Unveiling The Council of the European Union: Games governments play in Brussels* (Basingstoke: Palgrave Macmillan).

[82] See <http://ec.europa.eu/transparency/regcomitology/faq_en.htm>. In fact the Commission was legally obliged in the Decision of the Council from 1999 on procedures for the exercise of implementing powers conferred on the Commission (1999/468/EC; OJ L 184/23, 17 July 1999) ('the Comitology Decision') in Art 7 para 5 of that decision to create a register of Comitology documents which covers transmitted documents to the European Parliament in 2001. The Commission has also added—following a unilateral political commitment—a web-based repository to the register which enables the user to get direct access to certain documents which also contains a link for requesting the document, if is not made public in the repository (in accordance with the rules of the Regulation No 1049/2001 of the European Parliament and of the Council of 30 May 2001 (OJ L 145/43, 31 May 2001).

[83] <http://ec.europa.eu/transparency/regexpert/index.cfm>.

to websites of those Commission departments who publish more detailed information on expert groups on their own websites on the *Europa* website. In addition the question of lobbying transparency took more institutional form in the Commission's register of lobbyists (2008) that initially at any rate is a voluntary register.[84] The latter in particular can be considered to have come about as part of the Commission's European Transparency Initiative (ETI) launched by the Commission in 2006.[85]

8.3.3 Commission register(s) of documents disappoints

The main internal document register of the *Commission* mainly covers the Commission's legislative activity, namely proposals for acts presented to Parliament and the Council (COM documents) as well as autonomous Commission acts (C series). It contains legislative texts, adopted Commission reports and agendas and minutes of meetings of the Commission in full text. In addition it lists the working papers linked to legislative work as well as basic staff working documents (SEC series) and now also includes agendas and minutes of Commission meetings that are now 'accessible in full'.[86]

It transpires, however, that not all documents produced or handled by the Commission are included or even listed in a comprehensive and accessible manner. Indeed an empirical survey carried out in 2007 showed that for the Directorate General for Freedom, Security and Justice direct access to the full-text document (PDF file or equivalent) was only available for 43% of all

[84] Commission Register of Lobbyists, <https://webgate.ec.europa.eu/transparency/regrin/welcome.do?locale=en>.

[85] COM (2006) 194 final, 3 May 2005, Green Paper European Transparency Initiative, OJ C 151, 29 June 2006. The ETI contains a complex package of a number of different proposals referring to quite heterogeneous areas, some of which seem to have a rather loose link to the traditional transparency debate. The purpose of the ETI is first to follow up and further develop transparency policies that already exist. On the other hand it was designed to stir a transparency debate on new recent areas. The most important elements of this initiative included the development of a framework for lobbyists, the feedback on the first three years of application of the Commission's minimum standards for consultation, and the question whether Member States should be obliged to disclose information about the beneficiaries of EU funds, (see COM (2006) 194 final, p 4). These issues were subject to a public debate, based on which the Commission subsequently proposed further steps, see COM (2007) 127 final, 21 March 2007, follow-up to the Green Paper 'European Transparency Initiative'. The ETI also comprised certain 'inter-institutional aspects' including ethical rules and standards of Community staff, reconsidering the 'access to documents' legislation of the three institutions concerned, and the revision of the OLAF regulation to improve communication between Member States and OLAF. See further M Cini (2008), 'European Commission reform and the origins of the European transparency initiative', *Journal of European Public Policy*, 5, pp 743–60, p 750. See also COM (2006) 194 final, p 3 and AM Tournepiche (2007), 'Vers les nouveaux champs d'application pour la transparence administrative en droit Communautaire: Réflexions sur le Livre vert «Initiative européenne en matière de transparence»', *Cahiers de Droit Eeuropéen,* 1/2, pp 623–6, p 624.

[86] Commission Staff Working Paper, Annex to the Report on the application in 2004 of Regulation (EC) No 1049/2001 regarding public access to European Parliament, Council and Commission documents, SEC (2005) 1025.

relevant 'COM documents' (these relate to draft proposals, reports and communications, before their adoption), 21% of SEC documents (working papers and key administrative documents), and 0.5% of 599 Commission decisions and no minutes or agendas of meetings.[87] One wonders with regard to the category of Commission decisions whether their virtual non-existence in the relevant registers has to do with the fact that they were legal acts adopted by the Commission and that would be published in any event in the Official Journal of the EU.[88] Once acts (and their 'technical' annexes) that are obliged to be published according to Art 254 TEC have been published then there is no obligation it seems for them to be included in an access to documents register by the affected institution. The practice of not publishing binding rules is however not unknown in the context of the EU.[89]

If, on the other hand, documents were subject to a publication obligation but were not in fact published for the reason that they constituted 'sensitive documents' that had been 'classified', then they may well be legally null and void. The Commission recently had its fingers rapped for over-zealous (and illegal) efforts to keep documents out of the public domain and the Court of Justice has reaffirmed that it is under the treaty obligation to ensure that 'the law is observed'. Even where the subject matter is as 'sensitive' as airport security regulations and involved the adoption of a 'technical' implementation of an (unpublished) list of items prohibited in hand luggage fixed by a comitology committee, the Court did not 'turn a Nelsonian blind eye to the clear breach of a mandatory publication requirement, or make use of the exceptional power to maintain definitively, the effects of a defective measure'.[90] Rather, it ruled that a rule of conduct that was kept secret and with which individuals were required to comply has 'no binding force in so far as it seeks to impose obligations on individuals' and it explicitly ruled that the effects of its judgment should not be subject to any temporal limitation.[91] Implicitly, the ruling is to the effect that secrecy in such circumstances infringed the rule of law and could not therefore be enforced against individuals. Even an executive power that is given a specific mandate by the legislative power in terms of implementation and publication of specific rules applicable to individuals will not in any event escape control and scrutiny by the third power—the judicial power.

[87] See further Statewatch, <http://www.statewatch.org/foi/eu-ombuds-1-sw-response-to-com-detail.pdf>, in particular the Appendix.

[88] On this issue, see the opinion of 10 April 2008 of Advocate General Sharpston in Case C-345/06 *Gottfried Heinrich*, nyr and the subsequent Court of Justice judgment of 11 March 2009.

[89] See, in general, M Bobek (2007), 'The binding force of Babel: The enforcement of EC Law unpublished in the languages of the new Member States', EUI LAW Working Paper No 2007/06.

[90] Opinion of Advocate General Sharpston, para 100.

[91] Case C-345/06 *Gottfried Heinrich*, judgment of the Court (Grand Chamber), 10 March 2009, nyr, para 63.

But in a checks-and-balances perspective that is clearly evolving at the level of the EU political system, there may also be other actors who can put political—and legal—pressure on the Commission to behave more appropriately in view of the nature of the evolving political system. In this instance—and prior to the Court of Justice giving its final judgment—the European Parliament sued the Commission on the same matter before the Court of Justice. As a result of this political and legal pressure the Commission gave in and published—while the *Heinrich* case was still pending decision by the Court of Justice—the annex[92] and the European Parliament could withdraw its judicial proceedings against the Commission on this point.[93]

The general Commission Register does not bear up well compared to the Council Register (see below). It has been called a 'joke' and was the subject of a successful complaint to the European Ombudsman for 'maladministration' in failing to keep an adequate register of its documents.[94] The Ombudsman criticized the Commission for failing to '(i) deliver on its commitment to further develop its registers with any convincing action in that direction and (ii) provide any concrete indications as to the exact scope of the new centralized system, which seemed to be intended to be operational only in 2010'.[95]

The Commission's track record is thus in certain respects worse than that of the Council. For example, in its annual reports on public access it provides less detailed information than the Council and even failed to produce a report for 2005 at all in the calendar year 2006 as formally required in the Access to Documents Regulation. In the view of the Ombudsman, this amounted to 'maladministration' by the Commission.[96] The Ombudsman considers that the instance of maladministration revealed by this inquiry 'is especially deplorable since the publication of reports is a key mechanism of accountability to, and communication with, European citizens. The Commission should set a good

[92] Commission Regulation (EC) No 820/2008 of 8 August 2008 laying down measures for the implementation of the common basic standards on aviation security, OJ L 221/8, 19 August 2008, available at <http://eurlex.europa.eu/LexUriServ/LexUriServ.do?uri=OJ:L:2008:221:0008:0022:EN:PDF>.

[93] Case C-474/07 *European Parliament v Commission*. On 22 September 2008, JURI decided to recommend to the president of the European Parliament that Parliament discontinue the proceedings in Case C-474/07 *European Parliament v Commission of the European Communities*, with a view to Commission Regulation (EC) No 820/2008 of 8 August laying down measures for the implementation of the common basic standards of aviation security. The case was officially withdrawn on 17 December 2008.

[94] Decision of the European Ombudsman closing his inquiry into complaint 3208/2006/GG against the European Commission from 18 December 2008, available at <http://www.ombudsman.europa.eu/cases/decision.faces/en/3728/html.bookmark>.

[95] When the Commission rejected a draft recommendation by the Ombudsman, the latter wanted to refer the case to the European Parliament. However, he learned that the Parliament had already taken up this matter. He therefore decided to close the case 'with a critical remark'. See, for more information, <http://www.ombudsman.europa.eu/cases/summary.faces/en/3762/html.bookmark>.

[96] See decision of 10 October 2007, <http://www.statewatch.org/foi/eu-ombs-decision-2–668-2007.pdf>.

example to the many new Community agencies which have recently been established by giving high priority in future to the timely publication of reports.' In 2007 the Commission seems to have mended its ways by publishing the 2007 report in October 2008—within the formal requirements.[97] What is striking is the increase in number of requests for documents that in 2007 totalled 4,196 (up from 3,841 in 2006), of which 72% received an initial response granting the full access to the documents requested. Two hundred and seventy-three confirmatory requests were made in 2007, and in 15% of those cases (in which access to the documents was denied initially) full access was granted (up from 8.57% from 2006).

From the very early days the Commission has sought protection for what it terms 'documents of a purely internal nature' embracing 'summary reports of meetings, briefing notes, departmental opinions, mission reports, notes containing officials' personal thoughts or opinions etc'.[98] In so doing it attempts to draw a distinction vis-à-vis what it terms 'preparatory documents forming part of the legislative process (the framing of Commission initiatives and decisions)'; this category would cover both related preparatory and explanatory documents and other factual information. Such documents would fall within the scope of the general principle of access whereas 'documents of a purely internal nature' would not. This seems to be largely what it has implemented in practice in its General Register. It also, very systematically, excludes from the General Register documents relating to the Commission monitoring of the application of Community law that approximates a judicial or supervisory task. A very large proportion of access-to-documents applications relate to these documents and specifically to documents likely to support the applicant's position in a complaint concerning the alleged infringement of Community law or an administrative or judicial action.[99] A very high proportion of Commission refusals relate to this category of documents—23.48 per cent of refusals (as against 30.72 per cent in 2006).[100]

But this fragmented way of presenting information may require an interested member of the public (with a professional interest or otherwise) to trawl through various websites in order to access information that should, according to Art 11 of the Access Regulation, be available anyway. For example, in order to see the agendas for upcoming meetings of particular advisory/experts groups, the meeting documents and the minutes of the meetings once they have been held, the keen investigator will often be frustrated. Such information is generally not available on the Register of Expert Groups but will have to be tracked down, if at

[97] See 'Report from the Commission on the application in 2007 of Regulation (EC) No 1049/2001 regarding public access to European Parliament, Council and Commission documents', 10 October 2008, COM (2008) 630 final <http://eur-lex.europa.eu/LexUriServ/LexUriServ.do?uri=COM:2008:0630:FIN:EN:PDF>.

[98] European Commission, Discussion Paper on Public Access to Commission Documents, 23 April 1999, SG.C.2/VJ/CD D(99) 83, available at <http://www.statewatch.org/2comsw.htm>.

[99] Report from the Commission on the application in 2007 (n 97 above).

[100] Ibid, p 4

all, via this register to the specific policy website of a given DG. It seems that the practice may vary somewhat between different Commission DGs but, in general, this type of detailed information on who specifically is attending (names, affiliations etc), what documents are they discussing, and what decisions have they taken or discussed will not be available.[101] The only structured exception to this is with regard to 'comitology' committees (see below) and even then it appears from recent empirical research into the actual content of the register that the information provided may be very incomplete.

One of the most interesting developments in recent years relates to the creation and operationalization in December 2003, under the auspices of the Commission, of a specific register covering the work of the 'comitology' committees (see Chapter 5 above). This can be termed 'vertical' transparency within an institution, relating to the extent to which the documents of organs and committees established by institutions in order to assist them in the exercise of their tasks is covered by the obligation of public access as voluntarily assumed. The Commission initially attempted quite vigorously to shield the 'comitology' committees, in particular, from the requirement of public access since it felt that such committees could not be considered as part of the structures of the Commission as such. In so doing, it distinguished the position of such committees from what it referred to as consultative committees and expert groups that assist the Commission in its formulation of policy initiatives. The Commission readily considered the documents of these latter committees to be Commission documents as such and consequently to be covered by the general rules applicable to the Commission. It similarly has little problem, in its own analysis, with so-called scientific advisory committees.

In 2003, the Commission changed tack with regard to comitology committees specifically and made an elaborate database publicly available on the Internet. The purpose was, in effect, to provide a public window on the basic organizational and institutional 'facts' of comitology committees as well as enabling an interested user to follow their decision-making processes with a paper trail. In a leap of almost quantum proportions, comitology committees moved from being relatively invisible in structural and substantive terms to, in theory at any rate, one of the most structurally visible and documented of the institutional actors. The concrete value of this register, however, depends on its completeness. Are all comitology documents in fact made available through this public register? An initial pilot study was done by the present author together with two political scientists on the so-called 'comitology' committees of the EU.[102] Our aim was to analyse the nature and extent of transparency of comitology decision-making on

[101] See further the recent empirical work undertaken by an NGO, Alter EU (Alliance for Lobbying Transparency and Ethics Regulation in the EU), Secrecy and corporate dominance—a study on the composition and transparency of European Commission Expert Groups, <http://www.alter-eu.org/en/publications/secrecy-and-corporate-dominance-study>.

[102] See further GJ Brandsma, D Curtin, and A Meijer (2008), 'How transparent are EU 'comitology' committees in practice?', European LJ, 14/6, pp 819–38.

the basis of a concrete empirical study and assessment of comitology transparency in one specific year, 2005.

On the basis of the detailed empirical study of all documents available on the register for 2005 it was possible to reach the following conclusions. First, the resulting input transparency falls short of complete transparency: only 65 per cent of the agendas and 54 per cent of the membership lists are available through the register. The picture for throughput transparency is similar. Sixty-seven per cent of the summary records are available through the register. This means that citizens and stakeholders are not able to check what has been discussed in one-third of the meetings. Additionally, the quality of many of the summary records was limited. In general, the records provide only very brief information about the discussions within the committees. The resulting output transparency was the most disturbing. Voting records are generally available (87.3 per cent of the votes) but only 5.5 per cent of the draft measures were available through the online register.

The analysis conducted in this—limited—study shows that the resulting transparency is far below the transparency that could be expected if all comitology documents would end up in the public register. On the basis of the empirical research conducted, no explanation can be provided for this discrepancy. Theories about information systems stipulate that the outcome of complex systems is the result of interactions between a variety of actors with different perceptions and incentives.[103] Further research into these interactions is needed to explain why the resulting transparency falls short of the benchmark. Work such as this shows, it is hoped, how and why an empirical turn to such issues can actually shed less diffuse light on the degree of existing 'transparency' and the manner of its possible improvement as a matter of practice.

Table 8.3 Transparency in general of comitology committees in 2005

	Number of documents *expected*	Number of documents *available*	Percentage available
Agendas	946	616	65.1 %
Attendance lists	946	512	54.1 %
Summary records	946	641	67.8 %
Vote results	2715	2369	87.3 %
Draft measures	2715	149	5.5 %

Source: GJ Brandsma et al (2008).

[103] See further C Ciborra (2001), *The Labyrinths of Information: Challenging the wisdom of systems* (Oxford University Press); BA Nardi and VL O'Day (1999), *Information Ecologies: Using technology with heart* (MIT Press).

8.3.4 Council register evolves

The Council of Ministers, along with the other institutions of the EU, subscribes to the objective of a more active policy of making information available—but struggles to make it a reality. The Council was initially not very forthcoming in ordering its information in a user-friendly fashion, perhaps because it has had more difficulty in being candid about the scope of its expanded executive-type tasks in recent years.[104] In any event, the legislative role of the Council, both with regard to traditional EC policy matters as well as with regard to the new policy area of justice and home affairs, gradually became more visible over the years. For example, after the Council framework decision on the European Arrest Warrant was approved, few could deny that such measures constituted, in effect, binding general rules (legislation). Yet the reality was that they, the Council, adopted these rules in secret conclave, with no drafts made available on time (and no register in existence) for either parliaments or individuals to make any input in the debate and decision-making process.[105] If the Treaty of Lisbon enters into force, this area will have largely come full circle: with justice and home affairs, including police and criminal law legislation being adopted under the normal legislative procedure (co-decision) in the vast majority of cases.[106]

The state of the Council Register was the subject of some complaints to the Ombudsman in the early years. The Council initially excluded from its register all preliminary, restricted and confidential documents.[107] The Ombudsman, in a complaint brought before him, agreed that all documents put before the Council must be listed on the register 'in order to allow citizens to make proper use of their right to access to documents'; the Council's omission to do this constituted maladministration. Additional administrative work entailed for the Council would have to be accepted 'in view of the fundamental importance which the right of citizens to have access to documents held by the Council has in order to guarantee openness and transparency in the latter's decision-making'. In the aftermath of this complaint, the Council worked to ensure a much more complete cross-section of all its documents, including 'preliminary' documents.

Little or no sustained empirical research has been carried out, to my knowledge, as to the types of documents being made immediately accessible upon circulation within the Council or any of its preparatory instances. In formal terms it is laid down in Art 11 of Annex II to the Council's Rules of Procedure that

[104] D Curtin (2004a), 'European Union executives evolving in the shade?' in AE Kellermann (ed), *The European Union: An ongoing process of European integration. Liber Amicorum*, (The Hague: TMC Asser Instituut), pp 97–110.

[105] D Curtin (2001), 'The developing right of citizen access to information on EU asylum and immigration decision-making' in C Harlow and E Guild (eds), *Implementing Amsterdam* (Oxford: Hart Publishers), pp 34–63.

[106] See further JP Terhechte (2008), 'Der Vertrag von Lissabon: Grundlegende Verfassungsurkunde der Europäischen Rechtsgemeinschaft oder technischer Änderungsvertrag?', *Europarecht*, 2, pp 143–89, p 172 *et seq*.

[107] European Ombudsman, Annual Report for 2000, Complaint 917/2000/GG.

it is required that the register allows access to the full text of a large number of documents that must be made available to the public as soon as they have been circulated. This includes, in any event, the following categories of documents: provisional agendas for Council meetings and for its preparatory bodies (with the exception of certain bodies dealing with military and security questions); documents that are listed in the Council agenda as being subject to open/public debate (see below); and draft legislative texts and common positions etc, as well as documents regarding a legislative act once the common position is adopted or a legislative act has been finally adopted. What was not included in this list are the minutes of Council meetings and its preparatory bodies nor all those categories of acts that do not fall within the Council's Rules of Procedure.[108] Moreover, 'room documents' and *sans numero* documents are in any event excluded from the register—during the negotiation on the Regulation on Public Access to Documents, former Commission Vice President Loyola de Palacio explained that: 'Obliging institutions to divulge internal notes, in many cases, would only cause confusion among citizens ... sometimes an increase in misinformation results from an excess of information.'[109]

In any event the impression is that the Council register is including an increasingly wide range of documents from an ever growing number of actors, sub-councils, committees etc. No formal provision is made for access to the agendas, minutes, and documents relating to meetings of the European Council although, in practice, a certain number of these documents may be made available by the presidency of the Council of Ministers and also find their way onto the Council Register. This situation will change, in my view, after the entry into force of the Treaty of Lisbon and the formal institutionalization of both the European Council as an EU institution with a semi-permanent president. The formalized link in terms of administrative and other support by the Council General Secretariat should entail the listing on the Council Register of all its documents. The provisions on transparency in the TEU moreover will apply fully to the European Council and the rules of procedure of the European Council will have to deal squarely with the issue of access to its documents in a manner compatible with imperative treaty requirements.[110] Or will it, in parallel to the argument sometimes made with regard to the non-legislative activity of the Council of Ministers, seek to argue that there is a need for its intrinsically 'non-legislative' work to be afforded a comparable degree of confidentiality to any collective 'cabinet' type function in order to ensure an effectively

[108] See further, Article 11 of Annex II to Council Decision 2006/683/EC, Euratom of 15 September 2006, adopting the Council's Rules of Procedure, OJ L 285, 16 October 2006, p 47. Article 11 (3) of Annex II to Council Decision 2006/683/EC, Euratom provides that the following documents shall be published after having circulated: '1) provisional agenda for meetings of the Council in its various configurations ... 2) any text adopted by the Council and intended to be published in the Official Journal.'

[109] Statewatch, <http://www.statewatch.org/secret/freeinfo/ch7.htm>.

[110] See Art 15(3)–(4) TEU, Lisbon.

functioning executive?[111] It may not be successful in this regard, however, as the Court of Justice in particular seems to developing in its case law the relationship between a legitimate political system in the eyes of its citizens and increasing the citizens' confidence in the EU institutions 'by allowing divergences between different points of view to be openly debated'.[112]

The Council from the very beginning has defended its internal institutional 'space to think' that includes the ability to keep secret, even after legislation has been adopted, certain types of internal documents, in particular the opinions of its own internal 'legal service'. This practice was challenged in the recent *Turco* case. The Council refused access to the opinion of its legal service on a Council directive that had been adopted already. It took the view that the legal opinions of its own legal service were internal 'private' documents for the benefit only of the institution and not for 'outside eyes' and it fought tooth and nail through several courts (winning in the CFI and losing in the Court of Justice) in order to ensure that it had a more or less absolute right to keep the opinions of its legal service secret even after the legislation in question had been adopted. In the words of the Court: 'it is in fact . . . a lack of information and debate which is capable of giving rise to doubts in the minds of citizens, not only as regards the lawfulness of an isolated act but also as regards the legitimacy of the decision-making process as a whole.'

What are in any event more or less excluded completely from the Council register are the so-called 'sensitive' documents that have been classified according to the EU document classification system.[113] This issue was included in outline form in the Access to Documents Regulation 2001. Article 9(1) defines 'sensitive documents' as essentially classified documents 'originating from the institutions or the agencies established by them, from Member States or International Organizations'. The first point to the definition relates then to the wide scope of the actors whose classified documents are excluded. It is moreover not only the classification rules of the EU that apply (to its own institutions and agencies) but also of any other international organizations (NATO, United Nations, etc) and of any Member State or third country (no exclusions). The rules that apply are the rules of the organization or State, even if their rules are more restrictive than those of the EU. The classifications that the document in question must have received in order to be exempt from the public access rules are 'TRES SECRET/TOP SECRET', 'SECRET' or 'CONFIDENTIEL' with the further qualification that the document concerned must 'protect essential

[111] M Bauer (2004), 'Transparency in the Council' in M Westlake and D Galloway (eds), *The Council of the European Union* (London: John Harper Publishing), pp 367–88, p 388.

[112] Joined Cases C-39/05 P and C-52/ 05 P *Kingdom of Sweden and Maurizio Turco v Council of the European Union*, judgment of the Court of Justice of 1 July 2008, para 59.

[113] For the history of how these rules were adopted and the initial resistance by the European Parliament, which challenged the rules before the Court of Justice (but later withdrew the case when the Access Regulation was adopted), see Statewatch archives, <http://www.statewatch.org/news/2001/oct/11Aepsecreg.htm>.

interests of the European Union or of one or more of its Member States in the areas… notably public security, defence and military matters'. This means that the documents must have been classified at one of the appropriate levels *and* concern the protection of 'essential interests of the EU or its Member States in one of the given areas. The latter criterion is assessed by the institution that is asked to provide access to the document, rather than by the originator of the document.'[114] What might constitute the 'essential interests' of the EU and of its Member States (presumably these might be different) is not further defined.

There are in fact few shafts of light into the nature and types of document that fall under this category of 'sensitive documents'. In 2007 the annual report on access to documents notes that during this period 811 sensitive documents classified as 'SECRET UE' or 'CONFIDENTIEL UE' (representing roughly 10 per cent of the documents requested in 2007). This amounts almost to a doubling of the figures from 2006. These figures must moreover be read in conjunction with the fact that a very large proportion of such classified documents will not be even 'listed' in the Council Register.[115] Moreover the practice seems to be that once classified they will not even be considered for partial public access for the parts of the document where the demands of secrecy do not outweigh the general public interest. Detailed rules have been adopted for example by the Secretary General of the Council /High Representative for Common Foreign and Security Policy (CFSP) on how staff within the General Secretariat (see Chapter 6 above) have to protect and handle classified information.[116] A special agreement exists with the European Parliament as to how it will handle such classified information that it may be sent (see Chapter 9 below).[117]

The more general question is of the status of *security classifications* given to documents and to what extent documents bearing such classifications are in general excluded from the scope of application of the access rules in question.[118] The real problem lies in knowing that such documents exist in the first place rather

[114] F Riemann (2004), p 227 *et seq*.

[115] This risk is also emphasized by F Riemann (2004), p 228. Indeed, Art 9(3) of Regulation 1049/2001 provides that even the recording of such documents in the register depends entirely on the discretion of the document's originator.

[116] Decision of the Secretary General of the Council/High Representative for the Common Foreign and Security Policy of 27 July 2000 on measures for the protection of classified information applicable to the General Secretariat of the Council, 10703/00, Brussels, 8 August 2000. See the later Council Decision adopting the Council's security regulations, available at <http://www.statewatch.org/news/2001/mar/05775.pdf>, Council Decision 2001/264/EC of 19 March 2001, (OJ L 101, 11 April 2001).

[117] European Parliament, Rules of Procedure, Annex V11, Confidential and sensitive documents and information, 16th edition, February 2008.

[118] Legal scholars generally argue that access to sensitive documents is not *a priori* excluded, but is subject to special limitations and in practice is unlikely: H Bartelt and E Zeitler (2003), p 492 *et seq*; C Heitsch (2003), *Die Verordnung über den Zugang zu Dokumenten der Gemeinschaftsorgane im Lichte des Transparenzprinzips* (Berlin: Duncker & Humblot), p 68.

than necessarily being denied access in practice. The problem may however be more extensive in that it will be the Member States or third parties that have classified many of the 'incoming documents'. The practice of the Union in that regard is to accept the original security obligation and no procedure is provided for revision over the course of time. The status quo is that it is only after a period of 30 years have elapsed that any fresh consideration of the matter under the Archives Regulation takes place.[119] Council Regulation 354/83 lays down rules concerning the opening to the public of the historical archives of the EEC and the EAEC and provides that as regards 'documents and records received from a Member State or from another institution, the institutions shall abide by the classification established by the originator'. It can safely be assumed that if the institutions have this obligation concerning documents at the historical archives, then they have it prior to that, namely before the documents concerned are transferred to the historical archives.[120]

It would seem timely to review the issue of confidential information bearing a security classification. Why should such documents not be treated in principle as subject to the general rules on access to documents and document registers and subject only to the limits of one of the specific exceptions? In other words a security classification as such (either by an institution or by a third party) should not be capable of constituting an *automatic* disqualification from access/publication on the register.[121] In view of the manner in which the nature of the principle has evolved and the fact that the greatest possible access is to be granted, it cannot be considered acceptable that existing secondary legislation and other internal rule-making by the respective institutions provides an exception to the general principle, with no specific provision for review of classification over time, however marginal.[122] Reconsideration of this issue would seem even more timely now with evidence that several institutions have, in a low-key manner (via for example 'letters of exchange'), established a framework for the mutual collaboration and exchange of classified information—an example is the framework for exchanging classified information between Europol and the Council.[123] In other

[119] Council Regulation No 354/83 concerning the opening to the public of the historical archives of the EC and the EAEC, OJ 1983, L 43/1. Council Regulation (EC, Euratom) No 1700/2003 of 22 September 2003, OJ L 243, 27 September 2003, p 1–4.

[120] See, too, in this sense, P Dryberg (1999), 'Current issues in the debate on public access to documents', European L Rev, 24/3, pp 157–69.

[121] For example, F Riemann (2004), p 228. He interprets Art 9(3) of Regulation 1049/2001 restrictively by applying the principle of proportionality. In his view, only the content of sensitive information contained in the classified document should be subject to the originator's consent. Hence, the date of registration, a registry number and a note qualifying the document as 'sensitive' can and should be recorded in the register even if the document is classified.

[122] Some scholars contend that judicial review of at least the decision to refuse access to a avowedly sensitive document is possible, see C Heitsch (2003), p 68.

[123] Council Secretariat, 'Framework for mutual collaboration and exchanging classified information between Europol and the General Secretariat of the Council', 14050/05, Brussels, 7 November 2005.

words the web of classified information is spreading and being driven further underground.

8.4 The Inter-institutional Strategy

8.4.1 Inter-institutional dialogue

One of the ways that the European Parliament in particular worked to expand its own role (as we have seen already in earlier chapters) was by using more informal instruments than treaty-level change, in particular inter-institutional agreements in order to supplement transparency and accountability arrangements for both committees and agencies.[124] In other words, these are to a large extent 'own initiative' inter-institutional agreements not explicitly provided for or indeed envisaged in the treaties. They are informal in this sense but this does not necessarily exclude their being devoid of any legal effects.[125] For example the European Parliament has negotiated a series of informal agreements and institutional agreements with various actors regarding the provision of information to the European Parliament in a structured and mandatory fashion. One example is the series of informal agreements adopted between the Commission and the European Parliament imposing the obligation on the Commission to inform the European Parliament about the work of comitology committees (Chapter 5 above) and to send it all their draft implementing measures.[126] As a result of these agreements provision has been made for the electronic submission of these documents to the European Parliament as well as the possibility for committees of the European Parliament to request further draft measures not subject to the co-decision procedure.[127] One can infer however from the rather detailed and improved transparency measures to be included in the new PRAC (regulatory procedure with scrutiny) discussed in Chapter 5[128] that there is a need to improve

[124] Inter-institutional agreements are a long-standing phenomenon in the EC/EU context. See further J Monar (1994), 'Interinstitutional agreements: The phenomenon and its new dynamics after Maastricht', Common Market L Rev, 31/4, pp 693–719.

[125] J Monar (1994), ibid.

[126] See, for details, the Commission report on the working of committees during 2003, <http://ec.europa.eu/prelex/detail_dossier_real.cfm?CL=en&DosId=192392>.

[127] See, for details, the Commission report on the working of committees during 2004, <http://ec.europa.eu/prelex/detail_dossier_real.cfm?CL=en&DosId=193506>. Since December 2003 the Commission publishes a register (on the Internet) giving the references of all documents sent to the European Parliament under comitology procedures and also a repository that provides the public with the document in downloadable form. See Chapter 8 above.

[128] Council Decision of 17 July 2006 amending Decision 1999/468/EC laying down the procedures for the exercise of implementing powers conferred on the Commission, OJ L 200/11, available at <http://eur-lex.europa.eu/LexUriServ/LexUriServ.do?uri=OJ:L:2006:200:0011:0013:EN:PDF>.

the timing of receipt of information by the European Parliament on draft implementing measures as well as the Commission registry's functional specifications in order to enhance user-friendliness.[129]

In addition, the European Parliament has put elaborate arrangements in place to 'receive' and handle so-called sensitive information that may relate to a wide variety of subjects, including far-reaching 'executive' tasks of the Council of Ministers (and its General Secretariat) including in policy areas such as CFSP and justice and home affairs. One can infer from the fact that more than 50 per cent of the requests for access to Council documents that were submitted in 2007 refer to the areas of justice and home affairs and CFSP or ESDP[130] that these are the most 'secret'.

In terms of the further public nature of the rule-making on sensitive documents provision is made in the access regulation that the rules of the institutions in this regard are to be made public.[131] This could be interpreted as not entailing necessarily an obligation to publish (for example in the Official Journal) but to make 'public' if access is requested. The latter, in any event, seems to be the case with regard to the European Parliament. Moreover, it is explicitly provided that the Commission and the Council as the executive actors likely to have 'sensitive' documents within the meaning of the definition shall inform the European Parliament, presumably as the relevant 'accountability forum' in the institutional triangle, 'in accordance with arrangements agreed between the institutions'.[132] In other words the access regulation explicitly foresees the adoption of further implementing inter-institutional rules on how 'sensitive documents' will be transmitted to the European Parliament in a manner that will not involve them being made 'public' but will respect the confidential classification status.

What is interesting about the institutional arrangements in question is that they involve the European Parliament, the primary accountability forum in this context (see further Chapter 9), making arrangements to receive and 'handle' sensitive documents as defined in 'secure reading rooms' etc as the quid pro quo for being informed on the content of in particular the Council's security and defence policy.[133] It seems that such inter-institutional cooperation can add rules and specifications to those previously laid down in secondary legislation. Thus, for example, it is provided that one of the interests that classification is designed to

[129] See further, ibid, Commission Statement included in the Council minutes, Annex II.

[130] Council Report on Access to Documents, 2007 (n 61 above).

[131] Art 9(6) of the Access Regulation (n 29 above). In respect of the Commission the security rules are annexed to its rules of procedure, OJ L 308/, 18 December 2000, p 26 amended several times, consolidated version, see <http://europa.eu/scadplus/leg/en/lvb/o10004.htm>. See too, Council Decision of 12 July 2005, amending Council Decision 2001/264/EC adopting the Council's security rules, OJ L 23 July 2005, L 193/31.

[132] Art 9(7) of the Access Regulation (n 29 above).

[133] See further Inter-institutional Agreement of 20 November 2002 between the European Parliament and the Council concerning access by the European Parliament to sensitive information of the Council in the field of security and defence policy, OJ C 298/1, 30 November 2002.

protect is 'military or non-military crisis management' (which is not mentioned in the access regulation itself). Initially provision was made for the president of the European Parliament and a special committee composed of five specially selected members to 'ask to consult the documents in question on the premises of the Council'.[134] More recently it can be deduced from further rule-making within the European Parliament, and in particular by the president, that secure reading rooms have been established on the premises of the European Parliament itself, presumably to the satisfaction of the Council.[135] At the same time, pursuant to further inter-institutional cooperation between the Commission and the European Parliament,[136] elaborate provision is made for the forwarding of 'confidential information' to the European Parliament.[137] This includes the undertaking by Parliament that the following arrangements are actually put in place: a secure archive system for documents classified as confidential; a secure reading room (without photocopying machines, telephones, fax facilities, scanners, or any other technical equipment for the reproduction and transmission of documents, etc.); security provisions governing access to the reading room, including the requirements of signature in an access register; and a solemn declaration not to disseminate the confidential information examined.

8.4.2 European Parliament and the European Central Bank

The European Central Bank (ECB) may be in a special position it seems—one that the European Parliament in particular has grappled with. There is what can be termed 'a patent ideological division'[138] between two different schools of thought on the extent to which the ECB should be subject to the requirements of transparency. On the one hand some argue that the ECB should be fully transparent and that it should publish its individual voting records, the minutes of its

[134] Para 3.3 of the Inter-institutional Agreement.

[135] Decision of the European Parliament on the implementation of the Inter-institutional Agreement governing European Parliament access to sensitive Council information in the sphere of security and defence policy, P5 TA (2002) 0502 which provides that 'Parliament shall fit out a room specially designed for the holding of meetings to deal with sensitive information. The room shall be chosen with a view to guaranteeing a level of protection equivalent to that laid down for this type of meeting by Council Decision 2001/264/EC of 19 March 2001 adopting the Council's security regulations. It seems that the Parliament has only recently been able to implement this wish to have its own secure reading room approved by the Council. See further Decision of Secretary General of 21 November 2006 implementing measures for technical questions relating to operation of the Confidential Documents Service and transfer of confidential documents, on file with author.

[136] See Framework Agreement on Relations between the European Parliament and the Commission of 5 July 2000, OJ C 121/122, 24 April 2001, as revised by the Framework Agreement on relations between the European Parliament and the Commission of 26 May 2005, OJ C 177/125, 18 May 2006.

[137] Annex 1 of Framework Agreement 2005.

[138] P Magnette (2000), 'Towards accountable independence? Parliamentary controls of the European Central Bank and the rise of a new democratic model', European LJ, 6/4, pp 326–40.

deliberations, its inflation forecasts, and the other instruments used to take its decisions. This point of view is inspired by Scandinavian traditions of openness in this regard[139] and appears to be supported by some British central bankers[140] and many MEPs.[141]

On the other hand, accountability means for other actors, 'we do what we are supposed to do'.[142] In other words, an independent organ is accountable if it respects its mandate. According to this much less liberal point of view information should be channelled by the authorities and the ECB should be free to select the information that can be published and explain its decisions. On this view of the ECB, individual voting records and minutes should not be published because it would give rise to speculations about the attitudes of the members of the ECB.[143]

The ECB, as a matter of practice, publishes a monthly bulletin and holds press conferences. It refuses, so far, to publish inflation and other forecasts and minutes of meetings and votes, preferring explanations about the decisions and the reasoning behind them. In this respect, the transparency of the ECB falls short of that of other similar institutions such as the Federal Reserve System, the Bank of England, and the Bank of Japan.[144] Unlike the ECB, all of the aforementioned national banks publish both individual voting records and minutes albeit with varying periods of delay.[145] This has been justified by the ECB in light of the 'unconventional character' of the ECB, the specificity of its mandate that demands that the Governing Council take decisions for a 'multi-country economy.'[146] For example, the decisions not to publish voting records has been justified by the ECB by arguing that 'the publication of voting behaviour could lead to pressure and speculation about the motives behind the decisions of the individual members of the Governing Council, and could even allow the public to verify whether any attempts to exercise influence on voting behaviour had had the intended result.'[147]

The EP seems to have adopted a mid-way course, not requiring the publication of individual voting records but rather urging the ECB to include in its annual report 'a description and evaluation of recent inflation trends and an explanation of past monetary decisions' as well as making the reports more future-oriented, thereby enabling a 'sound public debate of the ECB's decisions' to take place, and

[139] See further, for example, C Gronbech-Jensen (1998) 'The Scandinavia tradition of open government and the European Union: Problems of compatibility', *Journal of European Public Policy*, 5, pp 185–99.

[140] WH Buiter (1999), 'Alice in Euroland', *Journal of Common Market Studies*, 37, pp 181–209.

[141] P Magnette (2000), p 334.

[142] O Issing (1999), 'The Eurosystem: Transparent and accountable or "William in Euroland"' *Journal of Common Market Studies*, 37, pp 475–95.

[143] P Magnette, p 335.

[144] ECB Monthly Bulletin, October 2000, p 53

[145] W Buiter, (1999), pp 191–4.

[146] ECB Monthly Bulletin, October 2000, p 53

[147] ECB Monthly Bulletin, ibid, p 54

thereby enhancing the centrality of the role of the European Parliament.[148] In seeking to carve out a political space for debating the EU's monetary and other economic policies, the European Parliament demands more transparency in the name of both efficiency and democracy. Thus it has demanded that the ECB determine its monetary objectives in a transparent way and that it publish the minutes of Governing Council deliberations.[149]

8.5 Shifting Fault Lines

8.5.1 Open meetings of the Council of Ministers

During the first, more legal, stage of transparency and access to information, the Council was adamant that it would not be appropriate to open up further its decision-making processes. In particular, it insisted in various court cases in the mid to late 1990s that its decision-making procedures could not be compared to those of a legislative body as, due to its composition by government ministers, it proceeded by *diplomatic negotiation* which depended on a large measure of secrecy and discretion. The question of opening up Council meetings to the public met traditionally with a lot of resistance among the Member States (with the exception presumably of Denmark which made a proposal for treaty reform in that respect and also of Sweden and the Netherlands[150]). The Council and many Member States argued that it is not possible to open up Council meetings, as this would damage the process of negotiation and compromise inherent in the way that EU legislation is adopted. If the meetings were more open, they felt that the Council would have great difficulty in reaching decisions at all.

Moreover, at least during the 1990s, a majority of the Member States rather persistently resisted attempts to open up further the Council proceedings, often voting against applications by individuals taken under the access-to-documents provisions in place at that time. Simultaneously, the same majority voted for changes to the Council's Rules of Procedure that only half-heartedly gave effect to the principle of public access to documents.[151] Less than a decade later the situation had changed quite dramatically—at least as far as (some) legislative acts are concerned.[152] There are indeed few who now argue that there should not be

[148] P Magnette, p 336.

[149] European Parliament Resolution on Democratic Accountability in the Third Phase of EMU, 2 April 1998.

[150] P Sherrington (2000), *The Council of Ministers: Political authority in the European Union* (London/New York: Pinter), p 170.

[151] See further D Curtin (1999); S Peers (2002), p 12.

[152] Art 7 of the Rules of Procedure of the Council (2006). See too Art 12(2) of Regulation (EC) No 1049/2001 of the European Parliament and of the Council of 30 May 2001 regarding public access to European Parliament, Council and Commission documents, OJ L 145, 31/05/2001, pp 0043–8 (that seems to be more widely drafted) and Art 11 Annex II which implements

full openness and transparency as far as the legislative activity of the Council is concerned.[153]

Following the adoption of an overall policy on transparency by the European Council in June 2006, a number of further measures were taken with a view to further improving public access to the decision-making process of the Council, modifying the relevant provisions of the Council's Rules of Procedure.[154] This provided for open public sessions in legislative procedures including those legislative acts adopted other than by co-decision (including framework decisions CFSP and PJCC)—it could also be said that the minutes of all such meetings should be included on the Council Register.[155] Yet it seems there are many 'black holes' left in terms of opening up Council legislative meetings (particularly with regard to some Council debates on non co-decision legislative points).[156]

As for legislative procedures other than co-decision, the 'first deliberation on important new legislative proposals' shall be open to the public. In general, it is for the presidency to decide which of the proposals are 'important', but 'the Council or COREPER may decide otherwise'.[157] The presidency may also determine that the following deliberations should be held publicly subject to the Council and COREPER not deciding otherwise.[158] Furthermore, the Council or COREPER may decide by qualified majority, that 'the Council shall hold public debates on important issues affecting the interests of the European Union and its citizens'.[159] The presidency, any Council member, or the Commission may make proposals in this regard.[160]

Apart from public deliberations on legislation, there are several types of policy debates that are open to the public. For example, the General Affairs and External Relations Council shall hold a 'public policy debate on the Council's 18-month programme'.[161] Also, a number of Commission's presentations to the

Regulation 1049/2001; M de Leeuw (2007), 'Openness in the legislative process in the European Union', European L Rev, 32/3, p 295–318; P Settembri (2005), 'Transparency and the EU legislator: "Let he who is Without Sin Cast the First Stone"', *Journal of Common Market Studies*, 43/3, pp 637–54.

[153] See, however, M Bauer, (2004) and B Driessen (2005), 'The Council of the European Union and access to documents', European L Rev, 30/5, pp 675–96.

[154] See, in particular, Art 8 of Council Decision 2006/683/EC, Euratom of 15 September 2006, adopting the Council's Rules of Procedure, OJ L 285, 16 October 2006, p 47.

[155] Art 9(1) of the Council's Rules of Procedure of 2006 provides that: 'In addition to cases where Council deliberations are open to the public under Article 8(1), where the Council acts in its legislative capacity within the meaning of Article 7, the results of votes and explanations of votes by Council members, as well as the statements in the Council minutes and the items in those minutes relating to the adoption of legislative acts, shall be made public.' This seems to provide an obligation to publish minutes of open Council deliberations.

[156] See further F Hayes-Renshaw and H Wallace (2006), *The Council of Ministers*, 2nd edn (Basingstoke: Palgrave Macmillan), p 126.

[157] Art 8(2) of Council Decision 2006/683/EC.

[158] Ibid.

[159] Art 8(3) of Council Decision 2006/683/EC.

[160] Ibid.

[161] Art 8(4) of Council Decision 2006/683/EC.

Council shall be public including the subsequent Council debate. This applies particularly to those 'of its five-year programme, of its annual work programme and of its annual policy strategy'.[162]

However, Hayes-Renshaw and Wallace point out that these improvements give little reason for enthusiasm since 'the cameras are... not present for the more interesting cut and thrust of negotiation and bargaining'.[163] In their view, the public session still 'amount to stage-managed events'.[164] In addition to that, certain problems remain. Some Council meetings were announced too late and sometimes the schedule of the meetings was changed without prior notice.[165]

A further bone of contention continues to be the Council's 'non-legislative' work, which in various tides of treaty reform has become much more visible than was previously the case but is still not adopted in an open fashion.[166]

8.5.2 Closed 'trialogue' meetings with the European Parliament

The story of the European Parliament as a determined constitutional agenda-setter steadily and incrementally introducing more 'public' moments into the process of holding other (executive) actors to account is however not necessarily a linear one. The European Parliament has, as part of the compromise surrounding its increase in legislative powers, agreed to at times quite far-reaching *non-public* moments prior to an account-holding process, thus making the latter more difficult and in any event incomplete with non-public 'enclaves' with regard to certain types of information. The downside in the dominant legitimation strategy of involving the European Parliament in a model of European parliamentary democracy has been the manner in which the Council of Ministers seems to have successfully influenced the European Parliament to shift a not insignificant part of its decision-taking and deliberations to *behind closed doors* 'negotiations'. This has to do with the manner in which the informal institution has evolved of so-called 'trialogue meetings' devised as an informal but structured means of bringing together a reduced number of participants by both sides (Council and European Parliament) in order to attempt to resolve contentious issues so that overall agreement (legislative co-decision) could be brokered.[167] In this manner, secret 'negotiations' take place on the content of legislation, making it difficult to include the entire process of legislation as part of the account-holding process.

Sometimes a minister of a Member State holding the presidency takes the lead for the Council in these discussions; but in the majority of cases the task falls to a

162 Ibid. 163 F Hayes-Renshaw and H Wallace (2006), p 126.
164 Ibid. 165 M Bauer (2004), p 373.
166 See further D Curtin (2004).
167 See further on the origins of the practice, M Schackleton (2000), 'The politics of codecision', *Journal of Common Market Studies*, 38/2, pp 325–42. See too T Bunyan (2007), 'Secret trialogues and the democratic deficit', available at <www.statewatch.org/analyses/no-64-secret-trilogues.pdf>.

(high-level) civil servant, or other civil servants.[168] Do, for example, members of the Council General Secretariat participate and 'negotiate' in trialogues with the European Parliament? It is inevitable that during ongoing trialogues, decisions have to be made on the spot without the chance to refer back to (a collectivity of) national capitals. In other words, COREPER and other 'representatives' of the Council (General Secretariat members?) will almost inevitably find themselves obliged to exercise *discretion* about the exact terms in which agreement is reached with the European Parliament. But how they do so and on what authority remains shrouded in mystery and a rather black shade of dark.

This is a worrying trend given their considerable expansion in use in recent years. It appears from recent studies of how and when legislation is adopted in practice at the EU level that at least 80 per cent of all agreements made under co-decision in the first three years of the current term of the European Parliament (2004–7) were either agreed during the first reading (64 per cent) or in an early second reading based on informal negotiations with resulting amendments directly integrated into the Council's common position.[169] In 2007 considerably more than half were being concluded at this very preliminary stage in the co-decision procedure as a whole.

The first reading does not have a time limit and is typically less formal than the subsequent stages in the procedure. 'Trialogues' between representatives of the three institutions during first or early second reading help to identify common ground and speed up the process, but they also remove the subjects under discussion from the realm of open political debate within and between the institutions, with the possible consequential loss of public involvement. This potentially affects the function of Parliament to adopt and deliberate on legislation in an open and public process. In this way the debate becomes 'de-politicized' and enters the realm of closed inter-institutional 'negotiations'. The Council, on this reading is enabled to tie the European Parliament into its 'cocoon of power'—negotiations behind closed doors. The Council has been facilitated by inter-institutional rule-making in the interstices of the formal rules that seems to be particularly paradigmatic in the context of co-decision.[170]

The risk now that so much of these behind closed doors inter-institutional negotiations are occurring before the first reading is that there is virtually no

[168] See further D Bostock, (2002) 'Coreper revisited', *Journal of Common Market Studies*, 4/2, pp 215–34, p 220. According to him legislative co-decision is not the only case in which members of COREPER collectively replace Ministers.

[169] See further S Kurpas, C Green, and P Maciej Kaczynski (2008), 'The European Commission after enlargement: Does more add up to less?', CEPS Special Report, available at <www.ceps.be>. See too, J de Clerck-Sachsse and P Maciej Kaczgński, 'The European Parliament – more powerful, less legitimate? An outlook for the 7th term', CEPS Working Document No 314/ May 2009.

[170] See further H Farrell and A Héritier (2003), 'Formal and informal institutions under co-decision: Continuous constitution-building in Europe', *Governance: An International Journal of Policy, Administration and Institutions*, 16/4, pp 577–600.

public moment of salient debate on the content of legislation. When this is combined with the fact that the Council's common position is also worked on in secrecy and largely behind closed doors with no means of non-national civil servants, diplomats, and politicians knowing what exactly various Member States are proposing during the course even of 'internal' Council negotiations, then it is clear that the parliamentary arm of governance is being put to one side in a very sustained fashion—both of the European Parliament and the national parliaments.

At the same time, there is some evidence that the European Parliament is engaged in a (balance of powers) strategy of sorts: to force the Council to come before Parliament and explain its views in committee, thereby forcing it to accept that it owes some accountability for its input into the legislative process to the European Parliament. The problem with this approach is that they are *co*-legislators and that in these circumstances it may well be difficult for the European Parliament to objectively hold the Council to account in some seriously substantive fashion in this highly specific institutional context (see Chapter 9 below). A wiser strategy may be for the European Parliament, now that it will acquire in the Lisbon Treaty its pivotal status as legislative partner in the *general* legislative process, is to insist that it does not compromise on its agora function of ensuring that legislation is as far as possible taking place in an open public process and arena and does not allow this core fundamental principle to be compromised by a form of executive privilege. This seems to be the direction that the European Parliament may be moving in. In its recent 'code of conduct for negotiating co-decision files' it insists on increasing 'transparency and accountability, especially at an earlier stage in the procedure'.[171]

8.5.3 Information in EU databases

One 'black hole' that continues to grow relates to the management by Union institutions (especially the Commission and the Council of Ministers) of information in distinct databases and to which access is never granted to individuals. Harlow has referred to this deficit in information provision as producing a 'mirage of transparency' in a 'surveillance super-state'.[172] The Europa webpage contains a list of *public* databases that can be consulted online.[173] There are also others not included in this list (such as the Commission Comitology Register,[174]

[171] See, for example, EP Code of Conduct for negotiating co-decision files, as approved by the Conference of Presidents at its meeting on 18 September 2008, on file with the author. See too, <http://www.europarl.europa.eu/code/newsletter/2008_01_en.htm>.

[172] C Harlow (2009). See too the proposals contained in European Commission Communication to the European Parliament and Council, 10 June 2009, COM (2009) 262/4.

[173] <http://europa.eu/geninfo/info/guide/dbatoz/index_en.htm>.

[174] <http://ec.europa.eu/transparency/regcomitology/faq_en.htm>.

the Register of Expert Groups,[175] and of interest representatives[176]). But there are also other distinct and often quite extensive databases housed within either the Council or the Commission and with very little, if any, digital public imprint. Examples of such databases include the Schengen Information System, the Visa Information System, the Customs Information System, the Europol database, and Eurodac. The issue is probably not that the content of the databases will never be made available online (because of confidentiality and data protection concerns) but rather that they may be 'supervised' in a secretive fashion[177]—and also that the manner in which amendments to existing systems evolve may ensure that 'function creep' takes place.[178]

Given the vast amount of information contained in such databases, the Ombudsman in a recent own-initiative report considers it problematic that the content of databases is not covered by the legislation implementing the right of public access to documents or by the 'proactive' practice of the institutions themselves. This has to do with the fact that the existing legal provisions relate to access to 'documents' as such whereas in the context of databases it is more appropriate to think in terms of a wider access to information. In the Commission proposal to amend the existing access regulation[179] it is proposed to effectively cut back on the definition of 'documents' as compared to the status quo, a matter that is considered controversial.[180] The Commission's view is that a database as such is not a 'document' and it will not modify the existing parameters of a database in order to be able to proactively retrieve information requested (as opposed to distinct documents via a standard search engine).[181] The Commission in its proposal for a revised EU access legislation proposes that 'data contained in electronic storage, processing and retrieval systems are documents if they can be extracted in the form of a printout or electronic-format copy using the available tools for the exploitation of the system'.[182] The European Ombudsman in a subsequent

175 <http://ec.europa.eu/transparency/regexpert/index.cfm>.

176 <https://webgate.ec.europa.eu/transparency/regrin/welcome.do?locale=en>.

177 See, for example, the Joint Supervisory Authority and Joint Secretariat for independent supervisory authorities, such as Schengen JSA, Europol JSA, and Customs JSA, <http://www.schengen-jsa.dataprotection.org/>. The internal rules provide for secret meetings and the respect of an absolute obligation of 'secrecy'.

178 See, for example, B Hayes (2004), *From the Schengen Information System to SIS II and the Visa Information (VIS): The proposals explained* (London: Statewatch).

179 Commission, 'Proposal for a Regulation of the European Parliament and Council regarding public access to European Parliament, Council and Commission documents', COM (2008) 229, final.

180 See, for example, T Bunyan (2008), 'Access to EU documents: When is a "document" not a "document"?', Statewatch analysis, available at <http://www.statewatch.org/news/2008/sep/access-to-eu-docs-eu-what-is-a-document.pdf>.

181 Quoted in European Ombudsman, 'Public access to information in EU databases', Strasbourg 2008, <http://www.statewatch.org/news/2009/jan/eu-ombs-databases-report.pdf>, p 7.

182 Proposed change to Art 3, Proposal for a Regulation (2008) (n 179 above). For a detailed commentary on the problems potentially inherent in each of these requirements/specifications, see European Ombudsman Report (2008) (n 181 above).

own-initiative report goes substantially further in recommending that: 'EU legislation regarding access should contain a right of public access to *information in databases*.'[183] Moreover, the needs of transparency should be taken into account in the design of new databases (and the amendment of existing ones).[184]

The point is that information (generally on individuals) stored in such databases is available to executive authorities both at the European level and at the national level. Authorized agencies in the Member States now routinely input data directly into the system, which includes data supplied by non-EU members and third parties. Moreover the so-called 'interoperability' between such databases is becoming increasingly common and incrementally reinforced in a variety of legal and institutional practices.[185]

The issue whether we must view such 'interoperability' in a technical way or whether it has broader social and even political implications is only just beginning to emerge at the EU level. The Commission (and presumably the other EU institutions too) is adamant that it is purely 'technical'. In a 'communication' to the Council and the European Parliament on improved effectiveness, enhanced interoperability, and synergies among European databases in the area of justice and home affairs, the Commission defined 'interoperability' as the 'ability of IT systems and of the business processes they support to exchange data and to enable the sharing of information and knowledge'.[186] This 'technical approach' seeks to avoid the political dimension and the fact that there may be lots of problems inherent in linking systems with, for example, police databases that are not serving law enforcement purposes.

There is another way of viewing the salience of 'interoperability'. In the words of de Hert and Gutwirth:

> Interoperability, made possible by law, disrespects the importance of separated domains and cuts through their protective walls. The use limitation and purpose specification principles are put aside. Data gathered by some are used by others for purposes that were never to be foreseen at the moment of their gathering. This is all the more problematic since the purpose specification principle is at the heart of the data protection according to which the processing of personal data is not banned in a principled way,

[183] Ibid.

[184] See too presentation by the European Ombudsman to the Committee on Civil Liberties, Justice and Home Affairs, European Parliament on the reform of Regulation 1049/2001 on Public Access to Documents, 29 November 2007, available at <http://www.statewatch.org/news/2007/dec/acceess-to-docs-reg-ombuds-ep.pdf>.

[185] See further P de Hert and S Gutwith (2006), 'Interoperability of police databases within the EU: An accountable political choice', TILT Law and Technology Working Paper No 001/2006, 1 April 2006, available at <http://www.tilburguniversity.nl/faculties/law/research/tilt/publications/workingpapers/>.

[186] Commission Communication to the Council and the European Parliament on improved effectiveness, enhanced interoperability and synergies among European databases in the area of justice and home affairs, COM (2005) 597 final, Brussels, 24 November 2005.

but allowed on the condition that the processing meets specified, explicit and legitimate purposes.[187]

A salient legal parameter with regard to the information contained in databases is the extent to which individuals can rely on EU legislation on data protection that enables them to discover what information is being stored on them in such databases and whether they can have it altered or deleted. To date the operationalization of this right is very limited.

8.6 Authoritarian Temptation

The diplomatic origins of international relations may help explain the innate drive towards secrecy of EU executive power. The dichotomy was initially—and to some extent still is—between diplomacy (international external relations) and democracy (national internal politics and policymaking). But, as Dahl reminded us many years ago, diplomacy and democracy are incompatible modes of decision-making. In the words of Beetham and Lord: 'By applying foreign policy methods to Union activities constructed around a domestic agenda, governments have extended executive privilege to the core of democratic politics and subjected them to a bargaining format that requires secrecy rather than transparency.'[188]

The natural inclination of the governing institutions of a totalitarian state is indeed to draw a veil of secrecy over their activities, their archives and, above all, their policy and legislative plans, and in the process elevating structural secrecy to the level of a principle for all areas of government. Open government cannot exist in such a state because openness implies the possibility of exercising public control over government and of empowering the opposition.[189] Authoritarian institutions seek dark shadows, if not complete secrecy, and exist in an environment where other institutions (and actors) are perhaps weak(er) or in any event not autonomous in their ability to carry out functions of accountability and control. The traditional view of access to information (or more widely open government) in increasing the transparency of the public administration is characterized as a measure of 'public hygiene' focused ultimately on the aim of improved democratic accountability and control. Transparency can also be considered a necessary condition for broad public debate on policymaking processes.

Transparency refers to the 'constant visibility of information'.[190] As such, it does not amount to accountability but it represents an indispensable element for

[187] P de Hert and S Gutwerth (2006). See further on the relationship between access to information and data protection the recent work by H Kranenborg (2007).

[188] D Beetham and C Lord (1998), *Legitimacy and the European Union* (London: Longman), p 73.

[189] See further D Curtin and H Meijers (1995b), 'The principle of open government in Schengen and the European Union: Democratic retrogression?' Common Market L Rev, 32/2, pp 391–442.

[190] R Lastra and H Shams, 'Public accountability in the financial sector' in E Ferran and C Goodhart (eds), *Regulating Financial Services and Markets in the 21st Century* (Oxford: Hart Publishing), pp 165–88, p 171.

an effective system of accountability. Whereas 'accountability is an obligation to give account or explain and justify one's actions . . . transparency is the degree to which information on such actions is available'.[191] In the absence of comprehensive and accurate information on the actor's actions, it becomes very problematic for the forum to overcome informational asymmetries and to be able to hold the actor to account for those actions in a meaningful manner. Transparency, in the sense of availability of all relevant information, is thus to be considered an essential prerequisite to specific account-holding processes (see Chapter 9 below).

[191] Ibid, p 172

9

Accountable Executive Power

9.1 Conceptualizing Accountability

Accountability is one of those golden concepts that are relatively uncontested in the sense that everyone intuitively agrees that public institutions or authorities should render account publicly for the use of their mandates and the manner in which public money is spent. The adjective 'accountable' is increasingly used in political discourse and policy documents because it conveys an image of transparency and trustworthiness. In the last two decades, the quest for greater accountability 'has penetrated all our lives, like great draughts of Heineken's, reaching parts that supposedly less developed forms of accountability did not reach'.[1] Accountability forces power to speak the truth, at least in ideal terms.[2] However, its evocative powers make it also a very elusive concept because it can mean many different things to different people, as anyone studying accountability will soon discover.[3] The concept of 'accountability' often appears to be used rather vaguely, as 'a garbage can filled with good intentions, loosely defined concepts and vague images of good governance'.[4] Its very elasticity represents both a challenge and a pitfall.

Accountability is indeed a broad term that reflects a range of understandings rather than a single paradigm. Until recently, accountability was not a term in common use, nor did it figure as a term of art outside the financial contexts of accountancy and audit.[5] Today as Richard Mulgan has aptly noted the word 'crops up everywhere performing all manner of analytical and rhetorical tasks and carrying most of the burdens of democratic "governance" '.[6]

[1] O O'Neill (2002), 'Lecture 3: Called to account: A question of trust', Reith Lectures on BBC Radio 4, available at <http://www.bbc.co.uk/radio4/reith2002/lecture3.shtml>.

[2] M Bovens and P Hart (2005), 'Evaluating public accountability', Paper International Research Colloquium Accountable Governance, Queens University in Belfast, available at <http://www.usg.uu.nl/download/Evaluating%20Accountability.pdf>.

[3] See further M Bovens (2010), 'Two concepts of accountability. Accountability as a virtue and as a mechanism', *West European Politics*, forthcoming.

[4] M Bovens (2005), 'Public accountability' in E Ferlie, L Lynne, and C Pollitt (eds), *The Oxford Handbook of Public Management*, (Oxford University Press), pp 182–208.

[5] C Harlow (2002), *Accountability in the European Union*, (Oxford University Press), p 1.

[6] R Mulgan (2000), '"Accountability": An ever-expanding concept?', *Public Administration*, 78/3, pp 555–73.

According to political theorists, accountability is not of necessity confined to democratic forms of governance, although it is in democracies that greater demands for accountability will generally be heard.[7] However more accountability is not necessarily to be equated with more 'democracy' (see Chapter 10).[8]

In the EU debate, those authors who focus on (the lack of) accountability in the evolving political system of the EU[9] tend to be concerned with the (broader) issue of making decision-making at that level more democratic as well as with the (narrower) issue of controlling delegated powers. The latter seems to be dominated by the former. Thus, in the words of Fisher, 'while accountability within the EU context is often characterized as the principle for an era of innovative governance unshackled from conventional understandings of the constitutional state it is doubtful whether accountability and accountability processes can operate outside the context of liberal democratic government'.[10] Others, like Moravcsik, defend the EUs 'democratic deficit' on the basis that it pretty much parallels what is found in the 'real world' of advanced industrial democracies; in any event, the EU is, on his findings, not 'an unaccountable technocracy' but is the subject of both direct and indirect mechanisms of democratic accountability.[11]

The purpose of this chapter is to further reflect on what a concept of 'public accountability' may mean in the specific context of the EU and to adopt a rather 'thin' definition of 'accountability', shorn of the inevitability of a link with the 'meta-norm' of democracy.[12] The idea is that understanding accountability as a social relationship (see below) enables it to be applied with regard to a range of (executive) actors engaged in the exercise of executive power under the auspices of the EU in one way or another. In so doing, account will be taken of the various legal and institutional practices that have grown up over the years in the manner in which various 'accountability forums' have put flesh and blood on relationships of accountability with various actors. The question is to what extent can one speak of the various executive actors active at the EU level being held to account in some fashion by forums either at the European level or at the national level? This is the question that this chapter will attempt to answer.

[7] D Robertson (2002), *The Routledge Dictionary of Politics* (London: Routledge), p 3.

[8] See, for example, I Papadopoulos (2010), 'Accountability and multi-level governance: More accountability, less democracy?', *West European Politics*, forthcoming.

[9] C Harlow (2002); A Arnull and D Wincott (eds) (2002), *Accountability and Legitimacy in the European Union*, (Oxford University Press).

[10] E Fisher (2004), 'The European Union in the age of accountability', Oxford Journal of Legal Studies, 24/3, pp 495–515, p 496.

[11] A Moravcsik (2002), 'In defence of the democratic deficit: Reassessing legitimacy in the European Union', *Journal of Common Market Studies*, 40/4, pp 603–24.

[12] A Wiener (2007), 'Contested meaning of norms: A research framework', *Comparative European Politics*, 5/1, pp 1–17.

9.2 Understanding 'Public Accountability' in the EU Political System

9.2.1 'Control' *ex ante*

What can be designated the original or 'core' sense of accountability is that associated with the process of being *called to account* to some authority for one's actions.[13] Accountability can be construed as an important organizing principle of democracy resting upon specific standardized procedures. In the modern state, accountability can be said to have two major meanings, which overlap.[14] In the context of a democratic state, the key accountability relationships in this core sense are those between citizens and the holders of public office and, within the ranks of office holders, between elected politicians and bureaucrats.[15] The former refers to more 'political' accountability and the latter more 'administrative'. In democracies, political accountability depends on the form and mechanisms of political representation, linking citizens to their legislators; and on the other hand, on the formalized relationship between legislative and executive powers.[16] Both types of political accountability rely 'on a rather weak power of control, for the position of the "agents" in those two relationships is comparatively stronger in terms of either their knowledge or their ability to control the agenda'.[17] Administrative accountability 'operates within a more defined hierarchical structure where there is a certain division of labour and competences, and where both the content and the process of public decision making, hence the role played by individuals, can be examined in more detail'.[18] This somewhat more technical use of accountability refers to those arrangements made for securing conformity between the values of a delegating body and those to whom powers are delegated (delegatee).

In contemporary national democracies the conditional designation of others to make decisions that the delegator (the party delegating) was originally authorized to do in their name and place tends to be viewed as one *single* chain of delegation. The single chain of delegation runs all the way from the voters to the civil servants that ultimately implement public policy albeit with several links. It is thus a single chain of delegation with multiple links.

In the EU context however, it is very difficult to establish a single chain of delegation (and thus of accountability) in this fashion. Moreover, it is difficult to conceive of each link in terms of a single principal delegating to a single or

[13] R Mulgan (2000), p 555. [14] D Robertson (2002), p 3.

[15] See, in general, K Strom, WC Muller, and T Bergman (2003), 'Parliamentary democracy: Promise and problems' in K Strom, WC Muller, and T Bergman (eds), *Delegation and Accountability in Parliamentary Democracies*, (Oxford: Oxford University Press), pp 3–32.

[16] See further D Castiglione (2006), 'Accountability' in M Bevir (ed), *Encyclopedia of Governance*, (Sage), vol 1, pp 1–7.

[17] Ibid. [18] Ibid.

multiple non-competing agents. Even if we view the national legislature (connected to the voters) as delegating power upwards via the national governments to the EU supranational actors (in particular the Commission, much less so the Council of Ministers), it is difficult to link that same authorization by the national legislature with the output of the EU actors. Moreover the national legislatures may be connected to the national voters but the elections are on purely national matters not on the output of the supranational actors. It is thus virtually impossible to conceive of a chain of delegation in singular terms. This has also emerged from the discussion in Chapter 2 of this book where we also concluded that we could not conceive of delegation in simple, singular terms from the 'political' Member State level to the 'administrative' EU level because of the fact that the EU political system is in some respects evolving in a non-linear and autonomous fashion. It includes delegation of powers from EU executive actors as political principals to EU executive actors as administrative or 'satellite' agents. At the European level we are forced to consider multiple chains of delegation with multiple links, largely due to the fact that it is not the legislature that is both directly connected to the voters and at the same time delegating its powers.

According to the classic delegation literature, principals engage in various forms of oversight of their agents. The literature on delegation identifies four major measures by which principals can contain agency losses,[19] namely contract design, screening and selection mechanisms, monitoring and reporting requirements, and institutional checks (and balances). The former two are mechanisms by which principals seek to contain agency loss *ex ante*; the remaining mechanisms operate *ex post*. But the principals may, de facto or *de jure*, 'control' their agent, in which case the need for either *ex ante* or *ex post* accountability may change. 'Control' in the Anglo-Saxon sense can be considered in conceptual terms as broader than accountability and can include both *ex ante* and *ex post* mechanisms of directing behaviour.[20] Control means 'having power over' and can involve very proactive means of directing conduct, for example through straight orders, directives, financial incentives, or regulations.[21] But these hierarchical, financial, or legal mechanisms are not mechanisms of accountability per se, because they do not in themselves operate through procedures in which actors are to explain and justify their conduct to (external) forums.[22] Control refers to a whole range of mechanisms employed by the controlling actor in order

[19] DR Kiewiet and M McCubbins (1991), *The Logic of Delegation* (Chicago: University of Chicago Press).

[20] C Scott (2000), 'Accountability in the regulatory state', Journal of Law and Society, 27/1, pp 38–60, p 39.

[21] M Busuioc (2009), 'Accountability, control and independence: The case of European agencies', European LJ, 15/5, pp 599–615.

[22] R Mulgan (2003), *Holding Power to Account: Accountability in modern democracies*, (Basingstoke: Palgrave), p 19

to direct, steer, and influence decision-making and behaviour of the controlled agents.[23]

Before evaluating accountability *ex post* and identifying deficits, it has to be ascertained *a priori* whether the executive actors in question really benefit from all the discretion and independence they are formally as a matter of legal rules said to possess. In her ongoing work, Busuioc has, for example, shown that, to the extent the 'parent bodies' (in particular the Commission but in some instances the Council too) are able to exert a large degree of control over a wide variety of EU *agencies* and to significantly limit their discretion, agency accountability *ex post* or the lack thereof becomes less problematic.[24] In other words her central thesis is that accountability as such precludes direct control from the principal. The need for accountability and the introduction of accountability mechanisms is relevant precisely because the principal has delegated powers to an agent and thus, renounced direct control. Following this line of reasoning, accountability is concerned with *ex post* oversight, with ascertaining after the fact to what extent the agent has lived up to its *ex ante* mandate and has acted within its zone of discretion. This is the focus in the rest of this chapter: on *ex post* accountability that comes into play when there is no (or little control). This can be illustrated by Fig 9.1 applied to the issue of EU agencies.

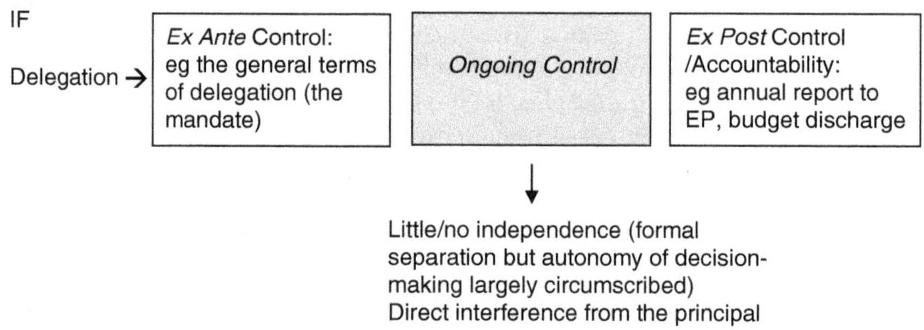

Fig 9.1 Controlled, little or no independence: EU Agencies?

Source: M Busuioc (2009), 'Accountability, control and independence: The case of European agencies', European LJ, forthcoming.

The argument is quite different with regard to the European Central Bank (ECB). One of the central arguments forwarded by those opposed to the introduction of accountability mechanisms for the ECB rests on the premise that accountability and independence are in a zero-sum relationship; that is to say, it is argued that rendering the ECB accountable would automatically result in a

[23] P Roness et al (2007), 'Autonomy and regulation of state agencies: Reinforcement, indifference or compensation?', Paper Presented at the 4th ECPR General Conference, Pisa, Italy, 6–8 September 2007, p 5.

[24] M Busuioc (2009).

decrease of the ECB's independence, which has been regarded as the 'essential condition of its efficiency'. This standpoint rests, as Busuioc's work show us, on the misplaced assumption that accountability is synonymous with what is termed 'direct control',[25] which would imply direct interference in decision-making processes. Whereas independence and control are indeed in a zero-sum relationship, accountability, and independence are not contradictory and *must* in fact coexist. Not only will the introduction of accountability mechanisms not jeopardize the 'sacrosanct' ECB independence but on the contrary, such steps should be undertaken in order to justify ECB's independence as well as to increase the bank's overall legitimacy.

Ex ante, by virtue of its mandate, the ECB has been granted a substantial amount of discretion to pursue its mandate. The ECB benefits from extensive powers and operational independence,[26] which, as we have seen in Chapter 6, have been raised to a constitutional status. Moreover, unlike its national counterparts, the ECB can also be said to display a substantial degree of implicit goal independence. Although the primary objective of the ECB (ie price stability) is specified by the treaty, the formulation of the operational expression of that objective is left to the latitude of the ECB and the bank has the discretion to change it when it deems necessary. More precisely, the treaty provides only a broad formulation of the primary goal and the ECB is the one that actually gives meaning and expression to this goal by setting the actual parameters. In this connection, it can be said that 'unparalleled power has been conferred on the ECB'[27] and that this is 'a characteristic that plainly distinguishes it from other models for central banks'.[28]

This extensive delegation has not been limited through ongoing intervention in the post-delegation stage. Unlike in the case of some European agencies where the Commission exercises ongoing controls over the respective agencies to the effect that part of the original delegation is neutralized,[29] the ECB is *de facto* independent in the fulfilment of its tasks. With the exception of the Court of Justice, no other institution or body of the Community has the power to approve, suspend, annul or defer decisions of the ECB, nor are they entitled to vote during the meetings of the Executive Board and the Governing Council. Thus, ECB benefits from a wide zone of discretion and real independence within its mandate. This needs to be matched by accountability mechanisms commensurate

[25] C Zilioli and M Selmayr (2000), 'The European Central Bank: An independent specialized organization of community law' 37 Common Market L Rev, 591–643.

[26] I Begg (2007), 'Contested meanings of transparency in central banking', *Comparative European Politics*, 5/1, pp 36–52.

[27] J De Haan and S Eijffinger (2000), 'The democratic accountability of the European Central Bank: A comment on two fairy-tales' *Journal of Common Market Studies*, 38/3, pp 393–407, p 395

[28] I Begg and D Green (1998), 'The political economy of the European Central Bank' in P Arestis and MC Sawyer (eds), *The Political Economy of Central Banking*, (Cheltenham: Edward Elgar), pp 122–35, p 124.

[29] M Busuioc, (2009).

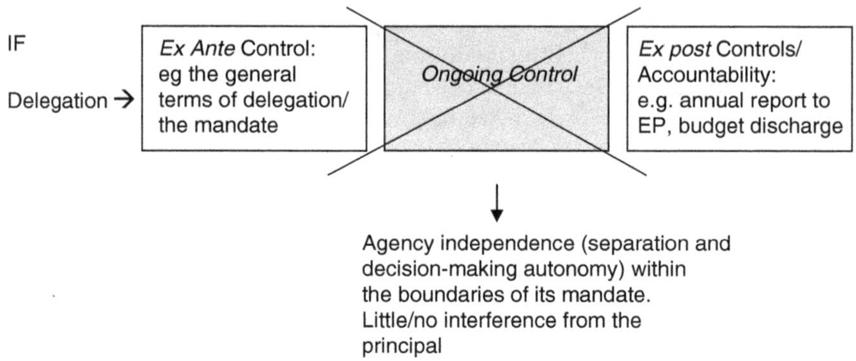

Fig 9.2 The ECB: Independent (little or no ongoing control) and accountable

Source: M Busuioc (2009), 'Accountability, control and independence: The case of European agencies', European LJ, forthcoming.

to its powers. That is to say, in the case of the ECB, where the actor enjoys far-reaching delegation of powers without ongoing intervention to limit that discretion, accountability becomes a necessity in order to ensure the actor's compliance with the terms of its mandate and the goals for which it was set up. In other words, precisely because of its extensive independence the ECB *must be* accountable.[30]

9.2.2 'Public accountability' *ex post*

As we have seen above, 'accountability' in the sense used here can be distinguished from 'control' (which will be generally *ex ante* or simultaneous[31]) and has a number of distinct features: it is external, it involves social interaction, and exchange and it implies rights of authority in that those calling for an account are asserting rights of superior authority over those who are accountable, including the rights to demand answers and to draw consequences, possibly including the imposition of sanctions. This sense of accountability is in line with the broad sense that Keohane and Grant describe: 'accountability' as involving the justification of an actor's performance vis-à-vis others, the assessment or judgment of that performance against certain standards, and the possible imposition of consequences if the actor fails to live up to applicable standards.[32] Accountability on this understanding is concerned with *ex post* oversight, with ascertaining after the fact, to which extent the agent has lived up to its *ex ante* mandate and has acted within its zone of discretion.

[30] I am grateful to M Busuioc for on-going discussions and a joint unpublished paper on this subject.
[31] M Busuioc (2009).
[32] RW Grant and RO Keohane (2005), 'Accountability and abuses of power in world politics', *American Political Science Review*, 99/1, pp 29–43, pp 29–30.

If one focuses largely on the EU level of governance, it is necessary to agree a working definition of accountability that could potentially be inclusive in terms of types and levels of actors and types and levels of accountability forums and that would link them in some fashion. In order to look more closely at the practice of accountability across a range of actors and to hopefully compare results, a working definition of accountability is required that will facilitate the operationalization of specific empirical studies, thus moving the debate one step beyond the level of conceptual generalizations. This can be done by focusing on the fact that the concept of 'holding to account' not only obliges actors to disclose information and justify their behaviour but also requires a *social relationship* between the actor and what can be loosely termed an accountability forum of one type or another, and moreover may require the establishment of a *mechanism*. In a much cited definition in the EU context,[33] Bovens views accountability as: 'a social relationship between an actor and a forum, in which the actor explains his conduct and gives information to the forum, in which the forum can reach a judgment or render an assessment of that conduct, and on which it may be possible for some form of sanction (formal or informal) to be imposed on the actor'.[34]

This rather focused definition of accountability as a social relationship between an actor and a forum is an excellent way of linking actors, any actors, and accountability forums, irrespective of the grand constitutional design. The attractiveness of the Bovens definition of accountability is that it provides a clear procedural and organizational framework with a focus on the relationship between the actor, potentially any actor (including, for example, actors that can never be understood as agents, such as networks), and an accountability forum—potentially any kind of accountability forum (it can be legal, administrative, financial, as well as the more obviously political). In addition, it limits the focus of accountability to the *ex post* and to those mechanisms that provide in some manner for the imposition of sanctions or consequences in a looser, not strictly legal, sense.

Moreover the very fact that accountability is given such a precise definition, with various steps and links, makes it possible to operationalize it in very specific institutional contexts and to study empirically the practices of accountability with regard to many different kinds of forums (courts, parliaments, auditors, ombudsmen, etc). The latter do not have to be in a principal–agent relationship with the actors and is inclusive and open in terms of mechanism or type of accountability forums. They can be legal, political, financial, administrative, etc irrespective of the grand constitutional design.

[33] See the various contributions to two (legal and political science respectively but with overlaps) special issues on 'Accountability in the European Union': European LJ, July 2007 and *West European Politics* (2010, forthcoming).

[34] M Bovens (2007), 'Analysing and assessing accountability: A conceptual framework', European LJ, 13/4, pp 447–68.

In this manner it is possible to explore, to greater or lesser extents, the nature of existing accountability deficits even if this was only with regard to very precise relationships and with nothing being said about wider aspects and concerns of political systems as a whole. This is its advantage in the short and medium term. Precisely the parsimony of the definition and the specific focus enable some concrete studies to take place across, at first sight, a range of very different governance levels.[35]

A further advantage of the Bovens definition is that the relationship between the rather precise notion of accountability as thus defined and much broader themes and even meta-norms of any political system is temporarily left to one side in the interest of being able to focus on establishing more neutrally to what extent one could speak of existing and evolving 'practices' of accountability at various different levels and with regard to various different types of actors or institutions. No claim is made that accountability as thus defined would solve the legitimacy problems of the EU nor that it will give rise to an appropriate and uncontested notion of supranational democracy at the level of the EU or anywhere else (however, see Chapter 10 below).

The most interesting finding from ongoing work on EU multi-level governance systems relates to the wide variety of actors that can be studied in terms of their relationship as a matter of legal, institutional and empirical practice with a wide variety of accountability forums. They vary from very formal and institutionalized actors (for example, the 'comitology' committees[36]) to much less institutionalized forums (for example networks[37]). We have seen in the previous chapters how legal and institutional practices have evolved that can be placed within a broad accountability framework and various mechanisms of accountability.

The 'multi-levelness' and interconnections between not only formal institutions but also individual actors and networks is an intrinsic part of the manner in which the EU conducts its business. Actors are not nested within one level but cross over into other levels or arenas without there necessarily being any clarity as to their authority or links back to their original level. In positioning the various types of actors at the European level and their relationship with both the national political systems and the horizontal EU political system, we need to use a framework of analysis that enables a broader understanding of

[35] See, for example, A Benz (2007), 'Accountable multilevel governance by the open method of coordination?', European LJ, 13/4, pp 505–22; Y Papadopoulos (2007), 'Problems of democratic accountability in network and multi-level governance', European LJ, 13/4, pp 469–86; M Koenig-Archibugi (2010), 'Accountability in transnational relations: How distinctive is it?', *West European Politics*, forthcoming.

[36] See further D Curtin (2007a), 'Holding (quasi-)autonomous EU administrative actors to public account', European LJ, 13/4, pp 523–41.

[37] Y Papadopoulos (2007); C Harlow and R Rawlings (2007), 'Promoting accountability in multilevel governance: A network approach', European LJ, 13/4, pp 542–62.

accountability in the sense of a procedural coupling between various actors and various forums. Carol Harlow and Richard Rawlings show that not only courts and ombudsmen institutions play today an important role in ensuring the accountability of rules in multi-level systems, but also that for accountability to operate efficiently this requires the establishment of *networks of accountability* (enabling exchange of information and cooperation between the EU and the national levels).[38]

In keeping with the Bovens' definition above it is proposed to divide the detailed consideration of various legal and institutional 'practices' into various discrete procedural stages in an attempt to get a view of the entire process, bit by bit. It is believed that a categorization that is more procedural and divided into the various stages (and procedural requirements of the process) may reveal more about the manner in which accountability mechanisms are developing as a matter of practice. These are essentially three: first the provision of information—mandatory, conventional, or informal; secondly, the manner in which a process of debate can occur between an accountability forum and the actor in question as well as subsequent processes of deliberation by the accountability forum; and finally, the issue of whether there is a carrot or stick attached to the process as a whole—can the accountability forum attach a sanction or any other consequence (annul a measure, impose a penalty, decrease the budget, etc) to reprehensible behaviour by an actor ?

The (mandatory or otherwise) provision of often rather general information cannot be considered without more as a neutral and objective account of what happened or what is happening. More is needed in the quest for accountability, namely the opportunity of hearing an explanation or justification of the actor's actions or decisions and for such an account to be debated and queried. In other words, as part of an *ex post* accountability process, provision must be made for a debate to take place between the actor being held to account and a relevant accountability forum on the interpretation of information made available. This may entail hearing witnesses, questioning representatives of the actors by the accountability forum, proactive investigations, etc, prior to internal deliberations by the forum itself as to the conclusions it wishes to draw from the facts and information presented to it in various ways. This will inevitably involve 'deliberation' in one form or another by the accountability forum itself. In considering the manner in which 'practices' have emerged in this regard, two specific types of accountability forums will be focused on: legal accountability (the Court of Justice) and political accountability (the European Parliament). This is not to deny there may well be others that are emerging. This particular model of accountability as a mechanism can be represented along the following lines (Fig 9.3).

[38] C Harlow and R Rawlings (2007).

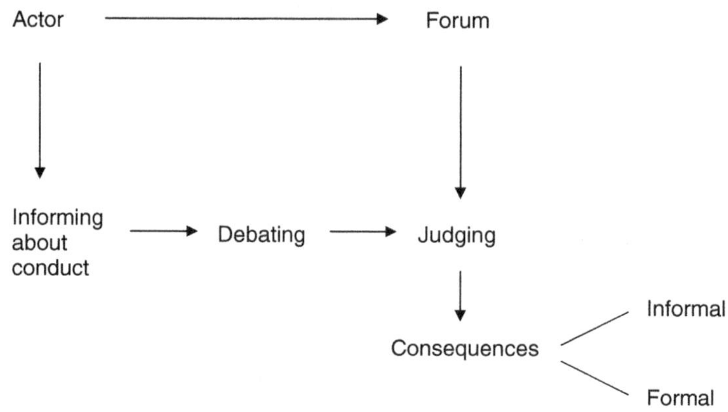

Fig 9.3 A model of public accountability

9.3 The Provision of Information

The provision of information is clearly an element of accountability although, without more, it cannot be regarded as synonymous with accountability. In other words, we can best view the provision of information in general terms (see also Chapter 8 above) as an essential prerequisite enabling actors to be held to account by accountability forums in various ways. The most basic form of providing information is quite simply *the act of reporting*. In a principal–agent relationship this involves the provision of information by an agent in a form, time, and place that is preset by a principal (traditionally in the constitutive document or institutional design). The role of the account-giver in the account-giving relationship (defined in advance in the contract design) is to provide information or feedback to the principal. The point however is that very often the form, content, and delivery by a designated agent is pre-established by the principal who requires nothing more from the reporting agent than formal compliance with the reporting requirements.

There are various types of issues that can be subjected to formal—and mandatory—reporting requirements. Examples of reporting of general activities of an actor include the annual reports of the EC prepared by the Commission, the annual reports prepared by the Council as well as, for example, the annual reports prepared by directors of independent agencies and organs and the annual reports made by the Commission on the working of comitology committees.[39] Originally in the context of the EU, the intention was to send such general reports

[39] See, for example and for other details, European Commission (2008), *Annual Report for 2007*. See too with regard to the proposed new European Systemic Risk Council (ESRC) Communication from the Commission, 'European Financial Supervision', COM (2009) final.

only to the formal principal but gradually this has been expanded, in line with evolving notions of political and public accountability within the EU framework, to include not only the parliaments (both European and, latterly, national) but also the public (and made easily accessible via active information on the Internet) and other institutional actors. From an accountability perspective it is clear that the provision of information is neither limited to formal 'reporting' arrangements nor to the existence of a principal–agent relationship. The provision of information is a necessary preliminary to the other stages in an accountability relationship; it is the beginning, not the end of the process of accountability forums being able to hold actors to account.

The formal situation is however less clear with regard to the reporting obligations of newer agencies and organs. Provision is made for an annual report to be drawn up and sent to, at the very least, the Commission and or Council; in a few more recent cases the European Parliament is also included explicitly in this list, in recognition undoubtedly of its expanded role both in decision-making and as the natural locus of political supervision of the Commission at any rate. This rule is copper-fastened with regard to executive agencies in their general statute and is also envisaged with regard to the operating framework for regulatory agencies. This general rule seems to apply equally to the Union agencies although in the case of Europol for some years only an abrogated version was made public and sent to the European Parliament, a practice that has been discontinued.[40]

There are also other types of reports that discuss more administrative and/ or managerial issues and that can be understood within the context of an actor's more internal mechanisms for accountability. Thus, with regard to the European Commission, a whole series of administrative reporting requirements have been imposed on various managers etc as the language and toolbox of New Public Management have made its entry at this level. For example, the Commission now produces informative annual activity reports.[41] Another well-developed form of reporting as account-giving is financial reporting and the range of financial mechanisms that have become institutionalized through legal requirements and professional standards. In general, the financial reporting agent is required to provide the relevant principals with the information needed to assess agent operations and to make decisions. In the context of the EU, financial reporting is institutionalized via the Court of Auditors for the primary institutional actors.[42]

The formal requirement of reporting has been backed up in recent years by the often proactive provision of extensive statistics, lists, registers, and databases, all of which make a contribution to shedding light on the various activities assumed by administrative actors. This has been highlighted in Chapter 8 above. In addition,

[40] On the differences between the 'public' and the 'secret' versions of the report historically see <http://www.statewatch.org/news/2001/mar/07accountab.htm>.

[41] European Commission, COM (2004) 418 and SEC (2004) 732.

[42] See further, C Harlow (2002), op. cit.

explicit provision may be made with regard to certain agencies for supplementary (scientific) reports to be made public and the practice is to make them available in PDF files on the respective websites.[43] Indeed, the amount of information being made available by some of the newer agencies, in particular via their own easily navigable websites, can be quite extensive.[44]

The notion of transparency, however, goes much further then than mere 'reporting' obligations at precise moments in time. Transparency implies constant visibility of information, not merely that the information is provided periodically or in response to information requests.[45] The broader term 'transparency' is about the provision of information and can best be understood in terms of the degree to which information is available. Transparency and accountability will thus mutually reinforce one another.

When it comes to comitology, as we saw in Chapter 8, the practice of the Commission in recent years has been to release to the public (via special databases on the Internet) quite extensive information on the membership of such committees, agendas of meetings, minutes of meetings etc, as well as draft measures. This practice has followed on from the imposition of horizontal requirements as to providing public access to documents of the Council, Commission and the European Parliament that has then been 'taken over' both in the context of comitology and in the case of the 'decentralized' agencies. One can discern a certain snowball effect in terms of legal regulation and developing, often further-reaching, proactive institutional practices, both formal and informal. In terms of agencies too, there is a tendency for them to often proactively release information on their decision-taking and consultation processes via their home pages on the Internet.

9.4 Debate and Deliberation

9.4.1 Public deliberation

Neither publicity nor transparency amount without more to *accountability* but represent preconditions for an effective system of accountability.[46] Publicity is a phenomenon that political actors and actions are exposed to; transparency is on the other hand a characteristic of the political process as such, and on an aggregate level of the political system as a whole. A transparent political process is one

[43] See, for example, the annual safety reports made available to the public by the European Aviation Safety Agency and the publication by the European Environment Agency of the scientific committee reports.

[44] See, for example, the web site of EASA, <http://www.easa.eu.int/ws_prod/index.html>.

[45] See, in general, C Hood and D Heald (eds) (2006), *Transparency: The key to better governance?* (Oxford University Press).

[46] See too D Naurin (2006), 'Transparency, publicity, accountability: The missing links', *Swiss Political Science Review*, 12/3, pp 90–8.

that is easy to follow for anyone who is interested; there is freedom of information or access to documents and easy access to decision-makers for the media. But there will be no publicity, ie no actual exposure of political actors and actions to a broad audience, no matter how transparent the policymaking process, if the available information about political actions is left unattended. The mass media is therefore a crucial link between transparency and publicity. Genuine publicity is necessary in order to foster democratic legitimacy and 'mere' transparency will be insufficient.[47]

By definition, democratic government functions through widespread *public deliberations* on important issues. There can only be public debate to the extent that information is made public. The criterion of public debate means that deliberation by (executive) policymakers has to be rendered public and debated in national and European media and through national and European parliaments.[48] From previous studies it is clear however that, as a matter of practice, only those citizens with expert knowledge of the policy subject make use of the possibility to read information about a particular policy, the process, and the actors involved.[49] It follows that increasing public access to documents will not automatically lead to a situation in which a majority of citizens feel sufficiently well informed on European matters to constitute an 'audience'.[50]

In public it is assumed that the 'force of the better argument' norm will rule. Public debate induces actors to replace the language of power with the language of reason—in other words they have to appeal to common norms and values.[51] From a normative point of view this shift in behaviour is described in the deliberative democratic literature as fostering the exchange of rational arguments concerning the common good, rather than bargaining or voting.[52] Deliberation is a concept that involves the willingness to listen to others, to express opinions, and to speak out when facing contradictory viewpoints.[53] Those who engage in deliberation are in principle forced to consider alternative perspectives, reconsider their own

[47] See too T Hüller, (2007), 'Assessing EU strategies for publicity', *Journal of European Public Policy*, 14/4, pp 563–81.

[48] See too C de la Porte and P Nanz (2004), 'The OMC: A deliberative democratic mode of governance? The case of employment and pensions', *Journal of European Public Policy*, 11/2, pp 267–88.

[49] L Cotino (2006), 'Theory and reality of public access to EU information' in D Curtin, A Kellermann, and S Blockmans (eds), *The EU Constitution: The best way forward?* (Kluwer), pp 233–44.

[50] See further D Curtin (2007b), 'Transparency, audiences and the evolving role of the EU Council of Ministers' in J Fossum and P Schlesinger (eds), *The European Union and the Public Sphere: A communicative space in the making?* (Routledge), pp 246–58.

[51] E Eriksen and J Fossum (eds) (2000), *Democracy in the European Union: Integration through deliberation?* (London: Routledge).

[52] Ibid.

[53] B Hardy, D Scheufele, and Z Wang (2009), 'Defining deliberation: Key determinants and distinct dimensions', Paper presented at the annual meeting of the International Communication Association, Sheraton, New York, available at: <http://www.allacademic.com//meta/p_mla_apa_research_citation/0/1/3/0/5/pages13051/p13051-1.php>.

perspectives and ultimately form reasoned opinions. An outcome of public deliberation is a clear understanding of all sides of a public issue.

The provision of information cannot be considered without more as a neutral and objective account of what happened or what is happening. More is needed in the quest for accountability, namely the opportunity of hearing an explanation or justification of the actor's actions or decisions and for such account-giving to be debated and queried. In other words, as part of an *ex post* accountability process, provision must be made for a debate to take place on the interpretation of information made available between the actor being held to account and a relevant accountability forum. This may entail hearing witnesses, questioning representatives of the actors by the accountability forum, proactive investigations etc prior to internal deliberations by the forum itself as to the conclusions it wishes to draw from the facts and information presented to it in various ways. This will involve 'deliberation' in one form or another by the accountability forum itself.

9.4.2 The European Parliament deliberates

The role of the European Parliament as an accountability forum where critical debate and deliberation can take place is a growing one in recent years. In general terms it can be said that the role of the European Parliament has evolved to such a point that it exists in a relationship of political accountability with the Commission in particular but also, at least in nascent form, with other actors, administrative or otherwise on the European stage. For example, the European Parliament began with carving out a political space for debating and deliberating upon the actions and inactions of the ECB even though this was only very weakly provided for in the constituent texts.[54] It monitored, for example, the ECB's reporting requirements and appointment processes in a 'very serious way'.[55] In the words of one author, 'MEPs want to transform the ECB's reporting obligations into occasions for real deliberation . . .'[56]

There is evidence of the emergence of an 'accountability game' between the European Parliament and EU-level agencies. Initially the general practice for the European Parliament was neither to debate the annual reports of the agencies nor to call in the directors for questioning in parallel with what it does for the Commission and the Council. In some of the more recent agencies (where it was also involved in the drafting, for example the European Aviation Safety Agency) the European Parliament is however mandated in the constitutive statute to invite the executive director to report on the manner in which the

[54] See too P Magnette (2000), 'Towards accountable independence? Parliamentary controls of the European Central Bank and the rise of a new democratic model', European LJ, 6/4, pp 326–40.

[55] See further N Jabko (2003), 'Democracy in the age of the Euro', *Journal of European Public Policy*, 10/3, pp 710–39.

[56] Ibid, p 724.

tasks of the agency have been carried out. With the European Agency External Borders Operational Cooperation the European Parliament sought to push out the frontiers even further: thus it may request 'at any time' a hearing with the executive director on 'any subject' related to the agency's activities.[57] The opening-up of these procedural possibilities enables those officials actually carrying out specific tasks in practice to engage in account-giving. The practice has developed of organizing annual meetings with the directors of many of the agencies on the basis of detailed documentation and questioning.[58]

The situation is however more problematic when it comes to an open public debate and deliberation on the performance of Union agencies. Traditionally for example, there was no formal right for the European Parliament to request an exchange of views on the annual report with either the Council presidency or the director of Europol on the activities of Europol. There was no practice (or possibility according to the original Europol Convention) to request the Europol director to appear before the competent committee of the European Parliament although the European Parliament has in recent years put questions to the presidency of the Council concerning the activities of Europol. In a subsequent protocol, provision was made stating that the director of Europol may appear before the European Parliament to discuss 'general' questions and only in order to assist the Council presidency.[59] The European Parliament itself was highly critical of these proposed amendments at the time pointing out that 'the European Parliament will keep its current role with regard to Europol: discussing without anyone listening and making reports without anyone implementing'.[60] In the new Council decision establishing the European Police Office (Europol)[61] on which the European Parliament gave an opinion,[62] it is explicitly provided that the director shall submit to the European Parliament 'at the latter's request,

[57] Report of 24 February 2004 drawn up on behalf of the Committee on Citizen's Freedom and Rights, Justice and Home Affairs on the Proposal of Council Regulation establishing a European Agency for the Management of Operational Co-operation at the External Borders, Amendment 40.

[58] See, for example, the work carried out by the European Parliament Committee on Budgetary Control on the annual budgetary discharge to the Agencies when an 'exchange of views' takes place with the 'representatives' (generally the directors) of (some of) the agencies. See Meeting documents of meeting of 1–2 December 2008. See too, EP Committee on Budgets and the annual meeting that takes place with EU Agencies. For 2008 see <http://www.europarl.europa.eu/meetdocs/2004_2009/documents/dv/200/200805/20080528_draft_agenda_en.pdf>.

[59] See further S Peers (2005), 'Governance and the third pillar: The accountability of Europol' in D Curtin and RA Wessel (eds), *Good Governance and the European Union: Concept, implications and applications*, (Antwerpen: Intersentia), pp 253–76.

[60] Report of 26 March 2003 drawn up on behalf of the Committee on Citizen's Freedom and Rights, Justice and Home Affairs on the initiative by the Kingdom of Denmark with a view to adopting a Council Act amending the Council Act of 3 November 1998 adopting Rules on the confidentiality of Europol Information (13875/2002-C5-0553/2002-2002/0823(CNS)).

[61] Council Decision establishing the European Police Office (Europol) of 6 April 2009, OJ L 121, 6 April 2009, p 37.

[62] Opinion of 17 January 2008 on the proposal for a Council decision establishing EUROPOL.

any information required for the smooth application of the discharge procedure for the financial year in question'. This is in line with the requirements of Art 146(3) of Regulation No 1605/2002 (the Financial Regulation) and already exists as a matter of practice.[63] The new provision relates to the obligation placed directly on the director of Europol as well as the chairperson of the Management Board (in addition to the presidency of the Council) to 'appear before the European Parliament at its request to discuss matters relating to Europol taking into account the obligations of discretion and confidentiality'.[64]

There is in fact nothing legally preventing the Council from voluntarily submitting other information it receives such as the reports from the Joint Supervisory Board to the European Parliament, nor to consult it and enable it to debate issues such as the budget of Europol and on Europol starting negotiations with third parties. With regard to the Council's role in common foreign and security policy (CFSP) the European Parliament had formally no role to play in account-holding either with regard to CFSP in general nor with regard to the High Representative CFSP in particular. Its role was to be purely marginal: it would be informed and consulted by the EU presidency on the basic choices and the progress in the CFSP.[65] The European Parliament had further the right to ask questions and to make recommendations to the Council. It has however attempted to exploit its role in the formal decision-making process in other areas by instrumentalizing certain substantive issues in order to bring the Council to concede certain 'informal' powers to it.[66] Thus, shortly before the first High Representative CFSP was appointed it 'insisted' on a 'confirmation hearing' of the Foreign Affairs Committee 'as a precondition for developing a close and constructive relationship between Parliament and the High Representative'.[67] The European Parliament even amended its rules of procedure in order to make this possible.[68] This has not yet happened in practice although it remains on the agenda from the Parliament's point of view.[69] Gradually it seems some relationship was established with the High Representative to come to a number of EP meetings a year but it does not

[63] OJ L 248, 16 September 2002, p 1.

[64] Art 48 of the new Europol Decision (2009) (n 61 above).

[65] Art 21 TEU.

[66] B Crum (2006), 'Parliamentarization of the CFSP through informal institution-making? The Fifth European Parliament and the EU High Representative', *Journal of European Public Policy*, 13/3, pp 383–401.

[67] See further European Parliament, 'Report on the Role of the Union in the World: Implementation of the CFSP in 1998', Rapporteur T Spencer, A4-0242/99, 23 April 1999.

[68] B Crum (2006).

[69] Almost a decade later the European Parliament continues to insist 'it would be particularly useful for candidates for the post of High Representative/Secretary General to present their programmes before the European Parliament's Committee on Foreign Affairs'. See European Parliament, 'Report on the annual report from the Council to the European parliament on the main aspects and basic choices of CFSP, including the financial implications for the general budget of the European Communities' (point H, para 40, of the Inter-institutional Agreement of 6 May 1999) -2005 (2006/2217 (INI), 4 April 2007, A6-013/2007, para 45.

seem to go much beyond that.[70] The introduction of the new style 'double-hatted' role for the High Representative CFSP (see Chapter 4 above) is not accompanied by any substantial revision of the European Parliament's role in the CFSP. To the extent only that the new style High Representative (post implementation of the Treaty of Lisbon) acts as a member of the Commission, his or her actions are implicated in all general Commission obligations vis-à-vis the European Parliament; *a contrario*, the powers of the European Parliament are significantly more limited when the High Representative acts within the competences of CFSP.

With regard to debate and deliberation with the Council on the main aspects of CFSP in general the European Parliament remains unhappy with the limited 'consultation that takes place'. It takes issue with the fact that the Council informs the Parliament *ex post* on the list of activities that have been undertaken in its annual report but does not consult with it *ex ante* on forthcoming aspects and choices—in violation in its opinion of the formal provisions of Art 21 TEU and of the Inter-institutional Agreement of 6 May 1999.[71] What the European Parliament seems to want is that it is 'consulted' at the beginning of each year by the Council and the High Representative CFSP on the main aspects and basic choices for that year and subsequent reporting to the Parliament whether—and, if so, how—Parliament's contribution has been taken into account. At the same time, there is some evidence that Members of the European Parliament are briefed and on an ongoing and regular basis by representatives of the Council. During 2007 for example it appears that such briefings took place on approximately 200 occasions.[72] In addition the Council responds to a large number of written and oral parliamentary questions concerning CFSP/EDSP.[73] Some contact exists between the European Parliament and the European Union Military Committee (EUMC), and senior Council General Secretariat officials who have also met on a number of occasions and been briefed.[74]

Finally with regard to comitology committees, the European Parliament has very steadily and gradually over the course of a decade, and without treaty change (prior to the entry into force of the Treaty of Lisbon), filled in its role as an accountability forum. At the same time, in seeking to acquire some 'control' over comitology draft decisions, it did so since 1993 as a co-legislative power. Nonetheless it implicitly accepted comitology, by agreeing in the so-called modus vivendi not to block implementing arrangements in such legislation in return for a minimal degree of transparency in the workings of the comitology

[70] B Crum (2006).

[71] European Parliament, 'Report on the annual report from the Council to the European parliament on the main aspects and basic choices of CFSP, including the financial implications for the general budget of the European Communities' (point H, para 40, of the Interinstitutional Agreement of 6 May 1999) -2005 (2006/2217 (INI), 4 April 2007, A6-013/2007.

[72] Council of the EU, Secretariat, Appearances by representatives of the Council in the European Parliament in the field of CFSP/ESDP in 2007, 6112/08, 5 February 2008.

[73] Ibid. [74] Ibid.

committees, but no real supervisory powers.[75] In 1999 the Parliament acquired, in respect of all draft measures to change the format subject to comitology, a 'right to information' which embraces the agendas, meetings, voting records, and summary records of the committee meetings, as well as the lists of the authorities and organizations to which the members belong. For measures which implemented acts adopted under co-decision, Parliament was entitled to receive the text of the Commission's draft, and to adopt a resolution indicating that the measure would exceed the implementing powers provided in the basic act, the so-called 'right of scrutiny'. In this case, the Commission was obliged to inform Parliament of the action it intended to take and of its reasons for so doing, but was not obliged to take account of, still less follow, Parliament's opinion. Where the Commission submitted a proposal to the Council under the regulatory procedure, Parliament was entitled to inform the Council that, in its view, the proposal exceeded the implementing powers provided in the basic act. The Council was not obliged to follow such an opinion either.[76]

In February 2000, Parliament concluded a complementary agreement with the Commission (but not the Council) on the application of the 1999 decision. This provides, for example, that Parliament receive the necessary comitology documents 'at the same time and on the same terms' as members of the committees themselves, and that it may on request have access to 'specific draft measures' other than those which implement acts adopted under the co-decision procedure. Rather remarkably, in view of the constraints on its working methods, Parliament agreed that it would have just one month in which to prepare and adopt resolutions objecting to draft measures on grounds of ultra vires.[77] As plenary sessions are usually only held once every four weeks, a draft measure tabled by the Commission in the week before one plenary session could only be examined by the committee two weeks later, and any resolution would be adopted after the expiry of the deadline. While it is true that some comitology measures are urgent, this is not normally so of those covered by the right of scrutiny. In practice little use has been made of the possibility that the European Parliament adopt a resolution on draft implementing provisions, with one exception.[78] In 2004 the European Parliament adopted a resolution concerning a draft Commission regulation in the field of animal nutrition asking the Commission to revise the scope of the draft measure that in its view exceeded the powers delegated to the Commission by the legislature. The draft decision was in fact modified in accordance with the

[75] KStC Bradley (1999a), 'Institutional aspects of comitology: Scenes from the cutting room floor' in C Joerges and E Vos (eds), *EU Committees: Social regulation, law and politics*, (Oxford, Hart Publishing), pp 71–93, p 76.

[76] See further KStC Bradley (2008), 'Halfway house: The 2006 comitology reforms and the European Parliament. A view from the ground floor', *West European Politics*, 31/4, pp 837–54.

[77] Ibid.

[78] See for example the Commission report on the working of committees during 2004, <http://ec.europa.eu/prelex/detail_dossier_real.cfm?CL=en&DosId=193506>. In 2009 the Parliament blocked the Commission's implementing measures to charge the format for the energy labelling of TV sets and called on the Commission to submit new draft measures by September 2009.

recommendations of the Parliament before being submitted to the Committee for vote and then adoption by the Commission.

In practice, it appears that the Commission has rather persistently failed to comply even with these limited obligations of information and consultation: according to the Commission itself there were some 50 occasions on which the Commission had failed to respect Parliament's rights under the comitology decision between December 2003 and February 2005. This admission was widely seen as providing concrete proof that the 1999 comitology arrangements were not working and gave added impetus for political action on a grander scale.[79] That political action resulted in 2006 in the adoption of a new procedure ('regulatory procedure with scrutiny') that enlarges the European Parliament's rights to scrutinize the documents and (draft) decisions of comitology committees considerably.[80] Parliament will have a period of three months, rather than one month, starting from the date of referral, in which to oppose draft measures approved by the committee, and four months from referral where the comitology committee has not approved the Commission draft. In the latter case, the Council is, in effect, first given two months to deliberate, and then Parliament a further two months to act in the light of the Council's position. In the view of one insider, 'this represents more than merely cosmetic progress'.[81] Once the Treaty of Lisbon enters into force then a shift in focus may well take place as the European Parliament will acquire a new right of 'call back' of implementing measures delegated to the Commission as such (and not to comitology committees) alongside that of the Council (see Chapter 5 above).[82] In the meantime a new inter-institutional agreement has been concluded between the European Parliament and the Commission on further procedures.[83]

9.4.3 The role of the courts

The role of the European courts (Court of Justice and Court of First Instance) in debating and deliberating, albeit in the highly proceduralized and not so 'public' context of legal review, should be very well established. Yet it has been difficult for the European courts to exercise substantive judicial control over agencies for the simple reason that provision was not always made for the judicial review of their decisions in their constitutive texts and, when it was, such provision was of a limited nature. The latter for a long time limited judicial accountability and

[79] See, for example, M Szapiro (2006), 'Comitologie: rétrospective et prospective après la réforme de 2006', *Revue du Droit de l'Union Européenne*, 3, pp 545–86, pp 567–8.

[80] For a detailed history of these measures, including the relationship with the so-called Lamfalussy procedure, see KStC Bradley (2008).

[81] KStC Bradley (2008) op. cit.

[82] Article 290 TFEU.

[83] Agreement between the European Parliament and the Commission on procedures or implementing Council Decision 1999/468/EC laying down the procedures for the exercise of implementing powers conferred on the Commission, as amended by Decision 2006/512/EC, 8 May 2008 (OJ 2008 C 143/1).

control to the contractual and non-contractual liability of the agencies. During the course of the 1990s however, the contract design of agencies included some provision for substantive judicial control over decisions and measures of various agencies at the instigation of either other institutions or individuals who could fulfil the highly specific criteria of 'direct and individual concern' (as well as staff cases).[84] Such provision extended the role of the Court of Justice to monitoring the legality of acts adopted by agencies that are intended to have binding legal effects. Later agencies tended to include a two-stage judicial system of appeals (one internal, although independent, and the final appeal external) especially where the tasks conferred on the agency are regulatory in nature or involve decision-making as such by the agency.[85] In the Treaty of Lisbon, explicit provision is made empowering the Union courts to review the legality of acts of agencies and other bodies.[86] Difficulty remains with regard to agencies established by the Council, as evidenced by the Eurojust case.[87] In the view of the Advocate General in that case, it was essential in a Union based on the rule of law that all Union institutions, as well as those of the EC, should be amenable to review when they produced legal effects vis-à-vis third parties. This view has not yet been confirmed by either the Court or the treaty-maker. The recent judgment of the Court of First Instance (CFI) in the *Sogelma* case (discussed in Chapter 6 above) confirms that this Court at any rate will not tolerate a 'legal vacuum' and a gap between treaty provision and institutional practices, even where the constitutive act of the agency makes no provision for judicial review.[88]

Once the access-to-the-Court issue is clear then the Court is in the driving seat in terms of not only obtaining the information it wishes from the actor being held to account but also in *debating* with the lawyers representing both sides (as well as possibly with other institutions and representatives of Member States) the manner in which the information must be interpreted. In addition, the Court can request to hear certain 'witnesses' including specific civil servants, including in an appropriate case directors of agencies.[89] The 'deliberation' by the Court includes the (often rather more revealing) 'opinion' of the Advocate General as well as ultimately the reasoned (albeit often terse) judgment of the Court itself on the specific issue of judicial review brought before it. In terms of

[84] See, for example, European Monitoring Centre for Drugs and Drug Addiction (1993).

[85] See the analysis made in Report by the Working Group, 'Establishing a Framework for Decision-Making Regulatory Agencies', June 2001, at 7. See for further details, D Curtin (2005a), 'Delegation to EU Non-Majoritarian Agencies and Emerging Practices of Public Accountability', in: D Geradin, R Munoz and N Petit (eds), *Regulation Through Agencies: A New Paradigm of European Governance*, (Cheltenham: Edgar Elgar), pp 88–119.

[86] Article 265 TFEU

[87] See, Case C-160/03, *Spain v Eurojust*, judgment of 15 March 2005. See further, P Craig (2006), *EU Administrative Law* (Oxford: Oxford University Press), chapter 5.

[88] Case T-411/06 *Sogelma v European Agency for Reconstruction (EAR)*, judgment of 8 October 2008, nyr.

[89] Rules of Procedure of the ECJ, Arts 45–50; Rules of procedure of the Court of First Instance, Arts 67–9.

its own self-understanding it can be said that there seems to be a growing consciousness by the Court, and its Advocates General in particular, of the need to ensure that administrative and other independent actors (including the ECB) fall under the rule of law and a general system of judicial accountability.[90]

Once the formal requirement of judicial review is satisfied, the Court can subject the action or decision of a given administrative/executive actor to substantive review. One interesting line of case law in recent years has been to build on a certain idea of 'good administration' that has now, to a certain extent, been codified in Art 41 of the Charter of Fundamental Rights (incorporated in the Treaty of Lisbon). One salient aspect in the current context of enabling (both legal and political) accountability forums to exercise their tasks of debate and deliberation relates to the issue of administrative (executive) reason-giving. Reason-giving can be understood as a 'social practice' with a long history.[91] In the words of the leading sociologist Charles Tilly, 'reasons provide organized answers to the question "Why does (did, should) X do Y?"[92]

Reason-giving is an entirely relational enterprise: 'giving reasons does a wide range of social work. That work always includes shaping the relationship between giver and receiver of reasons.'[93] Fitting reason-giving into the social relationship between an account (reason) giver and an accountability forum (reason receiver) it is clear that the presence of (sufficient) reasons enables the beginning of a dialogue of debate; if no reasons are given or they are tokenistic then it will not be possible for any dialogue or, ultimately, account-holding. In the absence of reasons an important procedural precondition is missing. When carrying out their administrative–executive tasks the administrator or actor is engaged in a relationship with other actors, including potential accountability forums that may be legal, political, administrative, and maybe even horizontal (see further below). The purpose of offering reasons to accountability forums of whatever nature is not only to enable a debate (and ultimately 'deliberation') to take place. It must also be seen against the backdrop of the powers (legal and otherwise) of the accountability forums to ultimately impose sanctions or other (unpleasant) consequences of one kind or another on administrators/actors who fail to explain themselves adequately.

Administrative actors have 'strong prudential reasons to give reasons. They need to supply justifications, or at least excuses, to avoid or mitigate unpleasant consequences, or to solicit cooperation or acceptance.'[94] Reason-giving relationships in the context of public accountability proceed according to the power

[90] See, in general on the role of the Advocate General, E Sharpston (2008), 'The changing role of the Advocate General' in A Arnull, P Eeckhout, and T Tridimas (eds), *Continuity and Change in EU Law: Essays in honour of Sir Francis Jacobs* (Oxford University Press), pp 20–34.

[91] See further C Tilly (2006), *Why? What happens when people give Reasons... and why* (Princeton University Press).

[92] Ibid, p 8.

[93] Ibid, p 180.

[94] J Mashaw (2007), 'Reasoned administration: The European Union, the United States and the project of democratic governance', George Washington L Rev, 76/2, pp 99–124, p 102.

relationships established by law and practice among public actors. They facilitate control, accountability, and coordination amongst institutions that have been placed in certain relationships to each other in the broad constitutional framework of a given political system.[95] In other words, a right to reasons facilitates hierarchical, legal, and political accountability. This is the perspective that is relevant in the context of this chapter on accountability; but some authors go even further to argue that a right to reasoned administration can be regarded as an individual (fundamental) right and not just a contingent feature of accountability regimes.[96]

One problem is that not all actors are subject directly to judicial review of their measures. Thus, neither comitology committees nor agencies as subjects/actors are included at the formal treaty–constitutional level but have come into being as a result of secondary legislation. At the formal level, comitology committees are not subject to the jurisdiction of the Court of Justice since the actual formal decision-making power does not lie with these committees as such. Either the Council or the Commission—depending on the circumstances—will be the subject of review proceedings (as having actually adopted the measure in question). Indeed, as detailed reviews of the Court's case law shows, the case law on comitology may even have influenced the design of evolving comitology arrangements.[97]

According to the Court, delegated regulations discussed in comitology committees may only amend or supplement 'certain non-essential elements of the law or framework law' not covering 'essential elements of an area'. This is an attempt to limit the remit of the tasks they carry out and to ensure that the underlying legislation (framework law) will guide the exercise of delegated power by the Commission and the comitology committees. The latter does not amount to a non-delegation doctrine such as that existing in the US where the courts can strike down delegations where the primary law is insufficiently precise in various respects. The opposite is rather true in the EU where the essential elements that must be specified in the primary law are traditionally defined rather loosely by the ECJ with the result that implementing regulations can legally have a rather broad remit.[98]

With regard to the statute for executive agencies the Commission has been given rather extensive power to review any acts of an executive agency and to take measures itself of a judicial nature, namely to suspend implementation of the measure of the executive agency in question, to prescribe interim measures, or to prescribe amendment of the agency measure in whole or in part, with the agency being placed under an obligation to comply with the Commission's decision in that regard. In the final analysis, an action for annulment can be brought to the Court of Justice to annul 'the Commission's explicit or implicit decision

[95] See too ibid. [96] See further ibid.

[97] See further KStC Bradley (2006), Comitology and the courts: Tales of the unexpected' in H Hofmann and A Türk (eds), *EU Administrative Governance* (Edward Elgar), pp 417–47.

[98] Ibid.

to reject the administrative appeal'.[99] With regard to the proposed operating framework for regulatory agencies, the Commission does not envisage a similar central role for itself in line with its thinking as to the more genuinely autonomous nature of such agencies.[100] Rather, in the case of decision-making agencies, it is envisaged that interested third parties will be able to challenge the legality of decisions taken by the agency—possibly with an internal system of boards of appeal—before the CFI as the competent court in addition to providing recourse to Member States and the institutions to challenge any breaches to the general principles of Community law.

Finally with regard to agencies established under EU provisions as such (as opposed to the original Community system) it is noteworthy that the provisions regarding independent judicial control are in some respects weaker. Thus, the Europol Convention in its Art 40(1) provided that disputes between Member States on the 'interpretation or application' of the Convention first have to be discussed in the Council 'with the aim of finding a settlement'. After six months, the Member States that are party to such a dispute, if they have not been able to end the dispute, are to agree among themselves how to settle it. The Convention itself did not include a provision guaranteeing that disputes about the Europol Convention will in the final analysis be sent to the Court of Justice for resolution, thereby clearly creating the possibility of deadlock. Fourteen of the fifteen Member States (at that time) however subsequently signed a declaration asserting that they would systematically send such disputes to the Court of Justice.[101] However, in the new Council decision establishing Europol adopted in 2008 it is explicitly provided that the normal jurisdiction of the Court will apply.[102]

In addition, a large number of Member States were keen to ensure that national courts would be able to send references for a (so-called) preliminary ruling on the Europol Convention (but not on the validity of measures implementing the Convention) to the Court of Justice. A protocol to the Europol Convention was initially adopted permitting Member States to decide for themselves whether to permit their own national courts to make such references to the Court of Justice or not.[103]

[99] Art 22(5) of Council Regulation (EC) No 58/2003, of 19 December 2002 laying down the statute for executive agencies to be entrusted with certain tasks in the management of Community programmes, OJ L 11, 16 January 2003

[100] As opposed to the European Parliament, which does envisage a similar role for the Commission regarding administrative complaints in the first instance against acts of regulatory agencies, similar to that played with regard to executive agencies. See Report of 4 December 2003 drawn up on behalf of the Committee of Constitutional Affairs on the communication from the Commission 'The operating framework for the European regulatory agencies', para 18.

[101] Convention based on Art K.3 of the Treaty on European Union, on the establishment of a European Police Office (Europol Convention), OJ 1995 C 316/32, 27 November 1995. The exception being the United Kingdom which fought vigorously to prevent the Court of Justice being given any role with regard to the Europol Convention or measures subsequently adopted.

[102] Council Decision establishing the European Police Office (Europol) of 6 April 2009, OJL 121, 6 April 2009, p 37.

[103] Council Act of 23 July 1996 drawing up, on the basis of Art K.3 of the Treaty on European Union, the Protocol on the interpretation, by way of preliminary rulings, by the Court of Justice of

In other words they could 'opt in' to the system of judicial control at their discretion and they could further decide whether to restrict the power to refer to their final national courts or to enable it more widely. Despite this wide jurisdiction over references no national court has yet sent any question concerning the Convention to the Court. It should be noted that this Protocol to the Europol Convention, while less than is the case with the rights and obligations of national courts under the general provisions of the EC Treaty, is still much more than has ever been expressly included in the constitutive texts of other agencies under the EC treaties.

9.4.4 The role of the Court of Auditors and the Ombudsman

Finally, mention can be made of the fact that other accountability forums exist where the possibility of probing questions, debate, and final deliberation can take place on the actions and inactions of administrative actors. Particularly noteworthy in this context is the role of the Court of Auditors and that of the Ombudsman. For example, with regard to agencies, by the time the European Environment Agency was established in 1990, the Court of Auditors was given its normal role to examine the Agency's revenue and expenditure.[104] This practice continued in all the later agencies financed from the Community budget. As a general rule, provisional accounts of the agency in question are to be sent to the Court and debate and deliberation take place in a dialogue of sorts between the Court, as accountability forum, and the actor/agency. The Court sends its 'observations' to the agency prior to its adoption of the final accounts.[105] Moreover, when returning the final accounts to the Court, the agency must reply to the Court's observations. In this sense a debate and ongoing deliberation can be said to take place with the Court of Auditors assuming an ever-more central role in this regard.[106] In a few very recent agencies, provisions are made that are more proactive and investigatory in nature with the Court of Auditors and the

the European Communities, of the Convention on the establishment of a European Police Office, OJ 1996 C 299/1, 9 October 1996. The Protocol entered into force on 29 December 1998 and 14 of the 15 Member States at that time gave the Court of Justice jurisdiction and 11 of these 14 decide to permit all their respective national courts and tribunals to send questions to the Court of Justice. See further S Peers (2004), 'Governance and the third pillar: The accountability of Europol' in D Curtin and RA Wessel (eds), *Good Governance and the European Union: Concept, implications and applications* (Antwerpen: Intersentia), pp 253–76.

[104] Art 13 of Council Regulation (EEC) No 1210/90 of 7 May 1990 on the establishment of the European Environment Agency and the European Environment Information and Observation Network, OJ L 120, 11 April 1990.

[105] See, for example, provision made with regard to the EMCDDA in Council Regulation (EEC) No 302/93, the European Agency for Health and Safety at Work in Council Regulation (EC) No 2062/94, the European Aviation Safety Agency in Regulation (EC) No 1592/2002, and the European Agency for the External Borders in Council Regulation (EC) No 2007/2004.

[106] See, in general, on the evolution of the tasks and role of the Court of Auditors, B Laffan (1999), 'Becoming a "living institution": The evolution of the European Court of Auditors', *Journal of Common Market Studies*, 37/2, pp 251–68.

European Anti-fraud Office (OLAF) being given the power to carry out 'spot checks' on the recipients of funding of the agency as well as those responsible for allocating it.[107] This arguably crosses the line to a more aggressive and independent checking of the facts as previously presented by the agent, the sanction presumably being delay in approving the final report (the Court of Auditors) and prosecution (OLAF passing the file to the national prosecutor).

It is precisely that extra element of coercion that is not present when it comes to that other relevant accountability forum in this context, the Ombudsman. The EU Ombudsman has certainly developed, in the decade or so of the post's existence, as an accountability forum in a looser and less strictly procedural sense (and consequently cheaper) than the judiciary. He can not only require that the actor in question produce all relevant information as explicitly requested but also provides an opportunity for debate (and further questioning of the actor) and deliberation and reasoned conclusion by the Ombudsman in the final analysis in his 'recommendations'. The Ombudsman 'promotes the principles of transparency, participation and explanation—underpinned by a philosophy of 'deliberative' administrative action'.[108] It is precisely the hybrid nature and status of the Ombudsman that enables him to 'combine the instruments of parliamentary scrutiny and judicial control in an original way'.[109] It can also be a disadvantage: unlike the Court of Justice or indeed the European Parliament, the Ombudsman has no power other than a voluntary and non-coercive one of the moral imperative of an actor following the recommendations made. And indeed, it appears from a recent judgment of the CFI that the Ombudsman may even be successfully sued in damages.[110]

9.5 Sanction and/or Consequences

The final procedural stage in the relational definition of account-giving is that the accountability forum may *pass judgment* on the conduct of the actor. It may approve of an annual account, denounce a policy, annul a legal measure, or publicly condemn the behaviour of an official or agency. In passing a negative judgment, the forum frequently imposes sanctions of some kind on the actor. It has been a point of discussion whether the possibility of sanctions is a constitutive element of accountability as a mechanism.[111] Bovens insists that the possibility of

[107] See the provisions of the European GNSS Supervisory Authority, Regulation EC 1321/2004; of the European Chemicals Agency, COM 2003/0644 final; and of the European Agency for Fundamental Rights, COM proposal for Council regulation (2005/0124 CNS).

[108] P Magnette (2003), 'Between parliamentary control and the rule of law: The political role of the Ombudsman in the European Union', *Journal of European Public Policy*, 10/5, pp 677–94, p 690.

[109] Ibid, p 678.

[110] Case T-412/05, *M v The European Ombudsman*, judgment of 24 September 2008, nyr.

[111] M Bovens (2007).

sanctions of some kind is a constitutive element of accountability as a mechanism and that it should be included in the definition.

The *possibility* of sanctions—not the actual imposition of sanctions—makes the difference between non-committal provision of information and being held to account. However, 'sanction' has a rather formal and legal connotation. It would exclude accountability forums, such as ombudsmen, who in many countries do not have the authority to formally sanction, but who can nevertheless be very effective in securing redress or reparation. Also, the term sanction would bias towards negative forms of scrutiny. Many accountability arrangements are not focused on finding fault with actors—forums will often judge positively about the conduct of actors and may even reward them. Bovens thus deliberately uses the more neutral expression: the actor may *face consequences*. These consequences can be highly formalized:

> such as fines, disciplinary measures, civil remedies or even penal sanctions, but they can also be based on unwritten rules, as in the case of the political accountability of a minister to parliament, where the consequence can comprise calling for the minister's resignation. Sometimes the negative consequences will only be implicit or informal, such as the very fact of having to render account in front of television-cameras, or the disintegration of public image and career as a result of the negative publicity generated by the process.[112]

There are above all two EU institutions who have been able to develop certain strong arm tactics or to enable the actor in question suffer some consequences as a result of having being held to account: the European Court(s) of Justice and the European Parliament. Neither is ever the formal principal but their role must be viewed much more broadly in the context of a system of legality and accountability. Once the issue of access to justice has been regulated then a consequence of information being supplied (during court proceedings) and debate and deliberation (highly proceduralized as befitting judicial procedures) is a sanction in the sense of a decision being declared null and void or someone being required to pay damages. For example, in the airport security case mentioned in Chapter 3 the consequence of the Commission illegally not publishing an Annex to a regulation in the Official Journal was that was that it was 'legally non-existent'.[113] This meant that it was null and void and could not be relied upon at all by any actor. In the case of comitology committees, for example, the substantive decisions come before the Courts as Commission decisions so these are *ipso facto* subject to challenge and *annulment.*

When it comes to the role of the European Parliament, it has followed a number of routes to be able to ensure that it can impose some sanctions on behaviour that it wishes to penalize. The fact that, for example with regard to agencies, the normal financial rules were followed (since the 1990s at any rate) meant that

[112] Ibid.

[113] Case C-345/06 *Gottfried Heinrich*, Opinion of Advocate General Sharpston, 10 April 2008. The Court of Justice in its judgment of 11 March 2009 upheld this view.

the European Parliament obtained an instrument giving it some power over the agencies via their budgets since it retained the ultimate power of discharge over non-compulsory expenditure. This has enabled the Parliament to, in certain instances, reorient (or threaten to do so as a preventive measure) the budget of agencies.[114]

The European Parliament used exactly the same strong-arm budgetary tactics previously with regard to the comitology committees and used the threat of budgetary power in order to get more of a foothold over scrutiny of the activities of comitology committees.[115] This was rather successful and, as a result of a series of informal agreements, the Commission is now obliged to inform the European Parliament about the work of the committees and to send it all draft implementing measures.[116] Following on its earlier strong-arm budgetary tactics the European Parliament in July 2006 succeeded in agreeing with the Council and the Commission by inter-institutional agreement a draft new procedure known as the 'regulatory procedure with scrutiny', which for the first time entitled the European Parliament to scrutinize certain comitology decisions (concerning quasi-legislative implementing measures delegated under the co-decision procedure) and, in the final instance, to reject or veto such measures.[117] In other words, a power to block the adoption of draft measures is introduced via the route of legislative amendment (of the original comitology decision).[118] This, for the first time, gives the European Parliament the possibility of exercising its role of holding certain comitology committees to account for decisions that they are intending to pass and to block their adoption. If they are blocked then the Commission can either make a new proposal for an implementing measure or it can table a draft legislative measure as such (for adoption by the two legislative partners). In the words of EP Rapporteur Richard Corbett, this new procedure 'is a good example of developing the institutional system without Treaty change

[114] LJ Brinkhorst (1996), 'The future of European agencies: A budgetary perspective from the European Parliament' in A Kreher (ed), *The New European Agencies*, EUI Working Paper RSC, No 96/49 (Florence: EUI), pp 75–81. See, most recently, the demands made by both the European Parliament and the Council as the two arms of the budgetary authority to the Commission in particular to provide annually a budgetary overview covering all existing and future Community agencies and to 'regularly evaluate the existing Community agencies, focusing particularly on their cost/benefit, and agree to assess the evaluation of the analysis prepared by the Commission for a selected number of agencies'. Annex II (Statements following the Trilogue of 18 April 2007) to European Parliament Resolution of 24 April 2007 on the Commission's annual policy strategy for the 2008 budget procedure, A6-0123/2007 in OJ C 074E, 20 March 2008.

[115] See further CF Bergström (2005), *Comitology: Delegation of powers in the European Union and the committee system* (Oxford, Oxford University Press).

[116] See, for details, the Commission report on the working of committees during 2003: <http://ec.europa.eu/prelex/detail_dossier_real.cfm?CL=en&DosId=192392>.

[117] Council decision of 17 July 2006 amending decision 1999/468/EC laying down the procedures for the exercise of implementing powers conferred on the Commission, O J L 200/11.

[118] See further B de Witte (2008a), 'Legal instruments and law-making in the Lisbon Treaty' in S Griller and J Ziller (eds), *The Lisbon Treaty: EU constitutionalism without a constitutional treaty?* (Vienna: Springer), pp 79–108.

	FORUMS				
ACTORS	**European Parliament**	**Court of Justice**	**National Parliaments**	**Ombudsman**	**Court of Auditors**
European Council	Weak	None. (Medium after Lisbon)	Weak–medium (individual)	None	None
Council of Ministers	Weak	Strong	Medium (individual)	Medium	Medium
European Commission	Strong	Strong	Weak	Medium	Medium
European Central Bank	Medium	Medium	None	Medium	Medium
Agencies	Medium	Medium	None	Medium	Medium
Comitology committees	Medium	Medium	None	None	Medium

Fig 9.4 Accountability Relationship Actors and Forums

in order to improve the governance of the Union. It will, wisely applied, be in the interests of all three institutions and enhance the democratic character of decision making.'[119]

A summary of the overall accountability relationship (qualified loosely as none, weak, medium and strong) between a selection of accountability actors and a number of accountability relationships is given for illustrative purposes in Figure 9.4 above.

9.6 An Organizing Principle, not a Meta-norm

There are different levels to the so-called democratic challenge: one at the level of the EU political system itself; secondly at the level of the national political system and thirdly the often intricate inter-actions between the two. This description already indicates that there is unlikely to be a single solution for Europe's democratic challenge at any level since national democracies are not only different but have been affected in critically different ways by ongoing processes of European integration. At the EU level, the problem is that concepts such as democracy, democratic accountability, and representation have in practice been filled in a manner that only compares very weakly with national counterparts and national traditions.[120]

[119] R Corbett, EP Report, Committee of Constitutional Affairs, 3 July 2006 (A6-0237/2006), http://www.europarl.europa.eu/activities/expert/reports.

[120] See, in general, D Curtin and A Wille (eds) (2008), *Meaning and Practice of Accountability in the EU Multi-level Context*, (Mannheim: CONNEX).

One aspect of the democratic tradition is what can be called the 'organizing principle' of accountability as opposed to the overall 'meta-norm' of democracy. Accountability can be construed as an important organizing principle of democracy resting upon specific standardized procedures. It is, as we have seen earlier in this chapter, a concept that is relatively uncontested in the sense that everyone intuitively agrees that public institutions or authorities should render account publicly for the use of their mandates and the manner in which public money is spent. In order, however, to look more closely at the practice of accountability across a range of actors and hopefully to compare results, we need a working definition of accountability that would help us to operationalize empirical study, thus moving the debate one step beyond conceptual generalizations. The Bovens working definition of accountability was analytically precise, consists of several distinct and discrete stages that could be rendered operational, and has the great merit of being able to link actors, any actors at any level, whether institutionalized formally or not with accountability forums. The latter did not have to be in a principal–agent relationship and was inclusive and open in terms of mechanism or type of accountability forums. They could be legal, political, financial, administrative, etc irrespective of the grand constitutional design. Emergent practices might be linked to systems of democratic accountability but were not limited in any way to this. Accountability as thus defined will not reduce the legitimacy problems of the EU nor will it give rise to an appropriate and uncontested notion of supranational democracy at the level of the EU. On the contrary, the relationship between the rather precise notion of accountability, as thus defined, and much broader themes and even meta-norms of any political system were temporarily left to one side in the interest of being able to focus on establishing, more neutrally, to what extent one could speak of existing and evolving 'practices' of accountability at various different levels and with regard to various different types of actors or institutions.

The embedding of the intergovernmental actors in an accountability framework is not only a European matter but also—and I would say ever more urgently—a matter for *national* political and constitutional systems. In many ways one of the greatest problems with the ongoing march of the European integration process is this failure to focus on the national level. More focus on the manner in which national ministers and national civil servants are held to account for their actions and inactions in Europe, and indeed in the context of other international organizations, is in my view one of the primary contemporary challenges. What is needed, in any event, is a better embedding of European decision-making in the national political process. Making European issues more political in a national context could contribute significantly to the much-required further politicization of European issues in general.

But one conclusion to already emerge from this book is that the different layers are already being related one to another in what can be referred to as an 'invisible EU constitution'. This robustly small 'c'—and in effect sedimentary constitution—is emerging from the nooks and crannies of ongoing practices and an at times interestingly proactive attitude of certain key accountability forums, in particular the European Parliament and to a sporadically visible extent the Courts in Luxembourg. In my view, the emerging sediments of this constitution, at times invisible (unless drawn into the light), are producing some countervailing power at the level of the EU political system and do not 'threaten' national constitutions in the way that a big 'C' political constitution was perceived to do so. What is now apposite is that, in line with Besselink's thinking on a composite constitution, the national actors (be they national parliaments or national constitutional courts) come to terms with their specific take on the accountability of 'their' actors but in a European context. That is properly the subject of a full length monograph in its own right however.

10

Making Visible the Invisible

10.1 The 'Invisible' Constitution

The EU does not have a written constitution as we have seen in the discussion in earlier chapters. It has however an unwritten constitution, in some sense not unlike some national constitutions (for example that of the United Kingdom). That unwritten constitution is partially visible and partially invisible and is not only composed of various 'bits and pieces'—some cohering, some less so—but it is also under construction by a number of different actors at different levels. It is a 'living' constitution growing incrementally and the emphasis in this book has been on the EU level. Nonetheless, it may be a *composite* living constitution put together by various actors (political, judicial, inter-institutional) at various levels.[1] The 'constitution' in question is robustly small 'c' and is in need of piecing together. The claim is not that it is complete or even coherent; rather that it is evolving, fragmentary, and at times even invisible. It is, after all, not only written constitutions (such as that of the United States) that may have underlying 'hidden' layers. Unwritten constitutions may also have visible and less-visible layers

In a powerful recent book, a leading US constitutional scholar has written of the so-called unseen constitution, impalpable but powerful, that accompanies the parchment version.[2] In the EU context we do not have the counterpart of the US Constitution, a tangible, visible, political, and democratic 'big C' Constitution. We have a complex set of treaties that seem to undergo almost constant amendment processes—at least that has been the case for more than a decade with a serial set of intergovernmental conferences throughout the 1990s and into the first decade of the new millennium. This is what we will have to live with, including the prospect of further treaty amendments if the Treaty of Lisbon is not ratified in the final event. On the other hand, my prediction is that if the Treaty of Lisbon finally enters into force as such then we will be entering a period when it is unlikely that there will be more formal treaty reform processes for the foreseeable future and where the more 'invisible' domain, in particular that of

[1] LFM Besselink (2007), *A Composite European Constitution*, (Groningen: Europa Law Publishers).

[2] LH Tribe (2008), *The Invisible Constitution*, (Oxford: Oxford University Press).

inter-institutional dialogue and agreement will be the way pushing what de facto amounts to constitutional development.

One of the primary purposes of this book has been to sketch with a broad-brush touch the contours of what can be considered an expansive and inclusive understanding of 'executive power' at the level of the EU political system. This too is part of the (in)visible constitution of the EU even if it is not often described and treated in this upfront fashion alongside the two more visible and sharply defined government powers: the legislative and the judicial. It has however been gradually emerging, bit by bit, actor by actor, policy by policy, over the years as part of an ongoing and evolving narrative, one that has culminated for the present in the provisions of the Treaty of Lisbon. But, as was said in Chapter 1, the Treaty of Lisbon and its ultimate entry into force is not critical to the story of how and where executive power has evolved in the political and administrative systems of the EU over the course of the past two decades. Rather we can view the incremental consolidation of EU executive power as, borrowing Lord Denning's striking metaphor, an intrusive 'incoming tide. It flows into the estuaries and up the rivers. It cannot be held back.'[3] An incoming tide is a highly suggestive metaphor as the waves of an incoming tide are relentless—they cannot be stopped. The failure to ratify the Treaty of Lisbon over time will not stop the ebb and flow of EU executive power but may rather force it underground.[4] The great virtue of the precursor of the Lisbon Treaty, the Treaty establishing a Constitution for Europe, was that it made the expansiveness of the tasks and powers of the executive (both national and European) more visible and more difficult to ignore also in terms of constitutional framing.

As pointed out earlier in this book an important (and often overlooked) component of EU executive power is that it is, to a significant extent, composed of *national* executive power (both political and administrative). In other words, and perhaps more than the other two government powers in the EU political system (the legislative power and the judicial power), it can be considered as a compound power in the sense that it is composed of different and largely autonomous elements—national politicians and civil servants and European politicians (Commissioners) and Eurocrats (European civil servants).[5] A compound (or its synonym composite) 'ecology' (or ecosystem), to continue the metaphor introduced in Chapter 1, suggests a conceptual whole made up of complex and related

[3] *Bulmer v Bollinger* [1974] 2 WLR 202.

[4] Ireland will hold a second referendum to be able to ratify the Lisbon Treaty on 2 October 2009; the Czech Republic will only ratify once there is a positive Irish vote. The legal challenges to the compatability of the German Constitution with the Lisbon Treaty were rejected by the German Federal Constitutional Court in a judgment of 30 June 2009 <http://www.bverfg.de/entscheidungen/es20090630_2bve000208en.html>, opening the way for German ratification.

[5] In 2007, S Fabbrini compared the American and European political systems under the label 'compound democracies' on the basis that they represent a union of states and of citizens. My analysis stresses rather the links in the actors and the levels of governance. See further S Fabbrini (2007), *Compound Democracies: Why the United States and Europe are becoming similar* (Oxford: Oxford University Press).

parts. In my view, this corresponds—and is another way of holistically representing the polity—with the reality of the conception and manner that the EU polity as a whole is evolving (embracing also the national level). National executives have, to some extent, become part of a European executive as well as still fulfilling purely national *and* international roles. The paradox is that the actors are often the same actors but performing different—and fluid—roles in the different layers of this complex ecosystem.

This final chapter places the subject matter of this book within the broader framing of some underlying meta-principles of any political system—these are the meta-principles of democracy and legitimacy in particular. After all, if one understands the EU as a political system then one can, on the whole, expect similar principles of legitimacy and democracy to be relevant. Issues of democracy, accountability, representation, and legitimacy have firmly established themselves at the centre of the debate on the contemporary EU. Is the EU legitimate? Is it democratic in the sense of respecting and enhancing the values and principles of representative democracy? Is the exercise (and abuse) of power by various (executive) institutions and actors subject to processes of (democratic, legal, and other forms of) accountability? Are there, in addition, less fundamental (secondary) norms (of European administrative law) that are evolving at the European level that are nonetheless of significance and political salience even with the overall legitimacy and the level of democratic decision-making remaining highly contested? Can these developments be considered in a positive light also from the perspective of global shifts in governance and the various legitimacy and democratic deficits that exist in that context too?

10.2 Dark Matter: Invisible Layers

The point is—as will also be clear from earlier chapters of this book, in particular those in Part III—that there is a shadow to the visible documents (the EU treaties in whatever shape or form). This 'darker' matter is always there and possesses some of its key meanings and values despite its absence on the written page. Some of the most fundamental understandings about the nature and significance of constitutional rights are not part of the written document (the treaties), but can only be deduced by piecing together hints and clues from the 'nooks and crannies' of EU law. In this context obviously the role of the Court of Justice (and its hierarchically inferior counterpart, the Court of First Instance) have been of crucial significance—to mention but two examples discussed earlier in this book: the *Kadi* judgment and the *Turco* judgment, both by the Court of Justice acting in its capacity as the highest constitutional court in the EU.

The *Kadi* judgment by the Court did something that could not be predicted on the basis of the wording of the pertinent legal provisions of the treaties nor general understandings of the nature of the EU as a special sort of regional international organization fitting within the hierarchy of public international law and in particular the hierarchy of the highest (political) organ of the global international organization, the Security Council of the United Nations. Yet the Court built upon its own earlier construction of the 'rule of law' in the EU context to give flesh and substance to a uniquely European version of constitutionalism that could in the final analysis offer judicial review to affected individuals who had been blacklisted on UN Security Council resolutions, a result that could not be achieved at the international level of governance.[6] The fact that in so doing it challenged very directly the hierarchy of public international law is beside the point in this context.

In other words, the Court developed, in the shadow of the formal treaty texts, very important meanings and values underpinning the process of European integration and gave further substance to the claim that the EU has already now what amounts to a small 'c' constitution. The other recent judgment in the *Turco* case made a very important statement as to why the principle of openness of the activities of the EU institutions, in particular of the Council, had to be considered so fundamental. This had to do with the very nature of the underlying EU political system and indeed implicitly also the very nature of its compound relationship with the democratic national political systems. In the Court's wording: 'this enables citizens to participate more closely in the decision-making process and guarantees that the administration enjoys greater legitimacy and is more effective and more accountable to the citizen in a democratic system'.[7] This applied in particular to the Council acting in its legislative capacity. But it also more than implicitly applies to institutions acting in their non-legislative capacity.

Again in the shadow of the formal treaty texts, the Court has filled in the nature of the EU political system, its relationship with and duties towards citizens, and the need for it to be legitimate, effective, accountable, and democratic. The Court has continued in such cases to detail the structure and the underlying principles of the invisible, small 'c' EU constitution. It reveals what lies beneath, beyond, before, betwixt and between the ink marks of the parchment treaty and its amendatory postscripts. At the same time, this process of an invisible constitution is not only within the remit of the compound judicial power, both at the European and the national constitutional level; it is also within the remit of the other actors, both political and administrative.

Political scientist Antje Wiener has documented in another recent book, *The Invisible Constitution of Politics*,[8] how the processes of the invisible constitution of politics matters also in the international and European context. She

[6] The jury is still out on the issue of whether the same result could be achieved at the national level by the national courts and on appeal by the regional human rights court, the Court of Human Rights in Strasbourg (see n 109, Chapter 7, above).

[7] Para 45.

[8] A Wiener (2008), *The Invisible Constitution of Politics* (Cambridge: Cambridge University Press).

too challenges us to look beyond the surface of formal texts and written norms, beyond the state. Based on extensive empirical research into how officials and other actors interpret and apply norms in transnational contexts, she challenges our understanding of core constitutional norms of non-state entities such as the EU. Indeed this ongoing and incremental process of the 'invisible' constitution of the norms and the manner in which they are further elaborated upon and evolve in the interstices of formal decision-making is one that has been referred to and elaborated upon in earlier chapters of this book (in particular in Part II), albeit more in the context of what is termed legal and institutional practices than 'social practices'. One particularly striking and salient example relates to the invisible constitution of politics (and law?) by the significantly growing phenomenon of inter-institutional agreements. Such agreements constitute an important layer in the sedimentary constitution of the EU.

10.3 Inter-institutional Engineering

Treaty amendments can provide a framework for institutional change and development but it takes tradition, conventions, and implementing law to provide the glue to hold it together in overall constitutional terms. Inter-institutional conventions or agreements have been referred to as the 'cartilage enabling the legal bones to move. Without it a certain constitutional arthritis is bound to occur'.[9] The instrument of 'inter-institutional agreements' has been much used as a relatively informal instrument to oil and even change the interrelationships among the institutions and introduce more checks and balances into the political system as a whole.[10]

In recent years, inter-institutional dialogue, and in particular the instrument of inter-institutional agreements, has gained considerably in importance in the EU's legal and political system. One role that such agreements may fulfill in the EU's institutional architecture is that of 'engineering' a particular result or practice that is agreed and carried out at what has been termed the 'sub-constitutional level'.[11] At the same time, endogenous institutional change involving informal and interstitial dynamics can in certain circumstances feed back into subsequent (treaty-level) institutional change as the detailed work of political scientists Farrell and Héritier has shown us.[12] The argument can be made that the

[9] B Driessen (2007), *Inter-Institutional Conventions in EU Law* (London: Cameron May), p 266.

[10] See, for a recent overview, B Driessen (2007).

[11] I Eiselt and P Slominski (2006), 'Sub-constitutional engineering: Negotiation, content and legal value of inter-institutional agreements in the EU', European LJ, 12 /2, pp 209–25.

[12] H Farrell and A Héreitier (2003), 'Formal and informal institutions under co-decision: Continuous constitution-building in Europe', *Governance: An International Journal of Policy, Administration and Institutions*, 16/4, pp 577–600; H Farrell and A Héretier (2007), 'Co-decision and institutional change', *West European Politics*, 30/2, pp 285–300.

European Parliament in particular has 'used' the instrument of inter-institutional agreements in order to pre-cook, in a sense and in certain respects, the content of intergovernmental (treaty reform) conferences.[13] A similar phenomenon can be discerned with the Commission in the driving seat, attempting to put and keep on the agenda the issue of the so-called 'operational framework' of regulatory agencies, first via a draft inter-institutional agreement and when the Council objected that there was no legal basis for the rather far-reaching measures proposed a 'declaration'.[14]

Upon entry into force of the Treaty of Lisbon it would be logical for the distinction to be dropped between Community agencies (first pillar) and Union agencies (second and third pillars, old style) and for the focus to be a more substantive one on the basis of the types of powers possessed (regulatory, operational, information, management etc). This is indeed the thrust of the argument the Commission has been making now for a number of years for an overall, horizontal approach to the key issues surrounding agency design and accountability concerns. In any event, provision is made in the Treaty of Lisbon for existing constituent acts to be replaced by new constituent acts but adopted according to 'community procedures' with a role for the Commission and the European Parliament in addition to that of the Council[15] (as happened preemptively with regard to the 'old style' Europol Convention).

Tracking the evolution of the European Parliament's competencies in three areas where inter-institutional agreements figure prominently—comitology, legislative planning, and the establishment of procedures to hold the Commission accountable—it has been shown by two political scientists that the European Parliament strategically uses inter-institutional agreements 'to wrest competencies for the Council and the Commission' and to 'create facts' through informal but politically binding inter-institutional agreements that may later be codified at IGCs.[16] This was the case with regard to the role of the European Parliament as 'codified' in the Treaty of Lisbon with regard to comitology type procedures but this 'path-making' route is not the only one that may be envisaged. Certain inter-institutional rules are simply adhered to by the institutions involved and may not require any further codification. The expectation is that, with the entry into force of the Treaty of Lisbon, the instrument of inter-institutional agreements will assume an enhanced importance given that so many details will need to be agreed among the three main decision-making institutions (the Council,

[13] See further D Kietz and A Maurer (2007), 'The European Parliament in treaty reform: Predefining IGC's through inter-institutional agreements', European LJ, 13/1, pp 20–46.

[14] See further European Commission (2008a), 'European Agencies: The way forward', Communication from the Commission to the European Parliament and the Council, COM (2008) 135 final, 11 March 2008.

[15] See Protocol no 36 on transitional provisions, annexed to the Treaty of Lisbon and Declaration no 50 concerning Art 10 of this protocol, OJ C 115, 9 May 2008.

[16] See further D Kietz and A Maurer (2007). See too, B Crum (2006), 'Parliamentarization of the CFSP through informal institution-making? The Fifth European Parliament and the EU High Representative', *Journal of European Public Policy*, 13/3, pp 383–401.

the Commission and the European Parliament) in order to make the procedures work at all. For example, the new procedure that is expected to replace to some extent the existing comitology procedures, that of 'delegated' executive acts to be adopted in future by the Commission, can only start functioning once all three institutions concerned have agreed how the procedure will operate and what the role of the various institutions will be as a matter of practice.

The question may be rightly put: is the very invisibility and shadowy process not problematic? The Court of Justice after all is itself a non-majoritarian institution that constitutes the 'oracle' of EU law in a manner that has no link with democratic process. At the same time, it might be argued, the ongoing and evolving practices of 'living' institutions in the interstices of formal rules may also be problematic because of its very invisibility and perhaps unpredictability. With regard to rule-making, in particular via the method of inter-institutional agreements, it is sometimes argued that these are concocted and applied with a non-democratic 'cocoon of power'.[17] The very fact that institutions meet largely behind closed doors to agree and apply rules with uncertain binding legal effect is regarded by some scholars as problematic from a democratic point of view.[18] In the words of one scholar:

> The findings about these 'sub-constitutional' changes as part of a self-referential inter-institutional game do not endorse the democratic quality of the EU *per se*. They rather seem to enhance integration by stealth, Or to put it differently, while the cocoon of power is ever growing through the formalisation of informal practices by creating legal instruments as sources of legitimacy, it does not resolve the problem of responsiveness and accountability *vis-à-vis* European citizens.[19]

We will now explore these wider issues, the meta-norms of any political system, legitimacy, and democracy and their relationship to the way executive power is exercised in the EU political system.

10.4 EU Executive Power and Fostering 'Legitimacy'

10.4.1 Formal and social legitimacy

Within contemporary debates, legitimacy is more often invoked than described and it is more often described than defined. Legitimacy can, in very general terms, be said to represent an umbrella evaluation that, to some extent, transcends specific adverse acts or occurrences; thus legitimacy is resilient to

[17] See, in particular, S Puntscher Riekmann (2007), 'The cocoon of power: Democratic implications of inter-institutional agreements', European LJ, 13/1, pp 4–19.

[18] See further I Eiselt and P Slominski (2006), 'Sub-constitutional engineering: Negotiation, content and legal value of interinstitutional agreements in the EU', European LJ, 12/2, pp 209–25.

[19] S Puntscher Riekmann (2007), p 19.

particular events, yet it is dependent on a history of events.[20] Over the years social scientists have offered a number of definitions of legitimacy, with varying degrees of specificity. When these concepts of legitimacy are applied to the EU, the theory is that when citizens know, or can find out, what the EU does, and even deliberate and participate in that process, their sense of being a European citizen may be strengthened. First, legitimacy may be understood in purely *formal* (legal) terms in the sense of the manner in which a particular structure of authority was constituted and acts according to accepted legal rules and procedures. Although many political scientists and lawyers focus traditionally on formal legitimacy, some stress the primordial importance of what is termed *social (empirical) legitimacy*. Social legitimacy refers to the affective loyalty of those who are bound by it, on the basis of deep common interest and/or strong sense of shared identity.[21] Social legitimacy will usually have to be created over time simply by the practice, and habit, of doing things together, and there is only so much that can be done to accelerate this process by symbol-building campaigns and communications strategies.

It is precisely with regard to social legitimacy that the EU has a long-standing problem—and this is widely recognized, not only by scholars[22] but also in the studies done in the context of EU treaty referendum defeats. However democratically legitimate the Member States may be in their own jurisdictions, a sense of social legitimacy will not be created simply by the attribution of rule-making competences to common institutions—although the welfare gains through integration, which should be made possible by the creation of those institutions, can be expected to facilitate it.

There are, however, many reasons to expect social legitimacy in particular to be an acute problem for the EU, and to remain so for the foreseeable future. The EU is, in the words of Lord:

> a new and unfamiliar political system; it has substantial powers to go into the nooks and crannies of member societies; its rules over-ride those made by national institutions; it takes decisions that affect ordinary lives; it demands sacrifices, sometimes with uncertain long-term reward; it takes from some in order to give to others; it affects deeply held values, including basic feelings of identity; and it is a large political system that often seems physically distant to its citizens.[23]

Should we then really be surprised in this intrusive and uncertain context that citizens feel a sense of alienation of feeling and of understanding of the EU as a whole? With regard to the executive power they can only feel that they do

[20] M Suchman (1995), 'Managing legitimacy: Strategic and institutional approaches', *Academy of Management Review*, 20/3, pp 571–610, p 574.

[21] See further D Curtin and A Meijer (2006), 'Does transparency strengthen legitimacy? A critical analysis of European Union policy documents', *Information Polity*, 11/2, pp 109–22.

[22] J Weiler (1991), 'The transformation of Europe', Yale LJ, 100/8, pp 2525–36.

[23] C Lord (2000), 'Legitimacy, democracy and the EU: When abstract questions become practical policy problems', available at <http://www.one-europe.ac.uk/pdf/P3Lord.PDF>.

not elect it for the functions it carries out, either at the national level nor at the European level and the deficit of affective loyalty cannot in these circumstances be considered surprising. But they also often do not see it visibly and do not recognize it for what it is (with elements of national executive power interwoven with the EU level).

10.4.2 Input and output legitimacy

A second way of looking at the legitimacy challenge is through the lens of *input legitimacy* versus *output legitimacy.* Output legitimacy means that people agree that a particular structure should exist, and even participate in rule-making, because of the benefits it brings. Social acceptance is thus instrumental and conditional, as well as independent of an affective relation. Input legitimacy, on the other hand, means that social acceptance of the structure in question derives from a belief that citizens have a fair chance (however understood) to influence decision-making and scrutinize the results. The ability to influence and hold accountable can be realized either through forms of representation which are held to be legitimate, through direct participation which is held to be meaningful, or some combination of the two. On the whole, the legitimacy of the EU and its decisions has tended to be focused on the output side of the equation[24] rather than on the input side.

In terms of Lincoln's famous description of the main elements of democracy, input-oriented legitimacy refers to government *by the people*, whereas output-oriented legitimacy refers to government *for the people.* The basis of legitimacy of these different kinds or rather different aspects of democracy is different.[25] From the perspective of input-oriented legitimacy, political choices are legitimate if and because they reflect the 'will of the people'—that is, if they can be derived from the authentic preferences of the members of a community. The input perspective derives its democratic legitimacy very largely from a pre-existing *collective identity.* As such a collective identity does not exist at the level of the Union, input-oriented legitimacy is out of reach for the EU for the foreseeable future. This can be considered true both at the level of democratic representation via a compound system of representative democracy (see below) or via the methods of direct democracy (in particular the use of referendums at crucial decision-making moments).

From the perspective of the more modest form of legitimacy—output-oriented legitimacy—political choices are legitimate if and because they effectively promote the common welfare of the constituency in question.[26]

[24] See, in particular, F Scharpf (1999), *Governing Europe: Effective and democratic*? (Oxford: Oxford University Press); G Majone (1996), *Regulating Europe* (London: Routledge).

[25] See further J Thomassen and H Schmidt (2004), 'Legitimacy and democracy in the EU', available at <http://www.mzes.uni-mannheim.de/publications/papers/Schmitt_26_1_04.pdf>.

[26] F Scharpf (1999), p 6.

Government for the people derives its legitimacy from its capacity to tackle problems requiring collective solutions. Identifying collective solutions still presupposes the existence of an identifiable constituency, but what is required is no more than the perception of a range of *common interests* that is sufficiently broad and stable to justify institutional arrangements for collective action.[27] Output-oriented legitimacy is thus *interest based* rather than *identity based*.[28]

It is often assumed that input legitimacy is out of reach in the context of the EU political system for the major structural reasons (no *demos*, no collective identity, no European public sphere, etc). Yet empirically it is noteworthy that there has been movement both in the political (and even treaty-reform) debate as well as in practice to introduce elements of a more participatory approach to executive rule-making, more grounded in theories of deliberative democracy and input legitimacy than might at first sight be assumed.[29] Deliberative democracy is in fact an ideal of political legitimacy. It claims that political decisions are ideally legitimate when they are made through a deliberative procedure, which implies publicly exchanging arguments 'offered by and to participants who are committed to the values of rationality and impartiality', and in which all those affected by the decision can take part directly or through their representatives.[30]

For some years now the perception among some scholars and practitioners has been that the model of *deliberative democracy* can have a role to play in increasing democratic legitimacy in the EU. In particular the perspective is that the 'civil society sphere' has a potentially significant role to play in widening and expanding the scope of the public debate at the EU level. Kohler-Koch opines, for example, in recent writings that 'civil society actors can contribute to *democratic* accountability if their intervention empowers citizens to evaluate executive behaviour, to pass a judgement and to impose consequences'.[31] Democratic accountability is used here specifically in the sense of 'we, the people' being able 'to reject one set of office-holders and public policies in favour of another, and to do so in a way that is genuinely effective'.[32] This is a different use of democratic accountability to one that focuses on the relationship between an actor and 'accountability forum' as detailed in Chapter 9 above on the basis that the nature of the forum will not always be an adequate criteria to assess the link between accountability of a certain kind and democratic legitimacy. For the

27 See too J Thomassen and H Schmidt (2004).

28 F Scharpf (1999), pp 11–12.

29 See further, in detail, J Mendes (2009b), *Rights of Participation in European Administrative Law: A rights-based approach to participation in rulemaking*, PhD thesis defended at the EUI on 16 March 2009, publication forthcoming.

30 J Elster (ed) (1998), *Deliberative Democracy* (Cambridge: Cambridge University Press), p 8.

31 B Kohler-Koch (2010), 'Civil society and accountability: The international and the EU discourse compared', *West European Politics*, 32, forthcoming.

32 S Gustavsson (2009), 'Putting limits on accountability avoidance' in S Gustavsson, C Karlsson, and T Persson (eds), *The Illusion of Accountability in the European Union* (London: Routledge,), pp 35–47, p 36.

latter purpose Kohler-Koch associates civil society for specifically *democratic* purposes with 'organized civil society' representing a constituency's interests.[33] The term 'civil society' has however given rise to a confused terminological jungle of multiple terms that may be identified for what is essentially the same phenomenon: organizations pressing government to act (or not, as the case may be). These include lobby groups, political interest groups, special interest groups, voluntary associations, pressure groups, organized interest groups, non-governmental organizations, non-profit groups, policy networks, etc.[34] Given the terminological and conceptual confusion even the most basic features of this 'sector'—its size, internal structure, financing and relations with other sectors are not always known in a solid empirical way.[35]

In the context of the manner in which executive power is exercised in the EU political system it is relevant to sketch briefly the manner in which certain attempts have been made to legitimize, at least very initially, this rule-making by virtue of having a more open and inclusive decision-making *procedure*. It may indeed be a far cry from 'government by the people' (see below on the different versions of the 'democratic deficit') but it does reflect the evolution of a nascent—and complementary—approach to inclusive public power. The term 'throughput legitimacy' is used to describe the more procedural ways that the decision-making procedure as such is or may be legitimized.

10.4.3 Throughput legitimacy

Throughput legitimacy asks *how* a decision is taken, who is responsible for it and which issues are at stake. *Transparency* and *fairness* are seen as important criteria for throughput legitimacy. They identify the quality and accessibility of gathering information or the equal opportunities to participate in decision-making, by means of transparency of procedures, negotiation, and decision-making processes, public access to documents, information, and participation via Internet and Intranet forums.[36]

[33] See further B Kohler-Koch and C Quittkat (2009), 'What is civil society and who represents civil society in the EU? Results of an online survey among civil society experts', *Policy and Society*, 28/1, pp 11–22.

[34] See further D Curtin (1996), 'Civil society and the EU: Opening spaces for deliberative democracy', *Collected Courses of the Academy of European Law*, (Oxford: Oxford University Press), pp 185–280.

[35] See, for example, L Salamon and H Anheier (1997), *Defining the Nonprofit Sector: A cross-national analysis* (Manchester: Manchester University Press).

[36] See, for this definition, R Nordbeck and E Kvarda (2006), 'New modes of governance for sustainability in Austria: Assessing the legitimacy and effectiveness of the Austrian biodiversity strategy and the Austrian forest dialogue', <http://web.fu-berlin.de/ffu/akumwelt/bc2006/papers/Nordbeck-Kvarda_Legitimacy%20and%20Effectiveness.pdf>.

Fairness refers to a fair participation and communication process in which all participants can participate on an equal basis or the participants accept that the restrictions upon participation are justified and legitimate.[37]

In the Treaty of Lisbon provision is made that the Union confers on 'every citizen the right to participate in the democratic life of the Union' (Art 10(3), TEU, Lisbon) in addition to the principle of representative democracy ('one man one vote'). Further, Art 11(2) TEU, Lisbon provides that the 'institutions shall maintain an open, transparent and regular dialogue with representative associations and civil society'. These new treaty-level provisions on so-called 'democratic principles' reflect ongoing work and existing empirical practices as it relates to notions of more 'participatory' or 'deliberative' democracy (in addition to principles of representative democracy) that have already some track-record of institutional and legal 'practices'. The thinking behind it is that process-related reform (relating to transparency and participation in particular) will feed notions of more throughput legitimacy.

In the context of the EU political system a variety of provision has been made over the years enabling organized civil society to participate in some manner in rule-making proceedings. Participation, in its simplest and most general form, can be described as the opportunity to take part in decision-making processes.[38] The Commission, in particular, has used a rather thin notion of 'public' participation as part of its search of more social legitimacy. Consultation of interested parties became one of the Commission's strategies of better lawmaking.[39]

Involving civil society in EU policymaking (and in particular the various Commission initiatives in that regard) was seen as a promise to improve the quality of decisions, not so much because of any superior scientific or technical knowledge but thanks to representing public attitudes and views that might have been neglected.[40] Over the years, EU NGOs have become professional experts in many policy fields. It has been argued that the recent trend towards including organized civil society in policymaking ('participation' in many institutional guises) may not really give such public-interest groups real benefits in terms of internal influence but may have the paradoxical effect that it empowers NGOs to exert their watchdog or accountability function. Participation provides insight so

[37] M Beisheim and K Dingwerth (2005), *Legitimität als Erfolgsfaktor für private Governance? Erste Überlegungen zu Kausalmechanismen* (Mannheim: DVPW-Sektionstagung).

[38] See, for example, on the different possible meanings of participation, J Mendes (2009a), 'Participation and participation rights in EU law and governance' in H Hofmann and A Türk (eds), *The Move to an Integrated Administration: Legal challenges in EU administrative law* (Cheltenham: Edward Elgar), forthcoming.

[39] See, in particular, European Commission (2002), 'Towards a reinforced culture for consultation and dialogue: General principles and minimum standards for consultation of interested parties by the Commission', Communication from the Commission, COM (2002) 704 final, 11 December 2002. See further D Curtin (2003), 'Private interest representation or civil society deliberation? A contemporary dilemma for European Union governance', Social and Legal Studies, 12/1, pp 55–75.

[40] B Kohler-Koch (2010).

that NGOs can 'act as transmitters and translators of highly specialised information... They may also provide the... audience with critical counter-expertise to challenge International Organizations and governments.'[41]

No matter how 'organized' it may be, civil society can clearly not compete with scientific expert decision-making that takes place, for example, in comitology committees and also in EU agencies. In this context too there has been quite some discussion about the relationship of such expertise and deliberative democracy. Joerges, with a number of other scholars, has made—and reiterated more recently[42]—the claim and produced some empirical support to this effect that comitology committee members become socialized into inter-administrative discourse patterns within the various committees and 'deliberate' among one another ultimately producing an epistemically good result.[43] Deliberation is contrasted with the more intergovernmental 'negotiation' one might expect from Member State representatives inputting their government view into the EU decision-making process.[44] However, as much as an epistemically good result is desirable, its legitimacy should be understood in a broader sense. Its transparency (or its lack in salient respects, despite the rhetoric) is also very important.[45]

10.4.4 From participation to procedures

The idea has been voiced for some years now of codifying and regulating the detailed participation of interested parties (both the profit and non-profit sectors) in an Administrative Procedure Act. Such procedural regulation would impose stringent requirements on the administrative and satellite executive in terms of rule-making, public participation, and high levels of judicial review.[46] Ideas akin to a notice-and-comment provision similar to the one that operates in the US through the Administrative Procedure Act 1946 is the most concrete idea to have been mooted and one that has had some limited ad hoc use in practice.[47]

41 J Steffek and MP Ferretti (2009), 'Accountability or "good decisions"? The competing goals of civil society participation in international governance', *Global Society*, 23/1, pp 37–57.

42 C Joerges (2006), 'Deliberative political processes' revisited: What have we learnt about the legitimacy of supranational decision-making', *Journal of Common Market Studies*, 44 (4), pp 779–802.

43 See too C Joerges and J Neyer (1997), 'From intergovernmental bargaining to deliberative political processes: The constitutionalization of comitology', European LJ, 3/3, pp 273–99.

44 M Pollack (2003), 'Control mechanism or deliberative democracy? Two images of comitology', *Comparative Political Studies*, 36/1–2, pp 125–55.

45 See, in general, GJ Brandsma, D Curtin, and A Meijer (2008), 'How transparent are EU 'comitology' committees in practice?', European LJ, 14/6, pp 819–38.

46 C Joerges and E Vos (eds) (1999), *EU Committees: Social regulation, law and politics* (Oxford: Oxford University Press); G Majone (2001), 'International regulatory cooperation: A neo-institutionalist approach' in GA Bermann, M Herdegen, and PL Lindseth, *Transatlantic Regulatory Cooperation: Legal problems and political prospects* (Oxford: Oxford University Press), pp 119–45.

47 F Bignami (1999), 'The democratic deficit in European Community rulemaking: A call for notice and comment in comitology', Harvard Int'l LJ, 40/2, pp 451–515.

In particular, it seems the EU agencies may be breeding grounds and learning sites for state-of-the-art participatory practices that ultimately may be generalized across the wider spectrum of Union administration. For example, the management boards of two relatively new agencies have themselves been proactive in developing participatory procedures for stakeholders prior to decision-making (essentially a system of notice and comment), namely the European Aviation Safety Agency[48] and the European Medicines Agency.[49] This is still streets ahead of the Commission's own thinking and practice, despite the rhetoric surrounding the implementation of its White Paper on Governance and the inclusion of a formal provision in the Treaty of Lisbon on the place of more participatory forms of democracy in the EU.

The tension is between a discretionary system (the existing one), where the emphasis is put on bureaucratic accommodation rather than legal right, and the introduction of a much more formal procedural framework within which participation can be exercised which would entail a considerable expansion of existing *locus standi* rules both in terms of input into the process and control *ex post facto*. The procedural route would consist of subjecting participation by all kinds of groups to detailed procedural rules. There are various precedents available, from a US-style Administrative Procedures Act to the provisions of the United Nations *Aarhus Convention* that provides an extensive framework for participatory rights for NGOs active in the environmental field. The advantage of the strictly procedural route is that the voice of such groups in the policy process would be facilitated as well as their access to the debate at specific moments. It would simply give as open and as inclusive a section of the public as possible a 'voice', a 'deliberative space' in the policymaking process.

The procedural option is in line with the idea of a more deliberative way of arriving at decisions after all possible viewpoints have been weighed but ultimately it is the responsibility of the formal political actors to choose among the different conceptions of the public interest presented.[50] The model of deliberative democracy stresses above all that 'spaces' be created which enable a proper public discourse and civil dialogue to take place and for institutional mechanisms which enable feed-back to the formal political institutions. At no stage and in no way does it recommend the possible replacement of the system of parliamentary or representative democracy in place, imperfect though it is. Moreover, what is not being discussed in this reform context, and rightly so in my view, is the prospect of giving the civil-society sector (or any new institution) real decision-making powers, enabling it as it were to take the place of the formal Union actors. This is, effectively, the model that has been chosen in the field of social policy and it is

[48] See further <http://www.easa.europa.eu/ws_prod/index.html>.

[49] See further <http://www.emea.europa.eu/>.

[50] E Eriksen and J Fossum (2000), *Democracy in the European Union: Integration through deliberation?* (London: Routledge).

open to a number of objections from the point of a healthy checks and balances in a constitutional system.[51]

10.5 EU Executive Power and Alleviating the 'Democratic Deficit'

10.5.1 The 'democratic deficit'

This book has deliberately not analysed the growing executive power within the framework of the 'democratic deficit' of the EU. There is, in any event, no consensus as to what the term 'democratic deficit' means in the context of the EU political system or a precise indication of its link with the constituent national political systems, despite the fact that it has been bandied about in scholarly and political debate for many years. Rather than looking for the crock of gold at the end of the rainbow, this book has preferred an approach more grounded in evolving legal and institutional practices and empirical reality while at the same time exploring (in Part III of this book) a (limited) framework of 'constitutionalism' (rule of law, transparency, and accountability) and the unveiling of the extent to which these principles are already being given some substantive content in the evolving political and legal orders of the EU.

One recurring theme in the vast literature on the EU system is the apparent *exceptionalism* of what has actually developed in post-war Europe. This is expressed in the notion that the EU represents an *n of 1*: it is neither a national state nor a conventional supranational or international organization. It is not part of the national political systems in Europe nor does it constitute a distinct political unit in its own right. Above all it is seen to be exceptional in that it lacks a so-called *demos*, a European people, and hence by definition, or so it is asserted, it is a system that *cannot* function democratically. This strange and ill-defined polity was moreover deliberately constructed in this way from the very beginning by national politicians. The puzzle is that they built it without any substantial room for politics or political parties. In the words of political scientist Mair: 'the EU is not conventionally democratic and can never be conventionally democratic for the simple reason that it has been constructed to provide an alternative to conventional democracy'.[52]

[51] G Britz and M Schmidt (2000), 'The institutionalized participation of management and labour in the legislative activities of the European Community: A challenge to the principle of democracy under Community law', European LJ, 6/1, pp 45–71.

[52] P Mair (2005), 'Popular democracy and the European Union', EUROGOV Working Paper, No C-05-03, <http://www.connex-network.org/eurogov/pdf/egp-connex-C-05-03.pdf>.

10.5.2 Policy without politics?

If the EU is viewed as a political system in its own right, though of a special kind, then the issues of democracy, representation, accountability, etc must be discussed and fleshed out at that same level. For those who view the EU as a quasi-federal state, citizen representation and accountability must be ensured for decision-making at the *European* level.[53] In order for a sense of democratic legitimacy to exist it is argued that there must be a basic system of electoral accountability with a match between the level at which the decisions are being taken and the level to which the electorate can, in the final analysis, hold the decision-makers to account. This is highly problematic in the context of the EU political system.

Much of the debate has traditionally focused on importing (elements of) a parliamentary system of government existing in the national Members States into the EU level, on the basis either that it was *sui generis* or ultimately evolving in the direction of a federal system/state. For many years the focus was on giving the European Parliament more powers in the EU legislative process and this has been overall a remarkably successful strategy, culminating in the Treaty of Lisbon with co-decision of the Council of Ministers and the European Parliament becoming the 'normal' and standard legislative procedure. The European Parliament indeed co-decides in an increasing number of policy fields and is, in theory at any rate, 'representative' of the European peoples, having been directly elected. This simple version is however highly contested at a number of levels; the most important is that these direct national elections are 'second-order' with no substantive discussion as to European policy or polity issues and no mandate resulting. Likewise, in national elections, no mandate is asked for or given regarding European issues.

The absence of politics and a real electoral contest fought out on European issues hampers the opportunities of citizens to hold MEPs accountable for their actions. Intergovernmentalists and others will respond that there is democratic representation in the adoption of legislative measures both through the Council of Ministers and through the European Parliament. The ministers (and civil servants preparing) are 'representing' their national interests and can be held to account in the national political systems for their actions and inactions at the EU level. This was certainly the original conception of 'representation' in the ESCS and EC as originally conceived and discussed in Chapter 3; the problem is that, with increased majority voting, there is no national veto and only rather artificial possibilities for national parliaments to hold their governments for account *ex post* to what was collectively agreed at the level of the Council of Ministers as a decision-making institution.

When we look at the Union and compare it to other political systems in the post-industrial world the most striking point is indeed its non-responsiveness

[53] F Decker (2002) 'Governance beyond the nation state: Reflections on the democratic deficit of the EU', *Journal of European Public Policy*, 9/2, pp 256–72.

in terms of elections, parties, and the conventional procedures of popular democracy. As Mair puts it: 'The efforts to displace conflict dimensions into arenas where democratic authority is lacking, as well as the efforts to depoliticize issues that relate to European integration, have led to the development of a distinct political system in which the exercise of popular control and electoral accountability proves very difficult.'[54] It is increasingly argued (by political scientists in particular) that the democratic deficit must be analysed as arising from the gap in *electoral accountability mechanisms* that apply at the EU level. In other words, the simple fact of direct elections of members of the European Parliament is not enough; what is problematic are the institutional deficiencies of the electoral and party system. This is precisely what Schmidt, refers to in her book, *Democracy in Europe*: the EU is, in her words, 'policy without politics'.[55] In addition, there is an absence of a common European identity that would be necessary for the acceptance of a fully majoritarian system of governance.

Indeed in recent years it has been argued that what the EU urgently needs is an injection of 'politics' along national lines.[56] Others take issue with the risk of over simplification in this regard.[57] They argue that the politicization of the EU is not plausible along a 'bipolar logic', and that the coupling of a system of politicized 'negotiation democracy' with mechanisms of direct participation are both plausible and desirable.

The advent of more legislative powers for the European Parliament (alongside the Council of Ministers) as well as a more proactive role as a forum of political accountability has not done away with either the reality, or the perception, of the 'democratic deficit'. The EU's institutions fall short of standards of democracy and accountability: popular representation plays only a minor role in many policy areas and mechanisms of accountability are thus not always well developed. Moreover, the evolving political system of the EU lacks the kind of integrated public sphere and civil society that sustain democracy and accountability in the nation states. In addition, the EU's policymaking system, as well as its political system, is not widely transparent, which prevents effective democratic control and accountability.

At the same time the pervasiveness of the phenomenon of 'depoliticization' in the political system of the EU goes beyond a lack of electoral accountability in all its facets. It has also to do with processes of placing (executive) power

54 P Mair (2004), p 339.

55 V Schmidt (2006), *Democracy in Europe: The EU and national polities*, (Oxford, Oxford University Press), pp 157–62.

56 See, for example, the debate by S Hix and S Bartolini (2006), 'Politics: The right or wrong sort of medicine for the EU?', Policy Paper No 19, Notre Europe, available at: <http://home.um.edu.mt/edrc/hix_bartolini_notre_europe.pdf>.

57 P Magnette and Y Papadopoulos (2008), 'On the politicization of the European consociation: A middle way between Hix and Bartolini', Eurogov Working Paper No C-08-01 / January 31, available at <http://www.connex-network.org/eurogov/pdf/egp-connex-C-08-01.pdf>.

at some distance from elected bodies, in non-majoritarian 'unelected' hands. As we have seen earlier in this book, this is a rapidly growing phenomenon, but as Vibert illustrates in his book *The Rise of the Unelected*[58] it is by no means confined only to the European level; it is prevalent at the (various) national levels and, of course, also at the global or international level.[59] The legitimacy issue can also be framed, above all, in terms of output legitimacy and there are those who argue that this is enough in the context of the 'regulatory state'.[60] This is contested however and increasingly it seems that emphasis is placed not only on core constitutional principles such as transparency and accountability (Chapters 8 and 9) but also on linkages or couplings back to the formal representative democratic circuit and, in any event, the realization that 'the shadow of hierarchy' (in the sense of democratic politics) is there and perhaps more pronounced than is often realized[61]—although much empirical research remains to be done, certainly in the EU system. The point is that, despite appearances or assumptions to the contrary, the linkages between more 'horizontal' satellite executive actors and the vertical 'core' executive actors tend to be there. They function in the 'shadow of the hierarchy'—the problem is that at European level the 'hierarchy' may be political but rarely directly *democratic*. This must be considered a salient difference with the national political level and the linkages with many and varied unelected organs and actors.

10.5.3 Politics without policy?

At the same time, there is increased recognition of the fact that part of the problem with the 'democratic deficit' of the EU lies at the national level and in particular the failure to link the 'politics' of the national level with the policy adopted at the European level. Even at the national level where politics is located, the Union, in common with an increasing number of issue areas, is not in fact the subject of *contestation* in real elections by the national political parties. At present we only find the conditions for electoral and party democracy at the national level and even these are weakening. In this case, says Schmidt, we are left with 'politics without policy'.[62]

One's perspective on the existence or otherwise of a 'democratic deficit' depends to a great extent on one's framing and broader perspective on the nature of the EU (discussed in Chapter 2 above). On an 'intergovernmental' view of

[58] F Vibert (2007), *The Rise of the Unelected: Democracy and the new separation of powers* (Cambridge: Cambridge University Press).

[59] See further ibid. [60] G Majone (1996).

[61] This was in fact the conclusion reached in the Dutch context of the so-called 'autonomous administrative organizations' (*zelfstandige bestuursorganen*): see T Schillemans (2007), *Verantwoording in de schaduw van de macht. Horizontale verantwoording bij zelfstandige uitvoeringsorganisaties* (Den Haag : Lemma).

[62] V Schmidt (2006), pp 163–78.

the EU, the assumption is that the 'democratic deficit' is largely a myth because democratic accountability will take place largely at the national level where the most politically salient decisions are taken anyway. This view does not conceptualize the EU as a polity or political system in the making but rather in more traditional terms as a more classic system of intergovernmental Member States taking certain collective decisions together.[63] On this view then the democratic input is to be found in the links between the (voting) citizens of Member States, Member State governments and, where applicable, the civil servants (and/or scientific experts) of Member States participating in various committees and networks. In the intergovernmental perspective then, ultimately democracy is assured through the *national political process*, supplemented by some weaker forms of politicization at the European level. In terms of accountability, legal and administrative accountability could be considered primordial in terms of the EU level itself. This is why authors such as Moravcsik stress, in addition, the presence of 'checks and balances' at the EU level and, overall, view the existence of a 'democratic deficit' as a myth.

The Union is of course institutionally part of the national political systems of the Member States as well as forming its own political system. Some of the key players in the EU political system right across the board are *agents* of democratic *principals* (ultimately the citizens) in the *national* political processes but they do not have a 'European' mandate as such (at least not one that has been part of the election process). Contrary to the belief that these national executive actors play a democratically legitimate role in the EU political system, having been elected and mandated in national elections, the reality is much more that these components of the national executive power have effectively become depoliticized when they operate in the European context. The problem is, however, that in neither national elections nor European elections are citizens given a decisive vote. This leads to what has been called the 'depoliticization of the Europeanization dimension in the national sphere'.[64] On the whole, at election time, European voters put their preferences regarding Europe on ice.[65]

In the opinion of the Dutch Scientific Council for Government Policy, the neglect of the national level goes a long way to explaining the Dutch 'No' vote in the referendum result on the Treaty establishing a Constitution for Europe.[66] For Dutch citizens, the results of European policy have remained largely invisible. They felt inadequately represented and had major doubts about the way in which

[63] A Moravcsik (2004), 'Is there a "democratic deficit" in world politics? A framework for analysis', *Government and Opposition*, 39/2, pp 336–63.

[64] P Mair (2004), 'The Europeanization dimension', *Journal of European Public Policy*, 11/2, pp 337–48, p 339.

[65] See further C van der Eijk and M Franklin (2004), 'Potential for contestation on European matters at national elections in Europe' in G Marks and MN Steenbergen, (eds), *European Integration and Political Conflict* (Cambridge: Cambridge University Press), pp 32–50, p 47.

[66] See further Dutch Scientific Council for Government Policy (2008), *Rediscovering Europe in the Netherlands* (Amsterdam: Amsterdam University Press).

'Europe' renders account for its policy choices. What is, in any event, needed is a better embedding of European decision-making in the national political process. Making European issues more political in a national context could contribute significantly to the much-required further politicization of European issues in general. This is also the conclusion reached by the Irish parliamentary committee that explored the consequences of the Irish 'No' to the Lisbon Treaty in the Irish political context.[67] The message coming through is indeed of the need to 'rediscover' the national in the European and to focus on the adaptation of national political processes to improve the fit with European policymaking.

One of the issues needing further reflection is how to address the fact that the national executive power continues to operate outside of its own national political and constitutional level. National executive power is active and engaged in decision-making at the European level and at the international or global level. It has, as a matter of practice, surmounted thinking in terms of hierarchical levels and may even be considered as engaged in a more fluid and composite governance process, as we have seen in earlier chapters of this book. This extends nowadays not only to government ministers and civil servants as well as more satellite actors, such as national (regulatory) agencies; it also extends to the *top* political level—to the prime ministers participating in the European Council. The 'disaggregated' state referred to in Chapter 2 is arguably reinforced and consolidated by further processes of European political integration. The fact is that the internal political actors are directly active at the European level, also in a disaggregated fashion, with their counterparts from other Member States, and that arguably the traditionally diplomatic 'foreign' ministries have lost much of their centrality and, to some extent, their purpose in a world where the 'disaggregated' actors actively network among one another, often invisibly, and considerably supported by modern information and communications technology as well as telecommunications. In this sense, too, traditional notions of (democratic) hierarchy are being outwitted and circumvented by modern 'networking'. This leads to increasing complexity, heightened structural invisibility, and the 'accumulation' of executive orders in Europe.

One real problem is that outside of the confines of the territorial nation states, executives are only to a very limited extent held to account for their actions and inactions. National parliaments, in particular, have not kept up with what their national executives are doing and not doing. While national parliaments have stayed put within their own neatly nationally fenced-off compartments, the executive has developed into a strongly interwoven, complex administrative network, beyond the horizons of many, maybe all, national parliaments.[68] But also

[67] Houses of the *Oireachtas* Sub-Committee on Ireland's Future in the European Union (2008), *Ireland's Future in the European Union: Challenges, Issues and Options*, available at <http://euaffairs.ie/sub-committee/Sub-CommitteeReport.pdf>.

[68] For an excellent account see L Besselink (2006) 'National parliaments in the EU's composite constitution: A plea for a shift in paradigm' in P Kiiver (ed), *National and Regional Parliaments in*

the national political hierarchy is not necessarily keeping up with what their subordinates are doing in the name of the national political system as a whole, for example in comitology committees in Brussels.

Besselink has argued that we need to shift our thinking on the role of national parliaments in evolving national political and constitutional systems if national executive actors are to be held to account for their action and inaction at the international and European levels of governance. Thinking outside the box in the next phase of European integration involves national parliaments in a more 'composite view' more proactively considering themselves part of a wider constitutional whole rather than just the microcosm of the national constitutional system.[69] The whole point of this more 'composite view' of the role of individual national parliaments is that it can also approach other institutions (than its own ministers or government) in that greater whole. In the words of Besselink: 'Why should only the French *Assemblee Nationale* enjoy the privilege of a real and lively debate with the President of the European Commission? Why could there not be an annual debate on the state of the Union in the respective national parliaments to hold the European institutions to account?'[70] Parliaments indeed need to stop feeling trapped within an enclosed national system and try and keep up with where power and rule-making has migrated and play a role in holding it to account.

The other critical importance of national parliaments in the democratic constellation of the compound EU is the fact that they provide space and voice to the political opposition. There has not been room for political opposition in the EU political system, at any level or in any space, for many years now. This is one of the chronic shortcomings of the EU political system. But, once political opposition cannot be organized in the EU since votes cannot be appealed for against a government in elections or in parliament, the risk is that it becomes opposition *to* the EU.[71] That is what we have effectively seen happen in the EU context in recent referendum results on treaty reform in particular.

The lack of opportunity for politicization, debate and opposition in the EU political system was referred to some years ago as being equivalent to 'the sleeping giant', arguing that the European issue is now 'ripe for politicization' and suggesting that 'it is only a matter of time before policy entrepreneurs . . . seize the opportunity . . . to differentiate themselves from other parties in EU terms.'[72] These words were written long before Declan Ganley (director of *Libertas*[73] that campaigned actively for a

the European Constitutional Order (Groningen: Europa Law Publishing), pp 117–31 (available at http://igitur-archive.library.uu.nl/law/2007-0313-201044/besselink_06_national.pdf).

69 See further ibid.

70 L Besselink (2007), *A Composite European Constitution* (Groningen: Europa Law Publishing), pp 113–23.

71 P Mair (2007), 'Political opposition and the European Union', *Government and Opposition*, 42/1, pp 1–17.

72 P Mair (2007).

73 <http://www.libertas.eu/>.

negative vote in the Irish referendum on the Lisbon Treaty) tried to rouse the sleeping giant from his lengthy slumber. Ganley indeed fits the category of a political entrepreneur who seized the opportunity to differentiate himself and his movement from other political parties in specifically EU terms and launched a pan-European campaign—unsucessfully—to contest the 2009 European Parliament elections on that basis. The fact that he has promised not to campaign against the Lisbon Treaty in the second Irish referendum in October 2009 must increase the chances that it will pass muster the second time around.

Shocks (such as the third negative referendum result in a row) may well provide entrepreneurs windows of opportunity that they may be able to exploit to accept change that would not necessarily be possible in less challenging times. Given the 'stickiness' of the EU institutions we have, and the manner in which executive power evolves and is given shape in the EU political system, part of a broader agenda of 'politicization' must be how can we ensure that certain requirements or 'standards' are met and actively applied by executive institutions and actors in ongoing governance processes?

One of the big problems is that notions of 'responsibility' are often left undetermined and at best 'shared'. Who can be held responsible for the conduct of complex (composite) institutions engaged in inter-institutional processes? The so-called 'problem of the many hands' comes into play particularly strongly in the EU context. As Thompson put it many years ago, in a very different context: 'because many different officials contribute in many ways to decisions and policies of government it is difficult even in principle to identify who is morally responsible for political outcomes'.[74] More recently, and closer to home, the Committee of Independent Experts when scrutinizing alleged fraud in the context of the exercise by the European Commission of its executive functions could not refrain from observing with a measure of despair that it was impossible to find anyone within the organization 'with even the slightest sense of responsibility'.[75] Will the concept of 'political responsibility' and the link with accountability applied in the context of the EU political system assist in this ongoing quest?[76]

10.6 From Active Responsibility to Active Accountability

'Responsibility' is not only conceptually contested but, like the sister notion of 'accountability', can be analysed and presented in a variety of different ways. Bovens analysed responsibility both actively (responsibility as a 'virtue') and passively

[74] DF Thompson (1980), 'Moral responsibility of public officials: The problem of the many hands', *The American Political Science Review*, 74/4, pp 905–16, p 905.

[75] Committee of Independent Experts (1999), *First Report on the Reform of the Commission*, Volume I, (Luxembourg: Office of Official Publications), p 144.

[76] See further M Tsakatika (2008), *Political Responsibility and the European Union* (Manchester: Manchester University Press).

(responsibility as *ex post* accountability).[77] Responsibility, as a virtue, involves behaving responsibly, or taking responsibility and addressing the question 'What is to be done?'[78] The political virtues of responsibility are those of reliability, trustworthiness, consistency, and prudence. These are qualities that enable the achievement of the goods internal to governance—predictability, order, and stability.[79]

Through active responsibility passive responsibility is created. Passive responsibility is largely what we have discussed in Chapter 9. We see that there is a web of formal accountability arrangements and relationships woven around the various executive actors, political, administrative, and satellite. The degrees to which the various accountability forums will actually use the oversight possibilities available to them may vary but there is unquestionably evidence emerging, in particular from ongoing empirical studies that some healthy accountability relationships are emerging. At the level of passive responsibility therefore, it is certainly not all gloom and doom. At the level of active responsibility there may also be a link to be made with an emerging debate on accountability as a virtue.

Active accountability has, in particular, been operationalized as a bundle of rules and principles regarding checks and balances on public power that belong to the broader family of good governance norms, and that may be institutionalized in various ways. It ties in with an understanding of accountability as a normative set of standards for the evaluation of the behaviour of (public) actors. It has been operationalized in a *Global Accountability Framework* developed by One World Trust using a broad, active notion of accountability and applied to large transnational organizations.[80] The accountability of an organization or actor is assessed according to how well it integrates four dimensions of accountability in its policies, procedures, and practice at all levels and stages of decision-making and implementation, in relation to both internal and external stakeholders.[81] These four dimensions are transparency, participation, evaluation, and complaint and response mechanisms. Each of these four dimensions is formulated as a standard for accountable behaviour.[82]

At the transnational level the emerging (administrative) principles in the Global Administrative Law literature[83] may be a helpful perspective on an emer-

77 M Bovens (1998), *The Quest for Responsibility: Accountability and citizenship in complex organisations* (Cambridge: Cambridge University Press).

78 Ibid, p 27.

79 See further M Tsakatika (2008), pp 48 *et seq.*

80 M Blagescu, L de Las Casas, and R Lloyd (2006), *Pathways to Accountability: The global accountability framework* (London: One World Trust); R Lloyd, J Oatham, and M Hammer (2007), *Global Accountability Report* (London: One World Trust).

81 See for the full text of the Accountability Framework and the operationalization of each of these principles, the 2008 accountability report that can be found at <http://www.oneworldtrust.org>.

82 R Lloyd, J Oatham, and M Hammer (2007), p 11.

83 E MacDonald (2008), 'The 'emergence' of global administrative law', paper at the 4th Global Administrative Law Seminar, 'Global Administrative Law from Fragmentation to Unity?', Viterbo, 13–14 June 2008.

ging culture of administrative law within global—and European—regulatory governance, despite some of the caveats that have been expressed in the literature.[84] Some principles (eg transparency and participation) have been identified as part of a growing body of global administrative law based on patterns of commonality[85] in its function as a mechanism of constraint and control.[86] The operationalization of accountability in practice can therefore be linked in with such normative principles and an attempt made to give these principles more flesh and substance in a highly developed institutional context such as that prevailing in the EU.

From this more global perspective, the EU can be studied with interest and perhaps some profit. Not only can one speak of more formal (alongside informal) institutionalization of executive power in the political system of the EU but one can also look to the manner in which attempts have been made to give flesh and substance, in an incremental fashion, to notions of 'checks and balances' in a much more advanced manner than one finds, on the whole, in other international arenas. In this optimistic sense some of what is emerging in the context of the constitutional order of the EU may well provide lessons and insights that are relevant in the context of international or global governance. At the end of the day, and for the conceivable future, the institutionalization and politicization of the EU, for all its gaps and 'dark holes' in democratic, legitimacy, and accountability terms,[87] is the closest we come in general terms to the allegory of good government and good governance in the post-national sphere. The challenge is to be neither complacent nor despairing but to rise to the challenge of banishing the demons of authoritarianism and secrecy as much as possible.

10.7 The End of the Beginning

The understanding of what is happening in the EU context as a living, evolving, sedimentary (small 'c') constitution may be helpful in enabling us to feel less anxiety about shadowy developments. Earlier in this chapter we have seen how problematic and contested the EU is and remains from a legitimacy and democratic point of view, in particular it seems because of the structural decoupling of systems of electoral accountability and processes of ongoing European integration. There are

[84] See, for example, C Harlow (2006), 'Global administrative law: The quest for principles and values', EJIL, 17/1, pp 187–214; B Kingsbury, N Krisch, and RB Stewart (2005), 'The emergence of global administrative law', Law and Contemporary Problems, 68/3–4), pp 15–61; S Marks (2004), 'Naming global administrative law', New York University J of Int'l L and Pol, 37/4, pp 995–1001.

[85] S Cassese, et al (eds) (2008), *Global Administrative Law: Cases, materials, issues*, 2nd edn (New York: Institute for International Law and Justice); B Kingsbury, N Krisch, RB Stewart (2005).

[86] RW Grant and RE Keohane (2005), 'Accountability and abuses of power in world politics', *American Political Science Review*, 99/1, pp 29–43.

[87] The term is that of C Harlow (2002), *Accountability in the European Union*, (Oxford: Oxford University Press).

probably at this point of time no easy, quick-fix solutions to 'fix' this, either in the short or even medium term. Perhaps we just have to accept imperfection, 'bits and pieces', dark shadows, and muddling through as an inevitable part of the constitutional canvas. What matters in the long run, in my view, is that we make visible the 'many hands' of European integration processes and that countervailing powers are present ('the many eyes'?) and develop incrementally some countervailing force in the interest of deeper values such as those of democracy, accountability, and the rule of law. There may well be no other way out of the labyrinth anyway. A gradual matching of the actors, all actors at all levels, with accountability forums, of all kinds and levels, may not be a bad starting point. The fact that it may lead to duplication and overlap does not necessarily make it redundant.[88] On the contrary, the more the better, although one should also not lose sight of the risk of overload (of information or of accountability processes), or what has been called 'the illusion of accountability in the EU'.[89]

The desirability of having a more empirical turn in studying the EU would dictate more empirical work on specific actors and networks at the European level. This could involve exploring the nature of existing accountability practices by the various accountability forums (eg, evolving roles in practice of European Parliament, European Court of Justice, Court of Auditors, European Ombudsman, etc). For example, it would be very informative, when studying the 'bigger picture', to look at actors such as the General Secretariats of the Council of Ministers and of the European Commission, and also at institutionalized networks such as the European-level network of financial regulators with European tasks (the CESR). This could build on existing empirical studies that have taken actors such as the European Council,[90] comitology committees,[91] and (regulatory) agencies[92] as their focal point of study.[93]

At the same time the focus of accountability studies can perhaps be shifted in addition also to the forums (and not the actors) and to question and investigate their role and input in the process. The 'accountability of the account-holders for their role in the process' is a very relevant point for a research agenda as it has direct impact on the effectiveness/success of the accountability arrangements in holding the actor to account.

[88] See, in general, M Landau (1969), 'Redundancy, rationality and the problem of duplication and overlap', *Public Administration Review*, 29/4, pp 346–58.

[89] S Gustavsson (2009), 'Putting limits on accountability avoidance' in S Gustavsson, C Karlsson, and T Persson (eds), *The Illusion of Accountability in the European Union* (London: Routledge), pp 35–47, p 36.

[90] M van der Steeg (2010), 'Accountability for European Council decision making' in M Bovens, D Curtin, and P Hart (2010), *Accountable European Governance: A comparative assessment* (Oxford : Oxford University Press), forthcoming.

[91] GJ Brandsma (2009), *Backstage Europe: Holding comitology committees to account*, forthcoming.

[92] M Busuioc (2010), 'The Accountability of European Agencies. Legal Provisions and Ongoing Practices', forthcoming.

[93] See further M Bovens, D Curtin, and P Hart (2010), *Accountable European Governance: A comparative assessment* (Oxford : Oxford University Press), forthcoming.

More empirical work can be undertaken that focuses on specific actors and explores the nature of accountability practices at the *national level* (national parliaments, national ministers, hierarchical superiors in civil service, other diagonal accountability forums, etc). For example, how are the members of the European Council held to account at the national level as a matter of practice? And what about weakly institutionalized networks of actors, such as those operating under the auspices of the 'open method of coordination' (OMC). Can we say that they exist in a social relationship with various accountability forums? What about the manner in which national comitology 'agents' are in practice embedded in hierarchical chains of accountability in the national context? The lesson from both quantitative and qualitative empirical work is that committee members may often be fully autonomous in organizing their own work. In such cases bureaucratic principals are usually informed of their agents' behaviour but tend not to engage in debating their agents' points of view that lie at the heart of their input in Brussels.[94]

There is a need for more conceptual (and empirical) work on the linkages between a concept of accountability as relatively precisely defined and other general 'themes' of any political system. This can include both meta-norms such as 'democracy', 'representation', and 'legitimacy' but also more secondary norms of the 'organizing principles' variety, such as 'transparency', 'administration', and 'civil society'. At the same time, there is a need to take the empirical work one step further by building on the insights from the empirical research. What do we learn from the empirical work? How we can contribute to or refine the existing theory? And what does that tell us about the substance of desirable law reform, procedural or otherwise?

There is a need for more conceptual focus on the normative and legal dimension. The EU is undoubtedly the most advanced example we have of an institutional normative order beyond the level of the nation state. To what extent is it given further shape and form in a context of multilevel interactions and challenges across legal orders (international, European, and national)? To what extent are the values of our constitutional states being eroded from above, and are there practices of account-holding by accountability forums that offer some sedimentation? What is the role of the EU as an autonomous actor in that context and is it being held to account for its actions by any forum?

Digging deeper into the interactions between the legal and political orders in the context of the EU, must the 'institutional balance' of the EU anno 2009 be revised in the light of the changing institutional realities? The 'institutional balance' is clearly not what it was anno 1959 when *Meroni* was decided and sooner or later the Court may need to reflect more deeply and provide more substantial guidance as to what the principle of institutional balance allows and does not allow in the contemporary political and legal systems of the EU. In any event

[94] GJ Brandsma (2010).

other actors are engaged in a process of self-reflection in this regard stressing the 'renewed and enhanced institutional balance within the Union' when the institutional innovations contained in the Treaty of Lisbon enter into effect.[95] This too is a salient topic for further research and reflection.

At the same time, a wider understanding of law and the role of practices may facilitate the creation of what can be called a 'space of dialogue' between lawyers and those increasing numbers of political scientists and experts in public administration working on understanding the nature of the EU and the way it works in practice. Such a dialogue is very necessary and valuable and it underlines the fact that disciplinary isolationism is of a bygone era. This book could not have been written by focusing exclusively on legal facts and understandings at various levels of several legal systems; it has been informed and enriched by the empirical work already carried out and ongoing by political scientists and those specialized in public administration and international relations in particular and by an ongoing dialogue with them. It is hoped that the result will be of relevance within the discipline of law (and European law more specifically), but also outside it, and may change somewhat the manner in which we view and understand the nature of the EU and the way that it is constantly evolving symbiotically as a matter of legal, institutional, and indeed social practice. The challenge is not a small one and we are only at the beginning of the conversation, the concepts, and the empirical focus.

The EU is however not the locus of the general problem of unfettered executive power in the international arenas. If the EU did not exist then many of the issues currently dealt with by the EU would not simply revert to the national (democratic) level, but would be dealt with through other instruments of international cooperation (bilateral or multilateral treaties, policy networks, etc) with an *aggravation* of the same phenomenon: overweening executive power and little if any countervailing power.[96] I hope that my book will put the more global phenomenon in its proper—and even more worrisome—perspective. From this wider perspective of international cooperation and rule making in transnational times, the EU harbours within its different modes of governance and decision taking some state of the art examples of transparent and accountable goverance. In this respect too we are at the end of the beginning and not the beginning of the end.

[95] Case T-264/07 *CSL Behring v Commission and EMEA*, action brought on 18 July 2007, OJ C 235, 6 October 2007, p 12. Committee on Constitutional Affairs of the European Parliament, *Draft Report on the impact of the Treaty of Lisbon on the development of the institutional balance of the European Union*, 26 January 2009 (PE405.890v02-00), para 1.

[96] See too P Craig (1999), 'The nature of the community: Integration, democracy, and legitimacy' in P Craig and G de Búrca, *The Evolution of EU Law* (Oxford: Oxford University Press). See more recently on the transnational level, G de Burca (2008), 'Developing democracy beyond the state', Columbia J of Transnat'l L, 46/2, pp 221–78.

Bibliography

Aberbach, JD et al (1981), *Bureaucrats and Politicians in Western Democracies* (Cambridge: Harvard University Press).

Abi-Saab, G (2008), 'The Security Council as legislator and as executive in its fight against terrorism and against proliferation of weapons of mass destruction: The question of legitimacy' in R Wolfrum and V Roben (eds), *Legitimacy in International Law* (Berlin: Springer), pp 109–30.

Ackerman, B (2000), 'The new separation of powers', Harvard L Rev, 113/3, pp 634–729.

Allen, D (1998), '"Who speaks for Europe?" The search for an effective and coherent external policy' in J Peterson and H Sjursen (eds), *A Common Foreign Policy for Europe?* (London, New York: Routledge).

Alvarez, JE (2003), 'The UN's "war" on terrorism', *International Journal of Legal Information: The Official Publication of the International Association of Law Libraries*, 31/2, pp 238–50.

—— (2006), 'International organizations: Then and now', American J of Int'l L, 100/2, pp 324–47.

Armstrong, K and Kilpatrick, C (2007), 'Law, governance or new governance? The changing open method of coordination', Columbia J of European L, 13/3, p 649 *et seq.*

Arnull, A and Wincott, D (eds) (2002), *Accountability and Legitimacy in the European Union* (Oxford University Press).

Aziz, M (2004), 'Mainstreaming the duty of clarity and transparency as part of good administrative practice in the EU', European LJ, 10/3, pp 282–95.

Bache, I and Flinders, M (eds) (2004), *Multi-Level Governance* (Oxford: Oxford University Press).

Balint, T, Bauer, MW and Knill, C (2008), 'Bureaucratic change in the European administrative space: The CASE of the European Commission', *West European Politics*, 31/4, pp 677–700.

Baratta, R (2002), 'Overlaps between European Community competence and European Union foreign policy activity' in E Cannizzaro (ed), *The European Union as an Actor in International Relations* (The Hague: Kluwer Law International), pp 51–75.

Barber, NW (2001), 'Prelude to the separation of powers', Cambridge LJ, 60/1, pp 59–88.

Barendt, E (1995), 'Separation of powers and constitutional government', Public Law, 21, pp 599–619.

Barents, R (2006), 'Case annotation of C-105/03, *Pupino*', *SEW—Tijdschrift voor Europees en Economisch Recht*, 1/2, pp 74–8.

—— (2008), *Het Verdrag van Lissabon: Achtergronden en Commentaar* (Deventer: Kluwer).

Barnett, M and Finnemore, M (2004), *Rules for the World: international organizations in global politics* (Ithaca and London: Cornell University Press).

Bartelt, S and Zeitler, HE (2003), 'Zugang zu Dokumenten der EU', *Europarecht*, 3, pp 487–503.

Bast, J (2005), 'The Constitutional Treaty as a reflexive constitution', German LJ, 6/11, pp 1433–52.

Bátora, J (2005), 'Does the European Union transform the institution of diplomacy?', *Journal of European Public Policy*, 12/1, pp 44–6.

Bauer, M (2004), 'Transparency in the Council' in M Westlake and D Galloway (eds), *The Council of the European Union* (London: John Harper Publishing).

—— (2009), *Reforming the European Commission* (Milton Park: Routledge).

Beach, D (2004), 'The unseen hand in treaty reform negotiations: The role and impact of the Council Secretariat, *Journal of European Public Policy*, 11/3, pp 408–39.

Beetham, D and Lord, C (1998), *Legitimacy and the European Union* (London: Longman).

Begg, I (2007), 'Contested meanings of transparency in central banking', *Comparative European Politics*, 5/1, pp 36–52.

—— and Green, D (1998), 'The political economy of the European Central Bank' in P Arestis and MC Sawyer (eds), *The Political Economy of Central Banking* (Cheltenham: Edward Elgar), pp 122–35.

Beisheim, M and Dingwerth, K (2005), 'Legitimität als Erfolgsfaktor für private Governance? Erste Überlegungen zu Kausalmechanismen', Presentation at DVPW-Sektionstagung, Mannheim, October 2005.

Bekkers, V (1993), *Nieuwe vormen van sturing en informatisering/New Forms of Steering and Informatization* (Delft: Eburon).

Benz, A (2007), 'Accountable multilevel governance by the open method of coordination?', European LJ, 13/4, pp 505–22.

Bergström, CF (2005), *Comitology: Delegation of powers in the European Union and the committee system* (Oxford: Oxford University Press).

Bermann, G (2005), 'Executive power in the new European constitution', Int'l J of Constitutional L, 3/2–3, pp 440–7.

Besselink, LFM (2006), 'National parliaments in the EU's composite constitution: A plea for a shift in paradigm' in P Kiiver (ed), *National and Regional Parliaments in the European Constitutional Order* (Groningen: Europa Law Publishing), pp 117–31, available at <http://igitur-archive.library.uu.nl/law/2007–0313-201044/besselink_06_national.pdf>.

—— (2007), *A Composite European Constitution* (Groningen: Europa Law Publishers).

Besson, S and Marti, JL (eds) (2006), *Deliberative Democracy and its Discontents* (Aldershot: Ashgate).

Beyers, J (2005), 'Multiple embeddedness and socialization in Europe: The case of Council officials', *International Organizations*, 59/4, pp 899–936.

—— and Dierickx, G (1998), 'The working groups of the Council of the EU: Supranational or intergovernmental negotiations', *Journal of Common Market Studies*, 36/3, pp 289–317.

Biesheuvel, B, Dell, E, and Marjolin, R (1980), *Report on European Institutions: Presented by the Committee of Three to the European Council* (Luxembourg: Office for Official Publications of the European Communities), available at <http://www.ena.lu/conclusions_wise_men_committee_dublin_29_30_november_1979–020003121.html>.

Bignami, F (1999), 'The democratic deficit in European Community rule-making: A call for notice and comment in comitology', Harvard Int'l LJ, 40/2, pp 451–515.

Blagescu, M, Las Casas, L de, and Lloyd, R (2006), *Pathways to Accountability: The global accountability framework* (London: One World Trust).

Blavoukos, S, Bourantonis, D, and Pagoulatos, G (2007), 'A president for the European Union: A new actor in town?', *Journal of Common Market Studies*, 45/2, pp 231–52.

Blokker, N (2009), 'Reviewing the review: Did the European Court of Justice in *Kadi* indirectly review Security Council resolutions? On the downside of a courageous judgment' in M Bulterman et al (eds), *Views of European Law from the Mountain* (The Hague: Kluwer), pp 315–26.

Blom-Hansen, J (2008), 'The origins of the EU comitology system: A case of informal agenda-setting by the Commission', *Journal of European Public Policy*, 15/2, pp 208–26.

Bobek, M (2007), 'The binding force of Babel: The enforcement of EC law unpublished in the languages of the new Member States', EUI LAW Working Paper No. 2007/6, available at <http://papers.ssrn.com/sol3/papers.cfm?abstract_id=973589>.

Boer, M den (1998), 'Steamy windows: Transparency and openness in justice and home affairs' in V Deckmyn and I Thomson (eds), *Openness and Transparency in the European Union* (Maastricht: European Institute of Public Administration), pp 91–105.

Bogdandy, A von (1999), 'The legal case for unity: The European Union as a single organization with a single legal system', Common Market L Rev, 36/5, pp 887–910.

Bostock, D (2002), 'Coreper revisited', *Journal of Common Market Studies*, 40/2, pp 215–34.

Bovens, M (1998), *The quest for responsibility: Accountability and citizenship in complex organisations* (Cambridge: Cambridge University Press).

—— (1999), *De Digitale Rechtsstaat: Beschouwingen over Informatiemaatschappij en Rechtsstaat* (Alphen aan de Rijn: Samson).

—— (13 August 2000), 'De Vierde Macht Revisited: Over Ambtelijke Macht en Publieke Verantwoording', *Inaugural Lecture, University of Utrecht.*

—— (2005), 'Public accountability' in E Ferlie, L Lynne, and C Pollitt (eds), *The Oxford Handbook of Public Management* (Oxford: Oxford University Press), pp 182–208.

—— (2007), 'Analysing and assessing accountability: A conceptual framework', European LJ, 13/4, pp 447–68.

—— (2010), 'Two concepts of accountability: Accountability as a virtue and as a mechanism', *West European Politics*, forthcoming.

—— and Hart, P (2005), 'Evaluating public accountability', Paper International Research Colloquium Accountable Governance, Queens University, Belfast, available at <http://www.usg.uu.nl/download/Evaluating%20Accountability.pdf>.

—— Curtin, D, and Hart, P (2010), *Accountable European Governance: A comparative assessment* (Oxford: Oxford University Press), forthcoming.

Bradley, KStC (1999a), 'Institutional aspects of comitology: Scenes from the cutting room floor' in C Joerges and E Vos (eds), *EU Committees: Social regulation, law and politics* (Oxford: Hart Publishing), pp 71–93.

—— (1999b), 'La transparence de l'Union européenne: une évidence ou un trompe-l'oeil?', *Cahiers de Droit Européenne*, 35/3–4, pp 283–362.

—— (2006), 'Comitology and the courts: Tales of the unexpected' in H Hofmann and A Türk (eds), *EU Administrative Governance* (London: Edward Elgar), pp 417–47.

—— (2008), 'Halfway house: The 2006 comitology reforms and the European Parliament: A view from the ground floor', *West European Politics*, 31/4, pp 837–54.

Brammer, S (2009), *Co-operation between National Competition Agencies in the Enforcement of EC Competition Law* (Oxford: Hart Publishing).

Brandsma, GJ (2008), 'Making comitology accountable', Paper presented at the Dutch and Flemish Political Science Associations Annual Conference, Nijmegen, 29–30 May.

—— (2010), *Backstage Europe: Comitology, accountability and democracy in the European Union,* forthcoming.

—— Curtin, D, and Meijer, A (2008), 'How transparent are EU comitology committees in practice?', European LJ, 14/6, pp 819–38.

Britz, G and Schmidt, M (2000), 'The institutionalized participation of management and labour in the legislative activities of the European Community: A challenge to the principle of democracy under Community law', European LJ, 6/1, pp 45–71.

Brouwer, O and Curtin, D (2009), 'Why? The giving reasons requirement of EU administration' in MK Bulterman et al (eds), *Views of European Law from the Mountain* (The Hague, Kluwer), pp 133–41.

Brink, van den A (2008), 'Van Rechtsinstrument naar Rechtshandelingen: "Lissabon" en de Introductie van een Europees Primaat van de Wetgever', *Sociaal-Economische Wetgeving*, 56/5, pp 166–70.

Brinkhorst, LJ (1996), 'The future of European agencies: A budgetary perspective from the European Parliament, The new European agencies', EUI Working Paper RSC, No 96/49, pp 75–81.

Buiter, WH (1999), 'Alice in Euroland', *Journal of Common Market Studies*, 37, pp 181–209.

Bunyan, T (1999), *Secrecy and Openness in the EU* (London: Kogan Page).

—— (2002), 'Secrecy and openness in the European Union: The ongoing struggle for freedom of information', available at <http://www.freedominfo.org/features/20020930-ch1.htm>.

—— (2007), 'Secret trialogues and the democratic deficit', available at <www.statewatch.org/analyses/no-64-secret-trilogues.pdf>.

—— (2008a), 'Access to EU documents: When is a "document" not a "document"?', *Statewatch analysis*, available at <http://www.statewatch.org/news/2008/sep/access-to-eu-docs-eu-what-is-a-document.pdf>.

—— (2008b), 'EU: Cementing the European state: New emphasis on internal security and operational cooperation at EU level', available at <http://www.statewatch.org/news/2008/feb/07lisbon-european-state.htm>.

—— Curtin, D, and White, A (2000), *Essays for an Open Europe* (European Federation of Journalists), available at <http://www.statewatch.org/secret/essays.pdf>.

Búrca, G de (1996), 'The quest for legitimacy in the European Union', The Modern L Rev, 59/3, pp 349–76.

—— (1999), 'The institutional development of the European Union: A constitutional analysis' in G de Búrca and P Craig (eds), *European Union Law: An evolutionary perspective* (Oxford: Oxford University Press), pp 55–82.

—— (2008), 'Developing democracy beyond the state', Columbia J of Trans'l L, 46/2, pp 221–78.

Burgess, M (2004), 'Federalism' in A Wiener and T Diez (eds), *European Integration Theory* (Oxford: Oxford University Press), pp 25–6.

Burnham, P (2001), 'New Labour and the politics of depoliticisation', *British Journal of Politics and International Relations*, 3/2, pp 127–49.

Busuioc, M (2009), 'Accountability, control and independence: The case of European agencies', European LJ, forthcoming.

—— (2010), 'The Accountability of European Agencies. Legal Provisions and Ongoing Practices', forthcoming.

—— and Groenleer, M (2008), 'Wielders of supranational power? The administrative behaviour of the heads of European Union agencies', Paper presented at the ECPR Standing Group on Regulatory Governance, 5–7 June Utrecht.

Cameron, I (2003), 'UN targeted sanctions, legal safeguards and the European Convention on Human Rights', Nordic J of Int'l L, 72/2, pp 159–214.

Caporaso, JA (1997), 'Does the European Union represent an n of 1?', *ECSA Review*, X/3 (Fall 1997), pp 1–5, available at <http://aei.pitt.edu/54/01/n1debate.htm>.

Cappelletti, M, Seccombe, M and Weiler, J (eds) (1986), *Integration Through Law: Europe and the American federal experience* (Berlin: Walter de Gruyter).

Castiglione, D (2006), 'Accountability' in M Bevir (ed), *Encyclopedia of Governance* (London: Sage), vol 1, pp 1–7.

Cassese, S et al (eds) (2008), *Global Administrative Law: Cases, materials, issues*, 2nd edn (New York: Institute for International Law and Justice).

Cater, D (1963), *The Fourth Branch of Government* (Boston: Houghton Mifflin).

Chalmers, D et al (2006), *European Union Law: Text and materials* (Cambridge: Cambridge University Press).

Chesterman, S (2008), 'An international rule of law?', American J of Comparative L, 56/2, pp 331–61.

Chiti, E (2000), 'The emergence of a Community administration: The case of European agencies', Common Market L Rev, 37/2, pp 309–43.

Christiansen, T (2001a), 'The Council of Ministers: The politics of institutionalised intergovernmentalism' in J Richardson (ed), *European Union: Power and policy-making* (London: Routledge), pp 135–54.

—— (2001b), 'Intra-institutional politics and inter-institutional relations in the EU: Towards coherent governance?', *Journal of European Public Policy*, 8/5, pp 747–69.

—— (2005), 'Towards statehood? The EU's move towards constitutionalisation and territorialisation', ARENA Working Paper, No 21, available at <http://www.arena.uio.no/publications/working-papers2005/papers/05_21.xml>.

—— (2006), 'Out of the shadows: The General Secretariat of the Council of Ministers', Journal of Legislative Studies, 8/4, pp 80–97.

—— and Laegreid, P (2005), 'Agencification and regulatory reform', Paper prepared for the CSANCOR/SOG workshop on 'Autonomization of the State: From Integrated Administrative Models to Single Purpose Organization', Stanford University, 1–2 April 2005.

—— and Lægreid, P (eds) (2006), *Autonomy and Regulation: Coping with agencies in the modern state* (Cheltenham: Edward Elgar).

—— and Piattoni, S (2003), *Informal Governance in the European Union* (Cheltenham: Edward Elgar).

—— and Vanhoonacker, S (2008), 'At a critical juncture? Change and continuity in the institutional development of the Council Secretariat', *West European Politics*, 31/4, pp 751–70.

Ciborra, C (2001), *The Labyrinths of Information: Challenging the wisdom of systems* (Oxford: Oxford University Press).

Cini, M (1996), *The European Commission: Leadership, organisation and culture in the EU administration* (Manchester: Manchester University Press).

—— (2008), 'European Commission reform and the origins of the European transparency initiative', *Journal of European Public Policy*, 5, pp 743–60.

Claude, IL (1964), *Swords into Plowshares: The problems and progress of international organisation* (New York: Random House).

Coleman, J (2006), 'The most dangerous branch? Mayors, governors, presidents and the rule of law. A symposium on executive power: Introduction', Yale LJ, 115/9, pp 2215–16.

Committee of Independent Experts (1999), *First Report on the Reform of the Commission*, vol I, available at <http://www.europarl.europa.eu/experts/default_en.htm>.

—— (1999), *Second Report on the Reform of the Commission: Analysis of Current Practice and Proposals for Tackling Mismanagement, Irregularities and Fraud*, vol II, available at <http://www.europarl.europa.eu/experts/default_en.htm>.

Committee for the Study of Economic and Monetary Union (1989), *Report on Economic and Monetary Union in the European Community* (Delors Report).

Comte, F (2008), 'Agences européennes: relance d'une réflexion interinstitutionelle européenne', *Revue du Droit de l'Union Européenne*, 3, pp 461–506.

Cotino, L (2006), 'Theory and reality of public access to EU information' in D Curtin, A Kellermann and S Blockmans (eds), *The EU Constitution: The best way forward?* (The Hague: Kluwer), pp 233–44.

Coussins, W and Crum, B (2003), 'Towards effective and accountable leadership of the Union: Options and guidelines for reform', EPIN Working Paper No 3, available at <www.ceps.be>.

Cox, RW and Jacobson, HK (eds) (1973), *The Anatomy of Influence: Decision-making in international organizations (*New Haven: Yale University Press).

Craig, P (1990), *Public Law and Democracy in the United Kingdom and the United States of America* (Oxford: Oxford University Press).

—— (1997), 'Democracy and rulemaking within the EC: An empirical and normative assessment', Jean Monnet Working Papers No 2/97, available at <http://www.jeanmonnetprogram.org/papers/97/97-02-.html>.

—— (1999), 'The nature of the Community: Integration, democracy, and legitimacy' in P Craig and G de Búrca, *The Evolution of EU Law* (Oxford: Oxford University Press).

—— (2003), 'The constitutionalisation of Community administration', European L Rev, 28/6, pp 840–64.

—— (2004a), 'European governance: Executive and administrative powers under the new constitutional settlement' in JHH Weiler and CL Eisgruber (eds), *Altneuland: The EU Constitution in a contextual perspective,* Jean Monnet Working Paper 5/04, available at <http://jeanmonnetprogram.org/papers/04/040501-12.html>.

—— (2004b) 'The Constitutional Treaty: Legislative and executive power in the emerging constitutional order', EUI Working Paper, Law no. 2004/7, available at <http://papers.ssrn.com/sol3/papers.cfm?abstract_id=635342>.

—— (2006), *EU Administrative Law* (Oxford: Oxford University Press).

—— (2008), 'The role of the European Parliament under the Lisbon Treaty' in S Griller and J Ziller (eds), *The Lisbon Treaty: EU constitutionalism without a constitutional treaty?* (Vienna: Springer), pp 109–35.

—— (2010), 'Shared administration and networks: Global and EU perspectives' in G Anthony, JB Auby, J Morison and T Zwart (eds), *Values in Global Administrative Law* (Oxford, Hart Publishing), forthcoming.

—— and Búrca, G de (2007), *EU Law: Text, cases and materials*, 4th edn (Oxford: Oxford University Press).

—— and Rawlings, R (2003), *Law and Administration in Europe: Essays in honour of Carol Harlow* (Oxford: Oxford University Press).

—— and Tomkins, A (eds) (2006), *The Executive and Public Law: Power and accountability in comparative perspective* (Oxford: Oxford University Press).

Crince Le Roy, R (1969), *De Vierde Macht*, (Den Haag: Vuga-Boekerij).

—— (1976), *De Vierde Macht : Een Hernieuwde Kennismaking* (Den Haag: Vuga-Boekerij).

Crosbie, J (2009), 'Support for Lisbon rises in Ireland', EuropeanVoice.com (1 June 2009).

Cross, MKD (2007), *The European Diplomatic Corps: Diplomats and international cooperation from Westphalia to Maastricht* (Basingstoke: Palgrave Macmillan).

Crum, B (2006), 'Parliamentarization of the CFSP through informal institution-making? The Fifth European Parliament and the EU High Representative', *Journal of European Public Policy*, 13/3, pp 383–401.

—— and Fossum, JE (2009), 'The multilevel parliamentary field: A framework for theorizing representative democracy in the EU', *European Political Science Review*, 1/2, pp 249–71.

Curtin, D (1993), 'The constitutional structure of the Union: A Europe of bits and pieces', Common Market L Rev, 30/1, pp 17–69.

—— (1996), 'Betwixt and between: Democracy and transparency in the governance of the EU' in JA Winter et al (eds), *Reforming the Treaty on European Union* (The Hague: Kluwer Law International), pp 95–121.

—— (1996), 'Civil society and the EU: Opening spaces for deliberative democracy', *Collected Courses of the Academy of European Law*, pp 185–280.

—— (1999), 'The fundamental principle of open decision-making and EU (political) citizenship' in D O'Keeffe and P Twomey (eds), *Legal Issues of the Amsterdam Treaty* (Oxford: Hart Publishing), pp 71–92.

—— (2000), 'Citizens' fundamental right of access to information: An evolving digital *passepartout*?', Common Market L Rev, 37/1, pp 7–21.

—— (2001), 'The developing right of citizen access to information on EU asylum and immigration decision-making' in C Harlow and E Guild (eds), *Implementing Amsterdam* (Oxford: Hart Publishing), pp 34–63.

—— (2003), 'Digital government in the European Union: Freedom of information trumped by "internal security"' in A Roberts (ed), *National Security and Open Government: Striking the right balance* (New York), pp 99–120, also available at <http://open.campbellinstitute.org>.

—— (2003), 'Private interest representation or civil society deliberation? A contemporary dilemma for European Union governance', *Social and Legal Studies*, 12/1, pp 55–75.

—— (2004a), 'European Union executives evolving in the shade?' in AE Kellermann (ed), *The European Union: An ongoing process of European integration. Liber Amicorum Alfred E Kellermann* (The Hague: TMC Asser Institute), pp 97–110.

—— (2005a) 'Delegation to EU non-majoritarian agencies and emerging practices of public accountability' in D Geradin, R Munoz and N Petit (eds), *Regulation Through Agencies: A new paradigm of European governance* (Cheltenham: Edgar Elgar), pp 88–119.

—— (2005b), 'Mind the gap: The evolving EU executive and the constitution', Third Walter van Gerven Public Lecture, University of Leuven (Groningen: Europa Law Publishing).

—— (2006), 'Making a political constitution for the European Union', European J of L Ref, 8/1, pp 65–76.

—— (2007a), 'Holding (quasi-)autonomous EU administrative actors to public account', European LJ, 13/4, pp 523–41.

—— (2007b), 'Transparency, audiences and the evolving role of the EU Council of Ministers' in J Fossum and P Schlesinger (eds), *The European Union and the Public Sphere: A communicative space in the making?* (London: Routledge), pp 246–58.

—— (2009), 'The Irish "no" to the Lisbon Treaty. Ireland's voice and Europe's exit', *Zeitschrift für Staats- und Europawissenschaften/Journal for Comparative Government and European Policy*, pp 31–50.

—— (2009), 'The Council of Ministers: The missing link' in L Verhey, P Kiiver, and S Loeffen (eds), *Political Accountability and European Integration* (Groningen: European Law Publishing), pp 126–35.

—— and Dekker, IF (eds) (1999), 'The EU as a "layered" international organization: Institutional unity in disguise' in P Craig and G de Búrca (eds), *The Evolution of EU Law* (Oxford: Oxford University Press), pp 83–136.

—— and —— (2002), 'The constitutional structure of the European Union: Some reflections on vertical unity-in-diversity' in N Walker et al (eds), *Convergence and Divergence in European Public Law* (Oxford: Hart Publishers), pp 59–78.

—— and Eckes, C (2008), 'The *Kadi* case: Mapping the boundaries between the executive and the judiciary in Europe', International Organizations L Rev, 5/2, pp 365–69.

—— and Egeberg, M (2008), 'Tradition and innovation: Europe's accumulated executive order' in D Curtin and M Egeberg (eds), *Towards a New Executive Order in Europe?, West European Politics*, 31/4, pp 639–61.

—— and Meijer, A (2006), 'Does transparency strengthen legitimacy? A critical analysis of European Union policy documents', *Information Polity*, 11/2, pp 109–22.

—— and Meijers, H (1995), 'The principle of open government in Schengen and the European Union: Democratic retrogression?', Common Market L Rev, 32/2, pp 391–442.

—— and Ooik, RH van (1999), 'Een Hof van Justitie van de Europese Unie?', *Sociaal Economische Wetgeving*, 47/1, pp 24–38.

—— and Wessel, RA (2008), 'Rechtseenheid van de Europese Unie? De rol van het Hof van Justitie als constitutionele rechter', *SEW—Sociaal-Economische Wetgeving*, 56/10, pp 369–76.

—— and Wille, A (eds) (2008), *Meaning and Practice of Accountability in the EU Multi-Level Context* (Mannheim: CONNEX).

Daintith, T (1997), 'Regulation' in R Buxbaum and F Mádl (eds), *International Encyclopaedia of Comparative Law*, xvii: *State and Economy* (Tübingen: Mohr Siebeck).

—— and Page, A (1999), *The Executive in the Constitution: Structure, autonomy and internal control* (Oxford: Oxford University Press).

Dashwood, A (2000), 'Decision-making at the summit', Cambridge Yearbook of European Legal Studies, 3, pp 79–106.

—— (2004), 'The relationship between the Member States and the European Union/ European Community', Common Market L Rev, 41/2, pp 355–81.

—— (2006), 'The EU constitution: What will really change?', Cambridge Yearbook of European Legal Studies, 7, pp 33–56.

—— (2008), 'Article 47 TEU and the relationship between first and second pillar competences' in M Cremona and B de Witte (eds), *EU Foreign Relations Law: Constitutional fundamentals* (Oxford: Hart Publishing), pp 53–78.

—— (2009), What can be salvaged if the Treaty of Lisbon is lost?' in MK Bulterman et al (eds), *Views of European Law from the Mountain* (Kluwer, The Hague), pp 335–44.

Davis, J (1998), 'Access to and transmission of information: Position of the media' in V Deckmyn and I Thomson (eds), *Openness and Transparency in the European Union,* (Maastricht: European Institute of Public Administration), pp 121–6.

Decker, F (2002), 'Governance beyond the nation state: Reflections on the democratic deficit of the EU', *Journal of European Public Policy*, 9/2, pp 256–72.

Deckmyn, V (2002), *Increasing Transparency in the European Union* (Maastricht: European Institute for Public Administration).

Dehousse, F (2005), 'Les caractéristiques fondamentales de la politique étrangère et de securité commune' in JV Louis and M Dony (eds), *Relations Extérieures : Commentaire J. Mégret: Le droit de la CE et de l'Union européenne* (Bruxelles: Institut d'Etudes Europénnes), pp 441–62.

—— and Coussens, W (2003), *Which Presidency for the European Union? The Convention's dilemmas* (Brussels: Studia Diplomatica).

Dehousse, R (2003), 'Comitology: Who watches the watchmen?', *Journal of European Public Policy*, 10/5, pp 798–813.

—— (2008), 'Delegation of powers in the European Union: The need for a multi-principals model', *West European Politics*, 31/4, pp 789–805.

Dekker, I and Wessel, R (2004), 'Governance by international organisations: Rethinking the normative force of international decisions' in I Dekker and W Werner (eds), *Governance and International Legal Theory (*Martinus Nijhoff), pp 215–36.

Dijkstra, H (2008), 'The Council Secretariat's role in the common foreign and security policy', *European Foreign Affairs Review*, 13, pp 149–66.

Dinan, D (1999), *Ever Closer Union: An introduction to European integration* (New York: Palgrave).

Dodson, S (2008), 'A Darwinist view of the living constitution', Vanderbilt L Rev 61/5, pp 1319–1347.

Driessen, B (2005), 'The Council of the European Union and access to documents', European L Rev, 30/5, pp 675–96.

—— (2007), *Inter-Institutional Conventions in EU Law* (London: Cameron May).

Drijber, BJ (2006), 'Europese integratie: Bottom up of top down?', *Nederlands Juristen Blad*, 81/26, pp 1418–22.

Drulák, P (2004), 'Metaphors Europe lives by: Language and institutional change of the European Union', available at <http://www.arena.uio.no/events/documents/Paper_001.pdf>.

Dryberg, P (1999), 'Current issues in the debate on public access to documents', European L Rev, 24/3, pp 157–69.

Duke, S and Vanhoonacker, S (2006), 'Administrative governance in the CFSP: Development and practice', *European Foreign Affairs Review*, 11/2, pp 163–82.

Dutch Scientific Council for Government Policy (2008), *Rediscovering Europe in the Netherlands* (Amsterdam: Amsterdam University Press).

Dutheil de la Rochère, J (2009), 'EU regulatory agencies: What future do they have?' in M Bulterman et al (eds) *Views of European Law from the Mountain* (The Hague: Kluwer), pp 355–66.

Easton, D (1953), *The Political System: An inquiry into the state of political science* (New York: Albert Knopf).

Eberlein, B and Grande, G (2005), 'Beyond delegation: Transnational regulatory regimes and the EU regulatory state', *Journal of European Public Policy*, 12/1, pp 89–112.

Eckes, C (2007), 'Annotation of Case T-228/02 (OMPI)', Common Market L Rev, 44, pp 1117–29.

—— (2008), 'Sanctions against individuals: Fighting terrorism within the European legal order', European Constitutional L Rev, 4, pp 205–24.

—— (2009), *EU Counter-Terrorist Policies and Fundamental Rights: The case of individual sanctions* (Oxford: Oxford University Press).

Editorial Comment (2005), 'The CFSP under the EU Constitutional Treaty: Issues of depillarization', Common Market L Rev, 42/2, pp 325–9.

Editorial Comment (2009), 'The second second Irish referendum: Finally a fair choice', Legal Issues European Economic Integration, 36/2, pp 101–4.

Eeckhout, P (2004), *External Relations of the European Union: Legal and constitutional foundations* (Oxford: Oxford University Press).

Egeberg, M (2002), 'The European Commission: The evolving EU executive', ARENA Working Papers, WP 02/30, available at <http://www.arena.uio.no/publications/wp02_30.htm>

—— (2006a), 'Balancing autonomy and accountability: Enduring tensions in the European Commission's development' in M Egeberg (ed), *Multilevel Union Administration: The transformation of executive politics in Europe* (Basingstoke: Palgrave Macmillan).

—— (2006b), 'Europe's executive branch of government in the melting pot: An overview' in M Egeberg (ed), *Multilevel Union Administration: The transformation of executive politics in Europe* (Basingstoke: Palgrave Macmillan).

—— (ed) (2006c), *Multilevel Union Administration: The transformation of executive politics in Europe* (Basingstoke: Palgrave Macmillan).

—— (ed) (2007), *Institutional Dynamics and the Transformation of Executive Politics in Europe* (Mannheim: CONNEX Report Series, 3).

—— (2008), 'European government(s): Executive politics in transition?', *West European Politics*, 31/1–2, pp 235–57.

—— and Trondal, J (2007), 'National agencies in the European administrative space: Government driven, commission driven or networked?' in M Egeberg (ed), *Institutional Dynamics and the Transformation of Executive Politics in Europe* (Mannheim: CONNEX Report Series No 03), pp 291–312.

—— Schaefer, G, and Trondal, J (2003), 'The many faces of EU committee governance', *West European Politics*, 26/3, pp 19–40.

Ehlermann, CD (1995), 'Reflections on a European cartel office', Common Market L Rev, 32/2, pp 471–86.

Eijk, C van der and Franklin, M (2004), 'Potential for contestation on European matters at national elections in Europe' in G Marks and MN Steenbergen (eds), *European Integration and Political Conflict* (Cambridge: Cambridge University Press), pp 32–50.

—— and Schmitt, H (eds) (2008), *The Multilevel Electoral System of the EU* (Mannheim: CONNEX Report Series No. 4).

Eijsbouts, WT (1996), 'Constitutional sedimentation', *Legal Issues of European Integration*, 23/1, pp 51–60.

—— (2000), 'De Raad van Opperhoofden: Over het Regeringsstelsel van de Unie' in AK Koekoek (ed), *Bijdragen aan een Europese Grondwet: Staatsrechtconferentie 2000* (Deventer: Tjeenk Willink), pp 59–87.

—— (2005), 'De Macht, de Mensen, het Model: Europa's Grondwet à l'Américaine', *Nederlandsch Juristenblad*, 80/20, pp 1024–34.

Eiselt, I and Slominski, P (2006), 'Sub-constitutional engineering: Negotiation, content and legal value of interinstitutional agreements in the EU', European LJ, 12/2, pp 209–25.

Elster, J (ed) (1998), *Deliberative Democracy* (Cambridge: Cambridge University Press).

Eriksen, E and Fossum, JE (eds) (2000), *Democracy in the European Union: Integration through deliberation?* (London: Routledge).

—— and (2007), 'Europe in transformation: How to reconstitute
democracy', RECON Online Working Paper 2007/01, available at <http://www.reconproject.eu/main.php/RECON_wp_0701.pdf?fileitem=5456091>.

European Commission (2000), *Reforming the Commission: A White Paper*. Part 1, 5 April 2000, available at: <http://europa.eu/documents/comm/white_papers/reform/com2000_200_part1_en.pdf> and Action Plan, <http://europa.eu/documents/comm/white_papers/reform/com2000_200_part2_en.pdf> and measures of implementation of the White Paper, <http://www.europa.eu.int/comm/reform/implementing/index_en.htm>.

—— (2001), *White Paper on Governance*, COM (2001) 428 final, available at <http://ec.europa.eu/governance/white_paper/index_en.htm>.

—— (2002), Communication, *Towards a Reinforced Culture for Consultation and Dialogue: General principles and minimum standards for consultation of interested parties by the Commission*, COM (2002) 704 final, 11 December 2002.

—— (2008a), Communication from the Commission to the European Parliament and the Council, *European Agencies: The way forward*, COM (2008) 135 final, 11 March 2008.

—— (2008b), *General Report on the Activities of the European Union* (Luxembourg: Office for Official Publications of the European Communities).

—— (2009a), Communication, European Financial Supervision, COM/2009/252 final, 27 May 2009.

—— (2009b), Communication from the Commission to the European Parliament and the Council, 'An area of freedom, security and justice serving the citizen', COM (2009) 262/4.

European Parliament (2009), Committee on Constitutional Affairs, *Draft Report on the Impact of the Treaty of Lisbon on the Development of the Institutional Balance of the European Union*, 26 January 2009, PE405.890v02–00.

Everson, M (1999), 'The constitutionalisation of European administrative law: Legal oversight of a stateless internal market' in C Joerges and E Vos (eds), *European Committees: Social regulation, law and politics* (Oxford: Hart Publishing), pp 281–309.

Fabbrini, S (2007), *Compound Democracies: Why the United States and Europe are becoming similar* (Oxford: Oxford University Press).

Fallon, RH (1997), 'The "rule of law" as a concept in constitutional discourse', Columbia L Rev, 97/1, pp 1–56.

Farrell, H and Héritier, A (2003), 'Formal and informal institutions under co-decision: Continuous constitution-building in Europe', *Governance: An International Journal of Policy, Administration and Institutions*, 16/4, pp 577–600.

—— and —— (2007), 'Co-decision and institutional change', *West European Politics*, 30/2, pp 285–300.

Featherstone, K (1994), 'Jean Monnet and the "democratic deficit" in the European Union', *Journal of Common Market Studies*, 32/2, pp 149–70.

Finer, SE (1970), 'Almond's concept of the political system', *Government and Opposition*, 5/1, p 5.

Fischer, F (1990), *Technocracy and the Politics of Expertise* (London: Sage).

Fischer, KH (2008), *Der Vertrag von Lissabon: Text und Kommentar zum Europäischen Reformvertrag* (Baden-Baden: Nomos).

Fisher, E (2004), 'The European Union in the age of accountability', Oxford Journal of Legal Studies, 24/3, pp 495–515.

Flaherty, MS (1996), 'The most dangerous branch', Yale LJ, 105/ 7, pp 1725–839.

Flinders, M (2004), 'Distributed public governance in the European Union', *Journal of European Public Policy*, 11/3, pp 520–44.

Follesdal, A and Hix, S (2005), 'Why is there a democratic deficit in the EU: A response to Majone and Moravcsik', *CONNEX*, No C-05-02, available at <http://www.connex-network.org/eurogov/pdf/egp-connex-C-05-02.pdf>.

Fouilleux, E, Maillard, J de, and Smith A (2005), 'Technical or political? The working groups of the EU Council of Ministers', *Journal of European Public Policy*, 12/4, pp 609–23.

Fratangelo, P (2006), 'L'Union européenne face à la lutte contre le financement du terrorisme', *Revue du Droit de l'Union Européenne*, 4, pp 815–41.

Friedman, B and Smith, S (1998), 'The sedimentary constitution', University of Pennsylvania L Rev, (147) 1, pp 1–90

Frissen, PHA (1996), *De Virtuele Staat: Politiek, Bestuur, Technologie. Een Postmodern Verhaal* (Schoonhoven: Academic Service).

Fromm, IE (2008), 'Rahmenbeschluss 2005/667/JI des Rates vom 12.7.2005 zur Verstärkung des strafrechtlichen Rahmens zur Bekämpfung der Verschmutzung durch Schiffe ist nichtig', *Zeitschrift für internationale Strafrechtsdogmatik*, 3/1, pp 168–77.

Galetta, DU (2007), 'Inhalt und Bedeutung des europäischen Rechts auf eine gute Verwaltung', *Europarecht*, 1, pp 57–81.

Garbagnati Ketvel, MG (2006), 'The jurisdiction of the European Court of Justice in respect of the common foreign and security policy', Int'l and Comp LQ, 55/1, pp 77–120.

Gearty, C (2006), *Can Human Rights Survive? The Hamlyn Lectures 2005* (Cambridge: Cambridge University Press).

Geradin, D (2004), 'The development of European regulatory agencies: What the EU should learn from American experience', Columbia J of European L, 11, pp 1–52.

Gerven, W van (2005), *The European Union: A Polity of States and Peoples* (Oxford: Hart Publishing).

—— (2006), 'Closing the accountability gap: And the rule of law', unpublished manuscript on file with author.

Geuijen, KP et al (2008), *The New Eurocrats: National civil servants in EU policy-making* (Amsterdam: Amsterdam University Press).

Gialdino, GC (1995), 'Some reflections on the acquis communautaire', Common Market L Rev, 32/5, pp 1089–121.

Goebel, RG (2006), 'Court of Justice oversight over the European Central Bank: Delimiting the ECB's constitutional autonomy and independence in the OLAF judgment', Fordham International LJ, 29, pp 610–24.

Goldsworthy, J (1997), 'Originalism in constitutional interpretation', Federal L Rev, 25/1, pp 1–50.

Goodhart, CAE (2003), 'The constitutional position of an Independent Central Bank', *Government and Opposition*, 37/2, pp 190–210.

Gornitzka, A (2008), 'Networking administration in areas of national sensitivity: The Commission and European higher education' in A Amaral et al (eds), *European Integration and the Governance of Higher Education and Research* (Dordrecht: Springer).

—— and Sverdrup, U (2008), 'Who consults? The configuration of expert groups in the European Union?', *West European Politics*, 31/4, pp 725–50.

Gosalbo Bono, R (2006), 'Some reflections on the CFSP Legal Order', Common Market L Rev, 43/2, pp 337–94.

Grant, C (2007), 'The view from 2027', Opinion paper (London: Centre for European Reform).

Grant, RW and Keohane, RO (2004), 'Accountability and abuses of power in world politics', IILJ Working Paper 2004/7, Global Administrative Law Series.

—— and Keohane, RO (2005), 'Accountability and abuses of power in world politics', *American Political Science Review*, 99/1, pp 29–43.

Graver, HP (2002), 'National implementation of EU law and the shaping of European administrative policy', ARENA Working Paper 02/17.

Grevi, G (2003), 'Time for a government of the Union', European Policy Center, Working Paper No. 4, 10 April 2003.

Grey, TC (1974–1975), 'Do we have an unwritten constitution?', Stanford L Rev, 27, pp 703–18.

Griller, S and Orator, A (2004), '*Meroni* revisited: Empowering European agencies between efficiency and legitimacy', NewGov-4/D40, available at <http://www.eu-newgov.org/database/DELIV/D04D40_WP_Meroni_Revisited.pdf>.

—— and Ziller, J (eds) (2008), *The Lisbon Treaty: EU constitutionalism without a constitutional treaty?* (Vienna: Springer).

Groenleer, M (2008), 'Building autonomous European Union agencies? Identity, legitimacy and leadership in a comparative perspective', Paper presented at the 3rd UACES Annual Conference, 1–3 September Edinburgh.

—— (2009), *The Autonomy of European Union Agencies. A Comparative Study of Institutional Development*, forthcoming.

Gronbech-Jensen, C (1998) 'The Scandinavian tradition of open government and the European Union: Problems of compatibility', *Journal of European Public Policy*, 5, pp 185–99.

Gross, T (2005), 'Die Kooperation zwischen europäischen Agenturen und nationalen Behörden', *Europarecht*, 1, pp 54–68.

Grzeszick, B (2006), 'Das Grundrecht auf eine gute Verwaltung: Strukturen und Perspektiven des Charta-Grundrechts auf eine gute Verwaltung', *Europarecht*, 2, pp 161–81.

Gustavsson, S (2008), 'The living constitution of the EU' in B Kohler-Koch and F Larat (eds), *Efficient and Democratic Governance in the European Union*, CONNEX Report Series Nr 09, (Mannheim: CONNEX Report Series), pp 325–38.

—— (2009). 'Putting limits on accountability avoidance' in S Gustavsson, C Karlsson, and T Persson (eds), *The Illusion of Accountability in the European Union* (London: Routledge), pp 35–47, p 36.

—— Karlsson, C and Persson, T (eds) (2009), *The Illusion of Accountability in the European Union* (London: Routledge).

Guy Peters, B (1994), 'Agenda-setting in the European Community', *Journal of European Public Policy*, 1/1, pp 9–26.

Haan, J de and Eijffinger, SCW (2000), 'The democratic accountability of the European Central Bank: A comment on two fairy-tales', *Journal of Common Market Studies*, 38/3, pp 393–407.

—— and Gormley, L (1997), 'Independence and accountability of the European Central Bank' in M Andenas, L Gormley, C Hadjiemmanuil and I Harden (eds), *European Economic and Monetary Union: The institutional framework* (Dordrecht: Kluwer Academic Publishing), pp 333–53.

Hage, F (2008), 'Who decides in the Council of the European Union?', *Journal of Common Market Studies*, 46/3, p 533–58.

Halberstam, D (2004), 'The bride of Messina or European democracy and the limits of liberal intergovernmentalism', Jean Monnet Working Paper No. 5/04 (New York: NYU School of Law), available at <http://www.jeanmonnetprogram.org/papers/04/040501.html>.

—— and Stein, E (2009), 'The United Nations, the European Union and the King of Sweden: Economic sanctions and individual rights in a plural world order', Common Market L Rev, 46/1, pp 13–72.

Hallstein, W (1965), 'The EEC Commission: A new factor in international life', Int'l and Comp LQ, 14/3, pp 727–41.

Hamilton, A, Madison, J and Jay, J (1961), *The Federalist*, BF Wright (ed), Essay No 48 (A Hamilton), Essay No 51 (J Madison), and Essay No 78 (A Hamilton) (Cambridge, MA: The Belknap Press of Harvard University Press).

Hannay, A (2005), *On The Public* (London: Routledge)

Happold, M (2003), 'Security Council Resolution 1373 and the Constitution of the United Nations', Leiden J of Int' L, 16/3, pp 593–610.

Harden, I (2002), 'The European Ombudsman's efforts to increase openness in the Union' in V Deckmyn (ed): *Increasing Transparency in the European Union* (Maastricht: European Institute of Public Administration), pp 123–45.

Hardy, B, Scheufele, D, and Wang, Z (2009), 'Defining deliberation: Key determinants and distinct dimensions', Paper presented at the annual meeting of the International

Communication Association, Sheraton New York, available at <http://www.allacademic.com//meta/p_mla_apa_research_citation/0/1/3/0/5/pages13051/p13051-1.php>.

Harlow, C (2002), *Accountability in the European Union* (Oxford: Oxford University Press).

—— (2006), 'Global administrative law: The quest for principles and values', EJIL, 17/1, pp 187–214.

—— (2009), 'Transparency in the European Union: Weighing the public and private interest' in J Wouters, L Verhey and P Kiiver (eds), *European Constitutionalism beyond Lisbon* (Antwerp: Intersentia), pp 209–38.

—— and Rawlings, R (2007), 'Promoting accountability in multilevel governance: A network approach', European LJ, 13/4, pp 542–62.

Hayes, B (2004), *From the Schengen Information System to SIS II and the Visa Information (VIS): The Proposals Explained* (London: Statewatch).

—— (2007), '"Terrorist lists" still above the law', *Statewatch analysis*, available at <http://www.statewatch.org/news/2007/aug/proscription.pdf>.

Hayes-Renshaw, F and Wallace, H (1995), 'Executive power in the European Union: The functions and limits of the Council of Ministers', *Journal of European Public Policy*, 2/4, pp 559–82.

—— and Wallace, H (1997), *The Council of Ministers*, 1st edn (Basingstoke: Palgrave Macmillan).

—— and —— (2006), *The Council of Ministers*, 2nd edn (Basingstoke: Palgrave Macmillan).

Heitsch, C (2003), *Die Verordnung über den Zugang zu Dokumenten der Gemeinschaftsorgane im Lichte des Transparenzprinzips* (Berlin: Duncker & Humblot).

Helliskoski, J and Leino, P (2006), 'Darkness at the break of noon: The case law on Regulation No. 1049/2001 on access to documents', Common Market L Rev, 43/3, pp 735–82.

Helms, L (2005), *Presidents, Prime Ministers and Chancellors: Executive leadership in Western democracies* (Basingstoke: Palgrave Macmillan).

Héritier, A (2001), 'Overt and covert institutionalization in Europe' in A Stone-Sweet, W Sandholtz, and N Fligstein, *The Institutionalization of Europe* (Oxford: Oxford University Press).

—— (2007), *Explaining Institutional Change in Europe* (Oxford: Oxford University Press).

—— and Lemkuhl, D (2008), 'Introduction: The shadow of hierarchy and new modes of governance', *Journal of Public Policy*, 28/1, pp 1–17.

Hermann, CW (2007), 'Much ado about Pluto? The "unity of the legal order of the European Union" revisited', EUI Working Paper RSCAS 2007/05.

Herrnfeld, HH (2009), 'Artikel 47 EUV' in J Schwarze (ed), *EU-Kommentar*, 2nd edn (Baden-Baden: Nomos), pp 230–6.

Hert, P de and Gutwith, S (2006), 'Interoperability of police databases within the EU: An accountable political choice', TILT Law and Technology Working Paper No. 001/2006, 1 April 2006, available at <http://www.tilburguniversity.nl/faculties/law/research/tilt/publications/workingpapers/>.

Herzfeld, M (1992), *The Social Production of Indifference: Exploring the symbolic roots of Western bureaucracy* (London: The University of Chicago Press).

Hillion, C and Wessel, R (2009), 'Competence distribution in EU external relations after ECOWAS: Clarification or continued fuzziness?', Common Market L Rev, 46, pp 551–86.

Hix, S (1994), 'The study of the European Community: The challenge to comparative politics', *West European Politics*, 17/1, pp 1–30.

—— (2002a), 'Constitutional agenda-setting through discretion in rule interpretation: Why the European Parliament won at Amsterdam', *British Journal of Political Science*, 32/2, pp 259–80.

—— (2002b), 'Why the EU should have a single president and how she should be elected', Paper for the Working Group on Democracy in the EU for the British Cabinet Office, available at <http://personal.lse.ac.uk/hix/Working_Papers>.

—— (2005), *The Political System of the European Union*, 2nd edn (The European Union Series; Basingstoke: Palgrave Macmillan).

—— (2007), *What is Wrong with the European Union and How to Fix It* (Cambridge: Polity Press).

—— and Bartolini, S (2006), 'Politics: The right or wrong sort of medicine for the EU?', Policy Paper No 19, Notre Europe, available at <http://home.um.edu.mt/edrc/hix_bartolini_notre_europe.pdf>.

Hoeksma, J (2007), *De Uitvinding van Europa: De Europese Unie als Nieuw Verschijnsel in het Volkenrecht* (Assen: Van Gorcum).

Hofmann, H (2003), 'A critical analysis of the new typology of acts in the draft treaty establishing a constitution for Europe', *European Integration Online Papers*, 7/9.

—— (2009), 'Legislation, delegation and implementation under the Treaty of Lisbon: Typology meets reality', European LJ 15/4, pp 482–505.

—— and Türk, A (2006), *EU Administrative Governance* (Cheltenham: Edgar Elgar).

—— and —— (2007), 'The development of integrated administration in the EU and its consequences', European LJ, 13/2, pp 253–71.

Homeyer, von I (2009), 'The evolution of EU environmental governance' in J Scott (ed), *Environmental Protection. European Law and Governance* (Oxford: Oxford University Press), pp 1–26

Hood, C and Heald, D (eds) (2006), *Transparency: The key to better governance?* (Oxford University Press).

Hooghe, L (2001), *The European Commission and the Integration of Europe* (Cambridge: Cambridge University Press).

—— and Marks, G (2003), 'Unravelling the central state, but how? Types of multi-level governance', *American Science Review*, 97/2, pp 233–43.

—— and —— (2008), 'European Union?', *West European Politics*, 31/1–2, pp 108–29.

Houses of the *Oireachtas*, Sub-Committee on Ireland's Future in the European Union (2008), *Ireland's Future in the European Union: Challenges, issues and options*, available at <http://euaffairs.ie/sub-committee/Sub-CommitteeReport.pdf>.

Hüller, T (2007), 'Assessing EU strategies for publicity' *Journal of European Public Policy*, 14/4, pp 563–81.

Hummer, W (2007), 'From "interinstitutional agreements" to "interinstitutional agencies/offices"?' European LJ 13/1, pp. 47–74.

Ipsen, HP (1937), *Justiz und Politik: Das Problem der justizlosen Hoheitskakte* (Hamburg: Hanseatische Verlagsanstalt).

Issing, O (1999) 'The Eurosystem: Transparent and accountable or "William in Euroland"', *Journal of Common Market Studies*, 37, pp 475–95.

Jabko, N (2003), 'Democracy in the age of the Euro', *Journal of European Public Policy*, 10/3, pp 710–39.

Jachtenfuchs, M (2007), 'The European Union as a polity (II)' in KE Jørgensen, MA Pollack and B Rosamund (eds), *Handbook of European Union Politics* (London: Sage Publications), pp 159–73.

—— and Kohler-Koch, B (2004), 'Governance and institutional development' in A Wiener and T Diez (eds), *European Integration Theory: Past, present and future* (Oxford: Oxford University Press), pp 97–115.

Jacobs, FG (2007), *The Sovereignty of Law: The European way. The Hamlyn Lectures 2006* (Cambridge: Cambridge University Press).

Jacobsson, K and Schmidt, H (2003), 'The European employment strategy at the cross-roads: Contribution to the evaluation' in D Folden and L Magnusson (eds), *Five Years Experience of the Luxembourg Employment Strategy* (Brussels: ETUI).

Jacqué, J-P (2004), 'The principle of institutional balance', Common Market L Rev, 41/2, pp 383–91.

—— (2007), 'Introduction: Pouvoir législatif et pouvoir exécutif dans l'Union européenne' in J-B Auby and J Dutheil de la Rochère (eds), *Droit administrative européen* (Brussels: Bruylant), pp 25–48.

Jasanoff, S (1990), *The Fifth Branch: Science advisers as policymakers* (Cambridge, MA: Harvard University Press).

Joerges, C (2000), 'Zusammenfassung und Perspektiven: Gutes Regieren im Binnenmarkt' in C Joerges and J Falke (eds), *Das Ausschusswesen der Europäischen Union: Praxis der Risikoregulierung im Binnenmarkt und ihre rechtliche Verfassung* (Baden-Baden: Nomos), pp 349–382.

—— (2001), '"Economic order"—"Technical realization"—"The hour of the executive": Some legal historical observations on the Commission White Paper on European Governance', Jean Monnet Working Paper No.6/01, available at <http://www.jean-monnetprogram.org/papers/01/012201.rtf>.

—— (2006), '"Deliberative political processes" revisited: What have we learnt about the legitimacy of supranational decision-making', *Journal of Common Market Studies*, 44/4, pp 779–802.

—— (2007), 'Integration through de-legalisation? An irritated heckler', European Governance Papers No N-07–03, available at <http://www.connex-network.org/eurogov/pdf/egp-newgov-N-07-03.pdf>.

——, Mény, Y, and Weiler, JHH (eds) (2002), *Mountain or Molehill? A critical appraisal of the Commission White Paper on Governance*, available at <http://www.jeanmonnetprogram.org/papers/01/010601.html>.

—— and Neyer, J (1997), 'From intergovernmental bargaining to deliberative political processes: The constitutionalization of comitology', European LJ, 3/3, pp 273–99.

——, Schepel, H, and Vos, E (1998), 'The law's problems with the involvement of non-governmental actors in Europe's legislative processes: The case of standardization under the "new approach"', Working Paper EUI, June, available at <http://cadmus.iue.it/dspace/handle/1814/154>.

—— and Vos, E (eds) (1999), *EU Committees: Social regulation, law and politics* (Oxford: Oxford University Press).

—— and Singh Ghaleigh, N (eds) (2003), *Darker Legacies of Law in Europe: The shadow of national socialism and fascism over Europe and its legal traditions* (Oxford: Hart Publishing)

Joint Study EPC, EGMONT and CEPS (2007), *Treaty of Lisbon: Implementing the institutional innovation*, Brussels, November 2007, available at <http://www.irri-kiib.be/SD/Joint_Study_complet.pdf>.

Jönsson, C and Hall, M (2005), *Essence of Diplomacy* (Basingstoke: Palgrave Macmillan).

Jorda, J (2001), *Le pouvoir exécutif de l'Union Européenne* (Aix-en-Provence: Presses Universitaires d'Aix Marseille).

Juncos, A and Reynolds, C (2007), 'The Political and Social Security Committee: Governing in the Shadow', *European Foreign Affairs Review,* (12) 2, pp 127–147.

Kassim, H (2004), 'The Secretariat General of the European Commission, 1958–2003: A singular institution' in A Smith (eds), *Politics and the European Commission* (Routledge), pp 47–66.

—— (2006), 'The Secretariat General of the European Commission' in D Spence and G Edwards (eds), *The European Commission,* 3rd edn (London: John Harper Publishing), pp 75–94.

Kavenagh, A (2003), 'The idea of a living constitution', Canadian J of L and Juris, 16/1, pp 55–89.

Keleman, D (2002), 'The politics of Eurocratic structure and new European agencies', *West European Politics*, 25/4, pp 93–118.

Keohane, RO and Nye, JS (1977), *Power and Independence: World politics in transition* (Boston: Little, Brown and Company).

Kickert, W (1993), 'Complexity, governance and dynamics: Conceptual explorations of network management' in J Kooiman (ed), *Modern Governance: New government-society interactions* (London: Sage).

Kietz, D and Maurer, A (2007), 'The European Parliament in treaty reform: Predefining IGC's through interinstitutional agreements', European LJ, 13/1, pp 20–46.

Kiewiet, DR and McCubbins, MD (1991), *The Logic of Delegation* (Chicago: University of Chicago Press).

Kiiver, P (2005), *The National Parliaments in the European Union: A critical view on constitution-building* (Maastricht: Maastricht University).

Kingsbury, B, Krisch, N, and Stewart, RB (2005), 'The emergence of global administrative law', Law and Contemporary Problems, 68/3–4, pp 15–61.

Koenig, T (2008), 'Why do Member States empower the European Parliament?', *Journal of European Public Policy*, 15/2, pp 167–88.

Koenig-Archibugi, M (2004), 'International governance as new *raison d'etat?* The case of the EU common foreign and security policy', *European Journal of International Relations*, 10/2, pp 147–88.

—— (2009), 'Accountability in transnational relations: How distinctive is it?', *West European Politics*, forthcoming.

Kohler-Koch, B (2010), 'Civil society and accountability: The international and the EU discourse compared', *West European Politics*, forthcoming.

—— and Quittkat, C (2009), 'What is civil society and who represents civil society in the EU? Results of an online survey among civil society experts', *Policy and Society*, 28/1, pp 11–22.

Koopmans, T (2006), 'De herontdekking van "hoger recht"', *Tijdschrift voor Privaatrecht*, pp 1747–61.

—— (2008), 'Confederalisme: Van de "Articles of Confederation" naar het Verdrag van Maastricht' in F Judo and G Geudens (eds), *Confederalisme?* (Gent: Larcier), pp 1–18.

Koutrakos, P (2006), *EU International Relations Law* (Oxford: Hart Publishing).

Kranenborg, H (2007), *Toegang tot documenten en bescherming van persoonsgegevens in de Europese Unie: Over de openbaarheid van persoonsgegevens* (The Hague: Kluwer Law International).

—— (2008) 'Access to documents and data protection in the EU: On the public nature of personal data', 45 Common Market L Rev, pp 1079–1114.

Krisch, N (2004), 'The rise and fall of collective security: Terrorism, US hegemony and the plight of the Security Council' in C Walter et al (eds), *Terrorism as a Challenge for National and International Law: Security versus liberty?* (Springer), pp 879–908.

Kuijper, PJ (2008), 'Of "mixity" and "double-hatting": External relations of the European Union explained', Inaugural Address, University of Amsterdam, 23 March 2008.

Kurcz, B and Lazowski, A (2007), 'Two sides of the same coin? Framework decisions and directives compared' in P Eeckhout and T Tridimas (eds), *Yearbook of European Law 2006* (Oxford University Press), pp 177–203.

Kurpas, S, Green, C, and Maciej Kaczynski, P (2008), 'The European Commission after enlargement: Does more add up to less?', CEPS Special Report, available at <www.ceps.be>.

Ladenburger, C (2008), 'Police and criminal law in the Treaty of Lisbon: A new dimension for the Community method', European Constitutional L Rev, 4/1, pp 20–40.

Laffan, B (1999), 'Becoming a "living institution": The evolution of the European Court of Auditors', *Journal of Common Market Studies*, 37/2, pp 251–68.

Landau, M (1969), 'Redundancy, rationality and the problem of duplication and overlap', *Public Administration Review*, 29/4, pp 346–58.

Larosière de, J et al, (2009) *The High-Level Group on Financial Supervision in the EU-Report*, Brussels, 25 February 2009, para 67, <http://ec.europa.eu/commission_barroso/president/pdf/statement_20090225_en.pdf>.

Lastra, RM (1992), 'The independence of the European system of central banks', Harvard Int'l LJ, 33, 475.

—— and Shams, H (2001), 'Public accountability in the financial sector' in E Ferran and C Goodhart (eds), *Regulating Financial Services and Markets in the 21st Century* (Oxford: Hart Publishing), pp 165–88.

Läufer, T (1990), *Die Organe der EG: Rechtsetzung und Haushaltverfahren zwischen Kooperation und Konflikt* (Bonn: éditions Europa-Union).

Lauwaars, R (2004), 'The president of the European Council: The beginning of a European government?' in J de Zwaan, J Jans, F Nelissen and S Blockmans (eds), *The European Union: An ongoing process of integration. Liber Amicorum Fred Kellermann* (Cambridge: Cambridge University Press), pp 71–6.

Lavrijssen, S and Hancher, L (2008), 'Networks on track: From European regulatory networks to European regulatory "network agencies"', *Legal Issues of Economic Integration*, 34/1, pp 23–55.

Lebeck, C (2008), 'Sliding towards supranationalism? The constitutional status of EU framework decisions after *Pupino*', German L Rev, 8/5, pp 501–32.

Lebessis, N and Paterson, J (1997), 'Evolution in governance: What lessons for the Commission? A first assessment', Working Paper European Commission Forward Studies Unit, available at <http://ec.europa.eu/comm/cdp/working-paper/evolution_in_governance.pdf>

—— and —— (2000), 'Developing new modes of governance', Working Paper, Forward Studies Unit, European Commission, available at <http://europa.eu.int/comm/cdp/working-paper/nouveaux_modes_gouvernance_en.pdf>.

Leeuw, M de (2007), 'Openness in the legislative process in the European Union', European L Rev, 32/3, pp 295–318.

Lempp, J and Altenschmidt, J (2008), 'The prevention of deadlock through informal processes of "supranationalization": The case of COREPER', *European Integration*, 30/4, pp 511–26.

Lenaerts, K (1991), 'Some reflections on the separation of powers in the European Community', Common Market L Rev, 28/1, pp 11–35.

—— and Nuffel, P van (2005), *The Constitutional Law of the European Union*, 2nd edn (London: Sweet and Maxwell).

Lenaerts, K and Verhoeven, A (2002), 'Institutional balance as a guarantee for democracy in EU governance' in C Joerges and R Dehousse (eds), *Good Governance in Europe's Integrated Market* (Oxford: Oxford University Press), pp 35–88.

Lequiller, P (2003), *Un Président pour l'Europe* (Paris: Fondation Robert Schuman).

Lewis, J (1998), 'Is the hard bargaining image of the Council misleading? The Committee of Permanent Representatives and the Local Election Directive', *Journal of Common Market Studies*, 36/4, pp 469–504.

Light, PC (1997), *The Tides of Reform: Making government work, 1945–1995* (New Haven, CT: Yale University).

Lindseth, PL (1999), 'Democratic legitimacy and the administrative character of supranationalism: The example of the European Community', Columbia L Rev, 99/3, pp 628–739.

——, Aman, AC and Raul, AC (2008), 'Oversight' in G Bermann, C Koch, and JT O'Reilly (eds), *Administrative Law of the European Union* (Chicago, ILL: ABA, Section of Administrative Law and Regulatory Practice).

Lloyd, R, Oatham, J, and Hammer, M (2007), *Global Accountability Report* (London: One World Trust).

Lord, C (2000), 'Legitimacy, democracy and the EU: When abstract questions become practical policy problems', available at <http://www.one-europe.ac.uk/pdf/P3Lord.PDF>.

Lucarelli, S (2007), 'The EU in the eyes of others: Towards filling a gap in the literature', *European Foreign Affairs Review*, 12/2, pp 249–70.

Ludlow, P (2002), *The Laeken Council* (Brussels: European Council Commentary).

Lyell, C (1990), *Principles of Geology* (Chicago: University of Chicago) (originally published 1830–33).

MacCormick, N (2004–5), 'The health of nations and the health of Europe', The Cambridge Yearbook of European Law Studies, 7, pp 1–16.

—— (2007), *Institutions of Law: An essay in legal theory* (Oxford: Oxford University Press).

MacDonald, E (2008), 'The "emergence" of global administrative law', Paper at the 4th Global Administrative Law Seminar, 'Global administrative law from fragmentation to unity?', Viterbo, 13–14 June 2008.

Maduro, MP (2004), 'How constitutional can the European Union be? The tension between intergovernmentalism and constitutionalism in the European Union in J Weiler and C Eisgruber (eds), *Altneuland: The EU Constitution in a contextual perspective,* Jean Monnet Working Paper 5/04.

Maes, M (2007), 'L'accès du public aux documents des Institutions de la Communauté européenne: Vers une révision du règlement (CE) 1049/2001', *Revue du Droit de l'Union Européenne,* pp 411–32.

Magnette, P (2000), 'Towards accountable independence? Parliamentary controls of the European Central Bank and the rise of a new democratic model', European LJ, 6/4, pp 326–40.

—— (2003), 'Between parliamentary control and the rule of law: The political role of the Ombudsman in the European Union', *Journal of European Public Policy,* 10/5, pp 677–94.

—— (2005), *What is the European Union? The nature of the European Union* (Basingstoke: Palgrave Macmillan).

—— and Papadopoulos, Y (2008), 'On the politicization of the European consociation: A middle way between Hix and Bartolini', Eurogov Working Paper No C-08-0, available at <http://www.connex-network.org/eurogov/pdf/egp-connex-C-08-01.pdf>.

Mancini, GF (1989), 'The making of a constitution for Europe', Common Market L Rev, 26, pp 596–614.

—— (2000), *Democracy and Constitutionalism in the European Union* (Oxford: Hart Publishing).

Maher, I (2007), 'Economic governance: Hybridity, accountability and control', Columbia J of European L, 13/3, pp 679–703.

Mahlmann, M (2003), 'Judicial methodology and fascist and Nazi Law' in C Joerges and N Singh Ghaleigh (eds), *Darker Legacies of Law in Europe: The shadow of National Socialism and fascism over Europe and its legal traditions* (Oxford: Hart Publishing), pp 229–42.

Mair, P (2004), 'The Europeanization dimension', *Journal of European Public Policy,* 11/2, pp 337–48.

—— (2005), 'Popular democracy and the European Union polity', Eurogov Working Papers, No. C-05-03, available at <http://www.connex-network.org/eurogov/>.

—— (2007), 'Political opposition and the European Union', *Government and Opposition,* 42/1, pp 1–17.

—— and Thomassen, J (2010), 'Electoral democracy and political Representation in the European Union' in P Mair and J Thomassen (eds), *Representation and the European Union,* special issue of *Journal of European Public Policy* (forthcoming).

Majone, G (1996), *Regulating Europe* (London: Routledge).

—— (2001), 'International regulatory cooperation: A neo-institutionalist approach' in GA Bermann, M Herdegen and PL Lindseth, *Transatlantic Regulatory Cooperation: Legal Problems and Political Prospects* (Oxford University Press), pp 119–45.

—— (2002), 'The European Commission: The limits of centralization and the period of parliamentarization', *Governance: An International Journal of Policy, Administration and Institutions,* 15/3, pp 375–92.

—— (2005), *Dilemmas of European Integration: The ambiguities and pitfalls of integration by stealth* (Oxford: Oxford University Press).

—— and Everson, M (2001), 'Institutional reform: Independent agencies, oversight, coordination and procedural control' in O de Schutter, N Lebessis, and J Paterson (eds), *Governance in the European Union* (Luxembourg: Office for Official Publications of the European Union), pp 129–68.

Mangenot, M (2002), 'L'affirmation du Secrétariat du Conseil de l'Union Européenne: Les transformations du rôle d'une institution non codifiée', Paper presented at the 'VIIe congrès de l'Association française de science politique', Lille, 18–21 September 2002.

—— (2003), 'Une "chancellerie du Prince": Le Secretariat général du Conseil dans le processus de decision bruxellois', *Politique Européenne*, 11, p 123–42.

—— (2009), 'European games and institutional innovation: The making of Eurojust (1996–2004)' Working Paper, Centre for European Political Sociology, University of Strasbourg, <http://prisme.u-strasbg.fr/workingpapers/WPMangenot.pdf>.

Mansfield, HC (1989), *Taming the Prince: The ambivalence of modern executive power* (New York: The Free Press).

March, M and Norris, P (1997), 'Political representation in the European Parliament', *European Journal of Political Research*, 32/6, pp 153–64.

Marks, S (2004), 'Naming global administrative law', New York University J of Int'l L and Pol, 37/4, pp 995–1001.

Marsh, JG and Olsen, JP (1989), *Rediscovering Institutions* (New York: Free Press).

Marshall, G (1971), *Constitutional Theory* (Oxford: Clarendon Press).

Martens, M (2005), 'Double-hatted agencies on the European scene? A case study of the IMPEL Network', ARENA Working Paper 05/12.

—— (2006), 'National regulators between Union and governments: A study of the EU's environmental policy network IMPEL' in M Egeberg (ed), *Multilevel Union Administration: The transformation of executive politics in Europe* (Basingstoke: Palgrave Macmillan), pp 124–142.

—— (2008), 'Voice or loyalty? The evolution of the European Environmental Agency (EEA)', Paper presented to ECPR Standing Group on Regulatory Governance, 5–7 June, Utrecht.

Martensson, M (2007), 'Mixed representation and legitimacy in the European Union', *European Integration*, 29/3, pp 285–302.

Mashaw, J (2007), 'Reasoned administration: The European Union, the United States and the project of democratic governance', George Washington L Rev, 76/2 pp 99–124.

Maurer, A (2008), 'Vermittlung, Steuerung und demokratische Verantwortung: Die Sollbruchstellen des Reformvertrages' in I Pernice (ed), *Der Vertrag von Lissabon: Reform der EU ohne Verfassung?* (Berlin: Nomos Verlag).

McNamara, K (2002), 'Rational fictions: Central bank independence and the social logic of delegation', *West European Politics*, 25/1, pp 47–76.

Meijer, AJ (2003), 'Transparent government: Parliamentary and legal accountability in an information age', *Information Polity*, 8/1–2, pp 67–78.

Meijers, H (1997), 'European cooperation: An authoritarian temptation', *Nederlands Juristen Blad*, 72/20, pp 890–1.

Mendes, J (2009a), 'Participation and participation rights in EU law and governance' in H Hofmann and A Türk (eds), *The Move to an Integrated Administration: Legal challenges in EU administrative law* (Cheltenham: Edward Elgar), forthcoming.

—— (2009b), *Rights of Participation in European Administrative Law: A rights-based approach to participation in rulemaking*, PhD thesis defended at the EUI on 16 March 2009, publication forthcoming.

Michelmann, HJ (1978), 'Multinational staffing and organizational functioning in the Commission of the European Communities', *International Organization*, 32/2, pp 477–96.

Milward, A (2000), *The European Rescue of the Nation-State*, 2nd edn (London: Routledge).

Missiroli, A (2003), 'Euros for ESDP: Financing EU operations', Occasional Paper 45, (Paris: EU Institute for Security Studies).

Molony, N (2007), 'The view from the financial markets: Institutional risks to law-making for the EC financial market in the post-FSAP environment', Paper presented at the Irish European Law Forum, 19 January 2007.

Monar, J (1994), 'Interinstitutional agreements: The phenomenon and its new dynamics after Maastricht', Common Market L Rev, 31/4, pp 693–719.

Monnet, J (1978), *Memoirs*, (Garden City: Doubleday).

Moon, MJ, Welch, EW, and Wong, W (2005), 'What drives global E-governance? An exploratory study at macro level', Proceedings of the 38th Hawaii International Conference on System Sciences, on file with author.

Moravcsik, A (1993), 'Preferences and power in the European Community: A liberal intergovernmental approach', *Journal of Common Market Studies*, 31/4, pp 473–524.

—— (2002), 'In defence of the democratic deficit: Reassessing legitimacy in the European Union', *Journal of Common Market Studies*, 40/4, pp 603–24.

—— (2004), 'Is there a "democratic deficit" in world politics? A framework for analysis, *Government and Opposition*, 39/2, pp 336–63.

Mouritzen, PE and Svara, JH (2002), *Leadership at the Apex* (Pittsburgh: University of Pittsburgh Press).

Mulgan, R (2000), '"Accountability": An ever-expanding concept?', *Public Administration*, 78/3, pp 555–73.

—— (2003), *Holding Power to Account: Accountability in modern democracies* (Basingstoke: Palgrave).

Münch, L (1997), *Die gemeinsame Aktion als Mittel der Gemeinsamen Außen- und Sicherheitspolitik* (Berlin: Duncker & Humblot).

Nardi, BA and O'Day, VL (1999), *Information Ecologies: Using technology with heart* (MIT Press).

Naurin, D (2006), 'Transparency, publicity, accountability: The missing links', *Swiss Political Science Review*, 12/3, pp 90–8.

—— and Wallace, H (eds) (2008), *Unveiling the Council of the European Union: Games governments play in Brussels* (Basingstoke: Palgrave Macmillan).

Nehl, HP (1999), *Principles of Administrative Procedure in EC Law* (Oxford: Hart Publishing).

Nettesheim, M (2007), 'UN sanctions against individuals: A challenge to the architecture of European Union governance', Common Market L Rev, 44/3, pp 567–600.

Neunreither, KH (1971), 'Transformation of a political role: Reconsidering the case of the Commission of the European Communities', *Journal of Common Market Studies*, 10/3, pp 233–48.

Nicolson, H (1969), *Diplomacy* (London: Oxford University Press).

Nieto, E (2005), 'The strengthening of the Commission competences by the Constitutional Treaty and the principle of the balance of power', RSCAS EUI Working Paper No. 2005/03.

Nolan, Lord (1995), *Standards in public life: First report of the Committee on Standards in Public Life* (London: HMSO).

Nora, S and Minc, A (1980), *The Computerization of Society: A report to the president of France* (Cambridge, MA: MIT Press).

Nordbeck, R and Kvarda, E (2006), 'New modes of governance for sustainability in Austria: Assessing the legitimacy and effectiveness of the Austrian biodiversity strategy and the Austrian forest dialogue', available at <http://web.fu-berlin.de/ffu/akumwelt/bc2006/papers/Nordbeck-Kvarda_Legitimacy%20and%20Effectiveness.pdf>.

Nørgård, GH (2006), 'National limits to transnational networking? The case of the Danish IT and Telecom Agency' in M Egeberg (ed), *Multilevel Union Administration: The transformation of executive politics in Europe* (Basingstoke: Palgrave Macmillan), pp 163–79.

Norris, P (1997), 'Representation and the democratic deficit', *European Journal of Political Research*, 32/6, pp 273–82.

Nuttall, SJ (1992), *European Political Cooperation* (Oxford: Oxford University Press).

—— (2000), *European Foreign Policy* (Oxford: Oxford University Press).

Ohler, C (2006), 'Die Verhängung von "smart sanctions" durch den UN-Sicherheitsrat: Eine Herausforderung für das Gemeinschaftsrecht', *Europarecht*, 6, pp 848–65.

O'Neill, O (2002), *A Question of Trust: The BBC Reith Lectures 2002* (Cambridge: Cambridge University Press).

Ooik, R van (2008), 'Cross-pillar litigation before the ECJ: Demarcation of Community and Union competences', European Constitutional L Rev, 4/3, pp 399–419.

Pahre, H (2008), *Das Recht des Europäischen Rates: Eine Untersuchung im Lichte aktueller Entwicklungen der Europäischen Union* (Frankfurt: Verlag Peter Lang).

Papadopoulos, Y (2007), 'Problems of democratic accountability in network and multi-level governance', European LJ, 13/ 4, pp 469–86.

Papadopoulos, I (2010), 'Accountability and multi-level governance: More accountability, less democracy?', *West European Politics*, forthcoming.

Peers, S (2002), 'From Maastricht to Laeken: The political agenda of openness and transparency in the European Union' in V Deckmyn (ed), *Increasing Transparency in the European Union?* (Maastricht: European Institute of Public Administration), pp 7–32.

—— (2005), 'Governance and the third pillar: The accountability of Europol' in D Curtin and RA Wessel (eds), *Good Governance and the European Union: Concept, implications and applications* (Antwerpen: Intersentia), pp 253–76.

—— (2006), *EU Justice and Home Affairs Law* (Oxford: Oxford University Press).

—— (2007a), 'The jurisdiction of the Court of Justice over EC immigration and asylum law: Time for a change?' in H Toner, E Guild, and A Baldaccini (eds), *EU Immigration and Asylum Law and Policy* (Oxford: Hart Publishing), pp 85–108.

—— (2007b), 'Salvation outside the church: Judicial protection in the third pillar after the *Pupino* and *Segi* judgments', Common Market L Rev, 44/4, pp 883–929.

—— (2008), 'Proposal on access to documents: Article-by-article commentary', *Statewatch analysis*, available at <http://www.statewatch.org/foi/sw-analysis-docs-june-2008.pdf>.

Pescatore, P and Dwyer, C (1974), *The Law of Integration: Emergence of a new phenomenon in international relations, based on the experience of the European Communities* (Leiden: A.W. Sijthoff).

Peterson, J (1999), 'The Santer era: The European Commission in normative, historical and theoretical perspective', *Journal of European Public Policy*, 6/1, pp 46–65.

—— (2006), 'Where does the Commission stand today?' in D Spence (ed), *The European Commission* (London: John Harper Publishing), pp 502–19.

Pocock, JGA (1975), *The Machiavellian Moment: Florentine political thought and the Atlantic republican tradition* (Princeton, NJ: Princeton University Press).

Poguntke, P and Webb, P (eds) (2005), *The Presidentialisation of Politics: A comparative study of modern democracies* (Oxford: Oxford University Press).

Pollack, M (2003), *The Engines of European Integration: Delegation, agency and agenda-setting in the EU* (Oxford: Oxford University Press).

—— (2003), 'Control mechanism or deliberative democracy? Two images of comitology', *Comparative Political Studies*, 36/1–2, pp 125–55.

Pollak, J and Puntscher Riekmann, S (2008), 'European administration: Centralisation and fragmentation as means of polity-building', *West European Politics*, 31/4, pp 771–88.

—— and Slominski, P (2009) 'Experimentalist but not accountable governance? The role of Frontex in managing the EU's external borders' *West European Politics*, 32/5, pp 904–24.

Ponzano, P (2007), 'Comitologie: Un point de vue de la Commission', *Revue du Droit de l'Union Européenne*, 2/2009.

—— (2008) '"Executive" and "Delegated" acts: The situation after the Lisbon Treaty' in S Griller and J Ziller (eds), *The Lisbon Treaty: EU constitutionalism without a Constitutional Treaty?* (Vienna: Springer), pp 135–41.

Porte, C de la and Nanz, P (2004), 'The OMC: A deliberative democratic mode of governance? The case of employment and pensions', *Journal of European Public Policy*, 11/2, pp 267–88.

Prechal, S and Leeuw, M de (2007), 'Dimensions of Transparency: The building blocks for a new legal principle?', Review of European Administrative Law, 0/1, pp 51–61.

Puntscher Riekmann, S (2007) 'The cocoon of power: Democratic implications of interinstitutional agreements', European LJ, 13/1, pp 4–19.

Raab, CD (1997), 'Electronic confidence: Trust, information and public administration' in ITM Snellen and WBHJ van de Donk (eds), *Public Administration in an Information Age* (Amsterdam: IOS Press), pp 113–33.

Ragnemaln, H (1999), 'The Community Courts and openness within the European Union' in A Dashwood and A Ward (eds), The Cambridge Yearbook of European Legal Studies, 2, pp 19–30.

Raworth, P (1993), *The Legislative Process in the EC* (Dordrecht: Kluwer Law and Taxation Publishers).

Rehnquist, W (1976), 'The notion of a living constitution', Texas L Rev, 54, p 693.

Rhodes, RAW and Dunleavy, P (1995), *Prime Minister, Cabinet and Core Executive* (Basingstoke: Palgrave Macmillan).

Riemann, F (2004), *Die Transparenz der Europäischen Union: Das neue Recht auf Zugang zu Dokumenten von Parlament, Rat und Kommission* (Berlin: Duncker & Humblot).

Rijken, C (2001), 'Legal and technical aspects of cooperation between Europol, third states and Interpol' in V Kronenburger (ed), *The European Union and the International Legal Order: Discord or harmony* (The Hague: TMC Asser Instituut Press), pp 577–603.

Rittberger, B (2001), 'Which institutions for post-war Europe? Explaining the institutional design of Europe's first community', *Journal of European Public Policy*, 8/5, pp 673–708.

—— (2007a), 'Constructing parliamentary democracy in the European Union: How did it happen?' in B Kohler-Koch and B Rittberger (eds), *Debating the Democratic Legitimacy of the European Union* (Plymouth: Rowman and Littlefield), pp 111–37.

—— (2007b), 'Original meanings: Ideas about representation in the making of Europe's first community', Paper presented at CONNEX Thematic Conference on Accountability, EUI, Florence.

Robertson, C (2008), 'Impact assessment in the European Union', *EIPA Scope* 2008/2, pp 17–20.

Robertson, D (2002), *The Routledge Dictionary of Politics* (London: Routledge).

Rogers, ML (2008), 'Republicanism' in WA Darity (ed), *International Encyclopedia of the Social Sciences*, 2nd edn (Detroit: Macmillian Reference USA), pp 188–9, available at <http://www.melvinlrogers.com/files/PublishedRepublicanism.pdf>.

Roness, P et al (2007), 'Autonomy and regulation of state agencies: Reinforcement, indifference or compensation?', Paper Presented at the 4th ECPR General Conference, Pisa, Italy 6–8 September 2007.

Rood, JQT (2008), 'De EU na het Verdrag van Lissabon: Naar een Nieuw Politiek en Institutioneel Evenwicht?', *Sociaal-Economische Wetgeving*, 56/4, pp 132–5.

Rutgers, M (2000), 'Public administration and the separation of powers in a cross-Atlantic perspective', *Administrative Theory and Praxis*, 22/2, pp 287–308.

Sabel, CF and Zeitlin, J (2008), 'Learning from difference: The new architecture of experimentalist governance in the EU', European LJ, 14/3, pp 271–327.

Safire, W (1998), 'On language: Transparency totally', *The New York Times*, 4 January, p 4.

Salamon, L and Anheier, H (1997), *Defining the Nonprofit Sector: A cross-national analysis* (Manchester: Manchester University Press).

Sanchez Barrueco, ML (2008), 'L'Agence européenne de défense : Un organe intergouvernemental au service d'une institution communautaire?', *Revue du Droit de l'Union Européenne*, 3, pp 507–42.

Sari, A (2008), 'Jurisdiction and international responsibility in peace support operations: The *Behrami* and *Saramati* cases', Human Rights L Rev, 8/1, pp 151–70.

Sbragia, A (2008), 'Distributed governance: The changing ecology of the European Union' in B Kohler-Koch and F Larat (eds), *Efficient and Democratic Governance in the European Union*, CONNEX Report Series No 09 (Mannheim: CONNEX Report Series), p 339–55.

Schackleton, M (2000), 'The politics of codecision', *Journal of Common Market Studies*, 38/2, pp 325–42.

Scharpf, F (1999), *Governing Europe: Effective and democratic?* (Oxford: Oxford University Press).

Schendelen, MPCM van (1996), 'The Council decides: Does the Council decide?', *Journal of Common Market Studies*, 33/4, pp 531–48.

—— and Scully, R (2002), *Machiavelli in Brussels: The art of lobbying the EU* (Amsterdam: Amsterdam University Press).

—— and Scully, R (eds) (2003), *The Unseen Hand: Unelected EU legislators* (London: Frank Cass Publishers).

Schermers, HG and Blokker, NM (2003), *International Institutional Law: Unity within diversity*, 4th rev edn (Leiden: Martinus Nijhoff).

Schillemans, T (2007), *Verantwoording in de schaduw van de macht: Horizontale verantwoording bij zelfstandige uitvoeringsorganisaties* (Den Haag: Lemma).

Schmidt, V (2006), *Democracy in Europe: The EU and national polities* (Oxford: Oxford University Press).

Schmitt, C (1936), 'Vergleichender Überblick über die neueste Entwicklung des Problems der gesetzgeberischen Ermächtigungen (Legislative Delegationen)', *Zeitschrift für ausländisches öffentliches Recht und Völkerrecht (ZaöRV)*, 6, pp 252–68.

Schmolle, KU (2006), 'Die Einbeziehung des Komitologieverfahrens in den Lamfalussy-Prozess: Zur Forderung des Europäischen Parlaments nach mehr Entscheidungsteilhabe', *Europarecht*, 3, pp 432–48.

Schön-Quinlivan, E (2007), 'Administrative reform in the European Commission: From rhetoric to re-legitimatization', *EU-Consent–Constructing Europe Network, Project No 513416*, available at <http://www.eu-consent.net/library/deliverables/D17_Team7_Schon2.pdf>.

Schout, A (2008), 'Agencies and inspection powers: The case of EASA as new of more of the same?' in E Vos (ed), *European Risk Governance: Its science, its inclusiveness and its effectiveness* (CONNEX Book Series: Mannheim: Mannheim University Press), pp 257–89.

—— and Schaik, L van (2008), 'Reforming the EU presidency?' *Journal of Comparative Government and European Policy*, 6/1, pp 35–56.

Schoutheete, P de (1980), *La coopération politique européenne* (Paris: Nathan).

—— and Wallace, H (2002), *The European Council* (Paris: Research and Policy Group—Notre Europe), available at <http://www.notre-europe.eu>.

Scott, C (2000), 'Accountability in the regulatory state', Journal of Law and Society, 27/1, pp 38–60.

Settembri, P (2005), 'Transparency and the EU legislator: "Let he who is without sin cast the first stone"', *Journal of Common Market Studies*, 43/3, pp 637–54.

Shapiro, M (1997), 'The problems of independent agencies in the United States and the European Union', *Journal of European Public Policy*, 4/2, pp 276–91.

—— (2001), 'Administrative law unbounded: Reflections on government and governance,' Indiana Journal of Global Legal Studies, 8, pp 369–77.

—— (2005), 'A deliberative "independent" technocracy v. Democratic politics: Will the globe echo the EU?', *Law and Contemporary Problems*, 68/3–4, pp 341–56.

Sharpston, E (2008), 'The changing role of the Advocate General' in A Arnull, P Eeckhout and T Tridimas (eds), *Continuity and Change in EU Law: Essays in honour of Sir Francis Jacobs* (Oxford: Oxford University Press), pp 20–34.

Sherrington, P (2000), *The Council of Ministers: Political authority in the European Union* (London/New York: Pinter).

Sjursen, H (2007), 'Integration without democracy: Three conceptions of European security policy in transformation', RECON Online Working Paper 2007/19, available at <http://www.reconproject.eu/main.php/RECON_wp_0719.pdf?fileitem=5456242>.

Slaughter, A-M (2004), *A New World Order* (Princeton: Princeton University Press).

Smismans, S (2004), *Law, Legitimacy and European Governance: Functional participation in social regulation* (Oxford: Oxford University Press).

Smith, ME (2004), *Europe's Foreign and Security Policy: The institutionalization of cooperation* (Cambridge: Cambridge University Press).

Smits, R (1997), *The European Central Bank Institutional Aspects* (New York: Aspen Publishers).

Snellen, ITM and Donk, WHBJ van de (eds) (1998), *Public Administration in an Information Age: A handbook* (Amsterdam: IOS Press)

Snyder, F (1994), 'EMU: Metaphor for European Union? Institutions, rules and types of regulation' in R Dehousse et al (eds), *Europe after Maastricht: An ever closer Union?* (Munich: Law Books in Europe), pp 63–78.

Söderman, J (1998), 'The citizen, the administration and Community law', General Report for the XVIII Congress of FIDE (Fédération Internationale pour le Droit Européen), Stockholm, 3–6 June 1998.

Solana, J (2002), *Preparing the Council for Enlargement*, Council of the European Union, General Secretariat, S0044/02, available at <http://ue.eu.int/ueDocs/cms_Data/docs/pressdata/EN/reports/69889.pdf>.

Spaventa, E (2007), 'Opening Pandora's box: Some reflections on the constitutional effects of the decision in *Pupino*', European Constitutional L Rev, 3/1, pp 5–24.

Spence, D (2006), 'The President, the College and the Cabinets' in D Spence and G Edwards (eds), *The European Commission* (London: John Harper Publishing).

Steeg, M van der (2010), 'Accountability for European Council decision making', in Bovens, Curtin and Hart, forthcoming.

Steffek, J and Ferretti, MP (2009). 'Accountability or "good decisions"? The competing goals of civil society participation in international governance', *Global Society*, 23/1, 37–57.

Stephanou, CA (2006), 'La nouvelle gouvernance Européenne: bilan et perspectives', *Cahiers de droit Européen* (No 1–2), pp 581–627.

Steunenberg, B, Koboldt, C and Schmidtchen, D (1996), 'Policymaking, comitology and the balance of power in the European Union', International Review of Law and Economics, 16/3, pp 329–44.

Stevens, A (2001), *Brussels Bureaucrats? The administration of the European Union* (Basingstoke: Palgrave).

Strauss, P (1984), 'The place of agencies in government: Separation of powers and the fourth branch', Columbia L Rev, 84/3, pp 573–669.

Strom, K (2000), 'Delegation and accountability in parliamentary democracies', *European Journal of Political Research*, 37/3, pp 261–89.

——, Muller, WC, and Bergman, T (2003), 'Parliamentary democracy: Promise and problems' in K Strom, WC Muller, and T Bergman (eds), *Delegation and Accountability in Parliamentary Democracies* (Oxford: Oxford University Press), pp 3–32.

Suchman, M (1995), 'Managing legitimacy: Strategic and institutional approaches', *Academy of Management Review*, 20/3, pp 571–610.

Suvarierol, S (2007), *Beyond the Myth of Nationality: A study on the networks of European Commission officials* (Delft: Eburon).

—— (2008), 'Beyond the myth of nationality: Analysing networks within the European Commission', *West European Politics*, 31/4, pp 701–24.

—— and Berg, C van den (2008), 'Bridge builders or bridgeheads in Brussels? The world of seconded national experts' in KP Geuijen et al (eds), *The New Eurocrats: National civil servants in EU policy-making* (Amsterdam University Press).

Svara, JH (2001), 'The myth of the dichotomy: Complementarity of politics and administration in the past and future of public administration', *Public Administration Review*, 61/2, pp 176–83.

Szapiro, M (2005), 'The framework for European regulatory agencies: A balance between accountability and autonomy', Paper presented on the 3rd ECPR Conference.

—— (2006), 'Comitologie: rétrospective et prospective après la réforme de 2006', *Revue du Droit de l'Union Européenne*, 3, pp 545–86.

Talberg, J (2004), 'The power of the chair: Formal leadership in international cooperation', Paper prepared for presentation at the Annual ISA Convention, Montreal, 17–20 March 2004, on file with author.

—— (2006), 'The power of the chair: Formal leadership in international cooperation', Paper presented at the Third Pan-European Conference in EU Politics, Istanbul, 21–23 September 2006.

Talmon, S (2005), 'The Security Council as world legislature', The American J of Int'l L, 99/1, pp 175–93.

Terhechte, JP (2008), 'Der Vertrag von Lissabon: Grundlegende Verfassungsurkunde der Europäischen Rechtsgemeinschaft oder technischer Änderungsvertrag?', *Europarecht*, 2, pp 143–89.

—— (2009), 'Artikel 11 EUV' in J Schwarze (ed), *EU-Kommentar*, 2nd edn (Baden-Baden: Nomos), pp 110–17.

Thatcher, M and Coen, D (2008), 'Reshaping European regulatory space: An evolutionary analysis', *West European Politics*, 31/4, pp 806–36.

—— and Sweet-Stone, A (2002), 'Theory and practice of delegation to non-majoritarian institutions', *West European Politics*, 25/1, pp 1–22.

Thedvall, R (2007), 'The EU's nomads: National eurocrats in European policymaking', Paper presented at the 10th EUSA Conference 17–19 May, 2007 in Montreal, Canada, available at <http://aei.pitt.edu/8046/01/thedvall-r-08j.pdf>.

Thomassen, J and Schmidt, H (2004), 'Legitimacy and democracy in the EU', available at <http://www.mzes.uni-mannheim.de/publications/papers/Schmitt_26_1_04.pdf>.

Thompson, DF (1980), 'Moral responsibility of public officials: The problem of the many hands', *The American Political Science Review*, 74/4, pp 905–16.

Tilly, C (2006), *Why? What happens when people give reasons... and why* (Princeton University Press).

Tomkins, A (2001), 'Separation of powers, ancient and modern', St Catherine's College, Oxford, available at <http://www.utexas.edu/law/conferences/oxford/>.

Torrent, R (1999), 'Whom is the European Central Bank the central bank of? Reaction to Zilioli and Selmayr', Common Market L Rev, 36, 1229.

Tournepiche, AM (2007), 'Vers les nouveaux champs d'application pour la transparence administrative en droit Communautaire: Réflexions sur le Livre vert « Initiative européenne en matière de transparence »', *Cahiers de Droit Eeuropéen*, 1/2, pp 623–46.

Tribe, LH (2008), *The Invisible Constitution* (Oxford: Oxford University Press).

Trondal, J (2000), 'Multiple institutional embeddedness in Europe: The case of Danish, Norwegian and Swedish government officials', *Scandinavian Political Studies*, 23/4, pp 311–41.

—— (2006a), 'Governing at the frontier of the European Commission: The case of seconded national experts', *West European Politics*, 29/1, pp 147–60.

—— (2006b), 'An institutional perspective on representation: Ambiguous representation in the European Commission', *European Integration Online Papers*, 10/4, available at <http://eiop.or.at/eiop/texte/2006–004a.htm>.

—— (2006c), 'EU committee governance and the multilevel Community administration' in H Hofmann and A Türk, *EU Administrative Governance* (Cheltenham: Edward Elgar), pp 391–416.

——, Marcussen, M, and Veggeland, F (2005), 'Re-discovering international executive institutions', *Comparative European Politics*, 3, pp 232–58.

Tsakatika, M (2008), *Political Responsibility and the European Union* (Manchester: Manchester University Press).

Underdal, A (1994), 'Leadership theory: Rediscovering the arts of management' in IW Zartman (ed), *International Multilateral Negotiation: Approaches to the management of complexity* (San Francisco: Jossey-Bass), pp 178–97.

Venit, JS (2003), 'Brave new world: The modernization and decentralization of enforcement under Articles 81 and 82 of the EC Treaty', Common Market L Rev, 40/3, pp 545–80.

Vesterdorf, B (1999), 'Transparency: Not just a vogue word', Fordham International LJ, 22/3, pp 902–29.

Verhoeven, A (2002), *The European Union in Search of a Democratic and Constitutional Theory* (The Hague: Kluwer).

Vibert, F (2007), *The Rise of the Unelected: Democracy and the new separation of powers* (Cambridge: Cambridge University Press).

Vile, MJC (1967), *Constitutionalism and the Separation of Powers* (Oxford: Clarendon Press).

Virally, M (1977), 'La notion de fonction dans la théorie de l'organisation internationale', in *Mélanges offerts a Charles Rousseau: La communauté internationale* (Paris: Pedone), pp 277–300.

—— (1981), 'Definition and classification of international organisations: A legal approach' in G Abi-Saab (ed), *The Concept of International Organization* (Paris: UNESCO), pp 50–66.

Visscher, C de, Maiscocq, O, and Varone, F (2008), 'The Lamfalussy reform in the EU securities markets: Fiduciary relationships, policy effectiveness and balance of power', *Journal of Public Policy*, 28/1, pp 19–47.

Visser, M de (2008), *Network-based Governance in EC Law. The example of EC competition law and EC communications law* (Nijmegen: Wolf Legal Publishers).

Vlcek, W (2006), 'Acts to combat the financing of terrorism: Common foreign and security policy at the European Court of Justice', *European Foreign Affairs Review*, 11/4, pp 491–507.

Walker, N (2006), 'EU Constitutionalism in the state constitutional tradition', Current Legal Problems, 59, pp 51–60.

Wallace, H (2002), 'The Council: An institutional chameleon', *Governance: An International Journal of Policy, Administration and Institutions*, 15/3, pp 325–44.

Weale, A (2000), 'Government by committee: Three principles of evaluation' in T Christiansen and E Kirchener, *Committee Governance in the European Union* (Manchester: Manchester University Press), pp 161–70.

Weatherill, S (1998), 'Safeguarding the *acquis communautaire*' in T Heukels, N Blokker, and M Brus (eds), *The European Union after Amsterdam: A legal analysis* (The Hague: Kluwer Law International), pp 153–78.

Weiler, JHH (1991), 'The transformation of Europe', Yale LJ, 100/8, pp 2525–36.

—— (1999), *The Constitution for Europe* (Cambridge: Cambridge University Press).

—— and Motoc, J (2003), 'Taking democracy seriously: The normative challenges to the international legal system' in S Griller (ed), *International Economic Governance and Non- Economic Concerns: New challenges for the international legal order* (Vienna: Springer), pp 47–77.

Welch, EW and Hinnant, CC (2003), 'Internet use, transparency, and interactivity effects on trust in government', Proceedings of the 36th Hawaii International Conference on System Sciences, available at <http://www2.computer.org/portal/web/csdl/doi/10.1109/HICSS.2003.1174323>.

—— and Wong, W (2001), 'Global information technology pressure and government accountability: The mediating effect of domestic context on web site openness', *Journal of Public Administration Research and Theory*, 11/4, pp 509–38.

Wendler, F and Vos, E (eds) (2006), *Food Safety Regulation in Europe* (Antwerpen: Intersentia).

Werner, W and Wessel, R (2005), *Internationaal en Europees Recht: Een Verkenning van Grondslagen en Kenmerken* (Groningen: Europa Law Publishing).

Werts, J (1992), *The European Council* (Amsterdam: Elsevier).

—— (2008), *The European Council* (London: John Harper Publishing).

Wessel, RA (1999), *The European Union's Foreign and Security Policy: A legal institutional perspective* (The Hague: Kluwer Law International).

—— (2000), 'The inside looking out: Consistency and delimitation in EU external relations', Common Market L Rev, 37/5, pp 1135–71.

—— (2004), 'Fragmentation in the governance of EU external relations: Legal institutional dilemmas and the new constitution for Europe' in J de Zwaan et al (eds), *The European Union: An ongoing process of integration. Liber Amicorum Fred Kellermann* (Cambridge: Cambridge University Press), pp 123–40.

—— (2009a), 'The constitutional unity of the European Union: The increasing irrelevance of the pillar structure?' in J Wouters, L Verhey and P Kiiver (eds), *European Constitutionalism beyond the EU Constitution* (Antwerpen: Intersentia), pp 283–306.

—— (2009b), 'The dynamics of the European Union legal order: An increasingly coherent framework of action and interpretation', European Constitutional L Rev, 1, pp 117–42.

Wessels, W (1991), 'The EC Council: The Community's decision-making centre' in RO Keohane and S Hoffmann (eds), *The New European Community: Decision-making and institutional change* (Boulder, CO: Westview).

Westlake, M (1995), *The Council of the European Union* (London: Catermill).

—— and Galloway, D (2004), *The Council of the European Union* (London: John Harper Publishing).

Wiener, A (2007), 'Contested meaning of norms: A research framework', *Comparative European Politics*, 5/1, pp 1–17.

—— (2008), *The Invisible Constitution of Politics* (Cambridge University Press).

Wiethölter, R (1972), 'Wirtschaftsrecht' in A Görlitz (ed), *Handlexikon zur Rechtswissenschaft* (München: Ehrenwirt), pp 531–9.

Wille, A (2007a), 'Bridging the gap: Political and Administrative leadership in a reinvented Commission' in M Egeberg (ed), *Institutional Dynamics and the Transformation of Executive Politics in Europe* (Mannheim: CONNEX Report Series, 3), pp 7–41.

—— (2007b), 'Senior officials in a reforming European Commission: Transforming the top?' in MW Bauer and C Knill (eds), *Management Reforms in International Organizations* (Baden-Baden: Nomos), pp 37–50.

—— (2009), 'Politicians, bureaucrats and the reinvention of the European Commission: From technical to good governance' in L Verhey, P Kiiver and S Loeven (eds) *Political Accountability and European Integration* (Groningen: Europa Law Publishing), pp 91–108.

—— (2010), *The Normalization of the European Commission: Politics and bureaucracy in an evolving executive*, forthcoming.

Wilson, W (1887), 'The study of administration', *Political Science Quarterly*, 2/2, pp 197–222.

Witte, B de (1998), 'The pillar structure and the nature of the European Union: Greek temple or French gothic cathedral?' in T Heukels, N Blokker, and M Brus (eds), *The European Union after Amsterdam: A legal analysis* (The Hague: Kluwer Law International), pp 51–68.

—— (2008a), 'Legal instruments and law-making in the Lisbon Treaty' in S Griller and J Ziller (eds), *The Lisbon Treaty: EU constitutionalism without a constitutional treaty?* (Vienna: Springer), pp 79–108.

—— (2008b) 'Legal instruments and decision-making' in J Kapteyn and P VerLoren van Themaat (eds), *Introduction to the Law of the European Union*, 4th edn (The Hague: Kluwer), pp 273–348.

Wittinger, M (2008), '"Europäische Satelliten": Anmerkungen zum europäischen Agentur(un)wesen und zur Vereinbarkeit europäischer Agenturen mit dem Gemeinschaftsrecht', *Europarecht*, 5, pp 609–26.

Woll, P (1963), *American Bureaucracy* (New York: Norton).

Wonka, A (2007), 'Technocratic and independent? The appointment of European Commissioners and its policy implications', *Journal of European Public Policy*, 14/2, pp 169–89.

Wouters, J (2004), 'The Union Minister for Foreign Affairs: Europe's single voice or Trojan Horse?' in J de Zwaan et al (eds), *The European Union: An ongoing process of integration. Liber Amicorum Fred Kellermann* (Cambridge: Cambridge University Press), pp 77–86.

Yataganas, X (2001), 'Delegation of regulatory authority in the EU: The relevance of the American model of independent agencies', Jean Monnet Working Paper 3/01, available at <http://www.jeanmonnetprogram.org/papers/01/010301.html>.

Zahle, H (1995), 'The polycentricity of the law or the importance of legal pluralism for legal dogmatics' in H Petersen and H Zahle (eds), *Legal Polycentricity: Consequences of pluralism in law* (Dartmouth: Aldershot).

Zilioli, C and Selmayr, M (2000), 'The European Central Bank: An independent specialized organization of Community law', Common Market L Rev, 37, p 591.

Zwaan, J de (1995), *The Permanent Representatives Committee: Its role in European Union decision-making* (Amsterdam: Elsevier).

—— (2004), 'The role of the European Commission over the years: Changes and challenges' in J de Zwaan et al (eds), *The European Union: An ongoing process of integration. Liber Amicorum Alfred E. Kellermann* (Cambridge: Cambridge University Press), pp 53–69.

Index

www.ingramcontent.com/pod-product-compliance
Lightning Source LLC
LaVergne TN
LVHW011908200926
848484LV00002B/564

9780199264087